Chinese and Indian Ways of Thinking in Early Modern European Philosophy

Bloomsbury Studies in World Philosophies

Series Editor:
Monika Kirloskar-Steinbach

Comparative, cross-cultural and intercultural philosophy are burgeoning fields of research. Bloomsbury Studies in World Philosophies complements and strengthens the latest work being carried out at a research level with a series that provides a home for thinking through ways in which professional philosophy can be diversified. Ideal for philosophy postgraduates and faculty who seek creative and innovative material on non-Euroamerican sources for reference and research, this series responds to the challenges of our postcolonial world, laying the groundwork for a new philosophy canon that departs from the current Eurocentric sources.

Forthcoming Titles in the Series:
Chinese Philosophy of History, by Dawid Rogacz
Chinese and Indian Ways of Thinking in Early Modern European Philosophy,
by Selusi Ambrogio

Chinese and Indian Ways of Thinking in Early Modern European Philosophy

The Reception and the Exclusion

Selusi Ambrogio

BLOOMSBURY ACADEMIC
LONDON • NEW YORK • OXFORD • NEW DELHI • SYDNEY

BLOOMSBURY ACADEMIC
Bloomsbury Publishing Plc
50 Bedford Square, London, WC1B 3DP, UK
1385 Broadway, New York, NY 10018, USA
29 Earlsfort Terrace, Dublin 2, Ireland

BLOOMSBURY, BLOOMSBURY ACADEMIC and the Diana logo are trademarks of
Bloomsbury Publishing Plc

First published in Great Britain 2021
This paperback edition published in 2022

Copyright © Selusi Ambrogio, 2021

Selusi Ambrogio has asserted his right under the Copyright, Designs and Patents Act,
1988, to be identified as Author of this work.

Series design by Louise Dugdale
Cover image © Olga Kurbatova/Getty Images

All rights reserved. No part of this publication may be reproduced or transmitted
in any form or by any means, electronic or mechanical, including photocopying,
recording, or any information storage or retrieval system, without prior permission
in writing from the publishers.

Bloomsbury Publishing Plc does not have any control over, or responsibility for, any
third-party websites referred to or in this book. All internet addresses given in this
book were correct at the time of going to press. The author and publisher regret
any inconvenience caused if addresses have changed or sites have ceased to exist,
but can accept no responsibility for any such changes.

A catalogue record for this book is available from the British Library.

Library of Congress Cataloging-in-Publication Data
Names: Ambrogio, Selusi, author.
Title: Chinese and Indian ways of thinking in early modern European philosophy : the
reception and the exclusion / Selusi Ambrogio.
Description: London ; New York : Bloomsbury Academic, 2020. | Series: Bloomsbury
studies in world philosophies | Includes bibliographical references and index.
Identifiers: LCCN 2020027551 (print) | LCCN 2020027552 (ebook) |
ISBN 9781350153554 (hardback) | ISBN 9781350153561 (ebook) |
ISBN 9781350153578 (epub)
Subjects: LCSH: Philosophy Europe–History–17th century. | Philosophy–Europe–History–
18th century. | Philosophy, Chinese. | Philosophy, Indic.
Classification: LCC B801 .A43 2020 (print) | LCC B801 (ebook) | DDC 181/.11—dc23
LC record available at https://lccn.loc.gov/2020027551
LC ebook record available at https://lccn.loc.gov/2020027552

ISBN: HB: 978-1-3501-5355-4
        PB: 978-1-3501-9141-9
        ePDF: 978-1-3501-5356-1
        eBook: 978-1-3501-5357-8

Series: Bloomsbury Studies in World Philosophies

Typeset by RefineCatch Limited, Bungay, Suffolk

To find out more about our authors and books visit www.bloomsbury.com
and sign up for our newsletters.

to Letizia,
remembering the days in Shanghai

Contents

Preliminary Note on Some Terms and Quotes		ix
List of Abbreviations		x
General Introduction		1
1	India and China between 'Prisca Theologia' and Barbarity	11
	1.0 Introduction	11
	1.1 The first rift in the perennial philosophy model: Otto van Heurn and India	16
	1.2 Jesuits and philosophia perennis: Xavier, Postel and Ricci	19
	1.3 The second rift in the perennial historical model: Georg Horn and China	31
	1.4 Chronology issues: La Peyrère, Isaac Vossius and Georg Horn	35
	1.5 China and India: problems of coherence among the theories about the diffusion of philosophy	40
	1.6 Thomas Burnet: modern Asia as 'wretched Barbarity'	42
	1.7 A first sceptic view of China: François de la Mothe le Vayer	52
	Conclusions of the first chapter	56
2	'Atheistic Asia': Positive and Negative Standpoints	59
	2.0 Introduction	59
	2.1 Missionary construction of the Asiatic negative myth in the seventeenth century: Buddhist atheism	61
	2.2 The reception of the negative myth of Asia in seventeenth-century Europe: François Bernier	70
	2.3 Pierre Bayle and the 'Oriental Spinozism'	76
	2.4 The effects of Bayle's 'Oriental Spinozism': a few instances of Histories of Philosophy in French	89
	2.5 Johann Franz Buddeus as critical follower of the 'Oriental Spinozism'	91
	2.6 The last effective perennialist philosopher: Leibniz	94
	2.7 Boureau-Deslandes: an anti-Bayle thinker with new insights	96
	Conclusions of the second chapter	102
3	The Complete Exclusion of Asians from Philosophy	105

3.0 Introduction 105
3.1 The Grecization of philosophy 107
3.2 German Eclecticism and Christian Wolff 108
3.3 Christoph August Heumann: the theorist of exclusion 111
3.4 Friedrich Gentzken: Asians lack morality and theoretics 119
3.5 Jakob Brucker: the unphilosophical nature of
    ancient Asians' thought 122
3.6 Jakob Brucker: the contemporary 'Exotic' Asians out of philosophy 131
3.7 Jakob Brucker's 'system of philosophy' and Chinese thinking 144

Conclusion: The Tight Shoes of Philosophy 153

Notes 167
Bibliography 209
Index 225

Preliminary Note on Some Terms and Quotes

We use several terms for Brahmins, as 'Brachmanes', 'Brahmanae', 'Baneanes', etc., because each of them was related to a period or to a particular author. For instance, 'Brachmanes' was the most common Latin transcription from the Greek and it was used often by historians in order to describe ancient Brahmins. Therefore, the incoherent use of these terms is due to the literature itself and it is our intention to respect the changing of the term.

Often we use the term 'Buddhism', however, in the period of our investigation, the term 'Buddhism' did not exist. Missionaries understood a clear similarity between Japanese and Siamese sects of 'Xekia' or 'Foe' or 'Thic', but Michel-Jean-François Ozeray coined the term probably in the year 1817 in French.* However, despite what Droit claimed (ibid.), the object 'Buddhism' was already largely discussed since the second half of the seventeenth century.

We use the term 'sect' and 'sects' because missionaries and historians employed these terms. The alternative terms, as 'religion', 'faith', 'philosophy', are even worse and more ambiguous. Therefore, it is not our intention to offend any followers; instead we use the terms as the thinkers of the time did.

We do not use the term 'Gentile' as a synonym of 'heathen' or 'pagan', since the etymology of the first word is usually related to persons who are not Jewish, while the two words we used are usually related to the non-Christians. Moreover, in the histories of philosophy we are concerned with, the term 'Gentile' never appears, instead 'pagan' and 'heathen' – in the different languages – are the terms used.

The few terms we retrace from the missionaries' transcription of Chinese are always in *pīnyīn* and traditional Chinese characters. The Sanskrit terms reconstructed are reported with diacritics in the stem form – i.e. not inflected root – as it is usual in the scientific literature concerned with Sanskrit. For instance, we write *karman* instead of the incorrect term *karma*, since the latter is the nominative case, while the first is the stem form. Simplified Chinese characters are used only when quoting from recent publications from the People's Republic of China.

All quotes that are presented in their original languages in the footnotes respect the orthography, italics, capital letters, etc. of the original source material. We do not reproduce italics and capital letters in translations when not necessary. The only orthographic change made is the replacement of '&' with 'et'.

---

* Roger-Pol Droit, *Le culte du néant. Les philosophes et le Bouddha*, 2nd enlarged edn (Paris: Éditions du Seuil, 2004), 25.

List of Abbreviations

MHP1 Santinello, alii, *Models of the History of Philosophy*, vol. 1 (see Bibliography)

SSGF1 Santinello, alii, *Storia delle storie generali della filosofia*, vol. 1 (see Bibliography)

MHP2 Santinello, alii, *Models of the History of Philosophy*, vol. 2 (see Bibliography)

SSGF2 Santinello, alii, *Storia delle storie generali della filosofia*, vol. 2 (see Bibliography)

General Introduction

'L'object de l'historie est par nature l'homme. Disons mieux: les hommes. Plutôt que le singulier, favorable à l'abstraction, le pluriel, qui est le mode grammatical de la relativité, convient à un science du divers.'
Marc Bloch, *Apologie pour l'historire ou métier d'historien*, 4

The purpose of this work is to examine the European understanding of China and India within the histories of philosophy from 1600 to 1744. The year 1600 is the publication of *Barbaricae philosophiae antiquitatum* by Otto van Heurn and 1744 the year of release of the last book of the *Historia critica* by Jakob Brucker, which was entitled 'De Philosophia Exotica'. Heurn's book is our *terminus post quem*, since in this work it was introduced for the first time in a 'history of philosophy' a chapter about modern or contemporary Indians, together with a chapter about ancient Indians. About Brucker, he provided a very long and detailed chapter on contemporary Asians in his widespread history of philosophy, while, after him, Asians were usually excluded from the histories of philosophy; that is the reason for choosing Brucker as our *terminus ante quem*. The two authors represent two opposite historiographical paradigms and the latter author openly rejected the method and the historical asset of the former. Therefore, we shall, on one side, investigate the description of these two Asian civilizations in a century and a half of 'histories of philosophy', on the other side, we shall try to understand the change of historiographical paradigms and appreciate the effects of these changes in the description of the two civilizations with which we are concerned.

However, it would be incorrect to investigate the chapters on Asians of the modern histories of philosophy without a precise awareness of the sources used by these historians, which were mostly accounts from missionaries preaching in these countries. Although for our investigation the 'histories of philosophy' are primary sources, these were secondary sources at that time, and the primary sources were obviously the accounts of missionaries and travellers from these distant lands. We shall necessarily come to terms with the – explicit or implicit – aims of these primary descriptions, and only after undertaking this analysis, will we be able to appreciate the personal – often apologetic – understanding of the selected historians of philosophy. Therefore, our research will follow parallel lines: on one side, the missionaries' descriptions, which led to the well-known 'rites controversy', and, on the other side, the critical interpretations of these sources by the European historians.

A preliminary and legitimate question that could be raised about our analysis is: why an investigation of the histories of philosophy, instead of the more dynamic French controversial pamphlets, letters, essays, etc.? The reasons for this methodological choice are several.

Firstly, the histories of philosophy – although their consistency is questionable in the period investigated[1] – are instances of a unique philosophical genre with a history itself. Therefore, a comparative investigation is more suitable and the references to one another are really recurring. Brucker was an author aware of almost every 'history of philosophy' written before him and he challenged the opinions and interpretations explicitly expressed by forerunner historians. To be more precise, he quoted Heurn, Horn, Burnet, Stanley, Bayle, Leibniz, Thomasius, Buddeus, Heumann and Deslandes, who are almost the entirety of historians we shall investigate.

The second reason for choosing the histories of philosophy was that these specific texts were not openly written for controversialist aims, instead they were composed in order to provide the complete figure of the philosophy of humankind since the creation of the world (or at least after the Deluge). Therefore, the introduction of India and China was refined and often challenging, since the coherence of the entire picture was relevant for these writers. A *philosophe* could be more incoherent than a historian in his use of foreign civilizations, since, this must be said, every history of philosophy we are concerned with reveals – more or less explicitly – an apologetic or demonstrative aim about what philosophy is and its role.

Our third methodological reason – we suspect it could be the more debatable – regards the greater consistency of these historians than the *philosophes* as representatives of the common European understanding of these civilizations. Usually, scholars present the 'Orientalism before Orientalism' – before the growing of the academic disciplines – as a question which regards libertines, Radical thinkers and *philosophes*. Therefore, the anti-orientalists are generally described as orthodox thinkers who despised or neglected Asia. Most of the available recent investigations are related to eighteenth-century France and focused on Voltaire, on the authors of the *Encyclopédie* or, as the only non-Enlightened philosopher, on Leibniz, who is usually reputed to be the philosopher of his age more concerned with Oriental cultures. The merits of these works are indisputable, since they highlight the critical use of China and India against the politics of the *ancien régime*, the religious violence and intolerance, the lack of meritocracy, the religious and theological control of the minds, etc. However, an investigation of a less harsh and controversialist literature, written by today less known authors, who often represent the common European perception of the Orient more faithfully and systematically, could be useful. Because in the process of writing a history of philosophy lies a double concern for the author: the perception of the self, as a modern European thinker, and the perception of the others, as thinkers of the past or of a distant land. The study of the works related to China or India, which belong to the Enlightenment, often suggests openness and a criticism of the European culture that could interrogate us when compared with the following Hegelian (and Kantian) exclusion of these civilizations from philosophy. While, if we concern ourselves with more moderate authors – as Horn, Burnet, Thomasius, Brucker, etc. – this rift with the following philosophers becomes tinier.

What we want to contend with this investigation is that the exclusion of every non-Greek and extra-European civilization past and present from 'the history of philosophy' was already contained in the precise time of the insertion of India and China as contemporary philosophic civilizations. The Hegelian description of the Orient, as contested by Said and by contemporary philosophers of China and India, was not an original product of the nineteenth-century colonialist and triumphant Europe, but instead a seed already rooted in both the Christian eschatological vision of the seventeenth century and in the opposed secularist scientific vision of the eighteenth-century European culture (and all intermediate positions). Summarising, the exclusion of China and India did not occur in the nineteenth century, but rather it was already argued in the early eighteenth-century histories of philosophy, where these peoples were described as unphilosophical, irrational, pantheistic, idolatrous, hyper-religious, lacking an effective morality, childish, etc. Furthermore, this must be said, these negative descriptions of Asians were certainly apologetical (both orthodox Catholic or Lutheran) but the Sinophilia or Indophilia of the Radical and Enlightened thinkers – following Israel's description – was not disinterested and not necessarily better grounded (on both the historical and philosophical standpoints). The programmatic use of China and India as weapons against orthodoxy was more concerned with the European debate than with a real process of understanding these two civilizations.

On the historiographical paradigms, we must draw attention to a few points concerning methodology. This research would have been impossible without the outstanding seminal work of the University of Padua led by Giovanni Santinello, *Storia delle storie generali della filosofia* [History of the general histories of philosophy] published in five volumes between 1979 and 2004, of which the first three volumes have been translated in English as *Models of the History of Philosophy* (MHP).[2] We will make use of the first two volumes, which cover from the Renaissance to Brucker. This pioneering work has been the subject of both praise and critique. Praises are mostly related to the usefulness and richness of this titanic work. Among the most relevant critiques we want to mention two, namely those raised by Leo Catana[3] and Dimitri Levitin.[4] Leo Catana in both one article and one outstanding monograph praises the MHP as a 'magisterial work', 'indispensable tool', 'pioneering work', 'highly recommended', etc. However, he raises one relevant objection: 'the history of the history of philosophy, including its analytic tools and evaluations, cannot always be explained on the basis of general histories of philosophy ...', therefore, it happens that in order to explain the reasons for specific historiographic choices it would be necessary to look at church history, biography and theology.[5] According to this objection, Santinello and his team made a dramatic research that could be lacking in explanatory power for the historical paradigms defined by some of the historians presented. This is actually a very relevant point we will try to consider in our investigation, particularly as it touches questions such as Original sin, Predestination, Grace, etc. Levitin, in his relevant and innovative history of philosophy in England during the period 1640–1700, dismisses MHP as 'old scholarship' and states 'they have almost nothing to say about the history of philosophy as it was practised by those who did not write works entitled *Historia philosophiae*, or the like'.[6] He offers as confirmation of his point the aforementioned article by Catana. However, Catana has never claimed that MHP are only interested in historians who authored monographs titled '*Historia philosophiae*'. This objection is actually exaggerated, since, of the around eighty historians catalogued and examined in the first two volumes of MHP, less than thirty had written something with a title similar to *Historia philosophiae*. Nevertheless, what both critics correctly point out is that MHP is much too rigidly divided into national schools (Italian, French, German, Dutch and English) and insists too much on the role of Cartesianism. However, those correct observations marginally touch our research, since we will use MHP as a tool in order to find 'histories of philosophy' that presented Asian thought within their expositions, while the partition presented often does not work with our investigation.

The historiographical paradigms we will use are quite general, and we will try to stress the specific stands of each author mentioned. We shall come across three of them: 1. Perennial philosophy or 'prisca theologia'; 2. Sceptical paradigm (i.e. Bayle) and 3. German Eclectic paradigm. The first paradigm suggested a history of philosophy which included all the ancient pre-Greek civilizations, since among these peoples the divine wisdom – preserved by the patriarchs – spread and, therefore, in modern times traces of this wisdom could still be detected among them. The original Neoplatonic perennialists – we should more correctly define them of the Platonic Renaissance – claimed that the wise men of these civilizations were closer to the divine source than Greek and modern philosophers. This paradigm, among the authors selected, concerns Otto van Heurn, Georg Horn and Thomas Burnet, although, as we will see, their perennialism was not univocal and they did not agree about the identity of the patriarch who propagated the wisdom (i.e. Abraham or Noah). Anyway, according to them, philosophy was connected with religion and its history should be inscribed within the biblical framework. However, Horn and Burnet, unlike the original Renaissance perennialists, reserved a relevant place for the development of modern philosophy, because of the European superiority guaranteed by both the Christian revelation and the recent scientific revolution. For instance, Horn acknowledged Chinese culture, but the highest unsurpassed model was already modern Europe. Burnet reserved an intriguing 'philosophical archaeology' to the pre-Christian civilizations, in order to retrace the seeds of ancient wisdom, however, he claimed that, at his time, these extra-European civilizations were barbarous and very far from the European standards of knowledge.

The second paradigm is the 'sceptical paradigm', which has Pierre Bayle as its best advocate. The Frenchman is usually acknowledged as the first theorist of the historical method because of his consistent use of sources, his sceptical reflections and his secularist – if not atheistic – positions. Bayle's image of China and India is influenced by the 'rites controversy' and by Bernier, influences which led the author to forge the idea of the Chinese men as moral atheists, Indians as Quietists and both as Spinozistic thinkers. These descriptions were largely shared by Radical and early Enlightened thinkers, but obviously contested by orthodox thinkers and Leibniz himself. As we shall see, the latter is the last exponent of perennial philosophy and he contended a universalism already far from the Eurocentric self-representation (which was shaped against foreign contemporaries or opposed faiths within the same Europe).

This Eurocentric vision has as best and more refined exponents the German Eclectics, who are often acknowledged as the real fathers of the scientific historical method in philosophy. This claim to be scientific is consistent with the presumption of universalism of the European culture. While the universalism of perennialists descended from the Christian religion as universal faith and was connected with the evangelic and ecumenical missions – which forecasted a diffusion of the revelation among new converts – the universalism of the German Eclectic thinkers was grounded on the Lutheran belonging and on the assumed superiority of the modern European philosophy, science and, more widely, rationality. Broadly speaking, we might say that the 'perennialist' and the 'sceptical' models, although on completely opposing and different grounds, were inclusivist. For instance, Bayle recognised the effectiveness of the Chinese (allegedly) pantheistic and atheistic theories, Wolff even felt them to be close to his own moral system. On the contrary, the German Eclectic histories of philosophy, particularly by Heumann and Brucker, supported a completely 'exclusivist' attitude, since only the Greek philosophies and the modern European philosophies deserved the rank of philosophies. Furthermore, whilst the 'perennialist' historians claimed a common original source of philosophy (although they believed that modern Asians were barbarians), the German Eclectic historians denied this common origin and, as we will see more clearly, they 'deceptively' distinguished religion and philosophy, thus they claimed a secular role for the latter, although they maintained Lutheran apologetic aims.

Throughout this investigation of the sequence of historical paradigms it is possible to identify specific images of the Chinese and Indians, which change consistently with the paradigm they are introduced within. Indians were depicted from Heurn to Brucker as idolatrous and superstitious; while at first the Chinese were acknowledged as respectable thinkers, but the definition of a 'Doctrina Orientalis' as an atheistic thought from Egypt to Japan, contested this claim and only Leibniz, Wolff and a few *philosophes* continued to suggest their morality, while most of the eighteenth-century thinkers followed the all-inclusive definition of one 'Asiatic philosophy', actually inferior to the European philosophy and which did not deserve to be named 'philosophy'. We shall also analyse the primary role of Buddhism, since this religion was the most dreaded by missionaries and its impressive spreading contended the universalistic role of Christian religion itself. Not by chance, while Brucker did not support the devilish nature of Indian and Chinese civilizations – which were simply irrational and inferior – he presented Buddhism as the Asian most hideous thought, which infected the others.

A further point that we shall stress regards the use of ancient and modern sources, which led to the writing of separate chapters or paragraphs on Oriental thought and, surprisingly, this is true from the first to the last author of this survey. Heurn wrote a paragraph on ancient and one on modern Indians, by separating ancient sources on one side and modern on the other side. So did Horn, who introduced China among the sixteenth-century European philosophers, because this civilization had been known – effectively – only at this time. The Eurocentrism of this claim is really intriguing, since it suggests that a civilization deserves to be introduced in history not according to its own chronology but instead at the time when Europeans had become aware of it. Afterwards, Burnet, Buddeus and Brucker did the same; they devoted sections to the ancients, where they made use of only ancient sources, and sections about the moderns written using modern sources. Modern and ancient sources were never contrasted and the ancient were often reputed as more reliable, since the modern sources were written by Jesuit missionaries involved in the defence of their conduct in Asia and in the 'rites controversy', while the Greeks were presumed to be impartial chroniclers.

The second issue we wish to raise in this Introduction is about the secondary literature available on these topics with which we are concerned. As far as we know, there are no monographs or essays devoted to the German Eclectics' exclusion of India and China from the philosophical history, and the same is for the introduction of these civilizations within the perennial historical paradigm. This is because Orientalism is usually acknowledged as a late-eighteenth-century and nineteenth-century topic, since this was the time of the first 'scientific/philological' translations from Oriental languages. However, Jesuits in China were already translating sources for publishing since the first half of the seventeenth century and, although these translations were apologetic – i.e. connected to their evangelic concerns – the impact of these texts was enormous in Europe and did not only regard the Radical or libertine thinkers, as it is often contended. On the other hand, it is true that translations of Indian texts were not realized till the birth of 'scientific' Orientalism, anyway, in the late seventeenth century, detailed accounts as that of Bernier and La Croze (§2.2 and §3.7.) already provided a very specific image of this civilization. Therefore, we need to acknowledge an 'Orientalism before the birth of Orientalism', since Indian and Chinese civilizations were already relevant topics among European thinkers, a century and a half before the presumed beginning of Orientalism. Moreover, the first (presumed) scientific translations of Indian and Chinese texts were obviously influenced by the already steady image of these civilizations.

Virgile Pinot[7] is the author of the first monograph devoted to the influence of Chinese issues in modern France; he explains effectively the Jesuit concerns and the concrete engagement of the French *philosophes* about this new topic. However, Pinot's aim is to prove the influence of China within the French debate, instead of providing the European (or French) image of China. David E. Mungello is likely the most relevant expert of the impact of China on modern philosophers and his essays and monographs are mostly devoted to the Jesuit accommodation,[8] Leibniz[9] and the French *philosophes*. His studies are rich with details and intuitions; however, his arguments likely regard only the second chapter of our investigation and also not the perennialism and the German Eclecticism. A recent investigation is the fourth volume of Pocock's wide research devoted to the complete understanding of the sources of Edward Gibbon's *The Decline and Fall of the Roman Empire*, which is entitled *Barbarism and religion*. In this fourth volume the author retraces the sources of the English historian about Barbarian civilizations, however he takes into account only the literature from the 1770s, completely disregarding the previous debates.

Several essays have been devoted to specific aspects of the impact of China on the European political debate from the end of the sixteenth century to the Enlightenment[10] or to the travel accounts from Asia. However, the first really effective works on the seventeenth century (proto-)Orientalism, which aimed at reconstructing the European image of India and China, are due to Urs App, who is both a renowned Sinologue

(Chinese Buddhism) and a historian of ideas. In his *The Birth of Orientalism*, he devotes a complete investigation to Voltaire, Diderot and Anquetil-Duperron and provides the sources behind each author, who are unfortunately all thinkers not investigated in our research, which ends with the 1740s. On the contrary, in 2012, therefore during the writing of our research, App published *The cult of emptiness*, the first effective study on the western discovery of Buddhism, from the early missionaries penetrating into Japan to Pierre Bayle. This work was of great help in our second chapter, since it proves the incontrovertible evidence of the shaping of an image of Buddhism – and therefore Asia – already at the end of the seventeenth century,[11] despite what is contended by Frédéric Lenoir[12] and, moreover, Roger-Pol Droit.[13] In effect, Droit suggests that the nihilistic vision of Buddhism arose in the 1830s with Eugène Burnouf, professor of Sanskrit at the Collège de France, whilst this negative judgement has already been fixed since the Jesuits who reached Japan and China after François Xavier.

The last three monographs we consider worth mentioning are *Orientalismo e idee di tolleranza nella cultura francese del primo '700* [*Orientalism and Ideas of Tolerance in early 18th century French Culture*] by Rolandi Minuti,[14] *India and Europe* by Wilhelm Halbfass[15] and *Anti-Europa* by Eung-Jeung Lee.[16] Minuti's work is devoted to the investigation of the use of Orientalism – i.e. Islam, China and India – as a critical tool against the violence, the intolerance and the obscurantism of European politics and society from the late-eighteenth-century thinkers to the age of Montesquieu. This composed essay traces the definition of a European identity in contrast to the Oriental otherness, particularly in the French early Enlightenment. What arises from Minuti's study is the great relevance of the orientalist challenge in the modern European debate, but also the limited interest of these thinkers in a real process of understanding of these foreign civilizations.

The work authored by Halbfass is likely the most relevant monograph on our topic concerning India, as it covers the issue of the shaping of Indian and European identities in a mutual confrontation. Halbfass includes a section entitled 'India in the History of European Self-Understanding', which, although being mostly devoted to India missionaries and to the most renowned philosophers, touches the historiographical questions and stresses the relevance of a research devoted to both the self-understanding of Europe and the understanding of others throughout the study of the western histories of thought.

The last book by Lee is a long and detailed collection of the most relevant ideas on China written by outstanding German authors since the early German Enlightenment until the debate of the late 1990s and it even provides a short introduction to the missionaries' literature. Though the research is erudite and full of impressive insights, it focuses only on the most well-known authors investigated in our analysis – i.e. Leibniz and Wolff – and neglects the all-encompassing turmoil about China and India in the seventeenth and eighteenth centuries. This book also regularly fails to retrace the origin of certain opinions on China, which can be followed only by examining those authors' primary sources, rather than their writings. Lee disregards the historical paradigms we already presented and, according to her, it seems that only in the second half of the eighteenth century in Göttingen University did the first universal historians (not of philosophy) begin to investigate Asia in their comprehensive works. This is completely imprecise, since universal histories of philosophy had already been written since the late sixteenth century. Despite the fact that, from our point of view, these are drawbacks, this work is pioneering and unavoidable since the analysis of the individual authors is completely outstanding.

A last unavoidable bibliographic consideration is about the antiquarian history research, which recently investigated the impact of the understanding of Asia in Europe during our period of investigation, with a focus mostly on geography, intellectual history, travel literature and religious debate. The most prominent expert in this field is Joan-Pau Rubiés, author of several essays and monographs. Two of his most recent essays are particularly connected to our investigation. In 'From Antiquarianism to Philosophical History: India, China, and the World History of Religion in European Thought (1600-1770)', he retraces the influences of missionaries' sources (Ricci, De Nobili, Martini, etc.) and the European historical debate on Voltaire's image of China and India. He also correctly stresses the religious and apologetic issues at stake. In 'The Discovery of New Worlds and Sixteenth-century Philosophy', he proposes an overview of the impact of knowledge about 'new civilizations' (Asia and America) on European philosophical and historical debate. The merit of this article is a rich analysis of the proto-ethnographic sources by missionaries. Although we are clearly indebted to this scholarly research, our focus is largely different, connected with the creation of the modern philosophical field, of the 'system of philosophy'.[17] We are actually engaged with the relevant question of 'what philosophy is or should be' in this historical frame and not the antiquarian attitude of intellectuals. We are interested in discovering the origin of the enduring parochial attitude of Philosophy more than we are in providing a complete coverage of the entirety of European knowledge about Asia.

The last issue we wish to point out regards the reasons for an investigation of India and China together. Usually scholars undertake an investigation of one of these two civilizations, because of personal interests and competences. For instance, Mungello is the most relevant expert of the reception and understanding of China; Halbfass devoted his research only to India. As far as we know, this is true for almost all the authors of monographs or essays about Orientalism. However, whilst this approach is correct when the subject of study is the 'scientific Orientalism', since China and India were arguments of two separate academic disciplines and chairs, this is questionable and problematic when we are concerned with the previous period. We mention the most relevant reasons in support of our claim. Firstly, China and India were usually included in the wide definition of 'the Indies', which covered from Persia to Japan, from Mongolia to South-East Asia. This is particularly true for India and China, because, as we shall see, since Horn the Chinese were mentioned in the chapter on ancient Indians and the reason was Buddhism, which was acknowledged as an Indian sect already at that time by the early missionaries themselves. The second reason is that the understanding of the thought of both civilizations was usually one unique process, as the study of Kircher, Bernier and Bayle might prove. The 'doctrina orientalis', the Asiatic atheism and pantheism, were theories which included China and India under one single devilish spreading. What was correct for Indian 'sects' was often claimed as correct for Chinese 'sects'. It is obvious that the link was Buddhism and thus an investigation of the difficult European acknowledgement of this thought shall be necessary. China and India were also the only ancient civilizations quoted by ancient sources which were still alive as such. On the contrary, Egyptian, Chaldean, Phoenician and Persian civilizations were extinct, because Muslims had conquered them and the ancient cultures had mostly been eradicated. Therefore, China and India were also connected because they were a historical exception, and this fact is evident when we study the modern histories of philosophy. The last evidence we adduce is the work by Minuti, where the question of tolerance is investigated as a topic raised by eighteenth-century philosophers who compared the European social and political model with Islamic countries, India, China, Japan and even South-East Asia reigns. In this respect, Urs App, although a Sinologue, is also always concerned in his works with both India and China, but also Japan and sometimes even Persia. Therefore, a study of India or of China as separate is certainly legitimate, but it could not reveal the complex phenomenon of this cross-cultural understanding, which is instead our aim.

1

India and China between 'Prisca Theologia' and Barbarity

> *'En sort qu'en bien des cas le démon des origines fut peut-être seulement un avatar de cet autre satanique ennemi de la véritable histoire: la manie du jugement.'*
> Marc Bloch, *Apologie pour l'histoire ou métier d'historien*, 7

1.0 Introduction

The origin of the genre 'History of philosophy' during the Italian Renaissance and its spread around Europe in the same years is usually a matter of agreement among Scholars. To be more precise, the place of birth of this philosophical field is considered to be the Florentine Neoplatonic School of Ficino (1433–99). For centuries, this Neoplatonic historical model of philosophy has been incredibly successful, being the leading one until the first half of the eighteenth century. It is also worth noting that this tradition did not begin in the Renaissance, but it dates back to the ancient Neoplatonic thinkers – i.e. Clement of Alexandria – passing on to Saint Augustine and Roger Bacon in the Middle Ages.[1]

Ficino's theory on the origin and diffusion of philosophy is usually named 'prisca theologia' or 'philosophia perennis'. As Charles B. Schmitt explains tersely, both theories consider philosophy as more ancient than Greek civilization, since it was already practised among Chaldeans, Persians and ancient Egyptians.[2] 'Prisca theologia' puts the stress on an enigmatic and esoteric wisdom carried out by wise men such as Zoroaster, Mercurius Trismegistus and, among the Greeks, by the Platonic – and pre-Platonic – lineage with Orpheus, Aglaophamus, Pythagoras and Plato. This theory was mostly grounded on Hellenistic fabricated texts, which claimed an ancient spiritual wisdom common to ancient civilizations. This ancient wisdom itself was that of Noah and Moses, if not of Adam himself, thus it was transmitted within patriarchs' divine lineage of wisdom. Following this theory, it was possible to trace this lineage back and rediscover all seeds of divine wisdom lost in the previous ages. The theory of the 'philosophia perennis', while sharing the same historical paradigm, does not entail the millenarian tone of the 'prisca theologia'. The 'philosophia perennis' is more neutral and claims simply a *fil rouge* across the history of philosophy, which if investigated carefully reveals traces of scientific truth in all ages. In both paradigms the historiographical task was to investigate all forms of thought and to compare whatever concept could seem similar among ancient civilizations. Schmidt-Biggemann, one of the foremost scholars of perennialism, summarizes suggesting that: 'Their theory consisted basically in the idea that Jewish-Christian theology and pious philosophy derived from participation in the same divine ideas, and that they revealed the same essential truths'.[3] This sentence illustrated all the relevance and urgency of this study felt by modern historians. The aim was to grasp God's archetypes, ideas, language and, in one word, wisdom, through the investigation of all ancient cultural expressions that could be acknowledged as related to His Splendour. However, it is necessary to point out that this 'paradigm' had numerous variations and that practically each historian proposed a specific interpretation. Therefore, we need to understand this paradigm not as a rigid school, but rather as a wide concept.

This Ficinian theory derived from the Neoplatonic *Theologia platonica* by Proclo, which claimed a common lineage of Orpheus and Plato. Gemistus Plethon began this lineage with the *Oracula chaldaica* (following Psello's analysis) and the Chaldean and Egyptian traditions of wisdom (i.e. Trismegistus). In his *Nómoi* (*Treatise of the Laws*), Plethon[4] suggested Zoroaster as the first lawgiver in history and among the first wise men of all times he listed Brahmans and Magi.[5] Before Plethon, Saint Augustine, in his *De civitate dei*, provided a genealogy of the transmission of wisdom derived from Clement of Alexandria and he undertook an investigation based on biblical chronology. Afterwards, we need to mention Roger Bacon, who elaborated and enlarged Augustine's genealogy in his *Opus Maius*. According to Schmidt-Biggemann: 'Bacon fills the gaps Augustine left in wisdom's genealogy by introducing Noah, his sons, and Abraham, who came from the town of Ur in Chaldea, as teachers of the Egyptians.'[6] As we shall see, the issue about which biblical patriarch moved to Asia was central among the sixteenth- and the seventeenth-century historians, as for instance in Guillaume Postel. Whilst for the true 'perennialist' all sons of Noah would have been bearers of wisdom, later historians divided this diffusion in more or less pure genealogies. For instance, in Bacon, Ham, who mocked his father Noah when drunk and naked (Genesis 9.20-27) and therefore had his descent damned by Noah himself, was the Father of Zoroaster, who invented magical arts.[7]

Ficino[8] elaborated all these Hellenistic, late Byzantine and Medieval influences into a global theory, obviously having Plato as a theoretical culmination, but with the aim of recovering the hidden unique source at the basis of the original theology.[9] According to Ficino, this research was the best accomplishment of the mutual penetration of philosophy and faith. In this project, besides Plethon, he was supported by an authoritative and widely followed father of the Church: Clement of Alexandria. In his *Stromata*, specifically in the first book, we find a definite denial of the originality of Greek thought and an accurate demonstration of its Egyptian and Jewish origin. Clement asserted the existence of an ancient wisdom coming from God. Obviously, he did not know many pieces of work of the 'eastern' tradition – as they were often Hellenistic fakes – thus he was not able to provide a real 'migration theory' of philosophy or simply a history of philosophy, as afterwards it was elaborated by the Platonic Renaissance philosophers and in the two following centuries. The main 'migration theories' and histories of philosophy were, since their modern spread, related to these paradigms of the 'prisca theologia' and the 'philosophia perennis'. Therefore, within this paradigm, philosophy was quite a wide concept, it corresponded with *sapientia* (wisdom).

Both these historical theories were expressions of a pure syncretic view, which tolerates dissent and tries to reconcile disagreements on every theoretical question. The opposed theory is exclusivism, which claims only one theory to be true and the others to be false. The exclusivist theory has always been represented among historians – or proto-historians – of philosophy. The best instance of this theoretical view is Diogenes Laërtius himself, who ascribed philosophy merely to the Greek thinkers, as a specific and new attitude arisen for the first time in this land. His *Lives and Opinions of Eminent Philosophers* is certainly the most refined and rich collection of philosophers written in ancient times. For this reason Diogenes' *Lives* was widely quoted by both syncretist and exclusivist historians of philosophy, although syncretists did not follow his first negative chapter on barbaric philosophy.[10]

As we said, almost all the first instances of 'history of philosophy' followed this perennialist historiographical model. These histories or proto-histories of philosophy usually provided more or less wide chapters on those barbarian civilizations. Among the ancient civilizations, whose thinkers were listed as 'prisci theologi', the most important were Chaldean, Persian, Egyptian and, obviously, Jewish.[11] Chaldea was the spreading source of the divine wisdom, usually being acknowledged as the country of patriarchs and the place of deluge. Persians were connected with the mythical figure of Zoroaster, who was considered the most important barbaric thinker. Egypt was not merely the place where sciences were cultivated at first and where religion reached a high level of sophistication, but also the bridge between ancient eastern culture and classical Greece. Obviously, Jews, historically connected with both Chaldeans and Egyptians, represented the first pure religious philosophy and the concrete origin of monotheism. According to fifteenth- and sixteenth-century philosophers, Jews and Greeks were the main direct sources of Christian philosophy: the former of religious thought derived from God – i.e. the Holy Covenant – and the latter of the philosophical method. However, these perennialist thinkers argued that Greeks were not properly 'prisci theologi', since they had elaborated and refined concepts and techniques derived from the aforementioned ancient East civilizations. In almost all these Platonic Renaissance histories, Chaldeans, Persians – i.e. Zoroaster – and Egyptians were steadily inserted, but many historians also added further civilizations. For instance, in the most complete historical lists we can also find Thracians, Scythians and even Indians as the farthest civilization reached by the aforementioned divine wisdom.

De Perenni philosophia[12] by Agostino Steuco (1497–1548) is universally acknowledged to be the first complete achievement of Ficinian historiographical paradigm[13] within a consistent and systematic early history of philosophy. Moreover, Steuco was the first to openly use the term 'philosophia perennis'. Like Ficino, Steuco reputed Plato as the best philosopher of all times, since he was the merging of the Adamitic (divine) wisdom, which had spread from the Orient – esp. Chaldeans, Armenians, Assyrians – to the countries of Jews and Egyptians, and afterwards reached the

West (ancient Greece).[14] In his analysis, Steuco did not introduce either India or China; nevertheless, this was the model in which these two civilizations were inserted into the following decades.

A remarkable instance of the insertion of India in this paradigm is the long list of civilizations provided by the Jesuit philosopher Benito Pereyra (1535–1610)[15] in 1588:

> It is displayed that in ancient times the wise men who worshiped [philosophy] were not Greeks, but mostly Barbarians. Such as Orpheus, who was Thracian, Thales was Phoenician, Mercurius was Egyptian, Zoroaster was Persian, Athlas was Libyan or Phrygian, Anacharsis was Scythian and Pherecydes was from Syros. In addition, among Spaniards the magistrates, men of great wisdom, ruled [people] with different nature, belief [in God] and morals. Gauls had the Druids, Egyptians the priests, among Babylonians the Chaldeans, among the Persians the Magi, among Indians the Gymnosophists and among Jews the Prophets.[16]
>
> ibid., IV, chap. 2, 191

This list of ancient 'barbaric' civilizations was one of the most complete. But, it was not completely original, being similar to the well-known list provided by Saint Augustine in his *De civitate Dei*: 'among other peoples that are supposed to have had wise men or philosophers: Mauritanians, Libyans, Egyptians, Indians, Persians, Chaldeans, Scythians, Gauls, Spaniards, ...'.[17] We need to notice that for Augustine, although those heathen civilizations possess wise men, it is only thanks to Mosaic revelation, grace and faith that men can carry out truly virtuous actions. Therefore, although he acknowledged all these ancient cultures as able to provide wisdom, Augustine maintained an exclusively Christian vision of what true religious wisdom was.

India was introduced among these civilizations and it was the most remote one, the concrete border of the spreading of ancient wisdom. Sources usually quoted for India were the ancient ones, particularly Megasthenes, Strabo, Philostratus and Clement of Alexandria. In the sixteenth century, although not copious, contemporary sources about India and America were already available, but early historians generally neglected them, since their historical focus was not on contemporary barbarians, but rather – as we said – on the roots of the ancient wisdom. India, together with all other civilizations, was mostly collocated in an ancient lost past. However, whilst all civilizations of the remote past of the Near East had actually disappeared and had been replaced, India was a historical exception, because in modern times it showed the same practices and traditions as they were described by the Greeks. The first historian who felt the necessity to provide details on contemporary Indians, was Heurn and we shall see that this necessity was not without consequences for the perennial historiographical paradigm (§1.1.).

This insertion is particularly consistent within the sixteenth-century phenomenon named 'antiquarianism', a field of study born of the research of the historian Momigliano. As Rubiés describes: 'European antiquarianism was born in the fifteenth century as the study of the customs, institutions, and material culture of the classical past'.[18] The study of ancient pagan cultures provided the 'tool set' for understanding unknown civilizations. Miller explains 'fascination with the details of life in ancient Rome, and especially with its structures of law and religion, provided the model used for dealing with the reality of living, breathing pagans in America and Asia'.[19] Most antiquarians dealing with Asians and Americans were guided by a thomistic and proto-secularist vision of theology as rational and natural, contending that, constitutively, humans rationality – belonging to God – can grasp some knowledge of God. Therefore, despite their cultural and geographic origin, all humans of the world can reach a certain knowledge of God, independently from the correct faith, the Mosaic revelation or the divine grace.[20] As we will mention further when dealing with Jesuit missionaries, Aquinas' natural reason and antiquarianism's anthropological epistemic instruments merged with *philosophia perennis*.

As we all know, in the late sixteenth century, missionaries' accounts and reports on China also reached Europe. One of the first thinkers who attempted the insertion of China into the perennial and syncretic paradigm was the orientalist Guillaume Postel. However, for a concrete understanding of China, Europeans had to wait until 1615, when *De Christiana expeditione* by Ricci was translated and published in Latin and French by Trigault. Missionaries' controversial descriptions of China were so influential that they need a detailed investigation, since these accounts entailed a refined historiographical paradigm consistent with their evangelic mission in Asia. About European historians, the first concrete insertion of China into a history of Philosophy was due to Georg Horn, who surprisingly introduced this civilization among European modern philosophers. In the same decades, missionaries reported the existence of the Chinese *Annals* and claimed that the history provided by these *Annals* was more ancient than the chronology deduced from the Bible, fostering a long chronological dispute in Europe. This dispute was really relevant from the historiographical viewpoint, because it could change the paradigm of the spread of the ancient divine wisdom from the Near East. As we shall see, the related issues had a chronological, a geographical and, obviously, a theological nature at the same time. For instance, either the Chinese *Annals* were an untrustworthy source, or the Chinese were more ancient than the Deluge (as Pre Adamists asserted).

In the late seventeenth century, Burnet introduced both India and China within his 'philosophical archaeology', providing a long Appendix at the end of his most important writing. Although he did not mention Heurn, Burnet proposed a similar theory: ancient Asians' cultures were suitable to be investigated by his 'philosophical archaeology' in order to find traces of the original divine wisdom, instead, modern Asians were barbarians, thus they have completely lost their original purity and their connection with wisdom. At the opposite side of Heurn and Burnet, Isaac Vossius and la Mothe le Vayer, both acknowledged as proto-libertines or proto-Radical thinkers, praised contemporary Asians, since they were both completely fascinated by the Riccian Jesuit description of China as a moral, tolerant and meritocratic empire. Furthermore, le Vayer's respectful appraisal of Confucius and Confucianism brings us to the next chapter, where Bayle's 'Chinese moral atheism' is investigated in detail.

1.1 The first rift in the perennial philosophy model: Otto van Heurn and India

The founding principle of perennial philosophy is the antiquity of the earlier philosophers, who were considered closer to the original divine wisdom. These ancient philosophers were named 'prisci theologi'. Therefore, they were presumed to be no longer alive in modern times. The sole contemporary philosophy, which was accepted by inclusivist – as well as exclusivist – philosophers, was the European philosophy, acknowledged as in continuity with Greek and Christian heritage. This heritage was recognized by most of the European historians. In every work on the history of philosophy we have mentioned, Oriental civilizations merely seemed to have 'prisci theologi', who lived in ancient and remote times. The only exceptions were Jews and Arabs (Muslims), as they were evidently part of the general root of monotheism; these were not as advanced as Christians from the philosophical viewpoint, but they shared the common biblical frame of a single God and they had been in continuous contact with Christians. On the contrary, all other ancient civilizations had disappeared as they had been in the past. At the time, Chaldeans, Assyrians, Persians (Zoroastrians), Egyptians, Thracians and all other civilizations listed by historians had already disappeared and their historical lands at that time mostly belonged to Muslims. While this claim was true for all these ancient civilizations, there was one exception: India.

Indian culture and society were described by ancient sources and by travellers or missionaries' accounts since Marco Polo almost identically. The divided classes and the Brahmans role as described by Megasthenes or Clement of Alexandria, were still reported in modern times almost unchanged. Although modern accounts claimed that superstition and barbarity prevailed in India, ancient and modern descriptions were compatible. The first historian of philosophy who recognized this unique continuity was Otto van Heurn (1577–1652), in his *Barbaricae philosophiae antiquitatum*.[21] He was a professor of theology at the University of Leyden, a philosopher and a doctor.[22]

The history of barbaric philosophy was devoted to antediluvian and post-diluvian philosophy before Greeks. As the author explained in the Preface, his work aimed at integrating Diogenes Laërtius' *Lives and opinions of eminent Philosophers*, where pre-Greek philosophy had been completely neglected. Heurn firmly believed in the superiority of Greek philosophy, however, he attributed the origin and the first development of philosophy and science to Chaldeans and Egyptians. He devoted the first book of his work to the biblical history of philosophy from Adam until the spread of philosophy into Greece. According to him, the first cradle of ancient philosophy after the Deluge was Chaldea; but when a famine obliged Abraham to move to Egypt, philosophy found there its second and most eminent home. In Egypt, Abraham met the local clergymen, thanks to whom the ancient wisdom had reached its greatest splendour. Since Chaldea and Egypt were the cradle of the biblical Abrahamitic lineage, Heurn focused his attention mostly on the description of these two civilizations, where the most important *prisci theologi* lived. Egyptians, in Heurn's opinion, were not only the first philosophers, but also even the first scientists, consistently with the 'philosophia perennis' model (for instance Roger Bacon). According to Eric Jorink: 'Heurnius's lifelong obsession with *prisca scientia* is clearly illustrated by his only philosophical work, the *Barbaricae philosophiae antiquitatum*, which appeared in 1600 ... Heurnius was certainly one of the [Dutch] Republic's most baroque advocates of the *sapientia veterum*.'[23]

The second book of the history is divided into four treatises: 1. Indians; 2. Babylonians and Phoenicians; 3. Egyptians and Judeans; 4. Impure magic. As usual, the first chapter is not devoted to Indians only, hence it opens with a long paragraph on Zoroaster (Bactrian), where the author quoted and translated many texts into Latin which had already been collected by Francesco Patrizi. Two chapters actually about India follow the first chapter of the second book. Although almost every civilization is investigated in several chapters, with each one devoted to a specific aspect – i.e. theology, physics, etc.[24] – only the two chapters on India are arranged chronologically: *De Priscorum Indorum philosophorum variis generibus* and *De recentium Indorum Philosophorum generibus*. This change is significant and intriguing, since India for Heurn was a concrete historical exception.

The chapter on ancient Indians ('priscorum Indorum philosophorum') begins with the biblical theory of Brahmans as descendants of Abraham and Keturah,[25] as claimed by Postel 'etymologically'.[26] Heurn attributed the knowledge of arts and sciences to this lineage, in particular as regards Astrology and natural Magic, which were still alive in India, as reported by contemporary Portuguese voyagers (ibid., 140–1). Heurn described Indians by quoting the common classical sources well diffused among antiquarians, as the classification of philosophers according to Strabo (*Geo.*, XVI, I, 59–60). Heurn also reported that Indians practised hard physical exercises and that they used to die without a moan into pyres. He commented:

> Insomuch as, that by means of several exercises they supplied their body with strength, to make their mind stable, and to stay immobile about judgements and decisions. All their philosophy had one aim and end: a pious death ended a good life.
>
> ibid., 142[27]

Heurn's comment reveals an unexpressed, but clear comparison with stoic ideals and moral life, aspects usually used as evidences of natural theology. Ancient Indian philosophers were presented as moral people, insensitive to pain and violent death, as according to classical Greek descriptions; and this morality of the ancients is relevant when compared to modern Indians.

Besides the ancient section, the real contribution to a new image of India is actually the chapter about contemporary Indians ('recentium Indorum Philosophorum'), wherein Heurn quoted extensively the recent 'Praefatio' by Giovanni Matalio Metello – Ioannis Matalii Metelli – to Jerónimo Osório,[28] *De rebus Emmanuelis Lusitaniae Regis invictissimi*;[29] a text devoted to Spanish and Portuguese conquests around the world, particularly in Asia. The *Preface* is a sort of collection of ancient and modern sources, merged together without any form of notes or captions, typical of the antiquarianism of the time. In his texts, Heurn separated ancient sources – generally well known and used in the previous chapter about ancient Indians – from modern ones. In doing so, Heurn expressed his clear intention to provide a chapter with pieces of information that concerned only modern Indians and, at the same time, he openly acknowledged the survival and continuity of Indian thought.

Heurn presented many unprecedented details found in Metello. The first clarification was the new classification of Indian thinkers, divided into 'Baneanes' and 'Bracmanes', although they were no longer named 'Brachmanes' (as for the ancients), a certain linguistic continuity was undeniable. Both groups had a strict moral code and alimentary prescriptions – i.e. vegetarianism – contained in sacred texts and taught by prophets ('prophetas', ibid., 145). These persons let their hair grow from childhood, and they wore a 'funiculum triplicem' with devotion (ibid., 148), namely the threefold thread of the Brahmin (in Sanskrit *yajñopavīta*). Heurn, following Metello, also reported the cult of cows and of several idols.

> Brahmans worship cows and they teach not to kill them. They believe that God is black, [because,] being familiar with this colour; it is wonderful in their eyes. These awful black idols are abundantly and impurely sprinkled with oil: so that [their] faces are gloomy and dirty, their aspect strikes terror into observers.
>
> ibid., 146[30]

People worshipped these idols daily with oblations of food and money, because Indian plebs were really superstitious and they feared disasters that could be caused by their possible religious negligence. Furthermore, Heurn noticed another preposterous practice against nature very diffused among Indians: polygamy (ibid., 147). From these excerpts we can figure out the shaping of an image of modern Indians as immoral and vicious, decayed heirs of the ancient 'Abrahamic Indians'. Whether ancient Indians were moral and strict ascetics, modern Indians were immoral, idolatrous and superstitious men.

Indian religion was esoteric, the secrets had to be protected and never revealed out of the inner circle of clergymen (ibid., 147). People were excluded from the heart of wisdom and were devoted only to idolatry. Wisdom and rites were taught in specific schools and uttered in a local language, which had a function similar to Latin (ibid.). Metelli and Heurn did not mention Sanskrit, but the reference is evident. Therefore, the description of contemporary Indians was already provided: they were superstitious, idolaters and subjugated to the class of clergymen. And we shall see this image had great fortune in the next two centuries. This fortune is due to the relevance of the concept of idolatry in the history and theology of the time. As Barbu[31] shows, idolatry was one of the labels of corruption used by Saint Paul, together with immorality, greed and drunkenness. For early Christian authors, this concept was often equated with polytheism, therefore the corruption of the original monotheism caused by demons. Aquinas suggested that if idolatry was only caused by demons, humans would not be considered responsible for it, therefore idolatry must belong primarily to human 'inordinate affections', which causes their attachment to living beings and enjoyment of them, instead of God. Demons according to Aquinas have a secondary role. This consideration helps us to understand the insistence of Jesuits, antiquarians and historians upon the stoic characters of good pagans. Their good and balanced nature was necessary in order to escape idolatry.

Two interesting details quoted by Heurn in his history reveal clearly that this was a description of India from the standpoint of missionaries preaching in India. The first is a surprising picture of the Indian God: 'They worship the God creator of heaven and earth repeating many times this sentence: "I worship [/pray] You, my God, for your eternal grace and help"'.[32] The contents and the words of this prayer remind to Christianity and they are not consistent with Indian culture, even if we compare them with followers of the devotional cults – as *bhakti* – therefore it had to be a Christian fabrication. Soon after this 'Christianized' prayer Metelli suggested obviously: 'Ingenio sunt acutissimo' ('regarding cleverness, [they] are extremely acute'). The second detail is about the interaction between missionaries and Indians: the latter consider taking food from the hands of Catholic clergymen as a sacrilegious act (ibid., 148). Although this refusal could be misinterpreted as an act committed specifically against missionaries, we know today that it fits perfectly with the Indian code of purity and impurity. An Indian could never receive food by an outcast and foreigners are *mleccha*, barbarians, hence they are ranked out of the Indian social castes.[33] Accepting food offered from the hands of a *mleccha* may involve tragic consequences, as diseases as well as the possibility of being refused by equals. These two details reported by Heurn are relevant, since they prove to which extent modern historians were influenced in the description of India and, as we shall see, of China by the accounts provided by missionaries.

Therefore, we find in Heurn the attempt to prove the continuity of Indian thought, but without the intention of claiming their current status as direct 'heirs of Abraham' or the surviving among them of 'prisca theologia'. Modern Indians had lost their purity since ancient times, the plebs were superstitious and their religiosity was impure. There was a clear ambiguity, introduced by Metello himself, between two opposite aims: on one side, missionaries needed to prove that Christian religion was necessary to save Indians, on the other side, they had to guarantee the possible compatibility of Christian religion with Indian culture. For these ambiguous reasons, Heurn's description merged positive and negative aspects, giving an incoherent image of India. Ancient divine wisdom and modern barbarity: these two were the poles of the description of Indians and this was a consequence of the merging of perennialist model, Aquinas' natural theology and the need to preserve a primary role to modern Christian Europeans.

The *Preface* by Metello (1580) was written before the great systematic work of Ricci on China[34] and the effective understanding of India had to wait two decades for Roberto de Nobili (1577–1656), who was harshly criticized for his 'Indianized method' and whose work was almost unknown among European thinkers. The image of modern Indians as already far from their ancient purity, hence already placed out of the perennial philosophy stream, became the leading one. This is the opinion of the most relevant historians of philosophy as for instance Burnet and Deslandes, although their general philosophical frames were very different from one another.

1.2 Jesuits and philosophia perennis: Xavier, Postel and Ricci

In the previous paragraph, we have seen how Heurn inserted India within his own perennial philosophy model, whilst China was still almost unknown to European thinkers. However, in the sixteenth century India and China had already been receiving Christian missionaries for a couple of centuries. At first, Thomas the Apostle came probably to India, Nestorians instead came to China and, in the thirteenth and fourteenth centuries, the first Christian missionaries reached China. They were the early Franciscans,[35] whose preaching left minor traces in China and passed almost unnoticed in Europe. However, it was only from the last decades of the sixteenth century that real accounts and reports on East Asia reached Europe. Authors were missionaries and, to a lesser extent, travellers (merchants), as in the previous centuries. What made the difference was that these missionaries belonged mostly to a new order, namely the Jesuit. As is well known, this order had two founders, Ignatius of Loyola (1491–1556) and Francis Xavier (1506–52). The first wrote the theoretical rules of the order – i.e. *Spiritual Exercises* – while the second was the first Jesuit missionary; he preached in India, Indonesia and even in Japan. In 1552 Xavier died while trying to enter mainland China, and because of his successful preaching became an extraordinary figure in the sixteenth century, his missionary life remaining as an evangelic model among Jesuits. Whilst many missionaries in India were devoted mostly to the European Christians living there, Xavier and the Jesuits who followed him started a real process of conversion of local people and tried to understand their civilizations. In doing so, Xavier wrote many letters reporting his experience to his European correspondents and, therefore, he provided unprecedented descriptions of eastern peoples.[36]

The first founders of the Jesuits were aware of their cross-cultural role and they believed firmly in a perfect Christian universalism, as typical in sixteenth-century Catholic Europe. 'Prisca theologia' is clearly a universalist theory, which claims a common origin of the whole thought of the world, whose origin was God's wisdom. Jesuits, without being openly perennialists, supported this opinion grounded on their religious and missionary aim which descended mostly from Aquinas' natural theology. The whole of humanity, in one way or another, shares a natural rationality and an innate idea of God. Following the widely diffused universal consent argument (*consensus gentium*), advocated by Cicero in particular (*De Natura Deorum*, II, 2–4), both Jesuits (counter-reform side) and Calvin (reform side), shared the assumption that total ignorance of God was impossible. Unlike historians, they found in that theory about the nature of the thinkers of ancient times the practical key for their mission in the present times, since they had to awaken and vivify the ancient seeds of monotheism lying in at least some – if not all – civilizations, and particularly China – despite their distance from Chaldea or Judea. According to Jesuits, these seeds of monotheism were to be discovered in ancient texts and rituals of foreign civilizations. Ethnographic observations, collaborations with locals, language skills, textual study and philology were the keys of their method. To a certain extent, Jesuits' action out of Europe might be considered as the culmination of the Counter-Reformation movement. According to their task, Jesuits were often refined men of letters and scientists, since they needed the qualities necessary to understand other cultures and to captivate local intellectual groups. That is the reason for inserting here the following analysis of the different interpretations of East Asian civilizations formulated by Jesuit missionaries from Xavier to Ricci. This multifaceted process of understanding determined the 'rites controversy' and the insertion of China within the historiographical works since the late seventeenth century to most of the eighteenth century. After Ricci, this process of interpretation continued and became mostly a debate over 'atheism' or 'idolatry', as we shall see in the next chapter devoted to the historiographical paradigm of atheism (§2.1.).

Xavier's letters were addressed to clergymen concerned with foreign missions; hence his accounts remained almost unknown to the intellectuals of the time. But there are relevant exceptions, among them there is Guillaume Postel (1510–81). Postel's viewpoint is intriguing for at least two reasons: 1. He was in direct contact with the Jesuit circle, since he knew Xavier and Loyola personally; 2. His 'prisca theologia' theory about Indians was very influential among historians. Postel studied in Paris with the first founders of the Jesuit order (in the 1530s) and he shared their evangelization project.[37] He is usually considered the first orientalist in Europe, as he knew Arabic, Syriac, Hebrew and other Semitic languages (i.e. he was a translator for the French embassy in Constantinople). He was also an astronomer and an advocate of religious universalism, which drove him to the quest for the 'lingua humana'.[38]

As we said, Postel was widely quoted by historians regarding the place of Indians within the biblical genealogy and that is why we need to investigate his thought, although he did not provide a history of philosophy. In *De originibus* and in *Abrahami patriarchae liber Jezirah*, he claimed a 'clear' philological connection between 'Brachmanes' and Abraham, based merely on phonetic assonance, typical of late Middle Age and early Modern (proto-)philology.

> Greeks called them Gymnosophists in reason of their nakedness and self-imposed poverty. Others, speaking of nowadays clergymen, in Gujarat and in other realms of India, called [them] Abrahmanes, Brahmanas, or Brahminos, from the same Abraham, authors of their disciplines ...[39]

The statement of Indians as descendants of Abraham and Keturah is an unmistakable instance of 'prisca theologia' and 'philosophia perennis', two theories strongly advocated by Postel. He believed that all religions of the world had a common root and that biblical history could incorporate each history of these religions, since Christian faith was the real universal faith. Therefore, the Abrahamic origin of Brachmans – argued historically and etymologically – was a natural consequence of his universalistic belief.

Besides this (pseudo-)philological claim, in a lesser known work Postel suggested a divine historical meaning of the Jesuit mission in the East and provided an astonishing comparison between Christianity and Buddhism, which deserves some attention. This minor book is entitled *Des merveilles du monde, et principalemét des admirables choses des Indes, et du nouveau monde*,[40] however, the title is simply the first paragraph of the book, whilst Postel named this work 'Histoire des Indes' [History of the Indies].[41] In fact, this is a history of Jesuit evangelization in India and Japan. Two chapters of the work are devoted to a detailed analysis of two letters about Japan written in India by Jesuits (ibid., 10v-38r).[42] The first letter was written by 'Françoys Schiabier' (ibid., 10r), who is clearly Francis Xavier, where he reported his first meeting with a Japanese during his stay in Cochin.[43] We understand that Xavier reports his dialogue with Anjirō, a Japanese man fascinated by the Christian message and who wished to meet

Jesuit missionaries.[44] According to this first letter written by Xavier, the second letter reported by Postel was written for him by a Portuguese merchant, probably Giorgio Alvares, who travelled from Japan to India with the Japanese man himself. We know that Anjirō invited Xavier to evangelize his country and that, when he became the first Japanese to be converted, he was named Paul. Postel reports that the translator of this second text is 'Paul governeur du College de la Saincte Foys aulx [sic.] Inde' (ibid., 12r), but Paul is probably Anjirō himself, since his complete Christian name was 'Paulo de Santa Fe'. However, this letter arouses undeniable problems: could a merchant know all these details about Japanese Buddhism? Moreover, the letter reveals a Christian theological expertise that was quite unusual for a merchant.[45] The answer to these issues may be found in *Documentos del Japon*,[46] where almost the same text is attributed to one of Xavier's companions, either Nicolao Lancillotto or Cosme Torres, and is entitled *Informacion sobre Japon*. Here the text is dated 28 December 1548 in Cochin, less than a month before the letter by Xavier according to Postel. Why did Xavier claim to have received this letter from a Portuguese man? Was it written by the Portuguese man and subsequently interpolated by one of the two Jesuits? However, Juan Ruiz-de-Medina, editor of the *Documentos*, suggested that the text was the report of Torres's interview with Anjirō.[47] Therefore, the role of the Portuguese merchant quoted by Xavier is quite mysterious. Besides the problems of attribution – Torres or Lancillotto – this second letter was the first account of Japanese religion before Xavier's arrival and Postel discussed it at length[48] in order to provide proof on behalf of his universal theory.

The central tenet of the second letter is the presumed (proto-Christian) monotheism of Buddhism, which was already presented as very similar to Christianity. 'The common argument of their sermons is that there is only a single God who created everything, that there is a Heaven or a place where good people go and, on the contrary, there is a specific place for bad persons, where the devil is the captain and chief, and lastly there is a place for intermediate persons, who need to be purified'.[49] Postel's comment on this point is of great interest, because it explains the real universalistic belief of Jesuits that was developed in Paris:

> This sentence confirms to me my doctrine of the 'Abrahamic' sons of the concubines of Abraham, who were sent by him under [his] positive influence into the Orient, and it is [also] proved by a letter written by F. Xavier to M. Ignatius of Loyola – leader of the Jesuit order, established 15 or 16 years ago in Paris – where Xavier wrote that there was one of the so-called Abrahamanes – that Marco Polo named Abrahmin, whilst they called themselves Brahmins eating the 'a' – who freely suggested the common seeds of their religions [i.e. Christianity and Indian thought]. Among many issues, he told him that they have the same Doctrine taught by our clergymen. However, this Doctrine is never taught to [all] the people and only the Brahmins can learn it for themselves. That is what is told by that Brahmin and I trust him. Because, although Abraham understood that the sons of the concubines would not obey Isaac and doing so they were renouncing [to be part of] the Catholic Church, equally he [i.e. Abraham] didn't sent them into the Orient without disclosing to them the Divine Doctrine, along with Magic or

Astrology [knowledge]. Thus, until today, they [i.e. the Indians] preserve the essence of [the Doctrine], that entails the Astrologic great knowledge of all the upper world, and it is the same in Japan.[50]

ibid., 18r–19r

Therefore, Postel suggested that Indians took part in the ancient doctrine of the patriarchs, since they were a branch of the same tree of wisdom. That was the reason why Indians and Christians had a doctrine of God, astrological knowledge and magical expertise, which were compatible. The common origin of European and Extra-European civilizations was the base upon which Jesuits could plan a natural and simple evangelization. In the above-mentioned letter, Francis Xavier also suggested his strong belief in a natural and rapid spread of Christian faith among Asian people, since this common origin constituted the pre-existing condition of the evangelic mission. Therefore, the conversion of Asian heathens was already planned by God.

The author of the *Informacion* – probably Lancillotto – considered Buddhism as the proof of the closeness of Christianity and Asiatic thought. He presented a story of Buddha ('Schiaca')[51] by giving him Christian attributes[52] and by describing him as destroyer of idols (ibid., 22r). Postel suggested that Asia could not have had a destroyer of idols since there had been only two in history: Jesus and Mohammed. Consequently, the Asiatic destroyer of idols must have been Jesus himself, who had such a great impact on men in ancient times to be known even in these distant lands (ibid., 22r-v). Buddha – or Jesus *deguisé* as Buddha – would have taught five commandments: do not kill, do not steal, do not fornicate, accept things as they are, do not look for revenge but rather forgive (ibid., 23r). The text also suggested that the Japanese have only one Law proclaimed by their god and which is very similar to the Christian one. After providing further examples, Postel was strongly persuaded and claimed: 'This is the true confirmation that XACA is worshipped there instead of JESUS CHRIST CRUCIFIED.'[53] This identification was proved also by means of Chronology: according to the Japanese account, Buddha went to China and Japan during the years of Christ's life (ibid., 35v).[54] It was even claimed that they worshipped the Virgin Mary, who they called 'Quamuon'.[55] Although the original letter is less explicit than Postel's comments, it shows the firm belief, among Jesuits, that Buddha was as a sort of embryonic Jesus – when not Jesus himself, as stated by Postel – and that the evangelization of Japan and China would have been be a light and natural process, already designed by God.

Among many other interesting arguments, which cannot be investigated here, Postel provided one of the first (if not the first) history of the Jesuit order, suggesting their strong universalistic vision of world history, which is already planned by God and that waited only to be accomplished by faithful man. Therefore, Loyola and Xavier were God's servants: their order was founded to carry out the complete evangelization of the world following God's providence (ibid., 78r and ff.). Postel considered himself as an active actor of this universal history, as the first historian of the Jesuit order and of their mission in 'des Indes'.[56] The history of Jesuit missions and activities was the fulfilment of the revelation of God and the incarnation of Jesus Christ (ibid., 83v). 'Having never left the knowledge of the King of Jews, this province of Cathay [China][57] must be considered as the most fortunate of the world.'[58] (ibid., 94r-v). Asian people received the original wisdom of the patriarchs, and they were also unconsciously aware of Jesus himself. Postel claimed openly that the Chinese and Japanese had always been included in God's revelation plan:

> In that way, we see the virtue of the power of our God and Father Jesus Christ, who wanted to plant and preserve at the two extremities of his world – without [a direct] transfer of power, of texts or of ceremonies – his holy doctrine and law, which are the most marvellous and necessary matters of the world.[59]
>
> ibid., 94v

Jesuits were simply doing God's will: they were bringing back these civilizations into the Roman Church. These idolaters were already aware of God and His Law; they needed only to reawaken their ancient wisdom, which was a seed of Christianity.

This was the first European interpretation of Buddhism, an unknown and diffused 'oriental religion'. During his stay in Japan, Xavier wrote sporadic letters to his European interlocutors. The early letters, written on the 5 November 1549, expressed a certain optimistic feeling, since Jesuits forecasted an unavoidable missionary success. However, in Letter nr. 90 we find the first critics to the Japanese monks, harshly accused of pederasty, as it had already been claimed in the *Informacion* itself. According to Xavier, Buddhist monks were so despised that the conversion of Japanese people could but be very easy. The next letters in our possession are dated between the end of 1551 and the beginning of 1552. Letter nr. 96 (29 January 1552) describes Japanese '*bonzi*' (Buddhist monks) and '*bonze*' (nuns) as negative oppressors of common people's minds, since they professed a confused system of sects and hideous doctrines. Among them, there was even a devilish sect of deniers of the immortality of souls. We could wonder what could have determined such a severe change in the description of Buddhists after only two years. The answer is simple: Buddhist people were not simple to convert and monks strenuously resisted evangelization, debating and taking advantage of nobles' protection.

The Augustinian missionary Juan Gonzáles de Mendoza, while waiting in Mexico for his mission in Ming China as Spanish ambassador and preacher – though he never reached China – collected all the available material on China. In 1585, this outline of sources was published in Spanish and entitled *Historia de las cosas mas notables, ritos y costumbres, del gran Reyno de la China*.[60] The success of the book was incredible: in 1586 a Italian translation was published,[61] in 1588 French[62] and English[63] translations became available, in 1597 it was translated into German and at last the Latin edition came out in 1655. Each translation was also reprinted several times. This book is the foundation of the myth of China as a moral, political and meritocratic realm. Mendoza wrote several chapters on Chinese education and public exams, as well as on the richness, beauty and size of the cities. The second book of the first part was completely devoted to Chinese religions and rites.[64] However, Mendoza was not really well acquainted with specific aspects of Chinese culture and he did not have a clear picture of the different sects. He proposed a vague description, presenting only the sect of 'Sichia', namely Buddha Śākyamuni, which was listed among other 'holy men' or 'gods'.

All sects were considered by Mendoza as an undefined whole. However, for the purposes of our investigation, there is something that is really worth noting in this account: Mendoza was the first to suggest to Europeans that Saint Thomas had a great influence on several aspects of Chinese religiousness. Mendoza traced back many elements of their culture, which he claimed to be clearly taken from Christianity, such as a statue representing the Trinity or the Virgin.

> the which being interpreted Christianly, may be understood to be the mysterie of holy Trinitie, that wee that are Christians doo worship, and is part of our faith: the which, with other things, seemeth somewhat to be respondent to our holy, sacred, and Christian religion: so that of verie truth we may presume that Saint Thomas the Apostle did preach in this kingdome, who as it is declared in the lesson on his day, after he had received the Holy Ghost and preached the holy Gospel unto the Parthes, Medes, Persas, Brachmanes, and other nations, he went into the Indias, whereas he was martyred in the city of Calamina, for his faith and holy Gospel that he preached.
>
> It is verified that when this glorious apostle did passe into the Indies, he travelled through this kingdome of China, where as it appeareth he did preach the holy Gospel and mysterie of the Holy Trinitie: whose picture in the manner aforesaid doth indure unto this day, although those people, by the great and long blindness which they are in with the errors and idolatrie, doo not perfectly knowe what that figure with three heads doth represent or signifie.
>
> ibid., 36–7

Mendoza did not claim that Christ moved to China, as Postel did, but that, before entering India, Saint Thomas preached in China, where several traces of his teaching could still be found in modern times. The theory of a direct spread of an original Christianity did not belong to Mendoza, but to the Dominican Gaspar da Cruz, largely quoted and a major source for this history of China. Da Cruz published his book on China in 1569.[65] This probably was the first book devoted to China to be published in Europe, but Portuguese was not properly an international language and the book was never translated. In chapter 27, da Cruz suggested that Saint Thomas's mission in China ('Apostolo sam Thome') was proven by the similarities between Buddhist practices and the Christian ones, as it was proposed again and finally claimed by Mendoza in the chapter that we have extensively quoted above. To summarize, this direct spread of Christianity through Saint Thomas was one of several theories argued by historians concerning the seeds of divine wisdom. Among these theories three were the most important: the first theory was the original spread of divine wisdom due to patriarchs, as consistent with 'philosophia perennis' and claimed for instance by Postel; the second was this direct diffusion of Christian thought thanks to Saint Thomas's mission to India as suggested by Da Cruz and Mendoza, whereas the third one, which was claimed by Ricci, consisted of a harsh criticism against Buddhism as 'polluter' of the original divine wisdom.

Before presenting Ricci's theory, we need to be aware of two different perspectives held among Jesuits, which played a crucial role in the 'Chinese rites controversy' since the 1670s. Alessandro Valignano, the successor of Xavier as Supervisor in East Asia, defined a new evangelization method in Japan, which consisted of the moderate rejection of all local idolatries because of their inconsistency with Christian faith. The understanding of Buddhism in Lancillotto's *Informacion* is very distant from Valignano's method; indeed the latter openly disavowed the accommodation ('acomodar')[66] method in his letters. In order to outline the correct evangelic method, he wrote the *Catechismus Iaponensis*[67] for young Jesuit missionaries and not for a general public. However, this text was partially edited in 1593 by the Jesuit Antonio Possevino in his *Bibliotheca selecta*,[68] thus it reached a quite large spreading, outside the Jesuit order. In the *Catechismus*, Valignano violently attacks Buddhism, depicted as a hellish sect based on four terrible doctrines: 1. Monism, according to which all things in the world can be explained in terms of a single substance; 2. Immanentism of the single substance in the world; 3. Mortality of the soul with the body; 4. The possibility of reaching the complete state of rest ('tranquillitatem') which pertains to the first principle (or God) by means of meditation ('meditando ... transertur in nulla re quietem adeptus' (Valignano 1586: 6v–7r). This description of Buddhism was quite detailed, however, even in the edition by Possevino, it did not have strong effects among European historians. It was more influential among Jesuits and entered the long-lasting debate about Chinese rites.[69]

Mendoza's account was superseded by the first book that really shaped the idea of Chinese sects and philosophies in Europe, authored by the well-known Matteo Ricci, who even today is the emblem of the 'accommodation approach', as opposed to Valignano's attitude in Japan. Ricci decided to insert local culture, habits and ceremonies into the Christian life, as this was the only way to convert people to a foreign religion. As we shall see in the next chapter, this evangelic attitude was not without heavy consequences, since it led to the 'rites controversy'. However, here we focus on the change brought about by Ricci in China in terms of the 'accommodation approach'. On one side, Valignano refused all local beliefs in Japan (particularly Buddhism), on the other, he allowed Ricci to create a refined hierarchy among Chinese sects, promoting Confucianism and blaming Buddhism. Therefore, we can also infer that Valignano understood Confucianism as different from Buddhism.

Ricci and Ruggeri entered China with the status and the appearance of a *tianzhu seng* 天竺僧 (i.e. monk from India) or *heshang* 和尚 (i.e. Buddhist monk or *osciano*). However, according to Ricci himself, the status of monk (*heshang*) or *bonzo* (a term coined by Francis Xavier from the Japanese *bozu* 坊主) was quite low and denoted an unlearned monk. Thus, with the approval of the general master (or supervisor) Valignano himself, in October 1594, changed their status and became 'learned/Confucian monks' (*ruseng* 儒僧) or 'superior monks' (*shangseng* 上僧). This is just their first change of status, because in April 1595, Ricci presented himself as 'a cultivated person with powers' (*daoren* 道人) or a 'residing scholar' (*jushi* 居士). Within twelve years, the Jesuit missionary became a 'lay monk with alchemical powers who came from the West', likely because this status was the highest he could reach.[70] Ricci said that adopting the look and the behaviour of a Buddhist monk was a disadvantage rather than help, and we know that this was for several reasons: 1. In China, Buddhism was a foreign religion as was Christianity; 2. Buddhism, as well as Christianity, was perceived as a western religion by Chinese people; 3. Christianity had too much in common with Buddhism, thus, in order to be accepted, the 'real faith' needed to distinguish itself and to be perceived as more compatible with the Chinese tradition (i.e. Confucianism) as compared to Buddhism itself; 4. During the Ming dynasty, Buddhist monks were regarded by Confucians as ignorant parasites, unable to fulfil Chinese social ethics. We see how, in only three decades, Buddhism lost the previous positive closeness with Christianity, even the points of agreement that were undeniable (i.e. morals, monasticism, missionary attitude, etc.), while, at the same time, Confucianism became the true interlocutor.

In this chapter, we cannot follow the interesting letters written by Ricci which clearly show his change of opinion, but we merely present the result of this change, that is his description of Chinese sects. According to his 'sinicization method', Ricci left the religious gown and instead he wears the literate robe, in order to be accepted as a scientist, rather than a clergyman or monk. He behaved and lived as a Chinese, studying Chinese classics. This new evangelization method, called 'assimilation', is consistent with the perennial theory. As he became a Chinese literate, he could deeply penetrate the original Chinese society and culture in its context; and Chinese Classics were the most crucial field for accommodationism. According to Ricci, Buddhism shared not the common seed of wisdom with Christianity and Buddha was not a hidden Christ as for the former Jesuits and Postel. In Chinese culture, there was only another defined sect that was Daoism, but the tenets of this sect were completely inconsistent with Christianity, since Daoism was dualistic, devoted to magic and alchemy. Although we do not share Jensen's theory of the Jesuit 'manufacturing' of Confucianism,[71] it is undeniable that the role of Confucius as first philosopher and father of Chinese thought owes a lot to the Jesuit reading. What is relevant to our research is that the description of Confucianism, and China in general, as observed by European philosophers, was the same outlined by Ricci and by his loyal followers.

We investigate here only the most important text written by Ricci, *Della entrata della Compagnia di Giesù e Christianità nella Cina*,[72] i.e. the original Italian version which remained unpublished since D'Elia edited it in 1942.[73] The worldwide edition of the text was made by Trigault, first in Latin in 1615[74] and then translated into many European languages, with the French edition being the most influential.[75] Trigault's edition is not always a simple translation, but rather it is at times even a different edition with slight changes. The analysis of the tenth chapter of the first book, devoted to a general presentation of Chinese 'sects', is useful to understand the radical change of viewpoint from Postel, to da Cruz/Mendoza and at last to Ricci.

Ricci claimed that in ancient times Chinese people worshipped one Supreme God and followed the 'divine reason' coming from that single, good God. The Chinese were monotheistic and they did not believe inappropriate things about deities as the Romans, Greeks and Egyptians did.[76] This comparison is a clear evidence of the antiquarian attitude we mentioned before. Chinese people conformed to a 'natural Law'[77] provided by God himself, therefore, their ancient philosophers were full of virtue, very pious and they gave good advice to other men. In short, these philosophers were certainly not inferior to our ancient philosophers. However, Ricci did not acknowledge the contemporary Chinese as monotheists, on the contrary, most of them were atheists and idolaters. By adopting the perennial philosophy vocabulary, we could say that according to Ricci the ancient Chinese were 'prisci theologi',[78] whilst modern Mandarins had lost the purity of this ancient wisdom, which did not disappear, but rather was overwhelmed by idolatry, as also happened to modern Indians (see Heurn). According to the Italian missionary, the true responsibility of this incoming impurity lay with a foreign religion, namely Buddhism, which came from India around the second half of the first century CE.

Before presenting Chinese sects, Ricci wrote about foreign religions already established in China, like Muslims out of Persia, ancient Christians (Nestorians) and Jews. All three were closed minorities, who were not really influential.[79] However, in his edition, Trigault decided to cut these paragraphs, maybe in order to present Chinese civilization as more detached from European and Mediterranean history. In this way, the only foreign influence on China became Buddhism, the most negative one, guilty of compromising the original monotheism.

In presenting the account of Chinese thought written by Ricci, a further specification is necessary: Ricci referred to Chinese schools or faiths by using the word 'leggi' ('Laws') and he used the same word for 'legge naturale' ('Natural law'). On the contrary, Trigault used two different words: 'secta' and 'lege Naturae', that were translated into all modern languages as 'sect' and 'Natural law'. Ricci did not use the word 'sect' extensively,[80] probably because he was influenced by the Buddhist word 'dharma' (Chinese *fa* 法), which means 'Law' and not 'sect' or 'religion'. The most common alternative Chinese words to *fa* 法 (law) were *jiao* 教 (school/teaching) and *xue* 學 (teaching), which were used for all the Chinese schools and not only for Buddhism. By using 'laws', Ricci preferred not to assign a strong religious meaning to Chinese thought, as Trigault did, because he always translated the Italian word 'legge' as 'secta' in Latin.

China had three 'laws', namely Confucianism, Buddhism and Taoism. Confucianism was the original local tradition founded by Confucius, who was said by Ricci and translated by Trigault as 'Auctorem seu Principem Philosophorum' (*De Christiana*, 102). Ricci, the first real interpreter of Chinese philosophy, described Confucius as the first Philosopher of China and the father of Chinese thought. Moreover, Ricci argued that Confucius's thought was not religious, but rather it was a thought devoted to moral and political issues. Confucianism was not an idolatrous sect, since its followers believed in the moral value of learning and in the consequent meritocracy. Furthermore, Ricci claimed that ancient Confucians believed in the immortality of the soul, the only possible foundation for an ethic of rewards and punishments after death (*Della entrata*, 94). On the contrary, modern Confucians believed that the soul dies when the body dies. Ricci suggested that this new, incorrect theory came from Buddhism, named 'sect of idols', whose adepts spread in China the hideous theory that:

> all this world is composed of a single substance, whose creator along with the sky and the earth, men and animals, trees and herbs, the four elements, are all one continuous body being these its members. From this one substance they [the Chinese] draw the charity that we are supposed to have mutually, because all men are similar to God, being them out of his substance. We are confuting this theory

not only through arguments, but even making use of the authority of their ancient [philosophers], who taught a deeply different doctrine.⁸¹

This paragraph is probably the first effective description of the Buddhist theory of *pratītyasumutpāda* that reached European thinkers. This theory claims the dependent origination of all things from one substance; hence everything is only an accident of this substance. Because of this doctrine, Buddhists and modern Confucians – influenced by the former – were atheists. This correspondence of the theory of the single substance with atheism would be an important issue at the end of the seventeenth century regarding the dispute over Spinoza and atheism (i.e. Bayle).⁸² Furthermore, Ricci explained in this excerpt his reading method, which consisted in philology applied to ancient Chinese texts, in order to find in these texts an original forgotten monotheism.

Confucianism was not a religion, since Confucians believed in the supreme God of Heaven (*tianzhu* 天主), but they did not build temples in his honour and they did not worship him. The only man who could worship God was the Emperor himself. All temples were devoted to minor cults, which were not really consistent with Confucianism. The effective temples of Confucians were their schools, where statues of Confucius and his disciples were collocated and regarded, as these men were Saints ('santi', *Storia*, 118), and where the Four Books were studied diligently.

> Therefore, they neither order nor forbid anything regarding what is believable of the afterlife, and many of them follow together with this doctrine one of the other two sects. We can conclude that this is not an effective religion ['legge'], it is more properly a School ['Academia'] instituted in order to [promote] a good government of the Republic, and that they [i.e. Confucians] may belong to this School and become Christians, since neither [their doctrine] in its essence includes anything against the essence of the Catholic faith, nor the Catholic faith prevents anything [claimed by their doctrine], but rather it [the Catholic faith] could help to preserve the quiet and peace of the Republic, which is what is requested by their books.⁸³

Confucianism was fully compatible with Christianity, since the first one was not a religion, but instead an ethic and political teaching. The only necessary change in Chinese thought, suggested by Ricci, was the restoration of ancient Confucianism, i.e. the alleged pure teaching of Confucius, which was lost because of the negative influence of Buddhist doctrines. Ricci aimed at assuming the role of a 'Confucian reformer', evidently influenced by the current Catholic Counter-Reformation, wherein the Jesuit order had arisen.

Buddhism, the second sect, had come from India around 64 to 65 CE, at the same time of the first Christian evangelization, while Saint Bartholomew was preaching in North India and Saint Thomas in South India. Ricci claimed that, because of the influential preaching of both Saints, the Chinese asked for the Gospel, but instead of it, they brought Buddhism back to China (*Storia*, 122–3, *Della entrata*, 99). This theory recalls Postel and Mendoza, however, whilst the French thinker claimed that Buddha was a 'modified Christ', Ricci objected that Buddhism was accepted by the Chinese instead of Christianity, although it contained nothing of the original holy message.

Therefore, Buddhists would have cheated the Chinese, who were in search of Christianity. In order to be more convincing, Buddhists also had taken many aspects of their doctrines from western philosophers[84] and from Christian theology, but they hid these seeds of truth with confusion and fairy tales. 'Since they say so many falsities they darken all the light – coming from the truth of the things taken from us – that might be perceived …'.[85] Ricci traced a short story of the introduction of this sect in China, stressing its uneven and sometimes difficult spread, also presenting both Buddhist monks and followers as vulgar and ignorant people, rejecting their main tenets.[86] The same is done in his Chinese writings as *The True Meaning of the Lord of Heaven*[87] and *Ten Chapters of a Strange Man*.[88] We need to remark that his knowledge of Buddhist concepts was really scarce when compared to his profound Confucian scholarship. As Hsia suggests: 'Their [Jesuits] ignorance of Buddhist texts reflected the disinterest in Jesuit missionaries. In Ricci's words, Buddhism represented "a Babylon of doctrines so intricate that no one can understand or explain it"'.[89]

The third sect was that of Laozi, namely Daoism. Ricci attributed to Laozi the rank of Philosopher ('Philosopho'[90]), like Confucius, but he was almost forced to do so, because of the Chinese character *zi* 子 that is in both names – *Kongzi* 孔子 and *Laozi* 老子 – and which acquires in this context the following meaning: 'master' or 'philosopher' (in Ricci's translation). Confucius is master or philosopher (子) Kong (孔); therefore, Laozi must be master or philosopher (子) Lao (老) and, since *lao* means old or honourable, Ricci translated it as 'filosopho Vecchio' ('old Philosopher'). However, Ricci explained that Laozi was not a philosopher like Confucius, but rather the spiritual father of a religious and mythological sect. Taoists lived as *osciani* (i.e. Buddhists) and they had a comparable idolatry, even though Daoists believed in the indissolubility of the soul and body. They practised magic, alchemy and haruspices. They had a leader – compulsorily a member of an ancient family of necromancers – who was highly esteemed by the Emperor.

Ricci added that although these sects/teachings were three, each of them was divided into a large number of minor sects. The Emperor, being tolerant towards religions, allowed fragmentation, confusion of sects and multiplication of statues everywhere. The most dangerous theory spread at this time was, according to Ricci, the unification of all three leading sects into one,[91] namely the *sanjiaoheyi* 三教合一 ('the three sects are but one'). This unification caused the problematic diffusion of the aforementioned Buddhist theory of the single substance among Confucians and Daoists. The conclusion of this chapter is that:

> [Chinese] wishing to follow all sects [leggi], hence not following properly anyone, they remain with no one [sect]. Many of them confess openly their incredulity, many others are cheated by the false conviction of believing, [therefore] the majority of them is lying in a deep Atheism.[92]

Modern Chinese were atheists – this time the word is used in its proper meaning – since they had lost the original message of Confucianism and they followed too many sects. Ricci was evidently claiming that Christianity was not only compatible with the original foundation of Chinese civilization, but also that his religion was the only way to preserve the Chinese Empire from the danger of chaos or, to use a modern word, anarchy. Atheism – namely Buddhism and modern Neo-Confucianism – was not merely a religious issue, but even a social menace. What, according to Ricci, the Jesuits had to do was bring Christian revelation and God's grace to China, since these two spiritual assets could easily take root thanks to the original monotheistic seeds.

This chapter, written by Ricci and translated by Trigault, provided the most relevant outline of Chinese philosophy for almost two centuries. The Preface of the *Confucius sinarum philosophus* (1687), probably the most influential book ever written on this civilization, was a faithful revision of this chapter by Ricci, with even a stronger apologetic view due to the growing 'rites controversy' (§2.1.).

1.3 The second rift in the perennial historical model: Georg Horn and China

As we remarked, Heurn claimed that Indian philosophy could not be relegated in a distant past as a 'prisca philosophia', as it could be done with the Egyptians. We might say that, with Heurn, Indian civilization began to be acknowledged as contemporary, although it was described as impure. The same, and even more clearly, happened to China within the *Historia philosophica* by Georg Horn,[93] who was indebted to the long process of understanding within the Jesuit order. He was also aware of the differences among the descriptions of China provided by missionaries, although the most relevant differences were to be known in Europe only in the late eighteenth century (§2.1.).

Georg Horn (1620–70) was a Protestant German historian and theologian, who, after having taught in several German Universities, moved to Leyden and held the chair that of the renowned historian Johannes Gerhard Voss.[94] He wrote many well-known essays, mainly regarding universal history, among which we mention only the interesting *De originibus americanis libri IV* (Hagae Comitis 1652), which was aimed at proving the Euro-Asiatic origin (Cantabri, Phoenicians, Chinese and Huns) of American natives.[95] His *Historia philosophica* was mainly written around 1640, during the late Thirty Years' War (1618–48), and only slightly rearranged in order to be published in 1655, when the United Provinces became independent from the crown of Spain, and gained a new role in world trade. In this book Horn's understanding of China was still in progress and it was systematized in the following years, when the author came to terms with the historical dispute over Chinese chronology.

Horn's historiographical system was typical of a Protestant religious thinker of the seventeenth century: like Heurn, he was committed to proving the religious task of philosophy. Wisdom could come only from God, and philosophies (always acknowledged as plural) were different paths leading to wisdom, hence to God himself. Philosophers had to make use of the 'philosophical critic' in order to create a 'new philosophy' leading to God, which would arise from the correct and useful aspects detected in the philosophies of the past. In Horn, 'philosophical critic' was a confluence of critical thinking, theology and philology. He refused as anti-philosophical every investigation based on the separation of religious wisdom and philosophy. Actually, a new philosophy was useful only when leading in an effective way to the perennial wisdom, which has been given at the origin by God himself.[96]

However, the critical nature of Horn's history entailed a distance from the bare syncretism of the Renaissance philosophers, indeed, he was not in all aspects a follower of the classic perennial philosophy model (i.e. Florentine Neoplatonism). He was one of the first historians of philosophy who argued that after the Deluge the three sons of Noah – Shem, Ham and Japheth – spread in all directions the divine wisdom remaining after Adam's fall and that among them the impious Ham did not carry the pure wisdom, but instead taught the impure knowledge of magic and the theories of the mortality of the soul and of the absence of a divine providence; therefore, he also corrupted the divine wisdom spread in the other directions by his brothers. The first man able to purify the ancient corrupted wisdom was Abraham, who restored the basis of the true religion in Egypt on behalf of the Israelites (Jews). Therefore, according to Horn, Indians benefited of the Noahic wisdom, although their philosophy was not as advanced or pure as the Egyptian and, above all, the Jewish. Globally, the whole of his chapters – on barbarian philosophies, Greeks, Christians and modern thinkers – adhered to the general biblical historiography of his time. However, although Horn provided the well-known biblical frame of references, his history of philosophy created a remarkable break or rift in the model with the insertion of China. It is necessary to remember that Calvin shared Cicero's *consensus gentium*, therefore, total ignorance of God could not exist, since the human mind possesses some sense of a Deity.[97]

The division of the *Historia philosophica* into seven books deserves to be reported, because something unprecedented was introduced into modern European philosophy:

1. The antediluvian period, where many myths of different civilizations were compared with the biblical history of humankind. In general, Horn did not refuse any of these theories, but rather he tried to find similarities with the Bible,[98] consistent with his theological and historical thought. The first philosopher was clearly Adam, the origin of wisdom among men.
2. The barbarians, such as Chaldeans (Assyrians), who were experts in astrology; Persian Magi (with Zoroaster); Egyptians (with Hermes Trismegistus), great ancient doctors and mathematicians; Ethiopians; Indians; Germans (Druids and Bards); finally, Jews.
3. Ancient Greek philosophy.
4. Mediterranean barbarians, such as Phoenicians and Scythians, Jews and Romans. All former philosophies were inferior to the Christian message, which was the highest expression of God's providence.
5. Barbaric invasions, late Roman philosophy and the spread of Christian faith, at first deeply Platonic. Ancient Hellenic philosophy and Arabs.
6. Middle Age philosophy (with the return of ancient texts). Chinese and Japanese philosophy. Renaissance philosophy and modern (atheists and reforms).
7. It is not a historical book, but rather it presents places, aspects and habits that were suitable for philosophical thinking around the world (consistently with his universalistic vision of wisdom that shows his antiquarian attitude).

The sequence of philosophies presented by Horn was the most common, similar to the classical perennial model, with antediluvian wisdom at the beginning and modern philosophy, which was obviously Christian, at the end. But there was a remarkable difference in the historiographical model: the insertion of China between Ockham and Marsilio Ficino, i.e. between Middle Age and Renaissance. Whilst all other ancient civilizations were inserted in the second book and Arabs in the fifth, according to the life of Mohammed, China reached a special status in modern times. Horn knew that the Chinese belonged to a real ancient civilization, as we shall see shortly when approaching the chronological issues (§1.4.), so this collocation was not due to a historical misconception.

As we said, in the *Historia* India precedes China being inserted in the second book. The chapter is not interesting because of its contents, but simply in order to contrast Horn's ideas on India with his vision of China. Horn only made use of ancient sources on Indians and his scarce interest in them is evident. Horn's only relevant statements on Indians pertained the philological investigation of terms such as 'Brachmanes' or names as 'Jarcha' compared with Greek, Hebrew and Chaldean allegedly equivalent words. Brucker, in the mid-eighteenth century, remarked, while he was writing on Indians, the unreliable philological illustration of this linguistic and religious community, in which those ancient civilizations would have been inserted. Moreover, Brucker stressed that Horn knew only some Hebrew and Aramaic, thus he did not have the philological competences to carry on this investigation.[99] Obviously, Horn's theory of a Noahic wisdom spread among those post-diluvian civilizations was unacceptable for a German Eclectic willing to prove the absolute superiority of Jewish revelation, among religions, and of Greek thought, throughout the history of philosophy.

But, as we already suggested, the most interesting chapter is the one related to China. According to Horn, the insertion of Chinese thought among modern European philosophies descended from an evident fact: until modern times, Chinese civilization was almost unknown in Europe, apart from some scarce Persian or Saracenic information and Marco Polo and John Maundeville's travel accounts, it was only with the Jesuits that a real knowledge of China reached Europe (ibid., 308). The only classical source quoted by Horn is *De Situ orbis libri III* (or *De Chorographia*) by Pomponius Mela, where the Chinese were praised as followers of Justice.[100] 'Afterwards, for many centuries they were forgotten and became unknown, European news [about them] was non-existent, until they were known again through Persians and after Saracens under the name of Cathai'.[101] Marco Polo was the first European who went to Cathai and after him John Mandeville, whose travel account, according to Horn, was full of interesting information about Chinese culture. Mandeville even described the 'Magnum canem'[102] (ibid.) – i.e. the Mongolian emperor of Cathai – as a philosopher, expert in Astronomy, Geometry and other sciences. Thanks to Portuguese travellers a real geographical knowledge of Cathai became possible.[103] However, only Jesuit missionaries provided detailed descriptions of Chinese culture and thought. Horn claimed that Jesuits where the first westerners who understood that the ancient land of Seres or Sina was the same region named Cathai by Persians.[104]

Horn revealed a great interest in Jesuit accounts, he quoted: Trigault's translation of Ricci (published in 1615); Martino Martini's *Novus Atlas Sinensis*, published in 1655

(Amsterdam); an unspecified letter of Niccolò Longobardo to Claudio Acquaviva and *Historia natural y moral de las Indias* by Acosta, which was published in 1590 (Seville) and translated very quickly into many European languages. These sources disagreed over the correct interpretation of Chinese philosophy. Trigault, following Ricci, praised the great Chinese knowledge in every cultural aspect, he even suggested that China was superior to ancient Athens (ibid., 309). On the contrary, Acosta, who never went to China, claimed that Mandarin studies were related only to the Chinese language, history, law, proverbs, because they were not skilled in sciences. Horn quoted Acosta's negative description:

> Academy in China until now was unknown; their studies are about Mandarin language, history, civil law, proverbs, and somehow they have Physics and Mathematics, but [they are] amethodical. They are really committed to tales and histories. All their erudition consists in mere reading and writing. They have not any Theology.[105]

Horn tried to find an agreement among those contrasting descriptions, suggesting that Trigault and Martini also would have said that Chinese philosophy was repetitive ('prolixe'), by which he probably meant traditional or learned by heart. Therefore, Horn concluded that the Chinese were not real scientists or empiricists, because their scientific knowledge and theories were out-dated and useless. The Chinese lack of scientific knowledge and empirical attitude from now on was very diffused among European thinkers – besides a few exceptions, such as Leibniz – and consequently Europeans were superior in the scientific and technical fields.

However, Horn agreed with the idea that the Chinese were refined moralists, and he supported the suggestion that their imperial system was a sort of realized Platonic Republic (ibid.). Obviously, their best philosopher was Confucius, who was still studied and followed by Chinese, as Pythagoras was by his adepts. Horn quoted two books attributed to Confucius: 'de adultorum disciplina' and 'de medio sempiterno', that are the *Great Learning* (*Daxue* 大學) and the *Doctrine of the mean* (*Zhongyong* 中庸).[106] Moreover, Horn added that all Chinese officials at any level were philosophers, skilled in Confucian ethics, who used philosophy to choose between peace and war and in general to rule the country. Horn explicitly wrote: 'Only in China philosophers rule [the Country], here Plato's wish finds its fulfilment' (ibid., 310).[107]

Horn also referred to China in the last book, where he compared European Universities with the Chinese scholar system, because they were the only two comparable educational models in the world. The Chinese system, as described by Longobardo, was very strict and serious; exams were really difficult, the candidate who passed them received glory and gained a possible place as an official. On the contrary, failure could cause the ruin of an entire family, because it was considered a terrible shame (ibid., 385–6).

We can conclude that Horn knew the latest books on China very well, some of which were published at the same time as his *Historia philosophica*. He was the first historian of philosophy to praise Chinese morality and even to compare their educational system with that of modern European countries. His insertion of Chinese thinkers among modern philosophers revealed the historical difficulty of coming to terms with a civilization completely absent in the biblical history. Horn did not try to prove the Noahic origin of Chinese wisdom, as there was no biblical basis in support of this claim. However, in the next years Horn could not keep on avoiding the issue of Chinese antiquity as he did in his history of philosophy, since Chinese chronology suggested a pre-diluvian origin of Chinese civilization conflicting with the biblical history, which was the European historiographical frame. Therefore, as we shall see, Horn also distinguished himself in the dangerous issue of chronology, where he revealed his universalistic vision of the history of all humankind, since he finally claimed the Noahic origin of Chinese Empire. A universalistic attitude that, as we already suggested, was less evident in his *Historia philosophica*.

1.4 Chronology issues: La Peyrère, Isaac Vossius and Georg Horn

At the beginning of the long-lasting 'rites controversy', one of the most dramatic debates was raised about Chinese chronology, because their *Annals* reported a history longer than the biblical one, thus the ancient Chinese would have been a pre-biblical (pre-Adamic) people. In the context of historiography, the chronological question plays a relevant role, since this dispute created a new vision of the past that contrasted the universalism and providentialism of the perennialist theory. However, because this analysis would entail complex biblical exegesis, in this chapter only the pivotal authors are mentioned and a general overview of the debate about Chinese chronology is provided.[108] Our focus in this section is mostly on Horn's introduction of China within the biblical frame, since this author, in his *Historia philosophica*, had not provided a coherent investigation of Chinese antiquity.

The first public trace of this debate may be found with the Augustinian monk Gonçales de Mendoza, who suggested that the original inhabitants of China should be at least the nephews or grandsons of Noah,[109] so they were not descendants of Abraham as Postel argued. He also provided the first chronology of imperial dynasties, which proved the Chinese to be antediluvian. Matteo Ricci, in the aforementioned *De Christiana expeditione*, translated by Trigault into Latin, made only a brief reference to Chinese antiquity and their Annals, by dating the origin of this culture to around 2500 BCE. In 1658, Martino Martini[110] published the first complete chronicle of Chinese imperial dynasties, where he dated the origin of this culture back to the year 2952 BCE, namely around 600 years before the Deluge following the version of the Jewish Bible (Vulgate).[111]

These references of missionaries, who translated, more or less faithfully, Chinese sources, created in Europe a real dramatic theological dispute. The issue was whether the Chinese were more ancient than the biblical creation (or at least the Deluge) as dated by the Hebrew version of the Bible (i.e. the Vulgate); either their chronologies were wrong or the Bible as a historical text was wrong. Many authors denied the validity of Chinese sources, whilst others found in the Septuagint version of the Bible,[112] instead of the Hebrew or Vulgate version, a possible conciliation, because in the former version the creation and the Deluge happened several centuries before. Another possible solution was to consider the facts reported in the Bible as a local history, i.e. the history of Jews, and therefore, the Bible was universal not as history of humankind but instead as allegorical teaching and spiritual doctrine. Evidently, the effective universality of the sacred and holy text was in real danger, at risk of being acknowledged as merely the 'national epic' of the Jews.[113]

Isaac La Peyrère (1596–1676), the author whose (bad) reputation is today still linked with this question, supported the most controversial theory. In his *Praedamitae*,[114] he analysed and tried to solve the contradictions in the Book of Genesis supposing the existence of mankind before Adam, since Cain, after having killed his brother, escaped from God's punishment and married a woman that was not a daughter of Adam and Eve (Genesis 4.14-17). In this *Exercitatio* by La Peyrère, Adam is described as the first Jew, the man who committed the sin, the man who prepared with his sin the coming of Christ (the second man), however, Adam himself was not historically the first man. We cannot analyse here the interesting and refined theory proposed by La Peyrère,[115] but only the most important practical effects that, according to the author, could descend from Pre Adamism, concern our investigation on China and India:

> [The real task is to] conciliate the Genesis and the Gospel with Astronomy, History and Philosophy of ancient [civilizations], even the most ancient. So that, whether the same Chaldeans – the most ancient astronomers, among which it is said since hundreds of thousands of years the properties of the orbit of stars has been determined –; or the ancient Egyptian historians of the glorious royal dynasties; or the same Aristotle; or with Aristotle the Chinese – philosophers and historians likely eminent –; or the wise men – when found – from an unknown Australian or Northern people among which – as for Chinese, Egyptian and Chaldean learned men – their historical events were passed on for millennia; [as all these men I mentioned] would have confront themselves [with the Bible] following my exposition, they could understand without pains the history of the *Genesis* and they could be willing to become Christians.[116]

We see that La Peyrère did not merely suggest that his own Pre Adamitic theory was a good solution for several contradictions contained in the Book of Genesis, but even that this theory would have been of great help for the evangelization of heathens, since Pre Adamism was historically the most universalistic theory compatible with the Bible.[117] All ancient civilizations that were already known or still to be discovered, because they were acknowledged as pre-Adamitic (then historically preceding the Bible), could have their chronicles respected and find a place among Christianity. Heathen peoples who own a long history could receive only Christian faith, without the historical restriction of the Hebrew text. In La Peyrère's opinion, this theory was not intended against Christian religion, on the contrary, he believed that it could even ease the spreading of this religion among learned persons of civilizations that were not yet Christian. Among the civilizations he acknowledged as pre-Adamitics, only the Chinese and a hypothetical 'people still to be discovered by Europeans' were alive at his time, and therefore susceptible to conversion. According to La Peyrère's theory, the fundamental element that every civilization needed in order to be integrated among

Pre Adamites was a great historical commitment. In those decades, the Chinese were acknowledged as a culture of great historical tradition and where a pure morality was taught, and both aspects deserved admiration according to La Peyrère.

Also, Isaac Vossius (1618–89) has been one of the most strenuous advocates of Chinese antiquity and of their moral qualities. He is listed by Israel among the first 'Radical thinkers' of the seventeenth century; he was a secularist and an erudite libertine.[118] His criticisms of the chronology of the Hebrew Bible were radical, but less subversive than La Peyrère's Pre Adamitic theory. Vossius proved, in the *Dissertatio de vera aetate mundi*,[119] the chronology of the Septuagint Bible to be more plausible and in accord with Chinese, Egyptian and Chaldean sources than the Hebrew version.

After a close comparison between the chronologies of the Hebrew Bible (Vulgate) and of the Greek version (Septuagint), the latter emerged as the more rational and compatible with the long and difficult colonization of the world before and after the deluge. As we said, Vossius supported his thesis by quoting the chronology of Chaldeans (chap. IX), of Egyptians (chap. X) and of Seres/Chinese (chap. XI). All these chronologies covered a longer time than the Vulgate chronology and, moreover, they went back to more ancient times. About the Chinese, 'they have authors more ancient than Moses'.[120] The beginning of their civilization dated from 2847 BCE (ibid., p. XLVI), thus their historical accounts covered till the year 1658 exactly 4,505 years (ibid., p. XLVII). Since, according to Vossius, the date of the Deluge of the Hebrew version was around 2300 BCE, the Chinese were evidently an antediluvian civilization. Vossius even claimed that the presumed unquestionableness of the Hebrew chronology was just a pretext provided to the Pre Adamitists, since when the date of creation and Deluge of this version were stated as the only acceptable chronology, these unorthodox thinkers were reasonably right in claiming a pre-diluvian humanity (ibid., XLIX–XLX). It was necessary to accept the Septuagint dates, which were consistent with the chronology of other reliable ancient cultures. Moreover, he claimed that the Deluge reported in the Bible was not universal, because there had been several deluges narrated in ancient sources from different countries, as Pre Adamists also said.[121] Vossius calculated the age of the world – based on these ancient barbarian chronologies – as 7,048 years old, thus the year of creation as 5390 BCE (ibid., LV).

We do not agree with Virgile Pinot when he says that the real aim of Vossius was merely 'to justify his frenetic admiration for China'.[122] In our opinion, Vossius came to terms with these chronological issues in light of a wider historical project, which derived, on one side, from the global historical vision of a modern libertine erudite and, on the other side, from his personal conviction about the coherency of all the polyhistoric or encyclopaedic knowledge. We suggest that Vossius's quest for order and coherence led him to search for a new date of creation for all humankind. There is something modern in Vossius, in accepting ancient chronologies beside the Hebrew Bible, in holding a non-dogmatic point of view on history and in being interested in China.

Vossius was deeply impressed by China and his admiration was so evident that critics hailed him for many decades.[123] For instance, he was chosen by Renaudot[124] as the best example of the anti-historical and unreasonable attitude of European erudites fascinated by Chinese culture as depicted by Jesuits according to the accommodation method (i.e. Ricci). In his *Variarum observationum*,[125] Vossius exalted China as the country with the biggest and most beautiful cities in the world. China was the most populated country in the world and even the better ruled: 'In all our World only Chinese have been able to preserve perpetually for more than five millennia now unchanged [their] literature . . .'[126] and 'only them, among all mortals, could preserve in total peace and tranquillity for more than four millennia their reign and government'.[127] In Vossius's opinion, Chinese culture was the evidence of the futility of violence, which was instead the common and leading factor of European history. However, China was not only well ruled, indeed it was a country full of arts and literature. Vossius praised the great continuity of Chinese literature (ibid., 69–70), their scientific knowledge, namely in Botany, Chemistry, Medicine, Architecture, Astronomy, Music, and any kind of art (ibid., 70ff). Among all these fields of expertise, Vossius underlined the 'ars typographica' (ibid., 81), because he firmly claimed that Chinese invented print almost 1,500 years before Europeans. Sinophilia, since Vossius, became the expression of a religious, political and social critic of European past and present. China became, among libertines, the emblem of freedom, justice and tolerance in contrast with theological orthodoxy. As Israel states: 'the first esprit fort, or "suspected atheist" . . . to hit on using Chinese culture as a subversive strategy within Western intellectual debate, was the Dutch Deist, Isaac Vossius . . .'[128]

We shall investigate afterwards libertines' image of China, but in this chapter we concern ourselves only with a few details about the reactions to Vossius's chronology. Among the historians of philosophy, we can mention Peter Lambec (1628–80)[129] and again Georg Horn. In his polyhistoric book, Lambec followed Diogenes Laërtius and denied strenuously both the Pre Adamism and the validity of the ancient chronologies contrasting with the Vulgate or Hebrew Bible. He stated that Chaldean, Egyptian, Indian and Chinese chronologies were fabulous and risible, if compared with the holy chronology of the Hebrew Bible. He also claimed that these ancient civilizations were not historically reliable and their mythology prevailed over every rational principle (ibid., 2ff). This reaction was quite common among 'orthodox' thinkers and it was one of the main arguments used against Jesuits in order to prove their 'manufacturing' of Chinese civilization, reversing Jensen's expression (see §1.2.). These were the same reasons argued by the German Eclectics as Heumann and Brucker, who refused to acknowledge the validity of the histories of ancient eastern peoples (§3).

Georg Horn, although defending the Hebrew biblical chronology (Vulgate), did not refuse so harshly the validity of Chinese history, as we have already seen in his *Historia philosophica*. At first, Horn replied to Vossius[130] and opened a direct debate that we cannot follow here. It is worth noting that Horn did not reject Chinese culture, rather he merely criticized briefly, and without producing any proofs, Jesuits' historical interpretation of their texts. He provided a more complex investigation only seven years later in his *Arca Noae*,[131] an impressive historical book, which is a sort of universal chronology and history of all imperial dynasties of the world. After having rejected the Pre Adamitic thesis and Vossius's thesis of the Bible as local history of the Jews (ibid., 12–13), Horn claimed that Chinese *Annals* were a mere peripheral and impure version of the antediluvian biblical history. Whilst Martino Martini simply showed the *Annals* as more antique than the Bible and their account of the ancient dynasties, Horn tried to prove a perfect compatibility of both chronologies. The Bible and the *Annals* were only the same account, which was in the latter case overwhelmed with myths and falsifications.

In order to state the equivalence between these chronologies, Horn used a method that merged together philology and chronology. He suggested that, since the Old Testament was the history of patriarchs before the Deluge and the *Annals* were the history of the Chinese mythical emperors, Chinese emperors could not but be the biblical patriarchs themselves. Following this historical assumption, he simply matched every biblical patriarch with a Chinese Emperor, suggesting an indubitable chronological and biographical conformity. For instance, the first emperor, 'Fohium' (Fuxi 伏羲) was Adam, because both were not born from parents (ibid., 14). 'Xinnungus' was Cain, being both founders of farming (ibid., 15). 'Hoangtius' was 'Hanoch' (Enoch), as the similarity of the name clearly proved (ibid., 16). And although the following emperor names and biographies were not similar to any biblical figure, Horn suggested these men belonged to the Enoch lineage. Lastly, 'Yaum' (Yao 堯), who was described as 'sanctissimum piissimumque' and lived at the same time of the Deluge, had to be Noah himself (ibid., 17).

> therefore, we could reveal the truth of the Holy Scriptures without obscurity and show to these peoples[132] the sources from which theirs [chronologies] had been taken.
>
> ibid., 19[133]

By this programmatic statement it should be clear that both La Peyrère and Horn, two tough and explicit opponents, shared at least the same evangelic concern. However, whilst La Peyrère believed that the solution was the restriction of the historical role of the Bible, Horn's opinion was on the opposite side, since he claimed that the Bible should be acknowledged as the source of all the ancient historical texts. According to him, the Bible contained the universal history of all humankind that was corrupted in several local histories, therefore China, although introduced among modern philosophers in his *Historia philosophica*, was an integral part of the Noahic spread of the divine wisdom.

What we wish to have proved reporting the chronological issues is the indubitable impact and relevance of China into the context of chronology and history during the second half of the seventeenth century.[134] Clearly, Chinese historiography undermined the authority of the Bible and of the Jews, therefore, the reliability of their *Annals* was necessarily contested and that was one of Eusèbe Renaudot's aims in his argument against Chinese culture.[135] According to him, the reliability of Chinese histories was contested not only by modern historians – influenced by the 'rites controversy' – but also by two ancient Muslim voyagers. And, after a few years, the German Eclectic Heumann translated Renaudot's argument, in order to reject the appraisal of Chinese culture and the validity of the 'barbaric philosophies'. The arguments against the 'oriental perennialism' of German Eclecticism shall be investigated in the third chapter.

1.5 China and India: problems of coherence among the theories about the diffusion of philosophy

Connected with the debate over the Extra-European chronologies and the historical authenticity of the Bible, the historians were also concerned with geographical issues regarding the origin and spread of philosophy or, more generally, of divine wisdom. In the second half of the seventeenth century, historical works often provided and discussed several theories about the spreading of wisdom, from the divine Adam to the whole of humankind. The most common theories were always consistent with the perennial philosophy model, which claimed that God was the origin of wisdom and Christian Europeans were his last and more advanced heirs. These theories were often repetitive and accepted by a large intellectual community. In this section, we shall see two instances among these theories, because it is essential to appreciate the great continuity of this vision and the attempt to insert and – at the same time – to marginalize modern India and China. Both de Villemandy and Thomassin were expressions of a traditional Christian vision of the role of philosophy and they were both against libertines' philosophies.

Pierre de Villemandy (1636/7–1703) – Calvinist professor at the Academy of Saumur – in his *Manuductio*,[136] provided two metaphors in order to describe the spread of philosophy: the human ages and the Sun's (apparent) daily movement. As regards the first metaphor, he divided the history of philosophy in three sections: 'Philosophiae nascentis sectae', 'Philosophiae adolescentis sectae' and 'Philosophiae adultae, et ad supremam perfectionem contendentis, sectae'. Therefore, the philosophical ages were childhood, adolescence and adulthood. Obviously, barbaric philosophies were a 'nascentis' philosophy, whilst Greek philosophy was 'adolescentis' and the adult age started with Christ and found its culmination in Descartes. In this apparently coherent system, the only strangeness is the collocation of Chinese philosophy at the end of adolescence (ibid., 70). De Villemandy claimed a chronological reason: Confucius was contemporaneous with Pythagoras, an 'adolescent' Greek philosopher. However, why did de Villemandy collocate Confucius at the end of the chapter and not at the beginning, where Pythagoras was discussed? There is not a possible answer to this question provided in the text. Moreover, the paragraph on Confucius is rather poor and it seems to be simply a required insertion, not really coherently placed in the whole book and written cursorily.

The second metaphor is the movement of the Sun from East to West. De Villemandy supposed the propagation of a 'prisca theologia' from Abraham and the Chaldean sects to the Christian West. At the heart of this common theology there were the bases of Christian catechism: 'The uniqueness of God, who created everything from nothing. The immortality of the soul. The wise Divine Providence that rules everything. The resurrection of bodies, etc.'[137] (ibid., 57). De Villemandy described the diffusion of this presumed monotheistic wisdom as follows:

> Actually, as rays of rising sun illuminated [illustrantur] at first the Oriental lands, then the Southern and at last the Occidental countries, in the same way the rays of the rising Philosophy illuminated [illustrate[138]] at first the Oriental lands, after they

were transmitted [trasmissi] to the Southern lands and in the end they were entrusted [deferrentur] to the Occidental [peoples].[139]

It is worth noting the syntactical differences between the two terms of comparison in this sentence. The movement of the rays of the sun, i.e. the first term, is expressed in three succeeding prepositions only governed by 'illustro' in the third passive person, whilst the spreading of Philosophy, i.e. the second term, is described through three prepositions with three different verbs in a precise sequence. These prepositions are as follows: 1. the Oriental lands are passive, with 'illustrate fuerunt'; 2. about the Southern lands the rays become passive ('trasmissi sunt') instead of the lands; 3. in the last preposition, about western lands, the rays are passive again with 'deferrentur'. Therefore, the eastern lands (i.e. peoples) were passive, they had received the spreading of wisdom, while the Southern and particularly the western lands (people) seem to have been more active in the reception. The verb 'defero' suggests the movement of philosophy as definitive, because among the most relevant meaning of the verb there are 'to bring till a certain point', 'to invest' and 'entrust'. Whilst the sun repeats his movement every day, the geographical movement of philosophy had as last destination the Christian West. Besides these apologetic aspects, this metaphor poses an evident problem: if Chaldeans were the first civilization blessed by wisdom and Brahmins and the Chinese received this wisdom afterwards,[140] the similarity with the solar movement does not fit properly.

A possible solution to this incoherence seems to be provided by a colleague at the Academy of Saumur, namely Louis Thomassin (1619–95), in his methodological work written for the teaching of philosophy,[141] where he suggested the diffusion of wisdom from a centre. The theory is more coherent, but it lacks the eschatological taste:

> From there, as from a commune source, humankind broadened out from one side to the Orient, where at the same time wisdom spread and brought to life the Brachmans or the Gymnosophists of the Indies[142]; and from the other side [spread] to the West, where among Phoenicians, Egyptians, and several further civilizations there were different wise men: because everything radiates from one commune source.
>
> ibid., I, X, 1, 107–8[143]

Thomassin suggested a common source for two geographical directions, East and West, which represented the real movement of human migrations (biblically speaking). This 'centrifugal' model was a good solution for China and India, which were excluded from the human spreading in the description proposed by de Villemandy, and this theory was consistent with the historical model of 'prisca theologia'. However, Thomassin, at the end of the section of the manual devoted to the history of philosophy, contradicted his multi-directional theory, providing the same comparison of de Villemandy:

> the natural course of human things, that seems to follow the course of stars, and to go always from the East to the West, as the same humankind does, because of the providence of the one who created and rules the Heaven and the Earth. This is an

effect of the natural progress of humans, and of everything related to them: usually the sequence of years and centuries adds new perfections to them [i.e. humans].

ibid., I, XXII, 262[144]

Thomassin, with Heurn, Horn and de Villemandy, showed the difficulties of collocating India and China, in particular, into a perennial model that should underline a necessary Christian – and European – eschatology or progress. The ultimate solution to this problem of coherence in the theory about the perennial spreading of the divine wisdom was the definition of an opposed line of diffusion to the Orient, which was not divine, but instead devilish. Kircher was the most eminent advocate of this stream of heresy and atheism, which originated from Egypt and diffused the most despicable religious opinions to China and Japan (§2.1.). The theory of a devilish line was already claimed by Horn, as he suggested that Noah's sons were the origin of world philosophy and obviously among them was Ham, the damned son (§1.3.). However, Horn did not argue, as Kircher did, that Ham went from Egypt to the East, instead he suggested that Ham went southerly to Ethiopia. In order to understand Kircher's 'anti-perennialist' thought, a detailed investigation of the creation of the doctrine of the 'atheistic Asia' is necessary, which we shall provide in the next chapter. Therefore, although these theories about the spreading of wisdom could seem poor and insignificant, they permit a visible understanding of the changes produced in the historiographical paradigms.

1.6 Thomas Burnet: modern Asia as 'wretched Barbarity'

During the seventeenth century, the English-speaking world did not show the same interest in historiography of philosophy, if compared with the numerous publications in France, Dutch Republic, Germany and Italy. In England, the concept of the 'history of philosophy' was peculiar, since it was connected with the Baconian 'historia litteraria', which was more interested in scientific progress rather than in religious or theological history.[145] However, there was a relevant exception: the *History of Philosophy*[146] by Thomas Stanley (1625–78), which was really famous and influential in the second half of the seventeenth century. This work was published in four volumes between 1655 and 1662. The last book of four, separately published, was entitled *Of the Chaldaick Philosophers* and was a great collection of annotated quotes and sources. It became famous when Jean Le Clerc translated it into Latin[147] and Goffredo Olerius integrated this edition almost fifty years later.[148] The Latin edition was very well known abroad and particularly in the Dutch Republic, and for decades many European historians appreciated the great erudition of Stanley. Besides the last volume published separately, Stanley never discussed Oriental philosophy and he dealt only with ancient Greek philosophy. In the very short *Preface*, Stanley simply mentioned the origin of philosophy from the East,[149] without providing any detail or discussion. His work started with Thales and ended with the Stoics. The book on Chaldeans was evidently a separate text with no intention of creating links between Greek and Asian philosophies, instead it was undertaken in order to investigate the Chaldaic, Persian and Sabaean peoples, among which the teaching of Zoroaster was the most eminent. Stanley stressed correctly that there was not only one man called Zoroaster, but rather several wise men with this name. From them originated Chaldaic wisdom, which Stanley did not acknowledge as divine. We shall see in the next chapter that Zoroaster was a very controversial historical figure, since he was accused of being the same as Ham, i.e. the origin of the devilish wisdom. However, in the book on Chaldeans, Stanley ended his investigation by presenting Persians and he surprisingly mentioned neither the Chinese nor Indians.

The only English historian, whom we found really engaged in the understanding of Indian and Chinese philosophies, is the theologian Thomas Burnet (1635–1715) in his *Archaeologiae Philosophicae* (1692).[150] This work had a very complex editorial process: it was translated and edited in several different ways over the course of thirty years. The first edition (1692) was written in Latin and composed of two parts: the first was a history of ancient philosophy, whilst the second was a history of the Earth, thus a geological text.[151] In the same year, a partial English translation of the second part was published and, in the following decades, many partial English editions of the geological section were edited. In 1729, Thomas Foxton wrote several remarks for a new comprehensive edition of the geological section.[152] In 1736, there was a new English edition of the same part by J. Fisher.[153] In short, the geological section was translated, while the philosophical section was never translated into English, but edited many times in Latin. There was an exception: the Appendix on the modern Brahmans (i.e. on Asians). As it was at the end of the entire work, it was translated into English and edited within the geological section, without the historical part to which it was a supplement.[154]

Burnet's history of philosophy – namely the first book of *Archaeologiae* – was not written with an academic or philosophical purpose, but rather was written in order to support the biblical theory of the creation that the author presented in the second part. Burnet acknowledged Philosophy as a preparatory discipline, useful and necessary in order to conciliate religious faith, reason and scientific theories (i.e. Newton). The history of philosophy – as asserted by Mirella Pasini[155] – was the history of the world 'a parte hominis', while the geological investigation was a philological and scientific analysis of the biblical theory of Genesis. Burnet claimed the possibility of a biblical exegesis free from the restrictions he attributed to the Catholic countries, as opposed to the presumed Anglican tolerance.[156] However, it is useful to mention that, because of the thesis formulated in the *Archaeologia Philosophica*, Burnet was accused of unorthodoxy by the eminent Archbishop of Canterbury and he was ousted from his role as chaplain of King William III.[157] Therefore, the tolerant Anglican England also kept under control any innovative and potentially dangerous interpretation of the Bible proposed by a rationalist and libertine Anglican theologian such as Burnet.[158]

Burnet opened his history with the threefold division of historical times by Varro: 1. *Tempus obscurum* (the antediluvian time); 2. *Tempus fabulosum* (from post-diluvian times till Olympic games); 3. *Tempus historicum* (ibid., 3). Obviously, eastern civilizations were collocated in the second period, which is a time not fully historical and clear. Furthermore, these Oriental civilizations spread from the descendants of

Noah and not of Abraham (as suggested by Postel), thus they were evidently post-diluvian civilizations (as Horn already claimed). In the second chapter, the author recalled the classification of peoples according to the *veteres*, which followed the four directions or 'quatuor Mundi plagas': 1. 'Scytharum in Septentrione'; 2. 'Celtarum, in Occidente'; 3. 'Aethiopum, versus Meridiem'; 4. 'Indorum, cum nulla fit vox latior, pro caeteris, Orientem versus' (pp. 4–5).[159] Therefore, Burnet clarified that the 'Indi' were a very wide cultural group, because this name gathered many different civilizations. A few lines later, he said: 'Under the name of the true Indians, many peoples were confusedly classified by the ancients, [now] having understood that, a new classification ['apparatus'] will be used …'[160] (ibid., 5) for Oriental peoples ('gentes illas Orientales', ibid.). The entire historical account is divided as follows: chap. 2 Scythians, Celts and Ethiopians; chap. 3 the so-called Indians; chap. 4 Assyrians and Chaldeans; chap. 5 Persians; chap. 6 Arabians and Phoenicians; chap. 7 Jews; chap. 8 Egyptians; from chap. 9 to 13 the Greek philosophy. The last chapter (chap. 14) is a general discussion on the origin of barbaric philosophy, where Burnet clarified several of his assumptions.

Consistently with his specification on the variety of 'Indians', he began the third chapter through a presentation of the Chinese. Burnet said that the ancients had called them 'Seres', while in modern times they were called 'Sinenses' and it was commonly accepted that they had an ancient and rich cultural history. The most relevant topic raised by Burnet is his denial of Chinese atheism, where the author rejected the ancient claim of Celsus (who said: άθεος). Celsus's lost *Against Christian* was quoted by Origen in *Contra Celsum*, and the sentence on the Chinese atheism is as follows: 'Let us now see what follows. "Let us pass on," says he [Celsus], "to another point. They [the Christians] cannot tolerate temples, altars, or images. In this they are like the Scythians, the nomadic tribes of Libya, the Seres who worship no god, and some other of the most barbarous and impious nations in the world".[161] Burnet rejected this accusation of atheism. However, he did not quote modern Jesuit texts, where Chinese ancient monotheism was claimed (consistently with Ricci's accommodation), but instead he discussed this accusation in its original historical context. He argued that, for Greeks, all men who did not worship or make sacrifices for gods were atheists, and the same accusation was levelled at Christians themselves (ibid., 14). Consequently, Burnet concluded that this accusation could not be trusted, as the Greek concept of atheism was incorrect. In the same years in France and the Dutch Republic, a great debate about Oriental atheism was increasing, particularly with Bayle, but in Burnet we cannot find any traces of it. Burnet answered the ancient accusation of atheism with an answer taken from an investigation of the ancients, disregarding (or avoiding) the intellectual impact of the topic in his time and the contemporary (mostly French) 'Chinese rites controversy'.

The conclusion of the author is that ancient sources on China were scarce and distorted by religious and ethnical beliefs. Instead of them, Burnet praised the modern sources of missionaries and travellers that made possible a true and deep knowledge of this civilization, the heart of which were the *Annals*. The author reported that many ancient texts had been destroyed in the 'books burning' ordered by emperor '*Zio*' centuries before Christ (ibid., 15),[162] but regardless the surviving books proved that China had a great cultural tradition.

They have conspicuous [traces useful for the] 'Archaeologia Philosophica', which regard the deluge, the [creation] of the earth from an egg and remarkable ancient astronomical observations.

ibid., 15[163]

Therefore, Burnet suggested that an investigation of ancient sources of wisdom in China was worthy of attention, because they had a really ancient philosophy, which deserved 'archaeological' investigation. We cannot forget here the 'geological' aim of our author, because his philosophical history was always related to the history of the human understanding of the Earth. According to this point of view, ancient Chinese sources related to this scientific issue might be of interest and should be better known, but whether Burnet's opinion was not negative about China, his description did not imply that he became a 'Sinophile', since, for him, only ancient wisdom was worth investigation, whilst modern Chinese philosophers were really below the scientific standard reached by Europeans:

When we compare nowadays Chinese with nowadays Europeans, I have no doubts that their [learning] is inferior to our, for instance when we look at theoretical and applied Mathematics and Physiology.

ibid., 15[164]

In this paragraph, Burnet expressed his opinion on Asians for the first time: they could be praised in consideration of their past splendour, but not as it regards their present state. This was quite a common opinion amongst historians, since in Heurn's history of barbarian philosophy, modern Indians were reputed inferior to their ancestors and the Chinese, following Ricci, were atheists although their ancestors were not so. It is evident the wall European thinkers were trying to build between the past and present of Asians, in order to exclude them from any kind of intellectual and scientific progress.

Burnet made only one exception to this dismissal of modern Chinese thought, which is a good appraisal of their ethics. Therefore, he shared the Jesuit claim of the high level of Confucian ethics, as stated since Ricci. Obviously, he quoted the equivalence 'Confucius, Sinensium Socrates' (ibid.) and the importance of this thinker also to contemporary learning, in order to have access to public offices. Even without mentioning Plato's *Republic*, he acknowledged the high role of Chinese philosophers in public life, because these philosophers were allowed even to blame the emperor himself (ibid.). Therefore, these Chinese philosophers, who could blame the ruler, did something not allowed, according to Burnet, in the Catholic countries, where intolerance and oppression were the common political strategy.

'Brachmanes' lived in the other hemisphere of the 'Indies' and they had been renowned as great philosophers among Greeks and Romans. Burnet, in a polyhistoric or antiquarian style, quoted several ancient sources, dividing the ancient ones from those of the Fathers of the Church. He also referred to modern sources, but – as for the Chinese – without reporting them. The absence of quotations from modern sources suggests already a clear separation '*à la* Heurn' between modern and ancient Asian philosophers. Brachmanes, according to the well-known ancient descriptions, were always absorbed in contemplation ('contemplationi semper vacabant', ibid., 15), they followed a strict moral code and practised sciences such as Physiology and Astronomy (ibid.). Burnet, in order to minimize their scientific consistence, quoted Strabo, where the latter suggested that Indian philosophy was based only on myths and tales, rather than on observation and rational theories. At last, after this polyhistoric presentation, Burnet criticized these ancient sources: 'This is what I [can] know of ancient Brachmanes, a lot is reported by ancient sources about their life, but very little about their doctrines' (ibid., 17).[165] This claim of Burnet was completely correct: Greek, Roman and early Christian sources on India were not so scarce as the sources on China, however, their philosophical quality was deplorably low. Ancient historians of the West had not been interested in a real understanding of the philosophical thought of Indians, instead they presented only the peculiarity of this foreign society and of their practices. Burnet observed also that later in the Byzantine *Suida* Indian laws and doctrines were mentioned, but never reported in detail.

Regarding contemporary Indians, Burnet wrote an interesting and rich paragraph worth quoting entirely:

> It is absolutely certain the survival of the institution and of the class of philosophers in India, as well as, it is true that they have preserved their philosophy, their sacred and extremely ancient language (that is not a popular one). And it is true that they remained faithful to their philosophy and their philosophical corpus, although variously distorted and actually encrusted with myths. This information reached us through learned men, who became experts living for a long time among Indians. When it will be the case, we will report the specific notions included in their texts in a following book.[166]
>
> ibid., 18

Therefore, according to Burnet, modern Indians were consistent with their ancient tradition, however, they had lost the original purity of their wisdom. This claim is clear from the perspective of perennial philosophy, as we have argued since Heurn's chapter on modern Indians. As the divine wisdom spread among Asians in ancient times, only European culture, thanks to Greek philosophy and Christian revelation, experienced a continuous progress following God's providence. Ancient Indians were closer to the divine wisdom than their heirs: the original purity was lost because of mythical and fabulous additions, which justified the actual European disdain about their culture. Heurn and Burnet, consciously or not, were accepting the missionaries' interpretation, which supported a 'prisca theologia' of Asians. These ancient civilizations had an original pure wisdom that needed to be cleansed from religious local impurities via the Christian faith and the modern European scientific knowledge. At the end of the excerpt, Burnet suggested that he would write a book in order to analyse Jesuits' accounts in detail and this mentioned book could not but be the Appendix.

As we said, chapter 14, the last of the first book – i.e. the history of philosophy – is about a general appraisal of barbarian philosophies. According to Burnet, barbaric thought was ineffective, and every reasonable tenet of this philosophy was derived certainly from a more perfect source, which could but be the divine Noahic wisdom. Barbarians were unable to produce real knowledge, because 'they pass on their dogmas bare and simple, they never proposed dissertations, and they are not grounded on rational [demonstrations]: by them orders and authority are acknowledged as teachings' (ibid., 191).[167] On that point he quoted Clement of Alexandria: 'Clement of Alexandria was in the right claiming that ancient-barbaric philosophy was insignificant and cursory, [structured] only on questions and answers. It was not argumentative and [articulated in] disputes as afterwards Greek was.'[168] (ibid., 192–3). Here Burnet referred to the first lines of the eighth book of *Stromata*, however, he betrayed Clement's sense. In this context, the father of the Church was blaming Greek philosophy for its artificiality, due to its search for fame, while he was praising Barbarians for their simplicity and their closeness to the divine wisdom. Therefore, Burnet overturned Clement's argument. For the Englishman the simplicity or 'bareness' of barbaric philosophy was not a value in itself, because a repetitive philosophy loses its original meaning. Burnet wrote: '[all I said] is enough to prove that: *Priscorum philosophia* was transferred [to Barbaric lands], thus handed down …' (ibid., 193).[169] Burnet's conclusion is that the barbarians had been philosophers, but they received philosophy from Noah. The core of this Noahic doctrine, which is the origin of the whole 'doctrina orientalis', is the emanation theory ('*ex nihilo nihil fieri*') opposed to the Christian '*creatio ex nihilo*', which was introduced much later and was lacking in previous philosophy.[170] The emanation theory and immanentism were taught in all ancient heathen philosophies (including the Greek one) and according to Burnet's side note: 'This [theory] is taught by today Brachmans in India'[171] (ibid., 64). The emanation theory was a central topic within the continental debate of the same years. However, Burnet did not claim the existence of a 'counter' perennial philosophy among heathen civilizations, which was opposed to the monotheistic and creationist faiths, as argued in particular by Athanasius Kircher (see §2.1.). On the contrary, the English author's perspective was the rational interpretation of ancient myths and faiths (even the Christian ones) in order to trace the Noahic wisdom. According to Burnet, the true philosophy of Noah was the emanative system, instead of Christian creationism, and this was the real object of his 'archaeologia philosophica', and the scientific study of the geological history of the Earth confirmed this theory. We cannot be surprised by the reaction of the Archbishop of Canterbury, who obviously judged this advocated 'Noahic emanative system' as a complete heterodox and subversive argument.

The last lines of the historical part of the *Archaeologiae Philosophicae* is a perfect example of 'prisca theologia' tenet, although Burnet was already far from the universalism or concordism of perennialism:

> The 'priscorum philosophia' is really a complex issue: although covered with stains and sordidly mucked, it reaches the fierce men [that] we are, namely the last and distant Noahic descendants. [Philosophy] is found and explored through the truths that proceed from a [divine] otherness, it is cleansed without efforts from these imperfections. In its [of philosophy] ancient gems, although faded because

of their oldness, sparks still vividly shine [and now] more frequently they are perceived with admiration.

ibid., 196–7[172]

Contemporary Europe was the last stage of the universal history of the world, it was the fulfilment of all the past experiences of mankind, because Europeans were also sons of Noah as all the ancients were.

The first note of the Appendix translated into English (both editions 1729 and 1736) refers to the chapter on Indians (the third) of the first book of the Latin version, since, as we said, this historical book has never been translated into English. If we consider this note and the reference made by Burnet on a future book on Indians in the first book of the *Archaeologiae philosophicae*, we can suggest that the Appendix was an integral part of the first book, planned since the writing of the historical section. Obviously, as the 'History of Philosophy' was intended by the author as a discussion on the origin and the creation of the Earth, in the Appendix he focused on the same topics as in the historical section. It is worthy of note that Burnet, as other modern historians, felt the necessity to provide an account of contemporary Asian thinkers, as Heurn did for Indians almost a century before and Brucker did around fifty years later with the book on 'exotic civilisations'. Therefore, from the seventeenth century until the first half of the eighteenth century, historians of philosophy were used to come to terms with contemporary extra-European cultures, however, this historical concern began to decay after Brucker's *Historia critica* (1742–4).

In the Appendix, Burnet remarked anew on the diverse peoples, which were included under the name 'Indians'. He mentioned the Chinese, Indostan or Moghul, Siam, Malabars, Cochincin, Coromandel, and he added: 'whatever others in the *East*[173] are known to us, who in some measure shaken off their Barbarity' (ibid., 2). This last sentence is very intriguing for at least two reasons. Firstly, Burnet reported that the equivalence between 'Asians' and 'Indians' was still quite common among Europeans; only Tibetans – although already known – were not mentioned in his list.[174] Secondly, he conferred a clear negative meaning to the words 'Barbarian' and 'Barbarity'. According to him, 'barbarity' was a sort of pre-historical or original wildness, which needed to be overcome by means of civilization. Indians, namely Asians, had been able to progress and to detach themselves from this original Barbarian state, obviously thanks to their received Noahic wisdom. However, Burnet stressed that they succeeded in this emancipation only 'in some measure', and not entirely.

Each of the quoted Asian civilizations had its philosophers or theologians. Both India and Siam had 'Brachmanes', who could be easily distinguished from the other classes, because of their peculiar way of life, social condition and mythological faith. They used a religious language called 'Hanscrit or the pure Tongue' (ibid., 3) and Burnet reminded to the alphabet letters written by father Henry Roth[175] and quoted in *China illustrata* by Athanasius Kircher.[176] Brachmanes followed a Cabala or 'Body of Learning' handed down from ancient times, which they spread in several Asian lands. Their literary corpus proposed many philosophical issues typical of antiquity: God, origin and end of all things (emanation), the periodical renovations of the Earth, human primitive state of nature, etc. (ibid., 2). They expressed these notions through mythical images; among which the most relevant was that of the Spider. In this myth, the Spider is the first cause of generation: it creates the world as it was an 'artistic web', over which it rules everything. When the Spider has amused and satisfied itself, it destroys the net swallowing all the threads. Therefore, their God is represented by a Spider who creates the world for its pleasure and destroys it to its liking (ibid., 3). Burnet rightly pointed out that this Indian myth of emanation was similar to many coeval myths of other civilizations[177] (ibid., 4). As further reading, the author suggested two books, one by captain Henry Lord, that should be *Discovery of two Foreign Sects*,[178] and one by the Gassendian philosopher François Bernier, probably the *Suite des Mémoires du sieur Bernier sur l'empire du grand Mogol*,[179] where the aforementioned myth of the Spider was reported. As we shall see in the next chapter, Bernier was one of the most relevant figures within the process of understanding Indians as atheists and quietists, and moreover he was the most important source on Indians for Bayle and for several German Eclectics, such as Buddeus and Brucker.

In these years in Europe took place a rapid – around twenty years – but intense debate over Siam, because of the books written by the Jesuit missionary Guy Tachard and the diplomat Simon de la Loubère.[180] Tachard wrote *Voyage de Siam des pères Jesuites, envoyés par le roy, aux Indes età la Chine*,[181] whose central focus was on the local sciences, namely astronomy, physics and geography. Siamese astronomy reported that Earth is cyclically destroyed by Fire and it comes again anew out of its ashes. This scientific concern explains Burnet's interest in this account and also his historical and cultural claim:

> It is really a most wonderful thing that a Nation half barbarous, should have retained these Opinions from the very Times of Noah; for they could not have reached a Knowledge of these Things in any other way than by Tradition; not could this Tradition originate from any other Spring than Noah and the Antediluvian Sages.
>
> ibid., 6–7

The argument is clear: Siameses believed in a theory so elaborated to be necessarily imported, because such a barbaric civilization could never have developed a refined scientific theory, whose content are also supported by Greek science. Therefore, Siameses – who according to Burnet were barbarians – were inserted in the 'perennial philosophy' lineage, which originated from Noah. Burnet was completely certain of this claim, but he provided no proof and he did not suggest a migration theory (as we have seen in §1.5). The Noahic origin of barbarian religious theories is clearly a dogmatic assumption, which is asserted in the whole book and it is consistent with his peculiar perennialist historical paradigm based on Noah as origin of culture and civilization.

After Siam, Burnet wrote a few lines on Coromandel[182] and Malabar.[183] On Coromandel, Burnet provided further details regarding the local theories on Earth, creation and ages, which were very similar to the Greek myths of Hesiod. As for Malabar, he suggested that Roberto de Nobili wrote books on Indian rites, but these books were completely undiscovered at his time, and Burnet did not know in which language they were written (i.e. Tamil). As we know today, Roberto de Nobili may be acknowledged as the 'Ricci of India', however his influence was only on Indian missions and on Malabarian literature, rather than on the European culture, whereas Ricci's influence was really considerable. For this reason, the debate on China took place during the seventeenth and eighteenth centuries, whilst an intense debate on India started only in the late eighteenth century, when the scientific Oriental studies were born.

As Burnet was not interested in morality and politics, modern China could not be of great interest for him. He quoted only their theory of the world: the first man was created out of an egg and this egg was depicted as the original chaos.[184] The second point to highlight is the admiration for Indian letters in China, and since Burnet believed that Chinese had not derived their philosophy from Indians, he could not explain this question:

> and although they do not seem to have derived their Philosophy or History from the *Brachmans*, yet they set so great a Value on their Letters and secret Alphabet, that as things Sacred, and of a very great Antiquity, they use to inscribe them on their Idols.
>
> ibid., 8

Nowadays, the reason of the use among the Chinese of Indian or 'Brahman' letters, namely Sanskrit, is easy to explain. Burnet, like his contemporaries, was confusing Confucianism and Buddhism, where the Sanskrit letters were used in the second sect for ritualistic aim and to recall the Indian origin. It is also evident that, as we said already, Burnet was completely disregarding the theory of the diffusion of civilizations from Egypt proposed by Kircher in the *China illustrata* that he knew and quoted (see §2.1.), since the latter provided his explanation of the use of Sanskrit in China, which was due to the devilish spread of Buddhism from India into East Asia.

Before closing this rich Appendix, Burnet added a few negative words on Muslims in Asia. They were in India, Persia, Egypt and in many other countries of Asia. Their presence was despicable from both the historical and cultural viewpoints, because they erased local cultures, as in Egypt and particularly in Persia, wherefrom Zoroastrians were forced to move to India in order to be safe. Burnet said about Muslims:

> These things exactly square with the *Mohametans*, wheresoever they are dispersed, they retain nothing of the ancient Wisdom; for the ambition of extending their Dominions has taken from them all manner of Love or Desire of Learning.
>
> ibid., 8

According to him, Muslims used to erase local wisdoms and they did not deserve a place in philosophy, as he stated in the last sentence. We perceive a lasting anti-Islamic Christian image of Muslims as violent oppressors, completely exterior to God's providence. However, we know that in India, the several Moghul rulers had different attitudes: some of them being really tolerant, others less so.

In conclusion, on one side, Burnet suggested a clear Noahic lineage among Asians and a few similarities between their cultures and Greek philosophy, but, on the other side, his concept of barbarity was very different from the original meaning consistent with the Renaissance perennialist historical paradigm. In a century and a half of Histories of Philosophy, the terms 'barbarian' and 'barbaric philosophy' had been used to denote and delimit a wide geographical area in the remote past, namely the pre-Greek history, also called the 'Fabulous time'. That was the attitude derived from Clement of Alexandria and widely diffused among historians. Ancient Barbarian civilizations were at the origin of philosophy and they had to be respected because of their closeness to the divine original wisdom. However, since Heurn's chapter on contemporary Indian philosophers, the ambiguity of the term 'barbarian' became necessary to safeguard the description of a 'prisca theologia' and, at the same time, the unquestionable superiority of European Christian culture. Contemporary Barbarians were undoubtedly inferior to Europeans in every field of knowledge, and they were also inferior to their ancient ancestors (effective 'prisci theologi' and heirs of Noah or Abraham). From the insertion of contemporary Indians into the perennial model, their inferiority necessarily followed. Although China passed almost unnoticed in ancient sources and its belonging to biblical history was debatable, several seventeenth-century authors acknowledge this civilization as eminent. The effective state of Chinese sciences was already disputable, but Chinese morality was not. As Burnet was interested in sciences instead of ethics, he reputed all Barbarians' knowledge as lesser than that of the Europeans and accordingly his use of the term, 'barbarian' was derogatory:

> This must be observed in general, of the modern *Pagans*, that there are (it is true) now remaining amongst them some *Footsteps* of the most ancient Tenets, which come to them by Tradition from their Ancestors, but quite overwhelmed with *Trash* and *Filthiness*, being for the most part clogged with fabulous Additions, even to the degree of being nauseous; insomuch that when you come to manly Arguments, they are of no manner of Validity. I cannot but pity the Eastern World, that the Place which was the first Habitation of wise Men, and one Day a most flourishing *Emporium* for Learning, should for some Ages past have been changed into a wretched Barbarity.
>
> ibid., 9

This excerpt is similar to the paragraph of the chapter 14 we quoted before. Burnet claimed that nowadays pagans were in such a dramatic barbaric condition that they must be pitied by Europeans, who were, on the contrary, more advanced and obviously superior to their ancestors and to all the other civilizations. It should be remembered that according to Burnet, as for the majority of Europeans, this superiority to both contemporary and past philosophers (or in general men) was guaranteed by Christian faith and God's grace, which had to be brought to all countries as the unique universalistic and redeeming message:

> I pray God grant that we may not undergo the same Vicissitude, and that in his Anger he may not withdraw that Light we now enjoy in the West; but it may be

more and more diffused on all sides, till *The Knowledge of GOD shall have filled the Earth, as the Waters fill the Sea.*

ibid., 9

With this evident Christian evangelical hope, Burnet closed the second and last book of his *Archaeologiae Philosophicae*. Now we can understand the reason for closing the first book with Greeks, thus investigating only heathens: there was no archaeology after them. 'Cultural Archaeology', in his perspective, was necessary for ancient civilizations, whose 'gems' of Noahic wisdom had become almost undetectable, because of their current degradation. In Europe, after Greek pagans, Christian religion brought the new light, and hence archaeology was unnecessary.

After Thomas Stanley, Thomas Burnet and Theophile Gale, the English histories of philosophy were less original and the lack of interest in Asians among historians became very common. This attitude changed slightly at the end of the eighteenth century with the first English orientalist Scholars, but their studies kept on influencing French and German readers more than the philosophers of the English Empire. This is particularly true for historiography.

1.7 A first sceptic view of China: François de la Mothe le Vayer

At the end of this chapter on the introduction of India and China into the histories of philosophy grounded on the biblical paradigm, we present François de la Mothe le Vayer (1588–1672), who interpreted Chinese culture with a completely different approach. His approach was similar to the above-mentioned praise of China by Isaac Vossius. Le Vayer was one of the most influential thinkers in seventeenth-century France, as he was also preceptor of Louis XIV of France and of his brother. He was elevated to be magistrate and advocate at the French Parliament, but he decided to sell his office in order to devote his energy to the humanities. He was a distinguished member of the Académie française and an appointed historiographer of France. He was also a friend of Molière. His fame allowed le Vayer to profess openly 'a sceptique chrétienne' ('a Christian scepticism'), different from atheism, and consistent with a real anti-dogmatic approach to religions, preceding Deism. He did not refuse Christian faith, instead he rejected the dogmatic assumptions added to the rational faith and which produced several absurd convictions. He represents perfectly the cultivated environment of Louis XIV's court, where the libertines' ideas and their morals were diffused and welcomed.

Le Vayer may be collocated at the undefined beginning of a very long stream of thinkers who claimed a social renewal grounded on anti-obscurantism and on cultural openness. According to Israel, le Vayer should be renowned as a precursor of the 'Radical thinkers':

For the perfecting of the erudite libertine techniques was chiefly a feature of the early seventeenth century – especially the work of Gabriel Naudé (1600-53) and François de la Mothe le Vayer (1588-1672) – when there was still little or no possibility of producing or propagating a systematic philosophy explicitly at odds with the prevailing orthodoxies. The *libertines érudits*, however seditious, were essentially precursors of the Radical Enlightenment operating behind a dense layer of camouflage.[185]

He was not an 'esprit fort' or atheist as Vossius, but he used theatre dialogues and irony in order to prove the ineffectiveness of orthodoxy and the despicable consequences of the penetration of religious power and dogmas into the social life of the nation.

Already in 1642 – before Horn himself – le Vayer published a book where he showed a great commitment to the interpretation of China, in a period when the majority of philosophers were still neglecting these new sources and historians were often adhering to the perennial interpretation of the biblical historical frame. In *De la vertu des payens*,[186] he aimed at proving that some ancient heathens – specifically, their moral wise men – could have gained salvation, despite being outside of Christianity. The pivotal point was not to know whether philosophers such as Plato or Aristotle would have been saved, but rather whether a moral behaviour and an educated life could be an adequate means of salvation, although without Christian faith. The author answered: 'Never a reasonable person could have doubted that Virtue does not deserve to be praised'[187] (ibid., 1). Could the virtuous pagan be damned when even the most dissolute Christian was saved? Le Vayer's answer was that a perfect virtuous life and loving God must be enough for salvation:

> That is why, as the [Christian] believers do not cease to be often vicious, it is not impossible that an infidel could practice some virtues, although these [virtues] do not go with the merit given by the grace deriving from faith.
>
> ibid., 4[188]

De la vertu des payens is entirely devoted to the investigation of heathens' virtuous lives and to their eventual salvation by means of that morality, a topic that anticipated Bayle's theory of the 'virtuous atheist' who does not need God's grace and seems to be untouched by the Original sin, two unavoidable aspects for Protestants and Jansenists.[189]

The work is divided into two sections, i.e. a historical and a biographical one. In the first, le Vayer traced a history of philosophy – or of culture – following the biblical frame. He divided the world history in three periods: 1. 'l'Estat du droit de Nature', from Adam to the circumcision of Abraham in the seventeenth book of Genesis; 2. 'l'Estat de la Loy', till Christ; and 3. 'l'Estat de la Grace', i.e. the spread of the Christian message (ibid., 17–18). Obviously, the Bible was the only source about the first stage. But the second stage was le Vayer's real focus, because it concerned pagan civilizations, among which he did not discuss India, but rather China.

He argued that, if ignorance of the Christian message alone were enough to result in eternal damnation, Jews also had to be condemned and they could never be considered to be on the path to salvation (ibid., 26). On the contrary, many pagans had 'une Foy tacite et enveloppée' ('a silent and hidden Faith') that only the Christian Holy Word could make explicit. Among them, le Vayer mentioned Confucius and his followers. He was certain of this claim about Confucius and he quoted Matteo Ricci, who 'did not doubt that many virtuous Chinese could have saved themselves only observing the simple Law of nature and by means of the special help provided by the one God they acknowledged as the author of the Heaven and the Earth' (ibid., 34).[190] The damnation of all heathens was an absurd and contradictory thesis, because when God sent his son, there should have been people ready to understand and believe in his message, otherwise the salvation process would have been impossible (ibid., 35). Salvation was possible because of pagan philosophers, who conceived the single God before the Christian truth reached them:

> So, the Heathens, who lived virtuously following the light of the Law of Nature and submitting their free will to the reason, they did all that was in their power since they did not know any other Law than the natural ... this law carved into our hearts, that includes all Moses' laws ...
>
> ibid., 35–6[191]

The natural Law and the law of Moses were innate, part of human nature, because they were rational. In the third 'State', that of 'Grace', the author mentioned the evangelic missions in Asia, in the New World and in Australia (ibid., 48ff). Coherently, le Vayer suggested that when we accept the salvation of few Greek philosophers because of their virtue and wisdom, the same must be true for all moral heathens. The only necessary condition a heathen man needed in order to be saved was the love for God – even if he did not know him through revelation – and to adhere faithfully to the silver rule, which is 'Do not do unto others what you would not have them do unto you' (ibid., 52).

The second part of *De la vertu des payens* is not arranged chronologically, but rather according to the importance of each philosopher. The first philosopher mentioned is not Pythagoras, as was usual in the histories of philosophy, but instead Socrates, because of his influential moral thought, which made him the most eminent heathen philosopher. The last chapter of the book is devoted to Confucius and, despite the distance from Socrates, the title revealed the great appraisal of le Vayer for him: 'De Confutius le Socrate de la Chine'. The author justified his insertion of a non-Greek philosopher by mentioning Saint Augustin's appraisal of Barbaric wise men as philosophers (see §1.0.). Confirmed by the authoritative saint, the French philosopher felt himself free to say that Confucius was the Chinese Socrates, the highest moral philosopher of China and one of the most eminent of all times. He followed Ricci's view of Confucianism as a natural and original monotheistic philosophy:

> The Chinese recognized from time immemorial only one God, whom they named King of Heaven. And we can see through their Annals that, for more than four thousand years, there never had been a heathen people who offended him less than them and who comply with what is prescribed by the right reason more than them.
>
> ibid., 280[192]

Among them 'the best man and the best philosopher who has ever lived in the Orient, was a man called Confucius the Chinese ...',[193] praised and beloved still in modern time. Le Vayer stressed that Confucius was not worshipped as a God, like only idolaters would do, but rather as a great man, emblematic of virtue and wisdom. Furthermore, le Vayer suggested that between the lives of Socrates and Confucius a few similarities could be detected, among which the most relevant were their moral thought and also a chronological issue: Confucius died in the same year as Socrates' birth.[194] 'Therefore, we can say that Confucius, like Socrates, did make the philosophy of Heaven descend on Earth, through the authority they both recognised to morality ...' (ibid., 281).[195] After le Vayer, this comparison of Confucius and Socrates became common among thinkers, for instance, Bordelon devoted a dialogue of his *Théatre philosophique*[196] to Confucius and Antisthenes, where the Chinese philosopher was taken as the expression of a moral and meritocratic society, not far from Socrates' ethics.

Following the general appraisal of Jesuits in China, le Vayer suggested that the high moral level reached by Chinese entailed that 'all Liberal Arts and Sciences in China evolved continually, like in our [western] countries' (ibid., 280–1).[197] They had all scientific expertise and a physics akin to the physics of Democritus and Pythagoras. However, the education and selection of politicians and ministers was not based on scientific knowledge, but instead on Confucius' collection of moral sentences (ibid., 282). The sect of Confucians, which ruled the military power, also influenced royal authority. Le Vayer commented:

> Actually, it's not a minor glory for Confucius, to have put the Sceptre in the hands of philosophy, and to have made the force obey easily to Reason.
>
> ibid., 283[198]

According to le Vayer, morality and true religion were completely reasonable and philosophy was the best expression of reason. Reasonable morality and reasonable religion were two tenets of libertines' thought and they were discussed extensively by Bayle.

In the same chapter on Confucius, le Vayer presented also Xaca, through the *Relatione*[199] by Cristoforo Borri (1631), in the French translation of the same year.[200] Borri was missionary in Cochinchina (Sud-Vietnam), where he had met South-Asiatic Buddhism, which is quite different from the Chinese one. However, through other missionaries' accounts, Borri described both Confucius and Xaca, in the Japanese and Chinese shapes. Xaca, according to Borri, was a great metaphysician, who denied the efficient cause and affirmed emptiness as the first principle. According to le Vayer, this theory was 'chimerical' ('chimerique', ibid., 286), because Buddhism entailed a refusal of positive morality and allowed idolatry for the satisfaction of common people, who were unable to accept emptiness as their destiny. Confucians, who believed instead in a Supreme Being ('Souverain Estre', ibid., 287), rejected the validity and the reasonability of this sect. As in Ricci's programmatic description (§1.2.), Buddhism and Confucianism were opposed, because the first sect was unacceptable and hideous, whilst the second sect was compatible with Christian religion. Le Vayer added:

> We condemn this Indolence, or complete refusal of pain, on which Xaca [i.e. Buddha] based the perfect beatitude; and we recognise that these terms related to God could not be accepted.
>
> ibid., 289[201]

In this paragraph, probably we find the first allusion to the question of Buddhist 'Indolence' or apathy ever written in a philosophical text.[202] This physical and moral apathy was unacceptable for le Vayer, who preferred the teaching of the great moralist Confucius, closer to Socrates. As we shall see in the next chapter, the question of 'Indolence' was connected with Quietism in the following decades and the most important actor of this connection was the philosopher François Bernier, who personally knew de la Mothe le Vayer and who wrote a few letters to him from Asia.[203]

Conclusions of the first chapter

In this composed chapter we aimed at tracing two problematic issues in the process of introducing India and China within the histories of philosophy: 1. the Asians as contemporaries; 2. the Asians as ancient barbaric peoples inserted within the biblical history of philosophy. The three main historians we investigated, i.e. Heurn, Horn and Burnet, came to terms with both aspects in different and intriguing ways.

Heurn was the first historian to write about modern Indians, since he divided his sources by whether they were related to ancients or moderns, where the sources about ancients were a wide collection of references from Megasthenes to Clement of Alexandria, while about moderns he used the accounts of missionaries and travellers in India. Heurn described modern Indians as barbaric and coarse people devoted to idolatry, as was claimed by his modern sources. At the end of the seventeenth century, Burnet proposed the same image of barbarity but enlarged to the entirety of Asia, since these peoples had overwhelmed with fairy tales and idolatric worships the purity of their original Noahic wisdom. In the 1640s, when not only Ricci's account – translated by Trigault – but also Chinese chronologies were available, China became a main philosophical topic. Le Vayer, following Jesuit descriptions, praised the morality and justice of the Chinese Empire, which was the fulfilment of Plato's 'philosopher-king' of the *Republic*. The same, as we said, was claimed by Isaac Vossius, but Horn also acknowledged Chinese morality and their models of education (i.e. the Mandarin exams). Le Vayer, who did not provide a real history of philosophy, even claimed that, since Confucius and Confucians followed a morality perfectly reasonable and believed in one God 'King of Heaven', they were suitable for salvation. If the sceptical attitude of le Vayer is evident, who opened to the later discussion about the reasonability of morality, as for instance in Bayle, who argued the perfect morality of Chinese atheists.

Simultaneously, the historians had to keep India and China within the biblical frame of the perennial historiographical model, therefore, all ancient civilizations had to come out of one unique stream. Heurn, following Postel, suggested that Indians derived their wisdom from Abraham and also that, as argued by Greek sources, they were devoted to a strict and moral life. Their contemporary heirs apparently preserved the morality and the seeds of wisdom of the ancient cultures, but the inner divine reasons of their habits were already lost and needed to be reinstated by Christian missionaries. Horn and Burnet, aware of the chronological antiquity of China – unlike Heurn who published his history in 1600 – suggested that the spreading of the divine wisdom began soon after the Deluge, when the three sons of Noah migrated in different directions. This change was relevant for at least two reasons: 1. the histories of the ancient barbaric peoples were more ancient than for Heurn, since they descended from Noah instead of Abraham and 2. of the three sons of Noah, Ham was damned by the father himself, thus one lineage of this biblical genealogy was preposterous and even could infect the wisdom of the other two. Usually, the legacy of Ham was connected with Zoroaster, master of Manichaeism and of black magic. According to Horn, Indians did not descend from Ham, however the pure divine stream claimed by concordists and perennialists could be described no more as completely pure. As we reported, Horn also claimed that the chronology of the Chinese was perfectly compatible with biblical history and that each Chinese emperor corresponded to one of the patriarchs since Noah. Therefore, we can infer that Horn followed to some extent the perennial model, but at the same time he participated in the deterioration of the perfect image of the pure divine spreading.

Burnet also aimed at recovering the ancient traces of the philosophy of Noah, but unlike Horn, he argued that the core of the ancient pre-diluvian philosophy was immanentism. He was not interested in moral philosophy, therefore, he disregarded Chinese ethics. On the contrary, he devoted a scrupulous investigation to any traces of immanentism detectable in all Asian countries, even in Siam, because all these civilizations descended from the Noahic wisdom he wished to retrace. However, Burnet claimed that those civilizations were at that time completely barbarian and were worthy of investigation only for 'philosophical archaeology' in order to detect the ancient seeds of wisdom. As we have said, the principle tenet of the Noahic wisdom was the theory of immanentism, which thus became the first metaphysical theory of humankind. Bayle claimed a similar opinion but completely on a different ground. For him, immanentism and atheism, being the most rational theories, were the natural state of human mind, which is overwhelmed with idolatry, religion, creationism and any dogmatic opinion (§2.3.). Not by chance was Bernier the source about the Indian immanentism for both Burnet and Bayle.

In the next chapter we shall investigate the emerging of the 'oriental atheism', which originated from the connection between the description of Buddhism as an atheistic plague within the Jesuit order (derived from Ricci himself) and the aforementioned biblical progeny of Ham, who was the same as Zoroaster according to Kircher. The description of the whole of ancient heathen civilizations as hideous 'atheists' met the accounts of the Gassendian philosopher Bernier, creating the image of a 'Spinozistic and Quietistic Orient', which was richly investigated by Bayle, who also emphasized Chinese morality as le Vayer did. And this description of Asia, although with some minor changes, reached the German Eclectics – i.e. Heumann and Brucker – and confirmed themselves in their refusal of the perennial model. Therefore, it would be impossible to understand Bayle's 'Oriental Spinozism' and Brucker's exclusion of exotic civilizations from philosophy without being aware of these previous histories of philosophy, which were influenced by the perennialist model but at the same time lost the universal and irenist meaning disclosed by the Renaissance philosophers. In the next chapter, we shall also present Leibniz: the unique philosopher who maintained the original perennialist universalism and who had exactly China as argumentative proof of the validity of this theory.

2

'Atheistic Asia': Positive and Negative Standpoints

'C'est d'oublier la force d'inertie propre à tant de créations sociales. L'homme passe son temps à monter des mécanismes, dont il demeure ensuite le prisonnier plus ou moins volontaire.'

Marc Bloch, *Apologie pour l'histoire ou métier d'historien*, 11

2.0 Introduction

In the first chapter we investigated the dramatic changes of the 'perennial' historiographical paradigm, which arose in the heart of the Italian Renaissance and survived until Leibniz. To some extent, these changes were caused by the introduction of India and China, both ancient and modern. We have identified Heurn, Horn and Burnet as the pivotal historians who tried to introduce India and China into their histories of philosophy. Heurn was the first to insert a chapter on modern India, where contemporary Indians were depicted as far from their (Abrahamic) original wisdom. Horn surprisingly introduced the Chinese between the philosophers of the Middle Ages and of the Renaissance, and he even praised Chinese education. He also discussed chronological issues, raised by the edition of the Chinese *Annals*, in order to save the historicity of the Bible (Vulgate). Burnet, although not openly, followed Heurn and built an insurmountable wall between ancient wise Asians – who derived their wisdom from a son of Noah – and contemporary idolatrous and depraved Indians – who instead had lost this original wisdom.

At the same time in the Catholic countries, particularly in France, two harsh debates, tightly connected, were spreading. The first debate was over atheism and Spinozism, since Spinoza was acknowledged as the most dangerous philosopher of that time by 'orthodox thinkers', because of his systematic and fierce criticism of Christian theology, ontology and ethics. The Spinozistic system was perceived as the worst and highest achievement of libertines' philosophy, i.e. the philosophers we might call 'Radical thinkers' following Israel. The accusations of atheism and Spinozism were the most dreaded and thinkers suspected to support the system of the Dutch philosopher could be also forced to abjure his thought. The second debate was the well-known 'Chinese rites controversy', which regarded the accommodation method of Ricci (see §1.2.). The pivotal question was the monotheism or atheism of the ancient Confucians. In the decades before the European controversy, the Jesuit missionaries, who were preaching in all of Asia, had already debated this question.

In this chapter, we try to outline, through a comparative investigation, how the myth of an Asiatic atheism arose at first inside the Jesuit missionary community and later on in the European intellectual environment. We shall see that in the shaping of the 'Oriental atheism', China and India were always connected, because they were two of the most important countries where the 'plague' of idolatry and atheism took deep root. However, the leading actor of this connection between India and China was not a missionary, but rather a philosopher and voyager in South Asia, namely François Bernier. According to his description, matured from the study of former accounts and his own journeys, China and India were part of a Spinozistic and Quietist cabala, a cabala that was appreciated right away by libertine thinkers. And the most relevant thinker who discussed the 'Oriental Spinozism' extensively and diffused this topic was Pierre Bayle, particularly in the entry 'Spinoza' of his *Dictionnaire*. Furthermore, Bayle did not develop this topic only in the two editions of the *Dictionnaire*, but also in three further writings that deserve a careful investigation as they reveal interesting insights on China and Confucianism that Bayle did not write in his most renowned work.

Thanks to Bayle, Atheism and Spinozism became a sort of 'carsic river' as opposed to Christian orthodoxy and to every religion. This 'carsic river' was discussed and interpreted by further historians, among them Pierre-Daniel Huet preferred to replace Atheism and Spinozism with Christian Scepticism, but he did not change the general aspect of the criticism against orthodoxy radically. A different follower of Bayle's 'carsic river' was Johann Franz Buddeus, who was not a Frenchman, but a German professor of theology belonging to the Eclectic school of Christian Thomasius. Buddeus followed the biblical historiographical model, the description of China as a moral country and Bayle's 'Oriental Spinozism', therefore, he provided quite a contradictory image of the Asiatic countries. In the third chapter, we shall see that the other German Eclectic thinkers more openly refused to acknowledge Barbarian and Asian wisdoms as philosophies, since they rejected the thesis of an ancient philosophy before Greeks.

In this chapter, we also mention Leibniz's writings about China, because, according to his theory of the universal harmony, he was the last great perennialist philosopher. After Leibniz, historiographical perennialism almost disappeared and it left room for a less syncretic and somehow more 'scientific' attitude towards the history of philosophy (although this attitude was still apologetic as we will see). This was the case of the aforementioned German Eclectics, but not of André-François Boureau-Deslandes, who wrote the first complete French 'History of Thought' (histoire de la pensée), but his work was so incoherent and was harshly criticized by several historians, including the German Eclectics themselves. Deslandes represented more the growing French interest in anthropology and in the description of cultural aspects of foreign civilizations – a kind of unsystematic antiquarian attitude – than a serious historian of philosophy. However, in the chapters devoted to Indian thought he provided a few unprecedented comments and insights which deserve our attention.

The central theme that links together the authors investigated in this chapter is the atheism and immanentism of Asian thinkers, an issue really multifaceted and debated. Jesuit missionaries described Buddhists as atheists, because they needed to fight local faiths in Asia and to find financing and support in Europe. At the same time, the opponents of the Jesuit order used the disagreement inside the order itself about the accommodation method to fight their power in Asia; the effect was the description of all Asians as atheists, from Persia to Japan. This atheism was obviously interpreted in many different ways by historians, either positively (i.e. Bayle) or negatively (i.e. Buddeus). In the third chapter, about German Eclectic histories of philosophy, we shall see a complete change of attitude: the question is no more the description of Asians, but rather the actual compatibility of their thought with a 'scientific' history of philosophy, because Asians lacked all the basis necessary for the development of an effective philosophy. In short, whilst among perennialists Indians and Chinese were inserted into the histories of philosophy – although merely their past was acknowledged as philosophical – afterwards they were depicted as dangerous philosophers appreciated by libertines (or Radical thinkers), whereas in German Eclecticism, we anticipate, they were excluded, since they were described as weak thinkers. These sudden changes of perspective suggest that Asians were among the main causes of 'the Crisis of the European mind' (i.e. Paul Hazard).

2.1 Missionary construction of the Asiatic negative myth in the seventeenth century: Buddhist atheism

As we have seen in the previous chapter, the leading text on China during the first half of the seventeenth century was *De Christiana Expeditione*, written by Ricci and translated by Trigault in 1615. In the Preface to the account of the missionary expedition, the description of the three Chinese sects was provided, which became the standard on the topic. However, not every Jesuit in China or Japan agreed with Ricci and his accommodation method. Broadly speaking, the Japanese mission followed Valignano, who mostly avoided any direct compatibility of local rites with Christian faith, and this method was considered to be more effective and coherent also by some missionaries in China. Valignano – who was the master of all East Asian missions – and Ricci never debated one against the other: at their time, the primary aim was only the conversion of heathens, the former permitted the latter 'to become Chinese among the Chinese'. The two strongest opponents of Ricci's method appeared after his death. They were Niccolò Longobardo and João Rodrigues, the former was the successor of Ricci in China and the latter was active mostly in Japan. As Urs App reports in his excellent *The cult of Emptiness*,[1] the different views on accommodation and on the use of Chinese classical terms among the Jesuits resulted in a meeting in Jiading (southern Jiangsu) between late 1627 and early 1628. On that occasion, Longobardo wrote a statement openly against the Riccian method, in order to explain and support his reasons. However, at the end of the meeting, the mission in China decided to reject Longobardo's reasons and to go on with accommodation.[2] These differences and oppositions were almost unknown in Europe, because of the wise editorial work made in Paris[3] by the Jesuit order in accord with the missionaries in Beijing: the anti-accommodation texts were not published or rearranged.

As regards the dispute, a further clarification is necessary: it regarded only Confucianism and Confucian rites and, in effect, Ricci himself never proposed to accept also Buddhist or Taoist doctrines or habits within Christian faith. The exclusion of both sects, i.e. Idolaters (Buddhists) and Magicians (Taoists), was a point of complete agreement. According to Ricci, these two sects were atheistic and false; they were both directly related to the sacred and religious practices. On the contrary, Confucianism was a political and social philosophy, concerned with morality (public and personal) and the good ruling of the country, a kind of perfect Stoicism. In Jesuits' view, the ancient books of the Chinese, considered by Ricci as the foundation of the sole Confucianism, confirmed the compatibility with Christian faith and suggested an original and lost monotheism, which needed to be restored by the missionaries themselves. And this restoration, as we investigated in the previous chapter, entailed a chronological analysis on Chinese sources and a difficult comparison with biblical history.

As we said, in 1627 the Jesuit 'dissidents' were defeated and the only image of China that could be presented in Europe was the leading one, mostly in accordance with Ricci. This was true until the publication of João Rodrigues's excerpts by Navarrete (1676) and the edition of the above-mentioned statement by Longobardo (1701), which should have been destroyed after the meeting in Jiading. However, first of all we need to focus on Buddhism during the period between 1627 and 1676 – i.e. before the time of the aforementioned publications – because, through the description of this atheistic and idolatrous sect, Jesuits created a new image of the Asian thought (i.e. the 'doctrina orientalis').

After Ricci and Valignano, the most important book to be published in Europe about Buddhism was the *Relatione*[4] by Cristoforo Borri (1583–1632) – written in Italian and translated in French – and was published in the year 1631 in both languages.[5] Borri is one of the first missionaries in Cochinchina, the South of today's Vietnam, where he found strong Chinese influences and the presence of powerful Buddhist sects. He was fascinated by Buddhists and by their founder, but at the same time, he was firmly aware of their 'diabolic' opposition. He said that 'it seems that the Devil wanted to make among heathens a portrait of beauty...' and that 'whether someone would enter [for the first time] in this Land [Cochinchina], because the Devil has so well imitated our things, he could easily suspect that here in ancient times there had been Catholics or Christians'.[6] Borri could not hide his admiration for the quality of thought of Xaca (Buddha):

> The sect of eastern heathens had their origin from a great metaphysician called Xaca, he was born in the kingdom of Siam, he was more ancient than Aristotle and he was not at all inferior to him with regards to capacity and knowledge of natural things. He was driven by the perspicacity of his intelligence, to the comprehension of nature and of the fabric of the world, and to the knowledge of principles and aims of all things, especially of human nature... [In that way,] he established that all things, both natural (or physical) and moral, were nothing from nothing and for nothing...
>
> ibid., 201–2[7]

According to this drastic metaphysical doctrine, Xaca (Buddha) 'concluded that, being all these things nothing ['nulla'], they had origin from a cause that was not efficient, but rather material, from a principle that was not simply nothing ['nulla'], but even a nothing ['nulla'] eternal, endless, immense, unchangeable, omnipotent and at last: 'God-nothing' ['Dio nulla'] and origin of nothing ['niente']' (ibid., 203–4).[8]

Moreover, Borri continued his account suggesting that given the failure of the 'doctrine of nothing' among common people, Xaca changed the doctrine into an idolatrous faith, merely designed to be agreeable and based on veneration, worship, punishment and reward. Borri also suggested, grounded on a clear chronological confusion, that the failure of the first doctrine of nothing occurred among the Chinese (ibid., 205), although we know that Buddhism entered China a few centuries after Xaca's death. Besides this error, Borri also reported that Buddha claimed that the doctrine of 'God-nothing' ['Dio nulla'] and the idolatrous one were coherent and compatible with one another.[9] The Jesuit claimed that this compatibility was possible only when speaking by means of beautiful metaphors and was not grounded on reason (ibid., 207–8). Borri added that the doctrine of nothing was not diffused in Cochinchina, where only the idolatrous doctrine might be found. Therefore, it is clear that, although Borri did not mention his sources, his description of the 'sect of nothingness' was taken from other Jesuit missionaries, who were preaching in China or Japan.

In 1645, the original Italian history of China of the Jesuit Alvarez Semedo (1568–1658) was published in French.[10] The piece was written by a missionary from China and not from South-East Asia such as Borri. Semedo had a stronger commitment with Chinese sciences and politics more than with sects and religious matters; perhaps because this was already an awkward topic within the order. In chapter 18, Semedo presented the three sects in this order: sect of Literati, Taoism and Buddhism. The first sect is described according to Ricci, although Semedo did not mention their claimed contemporary atheism, and he focused the attention only on their lack of any religious or ritualistic aspect, their positive laicism. Taoism, on the contrary, was the sect of magicians and soothsayers. Semedo suggested that only the sect of Xaca was actually religious and he described the monastic orders in detail rather than the doctrinal issues. He simply mentioned the inner and outer doctrines, but without speaking of atheism, and he qualified the inner doctrine simply as a monistic faith. In short, Semedo believed that Buddhist sects were not despicable but really weak and far from common people (ibid., 126).[11] This description contrasts with the sense of urgency, danger and fight inspired by all other accounts. Indeed, as we shall see, the description of Buddhism as a devilish doctrine was definitely dominant.

For instance, Buddhism was described as a diabolic enemy in *Histoire du Royaume de Tunquin* (1651) by Alexandre de Rhodes (1591–1660),[12] a Jesuit who lived for almost twenty years in Tunquin (Northern Vietnam), thus near Borri's mission. Rhodes opposed Confucius, author of a good ethic but very weak as a metaphysician (ibid., 63), to Thicca – local name of Xaca or Buddha – who was instead a refined atheistic thinker (ibid., 65), as already argued by Borri. The two Buddhist doctrines, the outer idolatrous and the inner atheistic, were described vividly as demonic:

> However, the Devils, which were dominating the soul of this ill-fated Prince [Buddha], did not ignore that Atheism is worse and more pernicious than Idolatry, as one who lays down in all sort of vices, [and] they had persuaded this impious

soul to withdraw [his doctrine] at the end of his life. He did so, not before the people, but rather only when he was with the most subtle, the most pernicious of his disciples, to whom he declared that the doctrine of Idols taught by him for forty years was only for the benefit of simple-minded [/common] people. [...] he was the author of [both these] two terrible errors: the former of Idolatry, into which the deceived and enchanted people threw themselves and still lay, because of the account of his [of Buddha] fairy tales; and the latter of Atheism, to which the finest minds still adhere, lapsing without fear into all sorts of vices...

ibid., 67–8[13]

Therefore, according to Rhodes, the devils persuaded Xaca to propose again, on his deathbed, the first doctrine that had no success among common people. The devils knew that the atheism of – using Borri's expression – 'God-nothing' was more dangerous than the simple idolatrous rites. As it is well known, Bayle proposed an opposite view of atheism and idolatry, since he claimed that idolatry, with its intrinsic violence and dogmatism, was really more dangerous than atheism (§2.3).

Rhodes, besides this interesting topic of atheism and idolatry, developed Ricci's theory of the Chinese embassy further, which was sent by the Chinese emperor to India to research the Christian faith. According to Ricci, Christian religion was already in India thanks to Saint Thomas and Saint Bartholomew, and it was mistaken for Buddhism. Whereas Rhodes claimed that the embassy was sent to the western lands ('aux quartiers d'Occident' ibid., 68), but for indolence it stopped in India. Therefore, Rhodes was supposing a sort of Chinese 'Three Wise Men' with the mission to search Christianity in the West and to take it to China. However, these disloyal ambassadors betrayed the imperial order, they 'halted [the quest] in India, where they asked the Brahmin ['Brachmanes'] and received back their [of Brahmin] Book and the doctrine of their Buddha ['Budda'] – that means the wise man, that is the name they gave to the Thicca we already mentioned – they [the ambassadors] brought all that to the King of China' (ibid., 68).[14] This paragraph is really intriguing, because it might show a direct connection with ancient sources. The Jesuit mentioned the name 'Budda', the same transliteration that could be found in Latin Christian sources,[15] and he also repeated the confusion among Brachmanes, Sarmanes (or Germanes), Gymnosophists and Buddhists as in the ancient and late Greek sources.[16] Rhodes also seemed to have understood that the ancient 'Budda' was Xakia, Xechia or Thicca (in the languages of Tunquin and Cochinchina). Therefore, on one side, Rhodes traced the complete range of Buddhist diffusion into a large part of Asia, on the other side, he revived an ancient misunderstanding: the connection of these two aspects made the diffusion of Buddhism even larger, because he wrongly considered the Brachmanes as disciples of Buddha. We know that Buddhism was born as an anti-Vedic and anti-class movement, against the privileges of Brahmin class and adverse to the ritualism of Vedic religion. Actually, this clear opposition between Buddhism and Vedism means that this misunderstanding could not have derived from Indian sources or from missionaries in India,[17] but rather from ancient Greek and Christian sources.

Seven years later, Filippo Marini (1608–82) provided a further version of the Chinese embassy theory.[18] He was a Jesuit missionary in Japan and Tunquin and in the account he reported his experience and the penetration of Christianity in these two lands. His version added new errors to the already confused understanding of Buddhism and Indian religions. Whilst Rhodes claimed that Buddhism was the religion of Brahmin, Marini knew that in India Buddhism had disappeared, maybe thanks to Indian missionaries' accounts he could read when he was the Dean of the Jesuit College in Macau. However, this awareness did not prevent him from making a fatal and greater mistake. He wrote:

> [the messengers sent by the Chinese Emperor] when arrived there [in India] did not intended to go further to more western realms, where it was well-known that there was a better Law, the one diffused in Cambaya [Khambat, India] and Sinde, near the river Indo [the Hyderabad area, Pakistan], where the people worshipped O My To, rather they saw that in India another Sect had more followers, because it was freer and more shameful, that of Rama, Idol newer than O My To ... The author of this devilish sect in India is called Rama, in China Xé Kiã, in Japan Faca, in Tunquin Thic Ca. This Hydra spread his poison in all the Realms in which Asia is divided, but, where this plague was more serious was in the Realms of India, of Bengal, Perú [namely Pegu, i.e. Burma], Siam, Cambodia and Laos. This monster was born in central India ...
>
> ibid., 107[19]

Marini claimed that Chinese messengers were not searching the Christian message – as Ricci and many after him claimed – but instead the doctrine of 'O My To'. However, 'O My To' is the Buddha Amitābha in the Japanese language, one of the several Buddhas in Mahāyāna Buddhism, the one worshipped in the devotional Pure Land Buddhism. Therefore, Marini did not know that, by quoting 'O My To', he was already speaking of Buddhism. This misunderstanding drove him to establish the equivalence between Rama and Xe Kia/Xaka/Thic, namely Buddha Śākyamuni. We know that Rama is the most important *avatāra* of Viṣṇu, who is one of the three major gods of the Hindu pantheon (together with Śiva and Brahmā). Rama has been worshipped and loved as the Supreme God only from the fifteenth to sixteenth centuries, when Buddhism had already left India. Although the sect of Rama was quite a recent phenomenon, Rama appeared in *ṚgVeda* and he was the protagonist of several epic accounts, always laying in the Vedic context, which we know is openly rejected by Buddhism. We propose two possible reasons for this disastrous mistake. The first is that Rama is an Indian prince like Buddha Śākyamuni himself. The second hypothetical reason is that both Buddhist sects and some Hinduist sects spread into South-East Asia and that led to a certain assimilation of elements, particularly in iconography, due to the common Indian origin.[20] However, it is worth noting that Marini did not really merge the two 'gods', but simply proposed the biography of Buddha, calling him Rama, as if this were his Indian name.

The Jesuit author also described 'Rama-Buddha' with ferocious words openly conditioned by the Counter-Reformation: 'in him we find all the art of hypocrisy of Pharisees; the impudence of Atheists' blasphemies and even all the sordid of Reformers' heresies, moreover of Luther and Calvin.' (ibid., 112).[21] Actually, Rama-Buddha represented all Catholic fears, in him all the new and ancient enemies found representation. Of course, in Rama-Buddha's doctrines there was nothing of Luther's or Calvin's thought, but he was forced into the same category of heresy and disbelief: Catholics were surrounded by heresy, atheism and reformation, in Europe and even in Asia. However, this assimilation should be better understood if we consider that the major aim of the books published by the Jesuits was, in Europe, to obtain funds to support their missions and, in Asia, to defend Jesuit missions from the harsh criticism from rival missions. This was an effective way to encourage the support of the courts and of the nobles, in order to suggest the urgency of the mission and the danger of these Asian doctrines.

This despicable equivalence of Rama and Buddha was widely diffused in Europe thanks to an influential book: the *China illustrata* (1667)[22] by the Jesuit Athanasius Kircher (1602–80). The fourth chapter of the third part of this book has a revealing title: 'Brahmin Institutions and How an Egyptian Superstition Passed by Means of the Brahmins to Persia, India, China and Japan, the Farthest Kingdom of the East'. By means of a wide spectrum of sources Kircher was analysing for decades, he suggested that Brahmins' birthplace was out of Egypt and that they were also the propagators of Buddhism. His description of Buddhism, which mixed many of the already quoted accounts, added more Indological details, since he provided a larger description of the Hindu pantheon. Concerned with the historical purposes of our investigation, the alleged common origin of Hinduism and Buddhism out of the same Egyptian source is extremely important.

Kircher's version of the spreading of the devilish lineage, began with the Persian King Cambyses's banishment of the Egyptian priests ('whole crowd of priests' ibid., 141), who escaped to the East, taking with them their devilish doctrines:

> they finally made their way along the Arabian Gulf, which borders on Egypt, and so they reached India, today called Hindustan ... The worship of these gods clings so tenaciously in the simple minds that it will never again be forgotten ... This preposterous superstition is found not only in the regions of India far and wide, but was also propagated in Cambodia, Tonchin, Laos, Concin China, as long as all of China and Japan. It has brought along its fanatic crowd of innumerable gods and goddesses ... The first creator and architect of the superstition was a very sinful brahmin imbued with Pythagoreanism. He was not content just to spread the doctrine, but even added to it so much that there is scarcely any one who is able to describe the doctrine or to write about it. He was an imposter known all over the East. The Indians called him Rama, the Chinese Xe Kian and the Turks Chiaga. This deadly monster was born in central India ... [He] instituted this abominable idolatry with Satan's help. Afterwards he infected the whole Orient with his pestilent dogmas [totum Orientem pestiferis suis dogmatis infectis].
>
> ibid., 141–2

The sources of these claims are clearly Borri and Marini, quoted along the text. For a better understanding of Kircher's theory, we need to remark that he claimed that even Greeks and Romans have derived their doctrines from Egypt, as all ancient heathens.

Heathens and Christian heresies were one single whole, which had originated in Egypt and was opposed to monotheism. This supposed origin of all heathen civilizations out of Egypt was not new, as we have seen in chapter one, since Egyptians were, together with Jews and Chaldeans, one of the possible origins of world wisdom. However, Kircher's claim was completely different, because he was not suggesting that Egypt was the outsource of civilization or wisdom (i.e. a *'prisca theologia'*), but rather of heresy and 'religious pestis'. He suggested that, among Noah's sons it was Ham and not Shem[23] who was the propagator of the Egyptian culture in Asia, thus Asians descended from the damned lineage. Already Horn and after Burnet suggested the origin of heathen wisdom from Noah, thus consequently one of the three lineages was damned, but usually this lineage was direct southerly to ancient Ethiopia and not easterly to Persia and India. Actually, Kircher's aim was not to mortify Asian thought, rather to restate the universality of Jewish history and the reliability of biblical chronology over Chinese, Egyptian or pre-Columbian annals.[24]

Among Jesuits missionaries in Japan, João Rodrigues (c. 1561–c. 1633) had already proposed a similar theory in the 1620s in his *Historia da Igreja do Japão*. In his unpublished work,[25] the author suggested that the Chinese civilization should have been established by Nimrod, Ham's grandson, the aforementioned damned son of Noah (see Genesis 9.20-27). Rodrigues claimed that the Chinese were part of this devilish descent, but also that Ham was the same as Zoroaster.[26] Despite what App suggests,[27] the equivalence of Ham and Zoroaster was a widespread theory in the Renaissance and it was supported in several books, among which the most famous were the *Opus majus* by Roger Bacon and the *Berosus* by Annius of Viterbo.[28] Therefore, this is not an original theory formulated by Rodrigues himself. Besides the origin of the theory about Ham and Zoroaster, what concerns us is that Kircher located the origin of the 'damned wisdom' in Egypt, whilst Rodrigues in Chaldea, Zoroaster being its founder, who moved personally to Persia, Egypt, India and, finally, China. The main point is that both authors overturned the 'philosophia perennis' model, since they did not find in pre-Christian civilization an original wisdom, but rather simply an epidemic heresy diffused everywhere. Whether for de Villemandy and Thomassin to compose India and China within an eschatological spreading was problematic (§1.5.), for Rodriguez and Kircher the problem was solved, since the spreading were two and opposed for qualities and directions: monotheism from Jews to Europe (westerly) and heresy from Egypt to Japan (easterly).

According to Kircher and Rodrigues, not only Buddhism and Taoism were devilish in China, but also Confucianism, both ancient and modern, in strong contrast with Ricci's theory, which suggested the existence of an original Chinese monotheistic *'prisca theologia'*. Rodrigues contradicted Ricci in several unpublished letters, because he claimed the atheism of all three Chinese sects, as all of them were the output of the same atheistic source.[29] Rodrigues's critic had no diffusion until his theories has been widely quoted in the *Tratados* (1676)[30] by Domingo Fernandez Navarrete (c. 1610–89), a Dominican missionary in China and bitter enemy of Jesuits in the 'Chinese rites controversy'. Around 1668 Navarrete obtained by the Franciscan – an order against Ricci's accommodation – Antonio a Santa Maria Caballero (1602–69) – also known as Antoine de Sainte-Marie – the allegedly lost treatise or statement against Ricci written in 1627 by the Jesuit Longobardo, together with Rodrigues's manuscript and a treatise of the same Caballero. The two Jesuits were 'dissident', since they contested the original monotheism or '*prisca theologia*' of Confucians, their morality and wisdom. Navarrete quoted these authors in his two-volumes *Tratados*. Although only the first volume was published, his claim was clear: 'The above-mentioned sect of Literati [Confucians] proclaims a pure Atheism, as we will show at the convenient place, by means of the most learned and serious missionaries of the Company [of Jesus]' (ibid., 80–1).[31] In this excerpt he did not explicitly quote the names of the missionaries, but he did when he listed: 'Longobardo, Sabathino e Ruiz [Rodrigues]' as opponents of the prevailing interpretation of 'Padre Riccio' and of his faithful followers (ibid., 249). In the next page Navarrete reported Rodrigues's theory on the Zoroastrian origin of all Asian doctrines:

> In that way, the Father Juan Ruiz [Rodrigues], in the Treatise he wrote on this controversy, proved that most likely Fo Hi [first Emperor of China] was Zoroaster himself, king of Bactrians and Prince of the Chaldean Magi, who gave rise to all western sects and afterwards came to this Oriental [land], where he founded the Chinese Kingdom together with the sect called of Literati.
>
> Therefore, because this Chinese sect has the same source of all the Heathens and together they are a work of the devil, they show a great resemblance, and with the same aim and method they keep the deceived men in the Hell.
>
> ibid., 250[32]

We know that Horn argued that the first emperor of China, i.e. Fo Hi, was the Chinese name for Noah himself, whilst Rodrigues and Navarrete were arguing that this first emperor was instead his devilish son Ham as Zoroaster. Moreover, whilst before Navarrete European thinkers knew that there was a bitter controversy about 'Chinese rites' between Jesuits and other missionary orders and the success reached by Jesuits in this land, this book testified the dramatic disagreement within the Jesuit order itself. As regards Buddhism and Taoism, all Christian orders shared the same opinion: these sects were atheistic, as Ricci said. However, as we have seen, Confucianism and its rites were considered by the 'Jesuit orthodoxy' to be compatible with Christian life, because it was not a religious sect and its related rites were simply social or political events. The evidence of these 'dissidents' – Longobardi, Rodrigues, etc. – was a clear weakness of the Jesuit order and of their reliability.

Navarrete described Buddhism as usual, also adding to the monistic description a further detail: 'the first principle, and last aim, was the material matter or Chaos, as signified by the two letters Kung and Hiu [空虛], which means vacuum ['vacuo'], and besides that there was nothing else to look at or to rely on' (ibid., 86).[33] Therefore, he added the idea of an original incoherence, because the first principle was at the same time the material matter or the chaos and it was also completely empty. Navarrete's aim was to show a clear metaphysical contradiction and hence the ineptitude of Buddhists. However, the real change introduced by Navarrete was not on Buddhism, but rather, as we said, on the description of Confucianism. After sixty years since *De Christiana expeditione* (1615) by Ricci, a missionary account rejected the leading theory and this change came out of the same religious order, from almost coeval missionaries with Ricci himself. Kircher's investigation was abstract and he never went to China, on the contrary Navarrete went to China and all his sources were important Jesuit missionaries who spent a long time in that land, thus he was clearly an authoritative source.

The *Tratados* were written in Spanish and the publication of the second volume was blocked, therefore their impact was limited. However, in 1682 the Jansenist Antoine Arnauld (1612-94), in his violent book against the Jesuits, namely *La Morale pratique des Jesuites*, translated important excerpts of the *Tratados*.[34] In this book, Arnauld attacked the immorality of Jesuits in Asia, their use of political power and influence, as well as the falsity of their theories about China and, particularly, about Confucianism. Arnauld aimed at uncovering Jesuits' lies and their Machiavellian morality by means of their 'dissidents'. The Jansenist wished to protect God's grace and the Original sin, two central Christian elements undermined by the 'holy morality' of Confucians.[35] The scandal caused by Arnauld and by the public disagreement inside the Jesuit order, required a strong reaction. The best way to prove Jesuits' honesty and morality was a great editorial effort, which was the *Confucius sinarum philosophus* (1687),[36] dedicated to Louis XIV of France. That book was not a polemical response, an attack against other orders, but rather a philological text, conceived to provide the first true and new authoritative canon or manual of Chinese sects, particularly of Confucianism. Jesuits went back to the originals, providing a complete and large Latin translation of ancient sources.[37] According to them, the best way to prove their correct understanding of Chinese culture was the reading of sources, where an original monotheism was clearly testified. Actually, the correct interpretation of ancient sources was the key of their evangelization method: accommodationism. The translations were provided with a long rich Preface, authored by Prospero Intorcetta (1626-96) and reworked by Philippe Couplet (1623-93), i.e. the general editor. App proves Couplet's wide rework and relevant changes. For instance, App reported a removed reference of Intorcetta to a missionary in Japan well acquainted with Buddhism, whom he identifies with Rodrigues,[38] clearly a *persona non grata* among Jesuit followers of Ricci.

In the Preface, ancient Confucianism was reported as an original lost monotheism that contemporary atheistic Confucians needed to rediscover thanks to the philological and religious help of Jesuits. Obviously, Taoism and Buddhism were described as in Ricci: the first was a sect of magicians and the second had a double doctrine, one idolatrous and one atheistic. Buddhism was depicted as usual, because its preposterous and dangerous atheism was not under discussion. The inner doctrine, for more advanced people, was both atheistic and immoral and Intorcetta and Couplet stated that: 'the first principle and origin of all things is *vacuum* and *inane* (*Cum hiu* [*kongxu* 空虛] in Chinese), there is nothing [else] to ask for and nothing [else] on which pinning our hopes' (ibid., p. XXIX).[39] Couplet did not accept Navarrete's concept of 'chaos', instead he used two terms which are almost synonyms: 'vacuum' and 'inane', i.e. empty in a physical sense and empty as ephemeral or evanescent, meaning also fictitious. The physical and concrete quality of this emptiness was really important, because Couplet stressed the reachability of the first principle, by means of meditation and annulment. The 'Buddhist' doctrine was described as metaphorical and obscure (ibid., p. XXIX), and he reminded also to the already classic relation with Pythagoras' philosophy (ibid., p. XXVII).

In particular, they – i.e. Couplet and Intorcetta – described one Buddhist school that was taken as the emblem of Buddhism and depicted as really powerful. They gave this sect a name in Latin that should recall something to all of us: '*nihil agentium secta*', 'non-action sect', hence it would be in Chinese the *wuwei* teaching (*wuweijiao* 無為教). Today, we know that this is not a Buddhist school, but rather a central Taoist tenet.[40] Besides the error in the name, the *Confucius sinarum philosophus* highlighted the role and importance of the Buddhist sect that we can call Chan (禪) or Zen and which played a major role in China and Japan, although it was not the only relevant sect. We might suggest that this emphasis on the sect of 'static meditation' was the simplest way to reduce the whole of Buddhism to an atheistic 'pestis', which destabilized the original Chinese monotheistic culture, as it was claimed by Ricci more than seventy years before (ibid., p. XXVII). This emphasis on the presumed 'static nature' and atheism of Buddhism constituted the connection with Quietism.

2.2 The reception of the negative myth of Asia in seventeenth-century Europe: François Bernier

In the previous paragraph we have seen the description of Buddhism as 'pestis' and how in Rodrigues and Kircher this devilish spreading included the whole of China, together with India, Persia and Egypt. In the same years, though less vivaciously, there was an analogous attempt to describe Indian thought. India missionaries – of whatever order – had been really less prolific than the China missionaries. There took place a 'Malabar rites' controversy, which involved Roberto de Nobili, however, its cultural effects and echoes in Europe were really limited. Roberto de Nobili and all other fathers in India were seldom mentioned by historians. For instance, Nobili's books were only a *desiderata* for Thomas Burnet. He was able to write in Tamil, and almost all his writings were written in that language, thus they were unavailable for European readers. The first who really tried to learn the language of Brahmans, deeply understand their culture and diffuse among European thinkers his learning, was the Jesuit Heinrich Roth (1620–68). In 1664, he met Kircher in Rome, by whom he was widely quoted in the *China illustrata*.[41]

However, as regards India, the most famous scholar was not a missionary, but rather a philosopher, namely the French Gassendian François Bernier (1625–88), who was also a doctor and physician. He visited many Near East countries and reached India, where he was acquainted with the Moghul court for almost twelve years. He met several wise men, influential people and also missionaries, among whom was the aforementioned Roth,[42] who explained to him many Indian tenets. While travelling, Bernier wrote copious letters, addressed to many of the most relevant European thinkers of his time, who proved themselves to be really interested correspondents. Among his letters, one is of particular interest for two reasons: first, it was widely quoted; second, it was the first description 'first-hand' available of Indian myths, and these myths were compared with those of the Persians and Turks. This letter was written on the 4 October 1667 and addressed to Chapelain.[43] We quote an extensive paragraph on the 'grande Cabale' ('Great Cabala'):

> You are doubtless acquainted with the doctrine of many of the ancient philosophers concerning that great life-giving principle of the world [Soul of the world], of which they argue that we and all living creatures are so many parts: if we carefully examine the writings of *Plato* and *Aristotle*, we shall probably discover that they are inclined towards this opinion. This is the almost universal doctrine of the *Gentile Pendets* of the *Indies*, and it is this same doctrine which is held by the sect of the *Soufys* and the greater part of the learned men of *Persia* at the present day, ... This was also the opinion of *Flud*,[44] whom our great *Gassendy* has so ably refuted; and it is similar to the doctrines by which most of our alchemists have been hopelessly led astray. Now these *Sectaries* or *Indou Pendets*, so to speak, push the incongruities in question further than all these philosophers, and pretend that God, or that supreme being whom they call *Achar*[45] (immovable, unchangeable) has not only produced life from his own substance, but also generally everything material or corporeal in the universe, and that this production is not formed simply after the manner of efficient causes, but as a spider which produces a web from its own navel, and withdraws it at pleasure. The Creation then, say these visionary doctors, is nothing more than an extraction or extension of the individual substance of *God*, of those filaments which He draws from his own bowels; and, in a like manner, destruction is merely the recalling of that divine substance and filaments into Himself; ... There is, therefore, say they, nothing real or substantial in that which we think we see, hear or smell, taste or touch; the whole of this world is, as it were, an illusory dream, ... But ask them some reason for this idea; beg them to explain how this extraction and reception of substance occurs, or to account for that apparent variety; or how it is that God not being corporeal but *biapek*,[46] as they allow, and incorruptible, He can be thus divided into so many portions of body and soul, they will answer you only with some fine similes: – That *God* is as an immense ocean in which many vessels of water are in continual motion; let these vessels go where they will, they always remain in the same ocean, in the same water; and if they should break, the water they contain would then be united to the whole, to that ocean of which they were but parts. – Or they will tell you that it is with God as with the light, which is the same everywhere, but causes the objects on which it falls to assume a hundred different appearances, according to the various colours or forms of the glasses through which it passes. – They will never attempt to satisfy you, I say, but which such comparisons as these, which bear no proportion with God, and which serve only to blind an ignorant people. In vain will you look for any solid answer.
> Bernier, Travels in the Mogul Empire, 345–8[47]

In this letter Bernier argued immanentism and monism to be the pivotal tenets of a long and continual tradition in heathen thought. In the past, the majority of Greek philosophers believed in these doctrines and, in the Europe of his time, Chemists and Cabalist thinkers followed it, among whom was Robert Fludd (who was contested by

Gassendi). In Asia, this doctrine was believed in the ancient past and was still held by the Persians and Indians, which belonged, according to the author, to a common Cabala. As Bernier claimed, Indians were the most extreme cabalists and, because of their incoherent doctrine, both materialistic and unmaterialistic, they believed that God was the efficient as well as the material cause, thus, at the same time, God was the soul and the body of the world.[48] Everything in the world was simply extension and retraction of God, the sole substance. We would say, through Spinoza's vocabulary, that everything is an accident of God's substance, without an individual ontological identity.

Bernier also provided a few Indian representations or descriptions of their ontological doctrine. Firstly, the metaphor of the spider producing a web out of its navel and afterwards eating it.[49] Secondly, the metaphor of the little flasks of oceanic water floating in the same oceanic water and which lose their water, upon breaking, and whose water gets back in the ocean.[50] Lastly, the third metaphor is God as Light, which is always the same but varies according to the shape and colour of the glass it passes through. These are three classical images of the Vedic and Upaniṣadic Indian tradition. However, besides the beautiful metaphors, the heart of the Indian argument is that nothing is real in the world, whatever is perceived is not real, it is an illusion or a dream ('une espece de songe et une pure illusion'). According to Bernier's account, illusion and ontological non-existence or nonentity were the pivotal tenets of Indian philosophers and of Persian Sufis. This description was followed by his negative opinion on Indian philosophy and traditions, as it was clearly shown by the last sentence of the letter: 'There are no opinions too extravagant and ridiculous to find reception in the mind of man' (ibid., 349).[51]

This description of the Indo-Persian philosophy as monist and immanentist, had a great effect on European thinkers. The excerpt we extensively quoted was mentioned and fully reported several times and particularly in Bayle's *Dictionnaire*. However, this was only the first step of Bernier's influence on the European understanding of Asiatic philosophy. The mention of Gassendi as an anti-monist and anti-cabalist philosopher was not accidental; indeed, we find almost the same account in the book Bernier devoted to his master. The first edition of the *Abregé de la Philosophie de Gassendi* was published in 1674 and the second enlarged edition – from which we quote – in 1684.[52] The circumstance for the mention of Asians was Gassendi's refutation of the immanentist theory, which was defined as an infection, according to the missionary description of the 'Buddhist plague' we investigated in the previous paragraph.

> I cannot prevent myself to be surprised at how this Opinion could take possession of men's souls, infecting a huge part of Asia, not to mention our Cabalists and most of our Chemists lost in it. When I was travelling, I have remarked that in these countries most of the Turkish Dervishes, Sufis or wise men of Persia are infected, and I have learned from very reliable persons that [this opinion] had penetrated even in China and Japan, thus, almost all of the Learned men in Asia are proud to say – although each one in his way – that they are pieces of the Divine Substance, and somehow little gods. I ask you to notice how far Brahmins pushed their fiction and reverie.
>
> ibid., 90[53]

Bernier, in presenting Gassendi, took a crucial step further: he established a clear line between his description of Indians, Persians and Turks, and the accounts on China and Japan by missionaries. According to this supposed 'agreement of theories', all Asians followed the same immanentist theories, because Bernier's account of Indian philosophy recalled the description of Xakia's doctrine (Buddhism) as given by the Jesuits. Whilst it seemed that Rhodes was influenced by classical sources on India and Marini had used and misinterpreted missionary sources (thus he created the 'Rama-Buddha' monster), Bernier could refer himself to his own direct experience in India, obviously mediated by his informers and his critical understanding, without the necessity to create fake gods. For this reason, Bernier was in Europe the most reputed and trusted source about Asia. His suggestion of a link between India and China was not new, but more authoritative, although he was providing the already classical image of the immanentist and monist doctrine infecting Asia as Kircher did.

Usually, Bayle is considered as the philosopher who established the link between the monistic doctrine of Asia – as described by the Jesuits and Bernier – and Spinoza. However, the first suggestion might be found in *L'Impie convaincu, ou dissertation contre Spinosa* (1685)[54] by Noël Aubert de Versé (c. 1642–1714), who was obliged to write this book in order to prove his anti-Spinozism. Whilst presenting the three theories on the first principle – namely, 1. the Christian tenet of the 'creation out of nothing' (*creatio ex nihilo*); 2. the dualist original division between God and matter; 3. the immanentism – he provided a sort of list of the followers of that last doctrine:

> This was the opinion of ancient Gnostics, of Priscillianists, and it is that of the Cabalists, new Adamites or illuminists, and an infinity of Philosophers of Asia and of the Indies.
>
> ibid., 7[55]

De Versé did not directly quote Spinoza, however he mentioned the Dutch philosopher a few lines later as the most important thinker of the doctrine of immanentism. It is likely that the first direct comparison of Spinoza and Chinese thought was made by Jean Le Clerc (1657–1736), editor of the *Bibliotheque universelle et historique*,[56] in his long review of the *Confucius sinarum philosophus*, written in December 1687, a few months after the first edition of the Jesuit book. There he described clearly the Chinese doctrine of 'Idolaters' as Spinozists:

> That we, all elements and all creatures, are parts of this emptiness and thus that there is a unique and single substance, diversified in each individual, which is [defined] simply through figures and quality or inner configuration. Approximately, like the water that is always essentially water, no matter if it is in the state of snow, hail, rain or ice. Those who want to learn more about the Philosophy of Indians and Chinese, which differs slightly from Spinoza's system, – whether it is still to be proved that they have a philosophy – may read the travel account of Hindustan by Mr. Bernier.
>
> ibid., 406–7[57]

The comparison of the sole substance with water was taken from *Confucius sinarum philosophus* (pp. XXXI–XXXII), but Bernier told an Indian metaphor which was very close to this Chinese comparison. This similarity even drove Le Clerc to invite readers to learn Indian and Chinese philosophy from Bernier's account. This suggestion reveals two European diffused concepts about Asia: 1. an account on India and Persia was perceived as also related to China, because of the enduring image of 'the Indies', therefore Bernier's account was useful in order to elucidate both Indian and Chinese civilizations; 2. Bernier's philosophical description was linked directly to the Chinese missionaries' books and both of them to the Spinozistic controversy. That is why the description of the 'Asiatic Cabala' provided by Bernier about India and Persia was extended to East Asian civilizations.

François Bernier was not only seventeenth-century France's foremost expert on India, he was also interested in Chinese thought, as were several of his contemporaries, therefore this connection of Bernier with China was not simply suggested by contemporary thinkers as the aforementioned Le Clerc, but instead proved by himself. On 8 June 1688, Bernier published in the influential *Journal des Sçavans*[58] some pieces of his epistolary exchange with Mme de la Sabliere regarding China. Despite the title, 'Introduction à la lecture de Confucius' ('Introduction to the lecture of Confucius'), the topic was not the *Confucius sinarum philosophus*, but instead Martini's *Novus Atlas Sinensis* (1655) and many not-quoted books. Like several European contemporaries, Bernier was interested in Chinese ethics and politics. He was positively impressed by the conformity of private ethics with public ethics or politics, as it was proved by the image of the Chinese prince (or emperor) as father. He mentioned the lack of method in Chinese philosophy, but at the same time the superiority of Confucius as a philosopher and man. He quoted François de la Mothe le Vayer as the first European philosopher who almost said: 'Sancte Confuci, ora pro nobis' (ibid., 22). However, Bernier did not only mention le Vayer, but also the review of *Confucius sinarum* published in the same *Journal des Sçavans*, attributed by him to Pierre-Sylvain Regis, the editor of the journal (ibid., 22). The review is dated 5 January 1688, a few days after the larger review by Le Clerc.

We clearly understand the ferment of the Chinese controversy around the years 1687 and 1688, and these three publications are only the tip of the iceberg. Bernier died on the 22 September 1688, and his last article appeared only a few days before: 'Memoire de Mr. Bernier sur le Quietisme des Indes', in *Histoire des ouvrages des Sçavans*.[59] The editor of this journal was Henri Basnage de Beauval, a very relevant Protestant thinker, who debated with the Jesuits on the forced conversions of heathens at length and who was an advocate of religious tolerance. This last contribution of Bernier shows a further topic that was exciting European minds: the correspondence between Quietism and Oriental philosophies.

The comparison between Quietism and Asiatic thought was not due to Bernier himself, who simply confirmed it. In the Preface to *Recueuil de diverses pieces concernant le quietisme ou Molinos, ses sentiments et ses disciples*,[60] the anonymous author – known today as Jean Cornand Lacroze – claimed that Couplet would have described the inner sect of Buddhism as a Quietism. The opposition between Molinists and Jesuits was harsh, the former ones accused the latter ones of forced conversions and false morality, whilst the Jesuits accused the Molinists of several heavy theological errors. As we have already mentioned, Couplet defined the inner sect of Xekia as devoted to the cult of nothing, thus it led to a contemplative and empty life, particularly within the *'nihil agentium secta'*. The author (i.e. Lacroze) claimed that Couplet had described the 'Idolatrous sect' (namely Buddhism) with the same words used to describe Quietism, and that this consonance was intentional, because he would have intended to cause in readers an assimilation of Quietists with this Asian atheistic doctrine (ibid., 24).[61] He closed the objection as follows:

> Father Couplet did not the comparison himself, but the readers understand clearly from the words we quoted, his whole description and his added arguments, that he wished to leave to the readers the pleasure of doing this comparison. Anyway, this [accuse] of reducing the whole religion to the contemplation of emptiness or to an idea vague and confused is the great accuse moved to the Quietists ...
>
> ibid., 25–6[62]

Not only did the author of this Preface claim this connection of Quietism and Asian thought, but he also proved that this was a topic commonly discussed in 1688. We might suggest that Quietism and Chinese philosophy were two major (libertine) topics of the year, thus a connection between them was really easy. In the article of September 1688, Bernier said:

> I have heard people speaking of nothing else but Quietism for five or six months now and this reminded me of our Quietists of the Indies and aroused my curiosity to pick up my old notes on these countries again.
>
> ibid., 47[63]

Bernier did not mention any author, but he confirmed right away the 'Asian Quietism'. He provided a description of the first principle according to the 'Joguis', namely Yogin, of India, who could adhere to the perfect state of the first principle by means of meditation. This first principle is immanent, pure, subtle, clear, limitless, perfect, 'and what is worth noting, in an absolute rest, in an absolute inaction, in one word in a perfect Quietism' (ibid., 48).[64] Suddenly, he proposed what was said by Couplet in the *Confucius sinarum philosophus* regarding the Chinese Buddhist inner doctrine, supporting it with his materials on Indians. As we said, Lacroze had claimed that Jesuits used 'Chinese atheism' – i.e. Buddhism and contemporary deviated Confucianism – against Molinism, but Bernier also added Indians, about whom he was a living authority. Turning back to the Indian doctrine of the first principle, Bernier argued that, although they described it as perfect, since it is immanent and reachable by a deep meditation, it could but be a corporeal principle. 'That is to make God corporeal, and thus divisible, corruptible, etc., thus whatever concept that contrasts with the Sovereign and absolute perfection of God' (ibid., 51).[65] Bernier knew that the accusation of materialism was extremely odious and that Quietists rejected it firmly. The last paragraph of this short essay is subtle and it is worth quoting in full:

I do not want to say here that [the doctrine] of the Quietism or Molinism – that is making so much ado – is the same as that of the Quietism of Yogin of Indies, or of Bonzis of China, or of Talapois⁶⁶ of Siam. I prefer to believe that there would be more devotion and extravagance [in Molinism] than evilness. However, the great relation between these two Quietisms, this hell of contemplation, that strong inaction, that union between our soul and God, and hundreds of other things, make me suspect and drive me to suppose that all this great and extraordinary devotion could lead to a kind of irreligion or libertinism. That is what someday we will investigate, when Molinos's original [texts] will be in our hands and if his friends judge that they are worthy of our reading.

ibid., 51–2⁶⁷

Clearly, Bernier was still not aware of the contemporary edition of Molinos's text by Lacroze, thus it is evident that the controversy over Couplet's allusion was quite diffused, even in Montpellier, where Bernier spent the last months of his life. We might argue that Bernier, who died on the 22 September, never read the text edited by Lacroze. However, he was the pivotal author who unified – according to either his own direct experience or by means of reading Jesuits' works – Persia, India, China, Japan, Siam, etc., in a modern 'Doctrina orientalis', defined as atheistic Spinozism and 'Quietisme des Indes'. Bernier offered a greater philosophical approach and influenced the debate at least till Brucker, and particularly Pierre Bayle's interpretation of Asia. From Xavier to Bernier we have traced the definition of a new concept of Asiatic *philosophia perennis* that was no more the sign of God's pre-Christian message, but instead the spreading of atheism and heresy, of which Buddhism was the leading propagator. It was not by chance that Bernier could mention libertinism and irreligion as two European allies of the Immanentist and Quietist Asiatic thought.

2.3 Pierre Bayle and the 'Oriental Spinozism'

Pierre Bayle (1647–1706) was one of the most complex and refined thinkers between the seventeenth and eighteenth century, an immense erudite who joined the knowledge of the polyhistoric with the historical vision of a modern historian, and he is usually considered the father of historical criticism. He took part in many disputes during his life and he had a plethora of enemies. We can say that he was on the side of pure anti-dogmatism, but at the same time he presented himself as a believer in Christian faith. He has been accused of atheism several times, whilst he presented himself as a coherent Christian sceptic, refusing any dogma.⁶⁸

In Bayle, it is possible to investigate the growing interest in Oriental thought across twenty years, from the *Pensées diverses à l'occasion d'une Comete* (1682) to the *Réponse aux questions d'un provincial* (1706), without forgetting the most famous writing of Bayle, namely the *Dictionnaire*. We began focusing on a few entries of the *Dictionnaire* because they were the first concrete achievement of his interest and his most influential work in the history of philosophy. All entries we quote are taken from the edition of 1740, which is identical to the 1702 edition, i.e. the second enlarged edition.⁶⁹ These entries are: Brachmanes, Gymnosophistes, Japon, Sommona-Codom, Spinoza and a few excerpts from further entries not related to Asia.[70] The first two are of little interest, because they are written only by quoting the well-known classical sources. On the contrary, the following entries are full of new quotes and arguments, the same arguments we investigated and traced in the previous two sections.

Regarding ancient *Brachmanes*, Bayle pointed out their abilities as strict teachers of ethics and of effective commitment,[71] their extreme practices,[72] their vegetarianism, their regulated sexual habits[73] and the question of Gymnosophists' nakedness.[74] According to Bayle, although their ethics was strict, from a theoretical point of view it was relativist, owing to their belief in a chain of rebirths, which provided new life in different social classes. This relativism did not lead to free actions, but rather to a process of 'indifference' or detachment from worldly life.[75] Their physics was unacceptable, but Bayle added that the physics of Greeks was equally unacceptable. These few questions include, more or less, all that Bayle said about ancient Indians, and these topics were common among historians.

At the end of the entry 'Brachmanes', we are not surprised to find 'Chinese Brachmanes', who were clearly the Buddhists, the third Chinese sect.[76] They believed in 'Foe' (Buddha), in the Law (*dharma*) and in their written rules (likely the *sūtras*). The most interesting topic is their 'strange sentiments about nothingness'[77] (*Brachmanes*, I, 653). Bayle devoted to this issue the rem. K of the same entry, where he quoted the Preface of *L'Histoire de l'Edit de l'Empereur de la Chine*, written by Charles le Gobien: Buddhists believe 'that the World is nothing more than an illusion, a dream, a prestidigitation; and that things in order to effectively exist, must cease to be in themselves and confuse themselves with the nothing, which thanks to its simplicity leads all beings to perfection'[78] (ibid.). This theory also entailed the ceasing of passions, actions and civil participation, in opposition to the Confucian theory. This abstention from passions and civil engagement reminded Bayle of the Quietists, but, in this entry, he even claimed that Brachmanes (i.e. Buddhists) were to be preferred, because their theory about the union with God was less meaningless than that of Quietists. This entry did not change from the first to the second edition, whilst the entry on 'Spinoza' was dramatically enlarged. In the new rem. B of 'Spinoza' in 1702, Bayle changed ideas and said that Chinese Buddhism was a form of Quietism. In the unchanged entry 'Brachmanes', Buddhists were called 'Brachmanes in China', while in Spinoza rem. B they were 'of the Chinese sect of Foe' (i.e. Buddha), therefore, it is clear that in both cases, although he used two different definitions, Bayle was speaking of the same Chinese Buddhists. Bayle also quoted the '*nihil agentium secta*' as a clear Quietist sect, after the suggesting of Couplet, Jean Cornand Lacroze and Bernier (see §2.2.), and he diffused the idea of the 'Oriental Quietism', which afterwards was argued also by Brucker (§3.5.).

The entry 'Sommona-Codom' – the 'supreme man' – clearly showed the difficulty in understanding that this deity Foe/Fotokue or Xiaka was Buddha himself. The true aim of this entry was not to present this deity, but to support one of Bayle's pivotal theories: the belief in Providence and the belief in God are not necessarily interrelated. He said: 'Chinese and Siameses are very different from Epicure, because they deny the existence of God, but they believe in Providence' (ibid., rem. A, 238).[79] Therefore, the faith in God and faith in Providence were not the same thing. One person, as the Chinese and Siameses, may deny the existence of God, but he can believe in a Providence that does not descend from God. In Siam, 'they claimed that laws and natural sympathies have connected virtue with happiness and vice with unhappiness, and these [connections] are incentives and restraints as powerful as it is to know that all [events] are the consequence of an Enlightened Providence'[80] (ibid., rem. A, 238). They also claimed that their god Sommona-Codom or Foe – different from Christian God – resides in the eighth Heaven, which is called 'Nireupan' or 'Nyruppam' (*nīrūpa* skr), namely 'absence of shape', described correctly by Bayle's source as: 'It is not a place, but rather a way of being, because, properly speaking, they say, Sommona-Codom is nowhere, he does not feel any happiness, he is without any power, and not in a state in which he could do good or bad to men: an expression that Portuguese translated with the word annihilation [anéantissement]'.[81] Here we have, quoted by Bayle in a widely diffused book of the eighteenth century, one of the first, if not the first, correct descriptions of *nirvāṇa*. However, Bayle was not pleased with this account, because missionaries also described several rites and cults in order to invoke Sommona-Codom's help. He felt that: 'their doctrines are so confused that they can affirm both black and white ... The notions of their minds are so different from the feelings of their hearts, that it entailed the disagreement of their theory with their practice' (ibid.).[82] Strangely, Bayle did not solve this contradiction by recalling the theory of the two Buddhist doctrines, the inner and the outer, although this would have been the correct answer and the knowledge of this theory was already diffused in Europe thanks to the missionaries' accounts we investigated (§2.1.).

Chinese thought was also mentioned in entries not related to Asia; they served as comparisons and rhetorical expedients, and that was the case, among many, of 'Cesalpin André' (Cesalpino Andrea) and 'Maldonat Jean' (a Jesuit). We cannot investigate here why the Chinese were quoted in these entries, but we remark only that in both cases it was claimed that they were materialist thinkers and they believed in a material Heaven that was their first principle. In 'Maldonat', the Chinese were presented as atheists (rem. L, 296), and the primary source used by Bayle was Arnauld, who strongly attacked the Jesuits, as we have already seen. The source was the *Cinquiéme denonciation du Philosophisme c'est à dire de la nouvelle heresie du Peché philosophique*,[83] where Ricci's theory of the original monotheism was openly rejected as a Jesuit's device given to hide, under a philosophical shape, Jesuit missionary failure and moral weakness.[84]

'Spinoza' is perhaps the most important entry of the *Dictionnaire*, not only for the purposes of our research but maybe in general, since it is also the longest and is devoted to one of the most dangerous topics of that time. Spinozism was the most disputed and harshly rejected philosophy of the second half of the seventeenth century, because both theologians and Christian philosophers understood the depth of Spinoza's radical criticism of the Christian practices (i.e. political and moral) and of the Christian ontology of substances. In those years, atheism and Spinozism were perceived as synonyms and the accusation of Spinozism was really dreaded. In the previous section we saw that Noël Aubert de Versé was forced to write against Spinoza to be rehabilitated. His was not an isolated case. Spinoza was the most influential source of the *philosophes*' philosophy of seventeenth and eighteenth centuries, a philosopher to reject or to follow without compromises.⁸⁵ Zoli traces two clear crossing lineages in French seventeenth- and eighteenth-century philosophical discourse: one connected to the libertine and unorthodox use of China, from la Peyrère and la Mothe le Vayer to Bayle and Voltaire; and one of the unorthodox biblical critics from la Peyrère to Spinoza (i.e. *Tractatus theologico-politicus* 1670), Richard Simon (*Histoire critique du Vieux Testament* 1678) and obviously Bayle.⁸⁶ The confluence of these two lines is blatant in the 'Spinoza' thirty-eight-page long entry, enriched by endless notes (i.e. remarks), where all the contemporary theories about the Dutch philosopher were widely reported and discussed. Among these theories and interpretations, the theory of the Oriental thought as a Spinozistic philosophy, gained the first lines of the entry into the revised edition:

> He was a systematic atheist with (A) an entirely new method, even though he shared the core of his doctrine with several other, ancient and modern philosophers from both Europe and the Orient. With regard to the latter one, it is enough to read what I report in note D of the article on Japan along with what I say here below concerning the theology of a sect of the Chinese (B).
>
> Spinoza, IV, 254–5⁸⁷

This paragraph was actually shorter in the first edition of 1697, it ended at 'new method', therefore, there was yet not any reference to the Oriental Spinozism in the body of the entry, the aforementioned note B did not exist and in this edition there was not the connected entry on 'Japan'. However, in 1697 Bayle already had the idea of an Oriental monism or immanentism shared by Asian philosophies and Spinoza. Indeed, in note A, which is identical in both editions, after a short but detailed history of the immanentist doctrine before Spinoza, he quoted the excerpt of Bernier's letter we have reported before (see §2.2.), where the metaphors of the Indian immanentism were discussed. Bayle clearly read the sources we investigated between 1692 (i.e. project of the *Dictionnaire*) and 1697 (i.e. 1st edition) and he decided to insert Bernier's description of Indian philosophy into a short history of immanentism or, as Bayle called it, 'the system of the Soul of the world' ('le systême de l'ame du monde').⁸⁸

It is necessary to remark that, in October 1700, something relevant changed, because the theological faculty of the Sorbonne in Paris censured the Jesuits' theory of accommodation. The Catholic Church in Rome was still arguing about the correctness of Jesuit theory, whilst the most important theologians in Paris decided to control this order and to favour its opponents. In 1704, by the decree *Cum Deus optimus*, the accommodation method was also condemned by Rome. The censure was a great and controversial scandal, the culmination of the enduring 'rites controversy'.⁸⁹ We can say that Jansenists, like Arnauld, and the minor orders have won their battle against Jesuits' power and influence. The 'rites controversy' did not end in 1704, but it signalled the beginning of the decline of the Jesuit order. Bayle clearly perceived the importance of the growing debate over the Chinese by the end of the 1680s. We should also notice that Bayle and the Jesuits had a common enemy, namely Eusèbe Renaudot, who wrote a pamphlet against the first⁹⁰ and several letters to the cardinal Bouillon, protector of the Jesuits, in order to persuade him of their errors and immorality.⁹¹ And, as we will see, Renaudot was the main source used by Heumann against Chinese thought and the European approval of it, which followed Jesuit descriptions (§3.3.).

In 1702 (i.e. 2nd edition), Bayle's idea of 'the Orient' was more complex and detailed. He could not consult the most important book on the Chinese, i.e. the *Confucius sinarum philosophus*, but we know from rem. B that he used two of its reviews: 1. *Nova acta eruditorum* (Leipzig 1688, 254–65) and 2. the aforementioned review by Le Clerc from the *Bibliotheque universelle et historique*. We also know that in this second review, the theory of a 'Spinozistic Oriental philosophy' was reported for the first time, and Le Clerc recalled in his review the same letter of Bernier that was quoted by Bayle in 'Spinoza' rem. A (already in the first edition of the *Dictionnaire*). Was that accidental or has Bayle read Le Clerc's reviews before 1697? Whether the second answer would be correct, why did Bayle write rem. B only into the edition of 1702? Did the censure of the Sorbonne cause the addition of a more explicit *remarque* on the 'Spinozistic Orient' in the entry? We cannot answer these questions, but it is really intriguing to investigate Bayle's process of understanding China and India between the two editions. Following the reviews of the *Confucius sinarum philosophus*, he also presented the two Buddhist doctrines and Buddha's deathbed confession (see §2.1.). Bayle confirmed the atheism of the inner doctrine, that of emptiness:

> Whether it is already monstrous to suggest that plants, animals and men are effectively the same thing and to base that [idea] on the claim that each particular being is detached from its principle, it is even more monstrous to assert that this principle does not have thought, power or virtue ... Even Spinoza was not so absurd ...
>
> ibid., rem. B, 254–5[92]

Bayle judged Buddhist theory as untenable, because the first principle was immanent to nature, as for Spinoza, but different from the Dutch philosopher, this Buddhist principle was lacking the active power of Substance to create accidents.

In the same rem. B Bayle dealt with Quietism, as in rem. K of the entry 'Brachmanes'. The discussion among Couplet, Molinists (i.e. Lacroze) and Bernier was clearly the source, but the French traveller and philosopher was not mentioned here. Instead Bayle quoted long excerpts from La Bruyère's *Dialogues*,[93] where Fenelon and Quietism were praised. The 'Vu guei Kiao' sect (*wuwei jiao* 無為教), described in *Confucius sinarum philosophus*, was introduced together with an alleged Confucian rejection of it, by means of one pillar of Aristotelian logical arguments: 'nothing comes from nothing'. However, Bayle did not simply report these critiques levelled against Buddhism (still not called as such), but started a very acute reflection about the concept of 'nothingness'. Bayle argued that nobody could assert such an untenable theory, therefore he suggested: 'I could never be persuaded that they [the sect of Idolaters, namely Buddhism] understand the word "nothing" in its proper meaning, instead I suggest that they understand it as people when they say that there is "nothing" in an "empty" box'[94] (ibid., 255). In contemporary philosophical terms, we could say that Bayle was distinguishing between ontological and logical, or linguistic, 'emptiness', because for him emptiness would be a property of the Buddhist first principle and not a negative ontology.

Grounded on this interpretation, the French historian even blamed the Confucians who rejected Buddhist 'logical' emptiness:

> Grounded on this [argument, we can say that] Confucius' disciples were guilty of the Sophism [or Fallacy] we call *ignoratio elenchi*, because they understood *nihil* as what has no existence, whilst their adversaries meant by the same word, what has not the properties of the sensible matter. I estimate that they meant by this word more or less what Modern scholars indicate with the word 'space'. I claim that the Moderns, which do not want to be neither Cartesian nor Aristotelian, argue that the space is distinct from bodies, and that its indivisible, impalpable, penetrable, immovable, and endless extension is a real thing. The disciples of Confucius proved that this concept could not be the first principle, whether it is without activity, as the contemplatives of China had understood it.
>
> ibid.[95]

The emptiness was the space and not a negative ontology (nothingness). However, Bayle refused to see this space as a productive first principle, because it is inactive. It is neither the contrary of Descartes's *res cogitans*, i.e. a body or at least a material thing, nor the space as a concept derived from the perception of motion, as in the Aristotelian physics, which rejects void because it would exist without the motion of a body. Actually, Bayle referred to a scientific concept of space, which seems the same of Newton as given in the *Philosophiae Naturalis Principia Mathematica* (published in 1687):

> Wherefore, entire and absolute motions can be no otherwise determined [definiri] than by immovable places [loca immota]; and for that reason I did before refer those absolute motions to immovable places [loca immota], but relative one to movable places. Now no other places are immovable [immota] but those that, from infinity to infinity, do all retain the same given position one to another; and upon this account must ever remain unmoved [immota]; and do thereby constitute immovable [immobile] space.[96]

Bayle showed, although cursorily, a surprisingly deep understanding of Buddhist philosophy. He related correctly the meaning of emptiness to the properties of the first principle, which is not definable through the same characters of common things, thus by means of words. The immanent principle is completely and strictly ineffable for Mahāyāna Buddhists from Nāgārjuna (*c.* third century CE) to the Chinese Chan (禅) or Japanese Zen, and that is something in common with several Indian schools of logic, indeed *chan* 禅 is the translation of *dhyāna*, the Sanskrit word for meditation. Therefore, Bayle correctly understood emptiness as an emptiness of mind, the silence of preconceived ideas on the single substance, which is the whole being. Bayle even approached this Buddhist first principle as 'space' and in so doing, he came very close to the concept of 'place' or *basho* 場所 as into the philosophy of the influential Japanese thinker Kitarō Nishida (1870–1945).[97] We think it is useful to stress that 'space' is a technical word in Buddhism, since *bhūmi* – from the root *BHŪ*- (to be) – means space, ground, plane, stage, level and state of consciousness. The *bhūmi*s are the 'stations' in the path of liberation of the Bodhisattva, thus they are metaphysical/psychological spaces and stages of freedom from worldly life. The main ancient text on this topic is the *Daśabhūmika Sūtra*, authoritative in ancient Indian Buddhism as in Tibetan, Chinese, Japanese and Mongolian Buddhism.[98] Therefore, besides the clear differences between the concept of space in Bayle and in Buddhism, what is intriguing is the deep understanding of emptiness as an epistemological issue far from any material/ontological aspects. What Bayle could not grasp was the refined idea of a changeable and variable single Substance, a concept that was not understood and explained by the missionaries themselves, who were more interested in banning Buddhism as atheism and in defending the approach of their respective order on Confucianism, than in undertaking an effective process of understanding.

It is possible to detect Bayle's growing interest in China not only through an investigation of the new edition of the *Dictionnaire* (1702), but also through three other books from the rich bibliography of the author, namely the *Pensées diverses* (1682–3),[99] the *Continuation des pensées diverses* (1704)[100] and finally the third part of the *Réponse aux questions d'un provincial* (1706).[101] We cannot investigate here these masterpieces of modern philosophical controversy, but we shall report briefly the parts where the Chinese are mentioned and how this argumentative presence had changed heavily in more than twenty years. The common threads of these three works are idolatry, superstition, 'universal consent' and atheism. According to the 'universal consent', the best proof of God's existence was the unanimous agreement of all human beings on his existence, according to Cicero's *De natura Deorum*. As we already underlined, this theory of the 'universal consent' was consistent with Riccian Jesuits' interpretation of Chinese civilization. The necessity of an original and ancient monotheism, in which all civilizations believe, was the most universalistic and inclusivist theory ever claimed within Christendom. The unquestionable proof of the existence of God and of his message throughout the world was perfectly inserted into the perennialist model; the consent was not simply a perfect theological, metaphysical and historical proof, but also a moral one. According to this theory, the faith in God's existence necessarily influences ethics and behaviour and every immoral habit had to be a local deviation from the original divine teaching that missionaries must rectify. Kors explained the importance of the topic as follows: 'For almost all early-modern theologians and philosophers, then, the argument from "universal consent" on behalf of God's existence, while not a demonstrative proof, was as strong a moral proof as one could imagine, and one, thus, that ought to persuade all reasonable minds.'[102] Bayle systematically rejected this theory from the *Pensées* to the *Réponse*, using the existence of atheists – i.e. people who do not believe in God – as proof against the presumption of the 'universal consent'.[103] Obviously, his opponents could reply that these atheists would have simply deviated from wisdom and would have fallen into an immoral life and thought. But Bayle rejected this argument and he mentioned several ancient heathen philosophers who lived morally, in a civil manner and with a tolerant attitude. The good or moral atheist – as already depicted by Le Vayer (§1.7.) – was the proof of the invalidity of 'universal consent' and of course of Christian universalism *tout court*, one of the most solid tenets of both Reformation and Counter-Reformation.

Kors reduces the argument of universal consent into the following syllogism: 'Major premise: what is universally believed by all people is true. / Minor premise: all peoples past and present have believed that God exists. / Conclusion: That "God exists" is true.'[104] Bayle rejected the major premise through his psychological theory, according to which humans are ruled by passions and impetus, not by rationality. Therefore, what people believed or believe is not a convincing proof of rational consent. Furthermore, according to Bayle's psychological model of passions, the atheist was the more rational and less easily deceived man: he has nothing to defend or to fight for. An atheist decides his activity only grounded on his reason and free will, never driven by fanaticism. On the contrary, whichever believer could be driven by religious impetus to even act immorally and against tolerance.[105] The virtuous atheist is the only man who could be completely rational. Therefore, 'Atheism is not more dangerous than Idolatry',[106] an issue that Bayle declared to have taken from Francis Bacon, quoted by la Mothe le Vayer (*Cinq Dialogues faits à l'imitation des anciens, par Horatius Tubero*). That was the rejection of the major premise. However, it is the minor premise that is the core of our investigation, because by describing all people who did not believe in – following Kors's syllogism – 'God exists', Bayle provided more and more cases of moral atheists in full detail.

In 1682–3, Bayle's *Pensées* revealed that he was not actually interested in the Indies, in effect, in this work the only mention about Asians was on Japan and it provides minimal and marginal contents. The context was the question 'Is atheism less dangerous than idolatry?' In the answer, Bayle quoted the Japanese as instance of the immorality and fanaticism of idolaters. They worship hundreds of gods but, when they do not obtain what they ask for, they outrage the statues in extreme rites. However, as we have seen, between 1697 and 1702, in Bayle the interest for Asian philosophies grew gradually, as the addition of several notes and entries in the *Dictionnaire* proves clearly. In 1704, Bayle went further in his understanding of Asia in *Continuation des Pensées* by reviewing almost the same topic. In chapter XVIII he rejected his opponent's counter thesis, which was 'Atheism appeared at the most among a few barbarian and wild peoples'[107] (ibid., 209). According to Bayle, those people were not wild and, most of all, they were not a few tribes. After a few chapters he mentioned the Chinese, regarding the issue of the massive conversions to Christian faith. He denied the authenticity of these conversions that were not due to a firm belief, but rather to the fear of missionaries' menaced punishments in Hell:

> We are surprised by the fact that so many heathens arrange themselves under the flag of a crucified God and that they agree with doctrines so in contrast with natural ideas. But since freethinkers [esprits forts] do not believe either in miracles nor in the inner action of grace, to motivate [force] this changing of faith they [*viz.* missionaries] had to find other principles and they found the most specious, that is to obtain Chinese [conversion] after shocking them with the fear of hells...
>
> ibid., 211–12[108]

Besides the relevant definition of Christian doctrines as against natural reason, the definition of the Chinese as freethinkers ('esprits forts') is extremely relevant. A few lines further, Bayle took the Chinese as a special example, since, whilst peoples from

America under the Spanish might be accepted as a case of barbarity, China emerged as a clear exception of a 'wise and clever country as no other',[109] thus, we can suspect, as the only civilization comparable with Europe as Horn said about Confucian educational system (§1.3.). Only fear could have convinced Chinese 'freethinkers' to convert, therefore for them Christianity was simply a religion of fear. Bayle's rejection of God's grace, providence and, at the same time, Original sin could not be more evident.

As we said, the effect of the censure of Le Comte's thesis on Chinese ancient monotheism[110] decided by the Sorbonne Faculty of Theology was really strong on Bayle. He devoted many pages to the rejection of this censure and he even said, in covert words, that the Sorbonne has been influenced and biased.[111] However, his real hidden aim was to prove the contradictions within this condemnation, because the same theologians, who rejected the monotheism of Chinese, pretended that the 'universal consent' was a correct logical and historical principle. This is because the censure of Le Comte – i.e. ancient Chinese as monotheists – entailed the existence of atheist people without the slightest idea of God, who lived perfectly morally in a stable and meritocratic empire. As Bayle often suggested, the confutation of the 'universal consent' was not his merit, but rather it was derived from the arguments of those Catholics who wanted it to be accepted. It was not possible to reject all non-Christian civilizations as atheistic and at the same time to claim that there were clear traces of knowledge of God among heathens.[112]

From chapter C Bayle dealt with the question of 'speculative atheism', a favourite topic of the last years of his life. This atheism was opposed to 'practical atheism', that was the atheism of former idolaters who rejected the idea of god or gods. In the *Continuation*, the speculative atheist completely lacks any knowledge of religious principles, among which the same idea of God. This condition was named by Arnauld, who was widely quoted here, 'philosophical sin' ('peché philosophique'). In the New World (America) and in the Indies, missionaries met several peoples and tribes they described as completely unaware of God, lacking the slightest idea about religion; therefore, those peoples were not properly idolaters, because they did not choose to worship a pagan god. Nobody preached about any god to them, neither a true nor a false one. And this point of view entailed several theological problems, as for instance: was not the idea of God innate? Bayle did not answer openly to this question, but his standpoint was clear, if we remember what he said about Greeks. The Greeks, even the philosophers among them, could have never had a correct idea of the Christian God, since they had a public cult that proposed materialistic ideas related to gods, opposed to the Christian God.[113] Therefore, according to this argumentative sequence, the idea of God was not innate, but rather must be learnt.

Bayle also rejected the prejudice that an atheist was certainly a less virtuous man than an idolater. He quoted several ancient atheists known for the absolute morality of their actions and lives, first of all Greeks philosophers (i.e. Epicurus), but he also added one thinker who was clearly not a heathen: 'for providing you an example not only more modern, but even more resounding, I have only to invite you to steal a glance at the morals of Spinoza.'[114] According to Bayle, the Dutch philosopher wrote the most systematic atheistic philosophy, associated with very good moral teachings. We can only suppose the scandal of this statement. Furthermore, immediately after mentioning

Spinoza, Bayle added the Chinese instance of atheism and morality, as it was clearly stated since the 2nd edition of the *Dictionnaire* (1702). However, also in this context, he did not speak only about Chinese literates, but also about Buddhists: 'I would not suggest that Confucius, who left remarkable moral precepts, was an atheist, [because] who asserts that meet several deniers, therefore, I present only unquestionable facts. The god Fo is the principle idol of China' (*Continuation*, chap. CXLV, 397).[115] And following the already famous 'deathbed confession' – which we presented in §2.1. – Bayle reported that 'Fo' (Buddha) taught atheism as his last doctrine and, as we know, this point was absolutely unquestionable among missionaries' accounts. Bayle reported the well-known theory of Buddhist atheism, which implied the atheism of all Chinese – even the literates – and he avoided asserting only the atheism of Confucius, namely of the ancient Chinese.[116] The Chinese, this was another common opinion, were renowned for their morality and this was asserted by followers of Ricci's accommodation as by many anti-accommodationists. Whereas Bayle's opponents would claim that the Chinese were not a good example of atheism, because they were well-learned and educated men, Bayle quoted also the 'barbarians' from the Antilles and Africa, peoples not learned but full of moral principles, dignity and even a sense of equality.[117]

In his *Réponse*, Bayle dealt with his two philosophical tenets for the last time: universal consent and atheism. On both themes China constituted his first explanatory case, and it was widely mentioned and considered as a decisive support to his arguments. Bayle came to terms again with universal consent[118] because the Calvinist Jacques Bernard had rejected the effectiveness of his dismissal of this theory in *Nouvelles de la République des Lettres*, in March 1705.[119] Bernard knew Bayle's answers as provided in *Continuation*, therefore, he tried to prove that travellers' and missionaries' accounts suggesting the existence of atheist sects were biased by the premeditated intention to prove the existence of atheism in these lands. Bayle opposed to Bernard the fact that, on the contrary, several missionaries and theologians had tried to prove the ancient monotheism of all civilizations, and they understood several local rituals as belonging to the ancient monotheistic root (in accord with 'prisca theologia'). Bernard also supposed that these atheists, when proved that they exist, had to be barbarians, savages and degraded people.[120] The rejection of this statement was easy for Bayle, since the Chinese, Japanese, Siameses, etc., had always been described as moral people, with a strong ethical commitment, even by the missionaries who were suggesting their absolute atheism.

Atheism was the most relevant issue of the *Réponse* and Bayle reached in the third part of this work a further level of refinement, the last one. In chapter 11, the pivotal point was the existence of 'Speculative atheists', who were different from 'practical Atheists', and the most effective instance of the former atheism were the Chinese:

> nothing is more to fear [for Bernard's thesis] than the accounts about the Atheism of Chinese Philosophers. This is not a simple negative atheism, as for the savages of the Americas, but rather a positive atheism, because those philosophers had compared the system of the existence of God and the opposite system. Outwardly,

they even adapt themselves to the idolatry of the country, to the laws of the State and they are engaged in politics. [121]

ibid., III, chap. XI, 925–6

Bayle also provided several further instances of Chinese positive atheism, from accounts of missionaries opposed to Ricci's accommodation, in order to prove the unquestionableness of his thesis. Bayle even claimed that all missionaries must be trusted in regards to Asian atheism, because: 'these missionaries do not speak as Controversialists, but rather as historians …'.[122] Whether this statement could be surprising, as Bayle often rejected and criticised Jesuits, he, as a historian, was persuaded by the convergence of all missionaries' accounts on Chinese atheism and good morals.

In chapter 12, Bayle provided further instances of atheists and closed his overview by claiming that morality was incompatible only with 'practical atheism', like that of savages, while it was compatible with 'speculative atheism', as proved by the example of Chinese literates. And when we consider that Bayle already claimed that morality could be incompatible with idolatries and even with religions (Jews, Muslims and Christians), because the morality of a religious man was always at risk of fanaticism, it is evident that 'speculative atheists' were the only effective moral men. In the next chapter, Bayle provided a complete examination and categorisation of atheists, a sort of ultimate list: 1. People who believe in God; 2. People who are not persuaded of God's existence. The first are divided according to the attributes they confer to God, while the second group is divided into two subgroups: 2.1. those who have never examined the question, i.e. 'negative atheists'; 2.2. those who compared atheism and theism, i.e. 'positive atheists'. 'Positive atheists' are also divided in two: 2.2.1. those who did not decide between atheism and theism; 2.2.2. those who decided for atheism. 2.2.1 atheists are again divided into Sceptical, who are still investigating the question, and Acataleptics, who stopped their search because the solution is insoluble. The atheists, who took a decision (2.2.2), namely adhere to atheism, either because atheism is more likely than theism or because they proved atheism to be true, anyway, are also said to be 'dogmatic atheists'. According to Bayle, Spinoza was an atheist of this last class, thus he is a dogmatic atheist.[123] As Kors explains with great clarity: 'Spinoza's *Ethica*, thus, became the touchstone that Bayle used to assay diverse accounts of ancient or other philosophies in order to determine less the absolute atheism in them than their degree of atheism.'[124] Whilst the classification may be somewhat confusing, what is more relevant is that all people classed from 2.2. down, i.e. who compared both the theories of the existence and the non-existence of God, are named 'speculative atheists'. They are opposed to 'speculative theists', people who decided for the existence of God after an investigation. 'As you might see to be non-Theist or Atheist, it is not necessary to assert that theism is false, [rather only] to see it as a problem …'.[125] The atheist is not an enemy of religion and of believers in God, rather he is someone who considers the act of believing as a question to be investigated and meditated. Therefore, speculative atheists do not choose a devilish doctrine, since they do not adhere to a heresy, but rather they suspend the act of believing and they avoid every extreme. 'Speculative atheists' are the expression of morality and balance, whatever they decide regarding God. That is so true that, afterwards in the same *Réponse*, Bayle claimed that a religious king was more to fear than a Spinozistic one, because the first would be prone to fanaticism and violence in order to have faithful subjects, while the 'atheist king' could be more tolerant and open to religious and moral diversities.[126] It would be interesting to question here whether Bayle was thinking of the Chinese emperor, often described as open to foreign religions and tolerant, or of a European king of his time still engaged in religious persecution.

Bayle even simulated the answer to a hypothetical question: shall the greatest part of 'speculative atheists' decide for affirmative atheism, therefore, shall they deny God's existence? Bayle answered by tracing a line between an atheist who has received the Christian teaching and an atheist who has never received it and who lived in an atheistic society. According to him, usually the first atheist, after an investigation and rejection of the proofs of God's existence, lies in a state of stable doubt, 'he stopped mentally to assert that there is a God, we ought to suppose that he abstain himself from denying God mentally, because the objections against atheism seem unsolvable. He should stay as a piece of iron between two equivalent poles' (ibid., III, chap. XIII, 933).[127] We could wonder: was Bayle providing a biographical insight of his personal challenge with (Calvinist) faith? Besides this personal aspect, if we follow his argument, the issue changes when the atheist was born in an atheistic society and has received only lately those religious teachings. The instance provided in this case is again the Chinese atheist:

> When we speak of the atheists of China, it is evident that the majority of them deny the existence of the Divinity. From childhood they learn a philosophical system that is a pure atheism. Usually most disciples of a philosopher assert all their lives what they heard he asserted and they disregard other philosophers. That is the case of the sect of Literates; they disregard the Bonzes or priests of Idolatry [i.e. Buddhist monks], who indeed are deplorable for both their doctrines and their habits.[128]
>
> ibid., III, chap. XIII, 933

The Chinese were atheists in an atheistic society, their change of conviction was really difficult, and therefore, Bayle suggested the ineffectiveness of Chinese conversion to Christian faith. The great number of new Christians in Asia was apparent: they adhered only because they were frightened by hell and damnation, not because they were persuaded of the Christian principles and dogmas, which are really far from the natural reason, as Bayle already claimed. The issue of the natural reason was really important for Bayle, because the natural state of humans is sceptical atheism, but humans have also a natural tendency to idolatry – on this specific point he was following Thomas Aquinas – thus atheism becomes rare although it is the original and most natural belief. Consequently, atheism is not infectious, it is not the 'Buddhist plague', as according to several missionaries and theologians as Kircher (§2.1.). Atheism is the natural state of mind, and atheism corresponds to the natural reason devoid of dogmas and theories. Bayle did not need a theory of diffusion for atheism as historians wrote for *philosophia perennis* or Kircher did for 'atheist plague', because rationality was the natural inner condition of every man before being influenced by the society he lived in. Bayle described this later religious influence on the atheistic natural mind as milk suckled by an infant. A person in his natural state or atheism has nothing to defend or to fight for; therefore, atheism was not dangerous. This is a clear example of Bayle's interest in tracing a pioneering 'histoire de l'Esprit humain', a project somewhat attempted within a history of philosophy by the early Enlightened philosopher Deslandes (§2.7.).

The third part of *Réponse* is closed by a long paragraph, which consists of a simulated dialogue between a Christian theologian and a Chinese mandarin.[129] The theologian accuses the mandarin of his lack of a stable basis for morality; the latter rejects the accusation and blames the theologian for ignoring his doctrine. The mandarin explains that the Chinese believe in virtue and they see that virtue as natural reason, thus their first principle is the eternal being, i.e. Nature, which is rational. The theologian claims that Nature lacks intelligence and will, which are necessary to create the world. The mandarin replies that physical, geometrical and arithmetical rules are true on their own:

> He [God] knew necessarily things as they are. As a result, their essence did depend neither on his [of God] intelligence or will, nor on his liberty ... Therefore, virtue was morally good before that God knew it, and it is not because God knew it that it has been what it is, on the contrary God knew virtue as it is, because virtue had been already as it is.
>
> ibid., III, chap. XXIX, 987[130]

According to the Mandarin atheist, things are necessarily as they are and God did not influence the essence of existing things. Because God himself is the essence of all things. This description of Chinese doctrine vividly recalls Spinoza's single substance (God) and this is in complete agreement with the theory of the 'Oriental Spinozism' asserted in the entry 'Spinoza' of the second edition of the *Dictionnaire*.

Bayle did not write a history of philosophy, but, as the Jesuits themselves, he highly influenced the historical debate about the Orient. Bayle created the image of an 'atheistic' and 'Spinozistic' Asian thought. For our investigation, Bayle is a pivotal historian at least for two reasons: 1. He proposed a history of human thought or human beliefs that were not religious, but rather focused on natural reason ('histoire de l'Esprit humain'); 2. Bayle's influence on historians and, particularly, historians of philosophy was really relevant, at least till the *Encyclopédie*.[131] Bayle's historical theories were the account of a degradation, which was not the degradation of the original divine message – as for perennialists – but instead of the natural reason that was overwhelmed by idolatry and fanaticism. As regards the second reason, the influence of the *Dictionnaire* does not need proof, but also his *Pensées*, *Continuation* and *Réponse* had a great impact. It should be enough to notice that Bayle's arguments on universal consent and atheism were reviewed between 1705 and 1707 at least twelve times in *Nouvelles de la République des Lettres* and eight times in *Journal de Trévoux*.[132] Bayle's opponent, Bernard, to whom Bayle devoted large parts of his *Réponse*, edited the first journal. The second journal was that of the Jesuits. Both were opponents, but the result of their harsh critiques was to make Bayle's ideas increasingly visible. In the 1740s, around forty years after Bayle's death (1706), Brucker published his *Historia critica*, where he challenged widely the opinions on Spinozism, atheism and 'Orientalism' of the Frenchman (see §3.5).

2.4 The effects of Bayle's 'Oriental Spinozism': a few instances of Histories of Philosophy in French

Bayle's influence on historians was remarkable, particularly with regards to the matter of 'Oriental Spinozism', and every writer after him had to come to terms with this historical theory. We shall not investigate those historians of philosophy who repeated barely Bayle's theories, but rather the authors who provided something original in their understanding of Asian thought.

The first of them is Pierre-Daniel Huet (1630–1721), a great churchman erudite and bibliophile. He wrote a *Traité philosophique*,[133] whose chapter XV was a history of Scepticism and not, as usual, a history of philosophy based on the biblical frame, as for perennialist histories and Theological histories. In about eighty pages, Huet traced his history of philosophy, which is mostly devoted to the Greek art of doubting, but he also wrote a few paragraphs about further civilizations. The Chinese were not mentioned, but Indians were:

> 59. Whether we move to the foreigner Nations, we find many of them sharing the same sentiment, namely that we need to suspend our judgment and our belief. Diogenes Laërtius reported that Anaxarchus and Pyrrho learned from Mages and Gymnosophists of the Indies [des Indes] this excellent method of philosophizing, which prevents to believe that nothing could be understood and that prevents to put our consent and faith on anything.
>
> 60. Brachmanes, according to the accounts of Strabo and Megasthenes, asserted that there is nothing good and nothing bad, since what seems good to one person, it seems bad to another. What I am saying is that the Sceptic Philosophy penetrated up to the extremities of the Orient.
>
> ibid., 164–5[134]

The 'carsic river flowing', according to Huet, was neither the divine wisdom, as for perennial philosophers (i.e. from Abraham or Noah), nor atheism, as for all missionaries, but rather Scepticism, actually a Fideistic Scepticism. Therefore, the true philosophical method was not based on religious consent, but strictly rational. For Huet, the correlation between religious history and history of philosophy was no more tenable. The same was true for Bayle, but while Heut provided a migration theory of Scepticism, which was intended as a learned philosophical principle, the author of the *Dictionnaire* had as principle a human feature, namely natural reason. We see how, among Christian Sceptics, both authors were (Heut) or pretended to be (Bayle), attitudes could be different. Although Huet was a Jesuit, he did not pay attention to the missionaries' accounts and only examined ancient sources on Indians. His aim was to prove Scepticism to be a good attitude also in religious issues, while Bayle's aim was deeper: he wanted to prove the natural atheistic disposition of humans, who could live better in a secular rather than in a religious state. Despite that, both philosophers proposed to reverse the perennial philosophy model, without being exclusivist historians, but rather they argued different inclusivist perspectives.[135] Perspectives, which were very diverse, since these thinkers were on opposite sides: Bayle could not hide his sympathy for Spinoza, while Huet was anti-rationalist (Descartes) and anti-Spinozist.[136]

In the following year (1724), Jean Lévesque de Burigny (1692–1785) published his *Histoire de la Philosophie payenne*,[137] a book that had a good fortune. The principle tenet of the book was that all heathen sects of philosophy have taught good principles, which were compatible with Christian thought, but as these peoples lacked the help of Revelation, each of them proposed at least a few religious errors. To prove his thesis, the author furnished a wide doxography, with plenty of quotes arranged by theological topics. Burigny was usually tempered and never took critical positions. The rich quotations and his moderate style were two reasons for the success of the book. In the first chapter, devoted to the existence of God, the Chinese were described as atheists who believed in a material principle, thus following the anti-accommodationist missionaries. In the second chapter, about God's essence, de Burigny followed Bayle's entries extensively, namely 'Japon' and 'Spinoza', thus he suggested the Spinozism of Chinese, according to the theory of the 'Oriental Spinozism'. Even more interesting is the long paragraph on Metempsychosis (XIV.4), where Indians are the main people investigated. Burigny presented this belief as a widespread opinion, from Egypt to China. He did not provide a real diffusion theory, however, this suggestion recalled a perennialist topic of the historiographies (see §1.5.).

The relevance of the 'Oriental philosophy' was evident also when this philosophy was not inserted within a history of philosophy to be discussed, since 'a philosopher of the Indies' could also be quoted as fictitious interlocutors. This is the case of the *Examen du Pyrrhonism*[138] by Jean-Pierre de Crousaz (1663–1750).[139] The Swiss philosopher was an adversary of Bayle's scepticism and the rhetorical use of this interlocutor was probably an open criticism of the 'Oriental Spinozism'. De Crousaz restricted this history of ancient and modern Scepticism or Pyrrhonism to the West and this decision was also against Huet. De Crousaz questioned this fictitious interlocutor as follows:

> I demand to allow me to be in conference somewhere in the Indies, with a conscientious philosopher, eager to know at which levels are Sciences in Europe. To please him, I shall start the investigation of the subject a little way back. I shall tell him that Sciences in Europe were born at first in Greece, or at least that we cannot go back any more, because we have not the books of other Nations, from which the Greeks could have taken their knowledge.
>
> ibid., 1[140]

The author followed Diogenes Laërtius, although he did not deny the possible oriental origin of philosophy, he judged this theory as empty of solid evidence. According to de

Crousaz, ancient oriental texts were lost and there was not any available evidence about them. The work of the philosophers and philologists of the two previous centuries on the oriental wisdom was not rejected, but simply neglected by de Crousaz. At the same time, this interlocutor from the Indies was taken as a rhetorical device: somebody who was unaware of European philosophy, to whom this history of philosophy must be taught correctly (in contrast to what Bayle taught). From this quoted excerpt, we might deduce that: 1. since the philosopher was from 'the Indies', probably he was not Indian, but rather a Chinese of the sect of Literates; 2. the author did refuse to trace a global history of Pyrrhonism, thus he placed his work out of what philosophers from at least Kircher had tried to demonstrate; 3. de Crousaz neglected also all the Greek mentions of an oriental origin of philosophy, which was downgraded as indemonstrable due to an alleged lacking of reliable sources.

2.5 Johann Franz Buddeus as critical follower of the 'Oriental Spinozism'

The German Lutheran theologian Johann Franz Buddeus (1667–1729), like Pierre Bayle, devoted several investigations to the question of atheism and to the historical approach related to philosophical topics. Here, we do not aim to provide a global analysis of this author, but rather we shall present a few issues in order to elucidate his philosophical vision of the Orient, inserted in the global history of philosophy he wrote. Buddeus was professor at the University of Leiden where he taught theology, but his interests in the history of philosophy were so remarkable that the great historian Brucker, one of Buddeus' most renowned disciples, felt himself indebted to him as a teacher of history and historical method.

In 1701, a few years after the first edition of the *Dictionnaire*, but before its second edition, Buddeus discussed two dissertations at the University of Halle: 'De superstitio mortuorum apud Chinenses cultu'[141] and 'De Spinozismo ante Spinozam'.[142] The first dissertation was about the dispute between the accommodationists, namely the Jesuits who followed Ricci and their opponents, who acknowledged all Chinese philosophy as atheist. The German professor showed a great knowledge of this topic and quoted from a large bibliography. He was almost equidistant between the two sides, but he betrayed a greater historical trust in the culture and understanding of Jesuits. In the second dissertation, which has a clear Baylean title, he described the atheistic immanentism before Spinoza. The main source was obviously the entry 'Spinoza' in the *Dictionnaire*, which was widely quoted here. However, as this dissertation was discussed in 1701, Buddeus could refer only to the first edition, which was less explicit on 'Oriental Spinozism'. In this dissertation, Buddeus wrote a short paragraph on the Chinese and Indians (§XXI), where he briefly reported the debate over Chinese atheism and materialism, together with the Spinozism of Indians. On Indians, Buddeus quoted the same excerpt from Bernier that was quoted by Bayle in the note A to the entry 'Spinoza' (see §2.2).

After a decade, in 1717 Buddeus published his *Theses theologicae de atheismo*,[143] taking part in the most important philosophical debate since the late seventeenth century. The *Theses* would be translated into French only in 1740¹⁴⁴ by Louis Philon, professor of the Sorbonne, together with Jean-Chretien Fischer, who rearranged and updated this edition. As this translation was co-written, we might suppose that the translation process began several years before the actual French release. In the Preface of this important book, which was conceived as a University manual, Buddeus quoted his dissertation on Spinoza along with the entry on 'Spinoza' written by Bayle. The French philosopher was also presented in §XXV,¹⁴⁵ where Buddeus wrote a very long note about him. Buddeus remarked that, although avoiding an open accusation of atheism, the excessive respect of Bayle towards atheist philosophers was suspect.

Buddeus divided the whole thought of 'Practical atheism' – the philosophical atheism, which did not follow from ignorance of God – by schools, in opposition to Bayle. These schools were only Greek and every reference to any foreign atheism was lacking. The schools were five and arranged on two sides: Sceptics and Dogmaticians, which were the Aristotelians, Stoics, Epicureans and Spinozists. In the last category, there were included the ancient Greek philosophers from which Spinoza has derived his systematic atheism. However, Buddeus did not quote the 'Oriental Spinozists', as Bayle did in the 2nd edition of *Dictionnaire* and in the books we mentioned (as *Continuation* and *Réponse*), whom Buddeus even quoted in the aforementioned note on the French thinker.¹⁴⁶ The difference in the interpretation and classification of atheism between the two authors was dramatic. For Bayle, atheism was the more natural state of the mind and his classifications of atheists followed the same process of believing or disbelieving, whilst Buddeus proposed again the division of the old Greek sects, by investigating the ancient philosophical opinions as universal instances, instead of the universality of human nature itself.

Buddeus, unlike Bayle, also wrote an actual history of philosophy, entitled *Compendium*,¹⁴⁷ which was published posthumously in 1731 and prefaced by his disciple Johann Georg Walch, who was a renowned Lutheran theologian. This history is divided into six chapters: I. *Philosophia generatim*, a methodological introduction; II. *Philosophia ebraeorum*,¹⁴⁸ from Adam and Moses to the Cabala; III. *Philosophia gentilium, speciatim barbarica*; IV. *Philosophia Graecanica*, till Epicurus; vol. *Philosophia Medii Aevi*, very short; and VI. *Philosophia recentiori*, late Platonism and Aristotelianism, late Hebraism, modern philosophy from Melanchthon to the eclecticism, which is Buddeus' favoured philosophy. Asian philosophies were obviously inserted in chapter II, but also at the end of the whole book, before the conclusion on eclecticism. Strangely enough, Pythagoras was not presented among Greek philosophers, but rather at the end of this chapter on barbarians. This arrangement was not intended to marginalize him, but rather was due to the fact that Buddeus reputed the Sicilian philosopher as the bridge between Greeks, on one side, and ancient barbarian philosophers, on the other.¹⁴⁹

Among *Indi* were included *Seres* or *Sinenses*, as usual, but the author stressed that: 'Since only today the study of their wisdom is cultivated, we will speak of them * when they have been known to the more recent [*recentiores*] philosophical sects'¹⁵⁰ (ibid., 59). The asterisk (*) referred to a note where Buddeus indicated 'cap. VI. §XXXVII'. The correct reference would be §XXXVI; this could be a misprint or a later change not updated in the note.¹⁵¹ Anyway, the long-lasting influence of Georg Horn's *Historia philosophica*¹⁵² (1655) is evident, because he was the first historian who mentioned the

Chinese in the chapter about Indians in order to refer to a later chapter about them, which was inserted among modern European philosophers. And we know that afterwards Brucker, a disciple of Buddeus, also did the same. However, Buddeus never did quote Horn and did not recognise the paternity of this division; this lack of reference is not strange if we think of the harsh critiques against Horn moved by the other German Eclectics (i.e. Heumann and Brucker). Buddeus' survey of Indian philosophy was very usual, he recalled several sources, both ancient and modern, as Megasthenes, Strabo, Palladius and Saint Ambrose (the last two were quoted less often) or Bayle (the entry 'Brachmanes'), Thomas Burnet, etc. He also quoted cursorily a more recent summary of missionary accounts on India, by the erudite M. V. La Croze,[153] who was the main source for Brucker about Indians (§3.6.).

More interesting is the sixth chapter, after the philosophy of Puffendorf, where there are five paragraphs on the Chinese and marginally on Indians (§XXXVI–XL), as the author already promised in the second chapter. Asia could be the origin of culture, but over barbarian philosophy there was a thick fog:

> Except the Indians, among which several traces of 'prisca philosophia' might still be found, and Chinese wisdom, which claims to be more ancient than all wisdoms of other peoples...
>
> ibid., 527[154]

According to Buddeus, in India there were still traces of the ancient wisdom, he called it openly 'prisca philosophia'; therefore, Indians were part of the 'philosophia perennis', even if they had lost the ancient purity of their wisdom and maintained only traces of it. On the other side, the Chinese claimed to be the most ancient civilization and Buddeus did not openly deny such a possibility. The leading source of Buddeus was *Confucius sinarum philosophus*, therefore the most representative book on behalf of accommodationism ever written, and not the anti-Jesuit books he had mentioned in the debate over Chinese rites (1701). Here, he presented Confucius as a great moral philosopher that was still worshipped by his disciples. Buddeus presented these rites as civil ones and not religious, therefore, he accepted Ricci's interpretation as reported by Couplet.[155] However, Buddeus did not accept all accommodation descriptions and held an eclectic vision of Asia. Therefore, whether Chinese morals and politics were really remarkable and advanced, Chinese were atheists and Spinozists on 'rebus naturalibus et divinis', namely metaphysics and theology,[156] since their first principle was the material heaven. And the definitive proof of the Chinese atheism was the sect 'FoeKiao' (*fojiao* 佛教) of the followers of 'Xekia' (Buddha), who taught a double doctrine on his deathbed. Buddeus presented the outer and inner doctrines of Buddhism as usual (see §2.1.), and the latter was the emblem of Chinese atheism and Spinozism. Obviously, not only was Couplet quoted, but even two entries of the *Dictionnaire*, i.e. 'Spinoza' and 'Japan', in this case from the 2nd edition (1702), that was, as we have seen, more explicit as regards Oriental Spinozism. Obviously, while for Bayle the Chinese Spinozism was the positive proof of the morality of (speculative) atheists, for Buddeus Spinozism was one of the most dramatic religious or theological errors in the history of mankind.

Buddeus was one of the leading figures of German Eclecticism, but his description of Asian people merged together aspects of perennialism and of Bayle. From 'perennialism', particularly Burnet, he took the idea of a relevant Asian 'archaeologia philosophica' devoted to 'prisca theologia', while from Bayle the Spinozism and atheism of the Chinese. But he did not mention Bayle's 'Oriental Quietism' as his disciple Brucker did in his *Historia critica*. The somewhat incoherent image of Asia provided by Buddeus keeps him closer to Burnet or Bayle – although on opposite sides – more than to his coeval German historians, and that is the reason for his insertion in this chapter.

2.6 The last effective perennialist philosopher: Leibniz

In the current investigation we do not aim to provide a complete analysis of Leibniz' sinological writings for at least two reasons: 1. there are already several effective researches and surveys on the topic; 2. Leibniz's point of view on the histories of philosophy about China was not original. In fact, Gottfried Wilhelm von Leibniz (1646–1716) was not the last, but one of the last renowned perennialist philosophers of the eighteenth century; therefore, as the perennial model was fading, the influence of Leibniz's historical view was not relevant as other aspects of his thought. Christian Wolff and Johann Franz Buddeus were inspired by his metaphysics, but his interpretation of China was accepted only by Wolff and rejected by eclectics as by pietist philosophers in Germany.

Modern scholars have often exaggerated Leibniz's interest for China, as Leibniz was presented as a historical exception for his commitment to the understanding of this country.[157] But, he was not such a great exception, because, as we saw, the interest in Chinese thought was quite diffused among European thinkers between the seventeenth and eighteenth centuries. Leibniz wrote a few important letters or short essays about China, he also devoted his attention to specific topics and interpretations, however he was not the only thinker in doing so. As Lai Yuenting correctly suggests: Leibniz's interest in China was more a strategy in order to combat disbelief than a disinterested fascination.[158] Thus, his commitment to China was not different from that of his contemporaries, as for instance Burnet, Bayle or Buddeus.

His works about China belong to three categories, the first regards his linguistic attempt to find a universalistic language, of which the Chinese worked for some time as the possible model (around 1677), an instance shared with John Webb.[159] The second category was the binary interpretation of the hexagrams of *Yi Jing* 易經 (or *I Ching*). This is maybe the most original and fascinating part of his view of Chinese culture, where he was influenced by the Jesuit Figurists, who claimed that China was the repository of the original divine Law, whilst the other countries had lost it after the punishment of Babel.[160] We add merely that the Jesuit Figurists shared Horn's and Burnet's opinion of the Chinese civilization as descended from Noah's son Shem,[161] instead of Ham, as contended by Kircher and Rodriguez (§2.1.). These Jesuits and Leibniz were advocates of the perennial system and they contended, as Ricci himself, that China had been one of the most relevant cradles – when not the cradle – of 'prisca theologia'.

Under the third category, in which we can divide Leibniz's works on China, we mention the Preface[162] to the *Novissima Sinica*, a collection of Jesuit news from China, and the Letter to Rémond (26 January 1716), usually entitled *Le discours sur la théologie naturelle des Chinois*.[163] The last two works are the most renowned and they are frequently quoted as expressions of Leibniz's commitment to Chinese thought and of his admiration, somehow even interpreted as proof of a possible influence of the Asiatic thought itself on his philosophy. The *Discours* was an open rejection of Malebranche's essay on Chinese theology.[164] Malebranche (1638–1715) was one of the most esteemed philosophers of his time, for that reason he was invited to write the *Entrétien d'un Philosophe Chrétien et d'un Philosophe Chinois* (1708).[165] The aim of the essay was to give a more refined philosophical appeal to the 'anti-accommodationist' theory, which claimed the complete atheism of all Chinese sects. We might suggest that this *Entrétien* intriguingly contrasted the dialogue written by Bayle at the end of the third part of the *Réponse*. However, Malebranche was completely unlearned on Chinese culture, scarcely documented and full of his philosophical preconceptions. He really created his stereotype of a rationalist philosopher that, not being supported by the light of Revelation, necessarily falls into the trap of atheism.[166] This atheist was not depicted through the accounts about the Chinese, but rather as a generic atheist, in effect, Malebranche reputed the *Entrétien* as also a refusal of Spinoza's system, which, he reported, was very similar to that of the Chinese.[167] On the contrary, in the *Discours*, Leibniz used the anti-accommodationist essays of Longobardi and Sainte-Marie (see §2.1.) and accepted the atheism of modern Chinese, but in order to claim the ancient monotheism of the Chinese to be true, and he exalted their natural morality, which drove directly to a natural theology, thus following Matteo Ricci.[168]

We cannot investigate the whole of Leibniz's arguments, but what is of interest to us is the continuity between his arguments on Chinese linguistics, history or philosophy and the whole of his thought: he aimed at demonstrating the universality of religion, morality and ontology, against scepticism and atheism. Therefore, the evidence of a moral but atheistic China was unacceptable before his eyes, and in contrast with his universalistic theory. We see clearly that Bayle and Leibniz moved from a common ground, that of the anti-Riccian description of China as an atheistic country – in contrast with their morality and the theory of the universal consent – but, while Bayle took as consequences of this description the morality of atheism – against superstition and idolatry – and the benefits of scepticism (even religious), Leibniz simply refused the description of ancient China as atheistic. In the *Discours sur la Théologie naturelle des Chinois*, Leibniz quoted only the accounts of Longobardi and Sainte-Marie, since he aimed at rejecting point-by-point their interpretation of Chinese philosophy as atheistic and materialistic. Leibniz claimed that these missionaries relied only on Chinese modern commentaries of ancient sources, but because modern thinkers were atheists – as it was known since Ricci – their understanding was evidently incorrect.[169] Therefore, Longobardi and Sainte-Marie contested the Riccian accommodation method because of their wrong use of Chinese sources, since the only reliable ones would have been the ancient ones. Leibniz argued also that the modern Chinese not only misinterpreted their tradition but that they even ignored several theological and scientific theories hidden in the ancient sources. It was thanks to the Figurist Bouvet and to Leibniz himself that the refined logic of exagrams (*gua* 卦), which dated back to the mythical founder of the Chinese Empire Fo Hi (Fuxi 伏羲), had been revealed, after centuries of oblivion.[170]

As we argued, Leibniz's understanding of Chinese culture was not original, but rather it was in continuity with both Jesuit accommodationism and perennial philosophy. Cook and Rosemont summarized: '[the *Discours*] is a sophisticated effort to provide an intellectual framework on behalf of the Riccian "accommodationist" position in the Rites Controversy so that the ecumenical movement could go forward and China could be brought more closely into the family of Christian nations.'[171] Therefore, Leibniz's investigation, although very rich on some aspects, was not truly original from the historical point of view, because it was a learned re-proposal of the Jesuit 'accommodationism', as his relationship with the Jesuit Figurists undoubtedly proved.

As we already suggested, accommodationism was compatible with the perennialist interpretation ('prisca theologia') and the same could be said of Leibniz's universalism. Charles B. Schmitt wrote an interesting article about the philosophical continuity of perennialism from Steuco to Leibniz, where he explains:

> Leibniz's whole philosophy of harmony is very similar to that expressed by Steuco and the others we have discussed, although in Leibniz the metaphysical foundations of such a *Harmonistik* are much more carefully worked out, recalling in some ways Cusanu's attempt to give a metaphysical basis to a 'philosophy of concord' ... In a sense, Leibniz is the most eminent defender of the tradition called by Steuco *philosophia perennis*. Moreover, Leibniz's attempts to bring about religious unity – in a century not reputed for its ecumenical spirit – hark back to Cusanus, as well as to Ficino and Pico.[172]

However, in the early eighteenth century, both perennialism and Jesuit accommodationism fell into a deep crisis, thus the same happened to Leibniz's harmony or universalism, and, consequently, his interpretation of China not only lacked influence, but it even gave opportunity to the opponents of his philosophy to reject and ridicule his thought (see §3.3. and §3.5.). As Oliver Roy said cleverly in the first lines of the conclusion of his *Leibniz et la Chine*: 'Is Leibniz and China the story of a defeat? Leibniz found himself in the champ of losers, both in the Chinese rites controversy and in the [research of a] universal language. Indeed, it was Irenicism the loser.'[173] And Irenicism in Leibniz's philosophy had the aspect of universalism and accommodationism.

2.7 Boureau-Deslandes: an anti-Bayle thinker with new insights

The most interesting French historian of philosophy during the early eighteenth century is also the one who wrote the first real French history of philosophy, which was afterwards harshly criticised by Brucker. His name is André-François Boureau-Deslandes (1689–1757), a real cosmopolitan man, who was born in India from French parents. He was a Commissioner of the Navy, but he was easily comfortable with the philosophical discussions at the court. Among many thinkers he knew, he was a friend of Malebranche. He wrote many books and one of his favourite topics was humour, which he reputed the best attitude of great men and women. He is usually considered to be midway between seventeenth-century libertines and eighteenth-century Enlightened thinkers, since he was also in acquaintance with Diderot and Voltaire.[174] His *Histoire critique de la Philosophie*[175] is an eclectic text, mostly an intelligent summary of different sources, which reproduced the general frame of the perennialist division of sects without adhering to it. It is evident that Deslandes's history was not properly a history of sects, but rather a 'histoire de l'Esprit humain', hence he conceived 'philosophy' in a wide sense (I, p. IV).[176] Deslandes showed in his history a great interest not only in theological and speculative issues, but also in sociological and anthropological arguments, because he wanted to provide the specific background in which each philosophy arose. According to Deslandes, the contexts involved local rituals, cultural attitudes, and even climatic conditions. Such a wide interest makes his history confusing, but rich in unprecedented detail. Although in a new way, this was an attitude typical of seventeenth-century antiquarianism, but much less interested in comparing the present with the past. For instance, on modern Indians, Deslandes provided an unprecedented description of schools of philosophy that we shall quote entirely.

In his history, Deslandes respected the general historical classification: pre-Greek philosophies, Greek and Roman philosophies, Arabic and Scholastic philosophies, Renaissance and modern philosophies. According to him, all ancient philosophies had esotericism as common character, which would have become less strict only within Greek philosophy. 'All the esteem and reputation accorded to Philosophy among Barbarians was the cause of its overload of endless symbols, allegories, enigmas and metaphors. Only priests and members of the royal family had the key; ... All other people were condemned to lay in a degrading and total ignorance' (I, 16–17).[177] All barbaric philosophy was an ambiguous twofold 'Enigmatic philosophy' ('Philosophie énigmatique', ibid.): public, on one side, and private, on the other. Public philosophy was false and its aim was the submission of minds, whilst the private philosophy, i.e. the true wisdom, was reserved to a limited number of people. Among the instances of the social function played by the philosophy of Barbarians, Deslandes quoted the idolatrous worship of the statues representing divinities in the Moghul India (I, 18–19), events that he probably saw with his own eyes before moving to France.

The classification of Barbarians provided by Deslandes follows the most classic model: the four directions of Ephorus, as reported by Strabo (*Geo* I, I). However, Deslandes added that there was little to say about Scythians (North) and Ethiopians (South), and the reason was that in the North it was too cold and in the South too warm: 'The diversity of Climate, of air and food, causes endless diversities in the souls, although they are immaterial' (ibid., I, 35–6).[178] Celts (on the West) were the European ancestors, but the real origin of philosophy was in the East, according to the perennial philosophy tradition. The 'Indies' were 'the cradle of humankind and the common source of Arts and Sciences'[179] (ibid., I, 36). Deslandes quoted the *Runaways* dialogue of Lucianus about the migration of Philosophy from the East to the West (ibid., I, 37) but, perfectly in agreement with Burnet, he stressed that those ancient wise lands were at that time lands of desolation and ignorance (ibid., I, 38). The author, before presenting the paragraphs on Indians – terms used to name the whole of Asians as was typical of the eighteenth century – repeated his expression of respect for their ancient wisdom: 'So far we traversed several ill-fated and sterile lands, where Philosophy could at the most drip a little bit ... The ancient Oriental wisdom was really more remarkable than what we normally think ...'[180] (ibid., I, 79). Actually, these positive words were not a praise of Indian or Chinese people, but, following the wide idea of 'the Indies', of Egyptians and Jews, whose cultural merging created the base for Christianity.

In the *Histoire*, the Chinese are presented as usual, reporting their three sects, Daoism, Buddhism and Confucianism. Confucianism was the leading sect, since it ruled politics and was followed by the emperors, however it was a materialistic philosophy, since it professed a material Heaven (ibid., I, 83–4). Deslandes did not acknowledge the Chinese as atheists, instead he only reported the ancient accusation of Celsus about the atheism of the Chinese and of other barbaric peoples, an accusation rejected by Origen of Alexandria (*Contra Celsus*, VII, 17),[181] who instead argued that for ancient Greeks an atheist was someone who did not worship images of Gods (i.e. statues). Strangely enough, Deslandes, like Burnet, did not mention the contemporary debate over Chinese pantheism and atheism (i.e. 'rites controversy'). According to him, the Chinese were materialistic thinkers, but not atheists. Deslandes even wrote that they had all arts and sciences, thus he agreed with Vossius, who was quoted in a lateral note (see §1.4.). It is completely inconsistent in this description of Chinese civilization the use of the Dominican sources against Jesuits, which discredited China as materialistic, together with Vossius' extreme appreciation. Here, Deslandes completely revealed his inaccurate use of sources as Brucker suggested in his *Historia critica*, because – as it should be clear having investigated the 'rites controversy' (§2.1.) – these two opposing viewpoints could not be composed so easily.

Following Vossius, Deslandes identified the enduring language as the cultural key point of Chinese civilization:

> What distinguishes China from the European countries is the use of the same language since the beginning of the Monarchy and their lack of interest in learning foreign ones. This sort of immobility of language allowed the Chinese to be aware of their origins, to understand their ancient authors and to perpetrate thought and attitudes that belonged only to them. Whilst other nations in less than three centuries had seen the change of their languages without possible solution.
>
> ibid. I, 87–8[182]

If the use of the same languages for millennia was the reason of Chinese imperial stability, the second point that deserved some attention, according to the French thinker, was their art of silk. It is unexpected to find silk and weaving mentioned in a 'History of Philosophy', but, as we said, Deslandes's understanding of philosophy is close to our modern concept of 'culture' and inherited antiquarian interests. He wrote an entire paragraph on weaving, where he reported several technical insights on the art of producing silk and working it out, suggesting that this art was one of the dominant aspects of Chinese culture. The 'Historire de l'Esprit' was, for Deslandes, the history of human intelligence and talent, in all its aspects. Deslandes represented the interest of Enlightenment in technical skills, moral aptitudes and achievements of the genius of men, as afterwards it would be evident in several articles of the *Encyclopédie*.

Before the chapter on Indians, Deslandes decided to leap over and presented Phoenicians. The reason for this displacement was obviously not geographical or due to a certain affinity, but instead he wanted to suggest a complete contrast between these civilizations: the Chinese people lived isolated and they did not travel out of their empire; on the contrary, Phoenicians were open and they navigated far from their homeland. As we have already seen, Deslandes gave great importance to those kinds of sociological arguments. The same sociological attention is turned to the Indians, whose caste system, with its inner injustice, was presented as the main relevant topic:

> How many talents have been annihilated for the injustice of chance, or for the ignorance of the people concerned? How many times the humble and timid merit has been left in such a deep darkness that the merit did not even try to escape.
>
> ibid., I, 95[183]

The second social or anthropological theory regarded the religious practices, of which the Indies were reputed, for Deslandes, the native place in the world:

> It is from Indians, or better from Orientals broadly speaking, that prostrations, genuflections, leaning of head or body, and finally all the exterior expressions of respect and deference, had come from. These expressions slowly came to the West, which is less explicit and less openly expressive.
>
> ibid., I, 98[184]

Indians – or in general the Oriental men – had a natural proclivity for any form of extreme submission and humiliation; their ceremonies were incredibly rich and Deslandes claimed that they taught to all other peoples how to worship and express respect. Europeans learnt from them, but their proud and discrete nature contrasted with these outrageous humiliations.

Whilst in those years the focus was mostly on Chinese or Buddhist atheism, Deslandes suggested the existence of atheism also among Gymnosophists, although he did not mention Bernier and his 'Cabala':

> With regards to Gymnosophists, they had not changed since the farthest ages. Several among them used to make public declarations of atheism and even so they lived wisely and moderately, they fulfilled all their social duties. This sect of atheists still exists and among them there are no forms of exterior religious worship ... But all the others admitted a God that gives life, fills and penetrates the Universe wherever ...
>
> ibid., I, 100[185]

Therefore, thanks to Deslandes, Europeans could learn that in India there were two main beliefs, one atheistic and one pantheistic. The first was the belief of several

Gymnosophists, while the second was the belief of the other Indians. Furthermore, common people were distracted from the one God by means of several deities, in accordance with the esoteric character of Barbarian philosophy claimed by Deslandes. The Indian wise man aimed at searching truth, but whereas he had the great chance to find it, he could teach his findings only to the few superior men belonging to his group. Strangely, in his presentation of atheism and pantheism in India, Deslandes did not quote Bayle and the current equivalence of pantheism, or Spinozism, with atheism. Although in the 1730s sentiments might have changed, we know that Bayle still played a central role in Brucker's *Historia critica* and in the *Encyclopédie*, thus Deslandes deliberately neglected the author of *Dictionnaire*. Since the Frenchman disagreed with the historical approach of conciliation – which, for him, forces thinkers from different contexts to agree with one another – it is likely that he preferred not to use 'Spinozism' as a transcultural concept, while 'atheism' entailed a universal meaning in itself.

Besides this neglect of the 'Oriental Spinozism', Deslandes provided a very interesting and original topic in his *Histoire*, regarding the Indian schools of philosophy, which he listed for the first time in a work devoted to the history of philosophy, and likely in all European literature. Deslandes's source should be a manuscript of 'Dom Franç. Rocio Arch. De Cranganor', as we can read in a side note two pages before (ibid., I, 101). The author is almost undoubtedly Francisco Roz, the first archbishop of Cranganore – nowadays Kodangullar – seat of the diocese of Angamale from 1608, who authored a manuscript on Nestorians in India around 1585–7.[186] Deslandes reported:

> The sciences [schools] cultivated by these Brachmans and on which they succeeded thanks to their force and intelligence, should be eighteen.
>
> The first is a kind of Grammar, which contains the principles and bases of *Grandham*, namely the privileged language they use to write and to speak to each other. The other sciences are listed in a very precise sequence, as they were steps from the simplest to the hardest, reaching what is arduous and difficult. At the end, the last school is named *Veddata* o *Vendata*, which means the end, the conclusion of all things. That is a kind of Metaphysics and Theology that Brachmans achieved not by means of investigation, but instead through a complete and fast submission. There are few innovators among them, because they lie in the constraining conviction that nobody can add something to what was thought by Ancestors: in that way they do not move forward and they improve nothing. Their souls stay immobile and never struggle or try to do something that may cause the risk to get wrong.
>
> ibid., I, 102–3[187]

The Indian schools of philosophy (*darśana* in Sanskrit) were eighteen, probably according to Roz, and not only one, as it could seem from the ancient Greek sources. The only two 'sciences' mentioned by name are: the first, that of Grammar, and the last one, which is evidently the Vedānta. Both schools were described shortly but correctly, the first was the very ancient spiritual and philosophical study of the word, which is related to the sound and meaning of the word itself. '*Grandham*', should refer to the 'Grantha alphabet' used by Tamil speakers[188] to write Sanskrit, thus it clearly refers to the same Vedic or ancient Sanskrit, namely the language of the *Veda*. Deslandes reported correctly that Vedānta, as the same name itself denotes, was the end of the *Veda*, thus the end of all things. The list of schools was presented according to the typical Advaita Vadānta doxographies, where schools were inserted in a precise order of importance and not according to chronology, as within western histories. The thinkers of Advaita Vedānta used to place their school at the top of all philosophies, as the fulfilment of the whole Indian thought. Very likely, the source used by Deslandes or Roz was the *Prasthānabheda* by Madhusūdana Sarasvatī (*c.* 1540-1640).[189] Since Madhusūdana was a contemporary of Roz, he was born in Bengal and he lived in Varanasi, while the archbishop preached in South India, such a widespread diffusion of the doxography into the whole of India raises some doubts. However, in support to this textual identification there is the use by Deslandes of the word 'Sciences', instead of 'Philosophies', which reflects Madhusūdana's use of '*vidyā*', namely 'science', instead of '*darśana*' ('school of philosophy' or 'vision'), which was really more common in Indian doxographies. Moreover, the *Prasthānabheda* lists eighteen schools as did Deslandes, while most of the Indian doxographies listed six schools or, at the most, fourteen. Whether the source behind Deslandes's unprecedented list of schools is Madhusūdana, this would imply an influence of Vedānta in westerners' understanding of India already in the seventeenth and eighteenth centuries, thus, before the early studies of the orientalist scholars and of the nineteenth-century philosophers such as Arthur Schopenhauer and Paul Deussen, who are proved to be highly indebted to this Indian school of thought.[190]

In addition to the order of the eighteen Indian schools of philosophy, Deslandes's stress on the lack of freedom and originality in Indian philosophy recalls our attention. He argued that authority had to be respected and what has been said in the past (i.e. in the *Veda*) must be repeated. Nowadays, we know that this presentation of Indian philosophical method was correct, however, that did not mean that there was no room for freedom, because the originality of each Indian thinker was expressed within tradition, as reinterpretation (often radical) of the tradition itself. There was a second possibility for 'unorthodox' philosophers, that was to place themselves out of tradition (i.e. *Veda* and rites), as Buddhists or Jaina had done. The submission to authority was real, but not blind. Anyway, besides this critical description influenced by his own theory of the Barbarian 'enigmatic Philosophy', Deslandes provided the first description of at least two Indian schools, which were presented as two among many. We must suggest that this pioneering philosophical approach of Deslandes, stayed completely unquoted and unimproved for several decades, until the first orientalist studies at the end of the eighteenth century.

Deslandes's history of philosophy and his criticism raised against Asiatic thought need to be contextualized within his general pessimistic view of human nature. At the end of the first book, he wrote a few pages providing his negative insights on human historical aptitudes, which fully disclosed a clear racist viewpoint:

> Africa reveals only monsters, hideous creatures, which are so degraded to have a lower instinct than that of animals. America is almost the same everywhere, this wide and unfortunate land [is] a cemetery of several murdered men, their throat slit, because [victims] of betrayal and inconceivable cruelty or because they satisfy

our [of Europeans] greed; and this horrible traffic [of humans] continues. The Australian lands have habitants whose human aspect is almost unintelligible and what of their nature still remains is deplorable. Asia seems somewhere politer. But still, what a culture! What a great difference between what [this culture] was and what it is now! How such a great barbarity has succeeded to such a great politeness? How have briers and thorns covered those formerly flowering gardens? Not to speak of Europe. What a mass of habits, systems [of thought], tastes, passions, laws, and customs can be found scattered here? We think differently in each country, and instead of tolerating mutually all these endless variety of opinions and instead of behaving gently, we harass and murder [each other] in cold blood.

ibid., I, 270–1[191]

According to Deslandes, Africa, America and Australia were barbarian countries, populated only by subhuman individuals. About Asia he suggested that, whilst in a far past Asians had been refined and learned men, in his age they were barbarians. They had completely lost their ancient pure and polite nature. This claim brings to mind Burnet and his Asian 'wretched barbarity'. Both authors accepted ancient Asians as philosophers, but they described modern Asians as degraded and subhuman. However, whilst the Anglican Burnet acknowledged (Protestant) Europe as the only polite and advanced land, thanks to the Christian Revelation and Reformation, Deslandes was not so optimistic about Europe. European states during the eighteenth century were in war one against the others; a secular religious intolerance between Protestants and Catholics was dominant and every cultural difference was a reason for violence. The inner violence and the deep intolerance described by Voltaire too, as by many Enlightened authors, was disconsolately observed and described by Deslandes, who accused the diffused human useless pride as the cause for all this worldwide pain (ibid., I, 276).

The *Historie de la philosophie* is not only the first instance of the French historiography, but also the first French critical history, and this history discloses several aspects close to the Enlightenment. For instance, the understanding of the word 'philosophy' in its widest meaning opened the investigation to new issues as sociology, politics, technology and psychology, since the 'phenomenon philosophy', in order to be correctly understood, needed to be critically investigated within its complete context. The historiography of philosophy, according to Deslandes, should not be confused with erudition, doxography or polyhistory. The historian of philosophy had to look for global reasons. Actually, Deslandes's historiographical attitude did not share the rigour of German Eclecticism, but it reveals the peculiarity of the French Enlightenment, which was displayed particularly in the heterogeneous articles of the *Encyclopédie*, of which also this history of Deslandes was a relevant source[192] together with Bayle and Brucker.

Conclusions of the second chapter

Whereas in the first chapter we came to terms with the histories of philosophy whose historical framework was the biblical chronology of patriarchs, and where modern

Asians were described as barbarians, in the second chapter the investigation came out of this frame. We investigated the growing and shaping of the 'doctrina Orientalis', a global definition of all the philosophy of Asia as atheistic, immanentist and Spinozistic. This vision arose among Jesuit missionaries from the description of Buddhism, the trans-Asiatic sect which was described as atheistic – since Matteo Ricci – and whose 'deplorable history' was enriched in the seventeenth-century accounts. The atheism of Buddhism was connected with Indian thought, from where this sect had already disappeared, and thanks to Kircher this sect became the emblem of the atheism of the whole heathen civilizations from Egypt to Japan. At the same time, the traveller Bernier described Indian and Persian thought as a pure immanentism and thanks to his writings and to the coeval description of China by Couplet – who followed Ricci's method – Asia began to be acknowledged as the land of Spinozism. To this description of the Asiatic Spinozism, Bernier added, before his death, the image of an 'Oriental Quietism', which was another relevant topic of late-seventeenth-century France.

Bayle made use of this 'Oriental Spinozism' in order to prove, on one side, the unreliability of the theory of the 'universal consent' and, on the other side, the morality of atheists. The Frenchman contrasted the missionary accounts about Chinese pure ethics and tolerance with the description of atheists as immoral and subhuman persons. With Bayle, China became 'Spinozistic', but in a positive sense, since, according to him, atheism was the natural state of human mind. Therefore, the Chinese were not opposed to the reasonability of Christian faith, but instead they represented the effective rational thinkers far from dogmatism. This problematic theory of Bayle was discussed by many authors, among which the most relevant was Buddeus, a German Eclectic theologian who accepted Bayle's description of an 'Oriental Spinozism', but who acknowledged 'Spinozism' in his negative philosophical meaning.

Whether the description of the Chinese as atheists was accepted and used by Bayle on behalf of his theory of moral atheism, Leibniz refused this description and claimed the original monotheism of the Chinese as argued by Ricci himself. Therefore, Leibniz was the last great perennialist philosopher and the strongest advocate of the Jesuit accommodationism. As we shall see in the last chapter, Christian Wolff acknowledged the rational morality of Chinese as Bayle did, and also their 'natural' monotheism following his master and friend Leibniz. But the historical universalism of Leibniz, which was the last relevant instance of perennial philosophy, faded together with the decrease of the influence of the Jesuit order. Among the historians of philosophy, the most strenuous opponents of Leibniz and Wolff had been the German Eclectics, whose pretended scientific definition of the philosophical field hid a clear apologetic aim, namely the identification and criticism of historical atheism and Christian heresies through the philosophical investigation.

On the contrary, Deslandes, although he provided a very incoherent history of philosophy, stood for the new historiographic model of the French Enlightenment. The wide interests of his historical investigation revealed the growing of new disciplines within the humanities, such as ethnology, anthropology and sociology. Deslandes's concept of history of philosophy was not scientifically grounded and aimed at describing the complex and often conflicting steps of the universal 'Historire de l'Esprit'. Besides this wide range of interests, he provided an unprecedented and correct description of the Indian schools of philosophy, although he argued the lack of freedom of those thinkers, since they could but repeat their tradition within their esoteric sect. Brucker disapproved Deslandes's history, because of the incoherent use of sources made by the French author and for his all-embracing concept of philosophy. Although our investigation shall finish with German Eclecticism and, particularly, with Brucker, Deslandes's history is consistent with our investigation for two reasons: he represented the first historiographical instance of the French Enlightenment, which was very different from the German Enlightenment, and together with Bayle and Brucker he was one of the most important sources of the philosophical entries of the *Encyclopédie*. Furthermore, to some extent, his critiques of the Indian social system could remind of some issues of Montesquieu's 'Oriental despotism', and he advanced the crisis of 'Sinophilia' which took place in the 1760s to 1770s.

3

The Complete Exclusion of Asians from Philosophy

'A chaque nouvelle formation d'esprit un pas en arrière se fait donc qui, par dessus la génération éminemment porteuse de changement, relie les cerveaux les plus malléables aux plus cristallisés.'

Marc Bloch, *Apologie pour l'histoire ou métier d'historien*, 12

3.0 Introduction

In this last chapter, we shall present the most relevant historians of philosophy that refused the perennialist historiographical model and placed the non-Greek civilizations out of the 'history of philosophy'. These 'exclusivist' historians of philosophy were various and they did not belong to one coherent group. On one side, as we argued presenting Burnet, there were the English historians, who were often not interested in Oriental philosophy. They simply neglected the insertion of India and China into their histories, without providing any reason for this exclusion. On the other side, several historians of philosophy explicitly refused this insertion; they rejected the arguments of the divine origin of wisdom and of the 'prisca theologia', because these questions did not concern philosophy and, furthermore, the Neoplatonic histories were reputed as completely unreliable. According to those thinkers, philosophy originated in Greece and not in the wide Orient. As Schmidt-Biggemann said efficaciously: 'It follows that the claimed monopoly of the Philosophia perennis not only vacillated, but even two kinds of history of Philosophy started to take shape, one that was oriented towards the Philosophia perennis and the other that followed the Greek guidelines of Diogenes Laërtius'.[1] Here we are concerned clearly with the second historical paradigm which followed Diogenes Laërtius.

As we investigated in the previous chapters, the inclusion of Asian civilizations among the philosophical people had several different reasons and the same is true for their exclusion. Broadly speaking, behind the exclusion there was not primarily a specific reason against a civilization, but rather a global conception of philosophy, which refused the Neoplatonic syncretic religious interpretation of philosophy. However, whilst a modern philosopher such as Bayle (except in politics) did not refuse the idea of an Oriental atheism and even of an Oriental Spinozism, those philosophers limited the spreading of philosophy to an ethnic area, very narrow and little, excluding all non-Greek civilizations. They agreed with Diogenes Laërtius' history and supported the idea of the ancient philosophy as equivalent to the Greek thought. All other civilizations could have created practical techniques for everyday life and religious beliefs, but not philosophy, which is different from all other outcomes of human thought.

Since Thomasius, the German Eclectic school opened a new way in the historiography of philosophy. According to this school, a good history of philosophy should first answer the question: what is philosophy? Thus a rigorous definition of the philosophical field was the first step. Philosophy was not religion and was not whatever outcome of the human thought. Philosophy was an investigative and demonstrative discipline able to analyse and understand reality by means of strict logical arguments, deductions and reasons. Consequently, although philosophy was different from religion, it could be of great help for religion in order to detect and defeat heresies and idolatries. Evidently, this definition was very far from the quest for divine wisdom, which was the aim of Neoplatonic and Renaissance thinkers. Philosophy was not the golden way to achieve some knowledge of God's nature – as for perennialists – but rather was a great argumentative and investigative instrument in order to detect human mistakes.

This idea of a delimited philosophical field and of the origin of philosophy out of Greece was quite diffused; also several French philosophers already shared the same negative opinions about barbarian thought. However, nobody was more explicit and resolute than Heumann, a distinguished follower of Thomasius's eclecticism. He openly rejected the historiographical method of perennial philosophy (Neoplatonism) and provided a definition of philosophy as an argumentative science which was opposed to the dogmatic restrictions of religion. According to him, Barbarian philosophers were clergymen who aimed at defending their personal interests, instead of being thinkers concerned with truth. The Greek historians called them philosophers, but Greeks evidently misunderstood their social role, which was religious and opposed to the freethinking of true philosophers. Heumann, reviewing a text of the aforementioned anti-Jesuit Renaudot, also devoted a long article to contrast the mythization of China. While in order to exclude the ancient Barbarian civilizations a new definition of philosophy was necessary, about the Chinese Heumann preferred to prove their irrelevance and to demolish their reputation of being a moral, ancient and meritocratic people. Brucker, who published the most complete, detailed and renowned history of philosophy ever written up to his time, more or less faithfully followed Heumann. His history was openly anti-Neoplatonic, it contested their perennial method and shaped the ultimate image of the Oriental thinker: traditionalist, unable to provide arguments and reasons, and with a low morality when not completely lacking ethical principles. That was the case of all ancient barbarians and of all modern Asians, particularly the Indians and Chinese.

As a result, whilst for perennialists all ancient civilizations were in continuous contact and contamination, those authors started the mythization and isolation of Greek society, considering this ancient culture as the origin of all forms of advanced civilization. Greece became the birthplace of morality, laity, justice, freedom, logical thinking and even beauty. Oriental countries were obviously at the other extreme, being religious, unjust, inequitable, irrational and full of horrible statues. The Barbarian countries had despotic regimes, because their rulers were heavily influenced by powerful clergymen, who did not share wisdom out of their own caste, but rather they subjugated all the other people in their own favour.

3.1 The Grecization of philosophy

Before the German Eclectic historians, it is necessary to mention that several French philosophers, as somehow the aforementioned Deslandes himself, also did not agree with the positive use of the Orient of several French thinkers. These philosophers were not a few anti-Jesuits or anti-atheistic (Spinozistic) orthodox thinkers, but rather belonged to very different cultural environments. It is true that from the late seventeenth century across most of the eighteenth century, French society lived an unbelievable 'Sinophilia',[2] a sort of obsession for Chinese arts and thought shared by Isaac Vossius, Gottfried W. Leibniz, Voltaire and Nicolas Fréret,[3] to name only a very few of them.[4] However, this 'Sinophilia' was not a coherent and univocal social movement and it did not touch all French thinkers. For instance, within the 'Querelle des Anciens et des Modernes' (Quarrel of the Ancients and the Moderns) at the France Academy,[5] authors of histories of philosophy of both opposing sides suggested the inconsistency of the thought of Barbarians. In short, the 'ancients' argued that the Greek literary art was unequalled and should be the model for modern writers. On the other side, the 'moderns' claimed that contemporary authors should have the chance to create new forms of art. This quarrel was really more than a literary dispute, because it involved political, scientific and moral aspects that surpass our investigation. What we need to know is only that on both sides the Barbarian philosophy was disregarded, if not completely refused. The reasons were obviously different: according to the 'ancients' Greek literature was superior to any kind of literature, while the 'moderns' claimed that all ancient forms of thought were inferior to the modern outcomes.

Rapin René (1621–87) and Coste Pierre were two relevant actors of the Quarrel, Rapin was for the 'ancients' whilst Coste was for the 'moderns'. Rapin was a Jesuit theologian and poet, his poems were written following the bucolic genre and so acclaimed that he was even named 'the second Theocritus', namely the ancient father of Greek bucolic poetry. He was a determined opponent of the libertines and radical philosophers. He proposed his theory of philosophy in both *Les comparaisons*[6] and in *Les Réflexions sur la philosophie ancienne et moderne*.[7] The first work brings to mind the comparisons between ancient philosophers of the Renaissance (who usually compared Plato and Aristotle), while the second title is evidently inserted in the 'querelle' (quarrel). In *Les Réflexions* the history of philosophy began with Greek sects and ended with a global refusal of all modern philosophy, from Humanist philosophers to his contemporaries.[8] In *La comparaison de Platon et Aristote* he was more explicit regarding the uniqueness of Greek philosophy: 'we all agree that the Greeks were the first philosophers of the world. That does not mean that the other Nations [civilizations], which came before, had no knowledge of parts of Philosophy, and that according to the nature and state of their countries, the necessity – which is the first master of all sciences – did not teach them but what was related to their needs' (*Oeuvres*, I, 283).[9] For the Egyptians geometry was necessary, for the Assyrians and the Chaldeans astronomy, for the Phoenicians sailing orientation, for the Jews religious wisdom. However, 'All these peoples knew those things only through experience and they did not reduce the knowledge they received to rules' (ibid., 284).[10] Therefore, all ancient civilizations learned only through experience, since that knowledge was necessary and not elaborated through a further rational deduction. Greeks were the first able to overcome necessity and to reach a mature and elaborated wisdom.

Coste Pierre (1668–1747) was a Protestant thinker, who was obliged to leave France when still young because of the revocation of the Edict of Nantes (1685). He lived for several years in the Netherlands where he met Bayle and in 1697 moved to England, where he knew Locke and translated a few writings of the English philosopher. Thanks to Locke himself, he became the tutor of the young Lord Shaftesbury and of the Duke of Buckingham. His 'Discours sur la Philosophie'[11] is a text written during his Dutch years directly to contrast Rapin's *Réflexions*, as a historiographical expression of the modernist side. According to Coste, the most relevant philosophers were the modern ones, such as Galilei and Descartes, because they made philosophy free from the authority of the ancient philosophers, who were praised in medieval times. He completely refused the perennialist model and even ridiculed it: 'Everybody claims that Philosophy came out of the Orientals, however, the Orientals do not agree on who is the first creator of this Science'[12] (ibid., 3). Are Chaldeans or Egyptians the fathers of Philosophy? Because that dispute was impossible to compose: 'No matter [who the creators are], this first Philosophy was so muddled, that it barely deserves that title. We should correctly call it *Superstitious Theology* ...'[13] (ibid.). Before the Greeks, there was only a confused 'Théologie superstitieuse', which cannot be properly named philosophy. However, as he was on the side of moderns, Coste even criticized Greek philosophers, praising only the role of modern philosophers who created the prerequisite for real freedom and for effective sciences.

As a matter of fact, those two philosophers, although opposed within the 'Quarrel of the Ancients and the Moderns', shared the same refusal of Oriental philosophy. That proves that the 'inclusivist' side and the 'exclusivist' side were both heterogeneous and hence difficult to list when we are grounded on the classification related to their historiographic vision of western philosophy instead of their vision of Barbarian thought (that's what happens with the *Models of the History of Philosophy*). Besides this problem of categorization, the effective description of the Oriental thought as inconsistent with philosophy and, consequently, inferior to the Greek thought – the only truly philosophical – took place within German philosophy, among the disciples of Christian Thomasius, where the real rigorous 'historia critica' was born.

3.2 German Eclecticism and Christian Wolff

Whereas Bayle is acknowledged as the father of French philosophical criticism, in German countries the most important historical school of philosophical historiography was that of Halle, started by the eclectic Christian Thomasius (1655–1728). He was a philosopher and a jurist controversist, he challenged the strict Protestant orthodoxy on several issues, as in the use of Latin at University (instead Thomasius used German), the pedantism of Aristotelians (Scholasticism), the prohibition of mixed marriage between Lutherans and Calvinists, the historical biblical authority, the Ecclesiastical law (opposed to the natural one following Grotius and Puffendorf). He was an anti-dogmatic thinker, close to several pietists' opinions (e.g. he was a friend of the pietistic theologian August Hermann Francke), but he disapproved the violent tones of the latter. Certainly, he was not a 'radical thinker' and he was very far from the philosophy of Leibniz and Wolff. Thomasius was an eclectic thinker and thanks to the prestige he garnered at the University of Halle, he deeply influenced the traits of German Enlightenment, more moderate and rigorous than the French or Dutch. Thomasius was an advocate of common sense and moderation, which – for him – were the only ways to connect divine wisdom and human sciences on a common ground.[14]

In 1688 Thomasius published his *Introductio ad Philosophiam Aulicam, seu Linae Primae libri de Prudentia cogitandi et ratiocinandi*, a programmatic explanation of his eclectic and moderate philosophy as the title itself says: 'Prudence in thinking and considering'. The book was re-edited and published in 1702.[15] The first chapter of the *Introductio* is a short history of philosophy entitled 'Philosophorum sectis'. It is an overview of all sects, ancient and modern, where the use of the word sect is somehow negative, because the only effective and rational sect is that of eclecticism, which is not properly a sect. As he stated at the end of the chapter: 'To whom objects that it is extremely difficult to be eclectic, I reply that (1) it is so for indolent and dumb people, (2) sectarianism is more laborious, because the eclectic philosophical task deserves free men, while the sectarian [philosophy] deserves asses'[16] (I, 44). Besides the harsh words used in this paragraph, Thomasius was a moderate thinker and we should not expect from him a radical secular historiographic renewal of philosophy, but instead a systematic appraisal of the eclectic method of philosophy in all ages.

The 'Philosophorum sectis' is a very short history, it displayed all the sects in around forty pages and 98 paragraphs. At first antediluvian and post-diluvian periods are presented, in the latter part barbaric and Greek philosophies are inserted. Among the barbaric ones there are only the most classic civilizations of the Near East, such as Chaldeans, Assyrians, Egyptians, Phoenicians, Persians and Indians. The Chinese are completely absent and that is surprising if we compare it with the current French debate over China. Regarding Indians only the classical sources are quoted, mostly Strabo. The whole barbaric philosophy is presented in three paragraphs of around half a page. Evidently Thomasius's interest in non-Greek philosophy was completely lacking.

In July 1721, Christian Wolff (1679–1754), in some issues (among which was China) a follower of Leibniz, delivered a public lecture (i.e. *Oratio de Sinarum Philosophia practica*) on Confucian philosophy,[17] arguing that Chinese morality was more natural and even more rational than the revealed ethics of Christian religion. He openly said gaining the conclusion of his speech: 'Here, Gentlemen, is the exposition of the principles of the wisdom of the ancient Chinese. They are in accord with my own principles, as I have frequently said publicly elsewhere[18] and as I hope to have shown convincingly to this illustrious assembly.'[19] Being that Wolff was a famous and esteemed professor, the scandal for this claim was dramatic and his pietist opponents denounced him for being Spinozist and thus atheist, according to the 'Chinese Spinozism' theory already diffused by Bayle. In 1723, Wolff was ousted from his chair at the University of Halle by King Frederick William I. He then moved to the University of Marburg, where he became probably the most renowned German philosopher of his age. Thomasius did not play a direct role in the expulsion of Wolff, being, as we said, close to the pietists but against their strict and violent acts. However, Thomasius blamed Wolff's appraisal of Confucian philosophy, calling the Wolffians 'Konfuzianer'[20] (Confucians), fully aware of the equivalence between Confucianism and Spinozism, thus, accusing more or less covertly Wolff of supporting atheism and pantheism.

It is also worth noting that the *Oratio* had a very complicated editorial history, which reveals the relevance of Confucianism within the European debate of the time. At first, Wolff decided not to publish this controversial text, which caused him so many troubles, but a first edition appeared in Rome in 1722, published by someone in the Catholic circle of the Office of the Inquisition (according to Wolff himself) [21] and this edition was reprinted by the Jesuits in 1725 in Trévoux. He disowned this edition, but by now he was forced to publish his own edition in January 1726 with several added notes. In February 1726, his pietist opponent Joachim Lange also published an allegedly more correct edition of the discourse with his own critical notes, where the atheism of Wolff was openly claimed.[22] Already in 1724, thus before the effective edition of the *Oratio*, Georg Bernhard Bilfinger, a former student of Wolff at Halle, wrote a monograph on behalf of the moral Sinophilia of his professor against pietists and Eclectists.[23] The debate continued and Wolff did not leave the field and in 1730 delivered the discourse *De rege philosophante et philosopho regnante* published the next year,[24] which was translated into English by Santhoroc in 1750. In this discourse Wolff not only stressed again his great commitment to Chinese civilization, but also depicted the Chinese political system as the realization of the Platonic Republic, rejoining through this claim several controversial philosophers such as Isaac Vossius and Bayle himself, together with their sources, namely the Jesuits. As Donald Lach points out, almost every writing of Wolff made at least some reference to China and brought to mind the similarities between Confucianism and his own moral thought. We can summarize that Wolff really connected the moral universalism of Leibniz coherently – without the ecumenical aim of the latter – with the French libertine debate on Scepticism and on ethics as an experimental issue. Clearly, Wolff's aim was not to defend an alleged 'Chinese philosopher', but instead to prove the universalism of his rational metaphysical and moral system (practical philosophy) against the theological theories of pietists. While a morality which descended from theology and religion was connected to a specific civilization, a morality which descended only from reason (deduction from common experiences and mathematical method) was universal and, this was Wolff's claim, it had already a great course in China.

In 1721, the same year of Wolff's delivering of the *Oratio* at the University of Halle, Johann Georg Walch (1693-1775), one of the most renowned disciples of Thomasius, wrote the *Historia artis logicae*.²⁵ This writing was one of the first comprehensive histories of logic, where the author refused resolutely to acknowledge any form of logic before the Greeks. The first book, after a complete bibliographical survey, is 'De origine artis logicae', which is divided into two chapters: 1. 'De falsa illius origine', 2. 'De vera illius origine et prima aetate'. Obviously, the 'false origin' was the divine or Adamitic origin of logic, because God and Adam had a clear and direct comprehension of truth, not requiring an art of logic. Therefore, logic was not a seed of the divine knowledge as claimed by the perennialists, and consequently there was not a spread of logic in ancient times. In the second chapter, Barbarians were quoted, and evidently their philosophy was presented as less sophisticated than that of the Greek: 'Simple [Simplex] was the manner of doing philosophy among them...'²⁶ (ibid., I, 495). Moreover, the Barbarian civilizations quoted were only from the classical list, without any mention of the Chinese, Japanese or Americans. We can deduce that if wisdom could be even a common ground of all civilizations, the same was not true for logic, which was without doubt only a Greek art. Walch specified that Arabs had learnt logic from the ancient Greek texts and had brought it back to Europe at the end of the Middle Ages. Consequently, all developments of this art belonged either to the ancient Greeks or to the modern Europeans, with the relevant Arab mediation. The philosophies of the Barbarians, both ancients and contemporaries, were 'simple' and the art of logic did not take root among them. In this history by Walch, the Asians were still listed among ancient Barbarians – although restricted to Indians and Persians – thus they were not yet formally rejected out of the History of Philosophy, but they were already out of one of the most important philosophical fields, namely Logic.

To stay in the German-speaking countries, the criticism against Oriental philosophy was not only related to logic, as in Walch, but also related to morality. We have already presented Buddeus, who dealt with the Oriental Spinozism – according to the *Dictionnaire* – not sharing Bayle's 'sympathy' for Spinozism. He was followed by Nikolaus Hieronymus Gundling (1671–1729), another of Thomasius's disciples, who was a professor at Halle University. In his *Historiae Philosophiae Moralis* (1706), he described Confucians and Indians as atheists, quoting Buddeus, Arnauld and Bernier (using Bayle's same quote in the entry 'Spinoza').

As a result, the hostility of the Eclectics towards Wolff and Bilfinger – due to their Sinophilia – was implacable and the anti-Confucianism of most German philosophers was really well known around Europe if Diderot in his article on the 'Philosophy of Chinese' wrote: 'It is true that Buddeus, Thomasius, Gundling, Heumann and other writers, whose Enlightened opinions are relevant, do not positively describe the Chinese...'.²⁷ Heumann, for his harsh and refined rejection of the Barbarians and Asians from the history of philosophy, deserves a specific investigation.

3.3 Christoph August Heumann: the theorist of exclusion

As Diderot pointed out, one of the most drastic deniers of the changeable but durable historiographic models of perennial philosophy was Christoph August Heumann (1681–1764), a brilliant German evangelical Lutheran theologian and historian, often undeservedly neglected by scholars. Although unsystematic and fragmentary, his thought was impressively modern and, on some points, he was even ahead of the authors at least two generations after him. Heumann was, with Thomasius, one of the fathers of a new systematic idea of philosophy and history of philosophy and Brucker's *Historia critica philosophiae* was in many aspects the fulfilment of his project.

Heumann was a reformer on the theological side: he supported a tolerant attitude to ease trans-confessional dialogue, at least among Protestants. In order to create a reunification of Protestant Churches, i.e. Lutherans and Calvinists, he proposed to abandon two controversial tenets: the concrete presence of God in the Eucharist and complete predestination. He even claimed that the light of Revelation and reason were fully compatible. For these and many other not perfectly orthodox opinions, Heumann's career at University was really slow and difficult; he was even obliged by orthodox Lutherans to ask for an early retirement.

Heumann's literary production is impressive, he wrote on philology, literature, law and obviously philosophy. He wrote in all literary genres: orations, disputes, academic dissertations, books, text editions, translations and articles for specialized reviews. What concerns the current survey is the review he edited and wrote from 1715 to 1727, namely the *Acta philosophorum, das ist: Gründliche Nachrichten aus der Historia philosophica*.[28] The *Acta philosophorum* was the first review written in German devoted to the History of Philosophy. As Mario Longo[29] reports, the first title of the review thought by the author was *Historia philosophiae philosophica*, thus a philosophical history of philosophy, but Heumann, aware of the enormous task, chose a less pretentious title, which allowed a more fragmentary publication in the form of 'acta' (i.e. reports).

Heumann's contribution is not only to the history of philosophy, since he provided a complete history in fragments or articles, but also to the definition of the precise extension of what is philosophical and what should be kept outside this field. Heumann devoted the long *Einleitung zur Historia Philosophica* (*Introduction to the history of philosophy*) to this relevant task and it was published in seven parts or chapters. Of the seven chapters the first one (I, 1, 63–92)[30] and particularly the fourth (I, 2, 179–236) regard Heumann's exclusion of Barbarians from the philosophical field. In the first chapter he defined philosophy as 'the research and study of the useful truths on solid grounds and principles'[31] (I, 1, 95). Therefore, the field of Philosophy was concerned only with speculation and it left no room for superstitions. Heumann, unlike the other historians, did not call Greeks heathens, thus employing a religious class, but rather 'Naturalisten' (Naturalists), stressing their scientific and empirical qualities. On the contrary, Barbarians were 'heathens', because, according to Heumann, all their thinkers were clergymen, thus they necessarily deserved a religious classification.

The definition of the whole thinkers that were not Greeks as clergymen is the pivotal argument of the second *Einleitung*. In fact, the German historian stated a rigid distinction between philosophy and whatsoever was related to religion (as authority, dogma and superstition). Clergymen could not be philosophers and, according to his (although somewhat unorthodox) belonging to Protestantism, he suspected that their aim was merely to manipulate followers and not to find the final truth. Subsequently,

Heumann excluded 'barbaric thought' from the context of philosophy, claiming that those civilizations could be inserted, at the most, among traditional forms of religious wisdom. He provided some further reasons for that exclusion. The first point is that superstition could never be compatible with philosophy, because history taught us that superstition has always been an instrument of clergymen to subjugate all other men, erasing free and effective thinking. Oriental philosophy 'is written by unworthy clerics [Pfaffe] in paganism and it is called philosophy' (I, 2, 209).[32] 'Pfaffe' is an untranslatable term in English, however it is worth noting that the use of this term by a Protestant such as Heumann entails a very negative meaning. Indeed, 'Pfaffe' was used to name Roman Catholic clergymen, hence it was a strong derogatory term[33] and that is why we added 'unworthy' to the translation.

The exclusion is already clear and the strongest words used by Heumann are as follows:

> I alone claim, grounded on the given reasons, that all these 'Collegia sacerdotum' of Egyptians, Orphics, Eumolpidies [of Eleusi], Samotraces, Magi, Brahmans, Gymnosophists, ... all of them are definitely not School of Wisdom, but rather of Ignorance, in which Superstition is raised to be *forma artis*, in order to succeed in subjugating all the peoples.
>
> I, 2, 210[34]

Heumann claimed that all Oriental thinkers (of the past) were 'sacerdos' or clergymen that propagated only superstition among their popular followers. Their schools did not teach wisdom, but rather the worst form of ignorance, that was superstition. Their aim was only to subjugate men and to keep them under control. All their practices and cults hid the true aim that was the dominance of the religious caste over the others. Heumann added that usually these castes guaranteed the power of a despot that was under their control, subjugated by means of superstition, magic and religious menace.

If clergymen and despotic politics were the heart of barbaric philosophy, this philosophy was clearly an 'anti-philosophy': 'thus the monarchic regime was prejudicial to [the existence] of philosophy in these lands'.[35] Since, if someone disagreed with the religious dogmas and superstitions, he was banned as atheist and often condemned to death. Of course, philosophy, as freethinking, was not only difficult to practise in these countries but even prohibited. Heumann suggested that the only civilization able to (at first) reduce and (afterwards) remove superstition (managed by clergymen) and despotism was ancient Greece, thus, only this land was the spreading place of Philosophy. We see how deeply Heumann erased the *philosophia perennis* model, dramatically reducing the spreading of philosophy. Each civilization that came first – before the Greeks – has only produced superstition and ignorance. All those peoples were evidently not heirs of a 'prisca theologia'. However, as we shall see, Jews were not listed among Barbarians. According to Heumann, they formed a special line, although not properly philosophical, because they were the precursors of the revelation of the Son of God.

In a less relevant article of his *Acta*, the *Eintheilung der Historiae Philosophicae* (*Classification of the history of philosophy*),[36] his critics to the classical perennialist list seem less harsh, but only apparently. In effect, Heumann started the article imposing an interesting dual model in order to divide schools of philosophy: 1. '*simplicem sive empiricam*', 2. '*scientificam sive theoreticam*'. The suggested philosophical focus was clear: what one needs in philosophy is epistemology and logical arguments (or simply logic), as the author learned from the school of Thomasius. The main theoretical ability was the deduction from particular experiences of universal rules or general principles and only this was the task of a mature philosophy.

When the author dealt with history of sects in ancient times he used the old list, dividing the history of philosophy between: 1. '*Graecanica*' and 2. '*Extra-Graecanica*'. However, there was a first change in the classification of the civilizations that were not Greeks, because they were divided between 2.1. '*Hebraeorum*' and 2.2. '*Barbarorum*', taking Jews out of the Barbarian world. Heumann's purpose was clear: he aimed at creating a pure monotheistic line from God to the Jews and after to the Revelation. This line of wisdom was pure from the religious viewpoint, but different from philosophy. Having safeguarded the religious line from which Christianity spread out, the historian explained to readers that among non-Greek civilizations: 'rigorously here we cannot find any philosopher ...'[37] (I, 3, 464). At the most, they could provide acceptable '*intervalla philosophandi*' ('philosophical moments') or '*particulas philosophicas*' ('philosophical pieces'), thus, only very partial philosophical fragments that afterwards had been converted into philosophy by the Greeks.

'Barbaros' (Barbarians) are divided into two geographical areas: 'der Orient', namely 'Asiaticam' and 'Africanam' and 'der Occident' (of the West). Under Asians: 1. Chaldeans, 2. Persians, 3. Indians, 4. Sabians, 5. Phoenicians. Under Africans only two peoples were worth mentioning: Egyptians and Ethiopians. About Egyptians, Heumann conceded that 'they have philosophized empirically a little bit ...'[38] (ibid.). The western barbarians are Romans, Gauls, Germans, Scythians and Thracians. Regarding the Romans, he simply added that the same Plautus considered them as Barbarians. The list of Barbarians complete, Heumann proceeded with the first effective philosophy, that of the Greeks, which before becoming pure and empirical had a phase of fairy tales (myths) and poetries like all the other civilizations. The division of the philosophical phases following the human ages – childhood, youth and adulthood – as used for instance by de Villemandy about the entire history of philosophy (§1.5.), is used here only to categorize Greek schools.[39] The claim was clear: in Greek philosophy the whole potential of ancient philosophy was deployed.

After several paragraphs on Greek and modern philosophy, Heumann wrote the last lines of the *Eintheilung* about the modern 'heyden' (heathens). Those heathens were the Chinese, which were the most renowned Asians among European philosophers, but he also mentioned the Japanese and the Siamese. This mention of the Chinese at the end of the history of philosophy is clearly a trace of the durable influence of Horn, reviewed by Heumann in the same *Acta* (I, 6, 1039–62). However, the German historian added that among those Chinese 'a method ['eine Art'] of Philosophy should be detected that, at the right time, *si per fata licet* [if I shall have the chance], I would investigate further'[40] (I, 3, 472). This further investigation reminds us also of that of Burnet, who wrote an Appendix to present modern Asians. Heumann was even more effective than the Englishman, since he wrote a very long article to harshly contrast the Chinese philosophical mythization of the libertines, the Wolffians and Leibniz himself.

Five years later, in 1720, Heumann fulfilled his task with a very long article of the *Acta* against Chinese philosophy.[41] To be more authoritative he did not provide a text written by him, but rather a translation[42] (or very faithful review) of the 'Remarques' of the *Anciennes relations des Indes et de la Chine*[43] by the French Catholic priest and orientalist Eusèbe Renaudot.[44] We know that afterwards this book has been fully translated into English (London 1733) and into Italian (Bologna 1749), but probably the first translation of the 'Remarques' was this in German provided by Heumann. Renaudot was a declared enemy of Jesuits – and Bayle – and in this book his aim was to use historical arguments to defeat them and their 'accommodation method'. Renaudot elevated the 'rites controversy' to the highest scientific level, moving from the apologetic or anti-apologetic register to the historical one.[45] This was an effective learned answer to the *Confucius Sinarum Philosophus* edited by Couplet, which was itself not written as an apology of Jesuits in China, but instead as the new canonical text of Chinese philosophy (see §2.1.). In effect, Renaudot used two ancient travel accounts by two Muslims to prove the falsity of the 'China myth'. Furthermore, his direct philosophical enemies were neither Jesuits nor Bayle, but instead Isaac Vossius,[46] who was harshly criticized as anti-historical and incompetent. Renaudot stressed that Vossius, although being a renowned thinker, could not speak Chinese and never went to China; on the contrary, those Muslims spoke Chinese and went there for a while, thus they were more reliable as sources.[47] Consequently, all the libertines' mythization of China was without value and lacked historical basis. Moreover, the two ancient Muslims, not being involved in any apologetical controversy, as that of the 'Chinese rites', could even be more effective and objective than the Jesuits themselves.

According to Renaudot, all extolled Chinese scientific knowledge was fictitious or modified (even invented) by Jesuits Missionaries. Heumann wrote:

> There is nothing relevant in Botany not even in Chemistry conceived by the Chinese. And moreover, whether someone finds something [interesting] in their writings, he should figure out whether these books are ancient or reworked and improved by missionaries. The same is true for Chinese astronomical texts.[48]
>
> II, 11, 732–3

Renaudot wrote that the cycle, the base of the Chinese chronological calculi, did not work well because it was 'aussi composé', a definition that Heumann translated even more critically with 'künstlicher Cyclus' ('factitious Cycle'). This argument entailed that Chinese calendars, which had proved the antediluvian antiquity of this civilization since La Peyrère, were completely worthless. As a result, all the erudite debate over the Bible – Septuagint and Vulgate editions – were irrelevant (see §1.4.). More clearly, Heumann wrote that the Chinese method of dating, namely their history, was 'simply a European invention, namely of P. Martini'[49] (II, 11, 741). In that way biblical universalism and historicity were guaranteed, whilst the renowned Chinese *Annals* were qualified as forged chronologies, since the Chinese themselves lacked the basis that was compulsory for the writing of an effective history.

Furthermore, ancient Greeks, Indians and Muslims never mentioned any Chinese philosopher, poet, wise man or scientist, and that testified the insignificance of the Chinese culture among the ancient civilizations.[50] All their rare correct opinions or tenets recalled Greek philosophy, particularly that of Pythagoras, and neither Renaudot nor Heumann reminded the long tradition about the Oriental influences of the Italic philosopher. Whilst almost all ancient western and eastern civilizations mentioned one another – thus, they could be part of a large original *koinè* – the Chinese were excluded. The consequence of this argument, even if not openly declared, was that Chinese could never have been *prisci theologi*, thus, they could not belong to the *philosophia perennis* (if there was one and this is not the case with Heumann).

Renaudot and Heumann, following the former, went deeper in their radical criticism. According to them, Confucius's philosophy was meaningless, since this thinker had clear opinions about nothing, first of all God. But even the ethical and political teachings of the 'Confucius Socrates de la China' – as Le Vayer called him – which had been admired for more than fifty years, were inconsistent and ineffective. Heumann claimed that the rare good Confucian arguments were not originally Chinese, but rather simplification of Persian, Indian or even Greek (again Pythagoras) arguments and the alleged ethical 'golden rule' was a European readjustment (II, 11, 763). However, the strongest criticism they argued about was the Chinese imperial system, which was appraised by libertines – since Isaac Vossius – as an emblem of justice and toleration. Instead Heumann wrote:

> For such a long time, it was suggested that a happy people was that whose rulers are Philosophers or [at least which is] regulated by Philosophers. Therefore, it was said sincerely that if this [happy] country exists, it was the Chinese Empire.[51] Until now those Mandarins, all people well learned and disciples of Confucius – thus philosophers – had ruled [the Empire] for centuries serving as aristocrats in the military arms and in the state apparatus.[52]
>
> II, 11, 767–8

But the morality of this class was a Jesuit invention, because Chinese people and even their thinkers lived immorally, because they were all vile and cowardly men. Moreover, their political system was unjust and it was grounded on the fact that they did not have a real moral code but instead, as Heumann said, only 'Common/popular opinions' ('gemeine Meynungen').[53] All the Chinese moral rules aimed at the stability of the ancestral bonds and not at the improvement of man's conditions. The political thought was weak and inconsistent, since in China there was an unequivocal 'pouvoir despotique' or 'Dispotische Herrschaft'[54] (despotic power or regime). According to Heumann, the alternative to despotism was the power in the hands of strong, brave and reliable men; the example provided by Renaudot are the Tartar kings – Yuan 元 – who conquered China. A good ruler should not be a philosopher, but rather a man with 'practical virtue', not willing to be pleased by a vile and parasitic class of bureaucrats. We see here the construction of a new political paradigm, of which

Heumann was probably one of the first German theorists, in opposition to the Chinese Empire and, we might suggest, to Louis XIV's reign.

If we compare this description of Chinese 'despotism' with a recent investigation into the history of the 'oriental despotism' provided by Rubiés,[55] we might see that the pivotal figures in the shaping of the concept were Giovanni Botero (1544–1617), Jean Bodin (1529/30–96), Jean Chardin (1643–1716), François Bernier (1625–88) and lastly the renowned philosopher of law, Montesquieu (1689–1755). Rubiés suggested that 'the philosophical travellers of the second half of the seventeenth century were using the category of despotism or equivalent formulations rather creatively, not in order to develop a common "European" position, but in order to interpret realities that were empirically diverse ...' (ibid., 156) and that only with Montesquieu a real theoretical debate over despotism arose (ibid., 157). Giovanni Botero and Puffendorf acknowledged Chinese government as despotic, but their concept of despotism was not negative as that of Montesquieu, since they praised the 'absolute monarchy' and they considered the non-European instances as evidence of the political effectiveness of 'despotism'.[56] Therefore, Montesquieu's 'Chinese despotism' is similar to that of Renaudot and Heumann, but very far from the political appraisal of Botero. According to Rubiés, the main source used by Montesquieu on China was the *Description géographique, historique, chronologique, politique, et physique de l'empire de la Chine et de la Tartarie chinoise* by Pierre du Halde published in 1735, thus seventeen years after the book written by Renaudot and translated by Heumann. Actually, we suggest that Renaudot in his anti-Jesuit attack should be acknowledged among the first theorists of 'Chinese despotism' (as we intend it since Montesquieu) and Heumann probably was one of the first philosophers in arguing this thesis in a philosophical work.

Furthermore, turning back to Confucius, Heumann claimed that his philosophical method was unacceptable and poor, since in his dialogues could not be found any real acceptable logical argument, as also the aforementioned Johann Jakob Walch suggested (§3.2.). The same Chinese language was equivocal and rigid, at the opposite side of the rich historical languages, i.e. Hebrew, Phoenician, Greek and Latin. This language, not having equivalence between characters and sounds, did not allow the development of an effective Rhetoric art and a rich Literature. Again Renaudot stressed the total lack of any references to Chinese literary arts in ancient Greek literature and in the same ninth-century Muslims' accounts.[57]

The core meaning of the 'Remarques' by Renaudot and of Heumann's 'translation' is condensed in this sentence:

> Finally, I do not understand how one can make of this Moral and Political [tradition] a great thought, when it lacks Principles, and it expresses itself only by means of Dialogues, without caring about human behaviour and human affections.[58]
>
> II, 11, 768–9; *Ancienne rel.*, 378

In the same volume of the *Acta philosophorum* (II, 7, 144ff), Heumann reviewed the *Historie der Heÿdnischen Morale* by Stolle,[59] who devoted many pages to Chinese and Indian philosophies. Stolle mostly made use of classical sources, but, when quoting the modern ones, he kept an impartial attitude, without taking part in the 'rites controversy' and specifically in the question of Chinese atheism. Obviously, Stolle described in detail those moral philosophies and Heumann, reviewing the sections of his book on Asians, suggested improperly that Stolle openly denied their morality. Heumann wrote that Confucius was an 'irrige Lehrer' ('false master') and that Asiatic 'people did not have Moral Philosophy, although somehow and somewhere they could have even produced one or another correct and useful Dialogue'[60] (II, 7, 146). According to Heumann, and thus not to Stolle, the literary form of Dialogue prevented the connections of effective arguments, thus this genre was not philosophically acceptable.

In substance, Heumann proved all Barbarian civilizations to be out of the philosophical field, for two main reasons: 1. they used the forms of Dialogue, Poetry and Tale, which do not allow a true logical construction of systematic principles or universal concepts, and 2. all their thinkers were clergymen, thus naturally unfaithful and not concerned with truth. We cannot avoid remarking that both reasons were properly speaking assumptions. However, it is true that those assumptions were due not primarily to Heumann himself, but instead to the missionary literature available. Therefore, the exclusion, argued by Heumann and still alive today in many histories of philosophy, was grounded on a complex process of misunderstanding of Asiatic civilizations. Religiousness and lack of logic are the two pillars of the contemporary interpretation of Asian people and Heumann was one of the first, if not the first, philosophical theorist of this interpretation. However, there were not only 'scientific' or textual reasons for that vision of Asia, but even strong apologetic aims that we cannot forget reading the supposed 'scientific' form of Heumann's history. Israel explains this remaining apologetic perspective as follows:

> *Historia philosophica*, held Heumann, summing up the German conservative enlightened eclectic agenda which in substance was that of Buddeus and Brucker too, equips students and the wider public to discern the true character and pedigree of ideas, and their implications, and hence determine whether they are 'good' or 'evil', 'Christian' or 'unChristian', desirable or undesirable, 'corrupt Catholic' or 'upright Protestant'. History of philosophy, he, like they, urged, is a way of defending faith, authority and tradition critically and reasonably without relying on mere authority, indeed freeing the mind from the shackles of 'authorities' while simultaneously opening the door to genuine philosophizing. For those thinkers believed only the modern Eclectics, sifting the full range of what is available with expertise, discernment and a Christian conscience, deserved to be called true 'philosophers'. Here was a crucial ideal in the history of mankind which Heumann deemed part of a wider transformation of modern thought and culture, one which he attributed to the younger Thomasius who, in his eyes, had set out to and succeeded in reforming everything in the world of erudition and thought in the right direction – ideas, criticism, history of philosophy and the education of the general public – and so by means of the incomparable new Eclectic method. Christian Thomasius, he proclaimed, was truly the 'Luther' of philosophy.
>
> Israel, *Enlightenment contested*, 495

Heumann's 'scientific' attitude and his concept of philosophy came out of the Eclectic agenda, which on many aspects coincided with that of the Lutheran philosophy. Among Protestants and particularly in Germany, the issue of religious universalism was not as important as in Catholic countries (i.e. France), because the former more or less strictly believed in predestination. The same 'histoire de l'Esprit' was very different from the Eclectic view, since the latter focused on the definition of philosophers as useful or useless, namely dividing them in eclectics and dogmatists. Oriental thought was described as dogmatic, hence not truly philosophical. According to Bayle[61] and many French authors, Chinese and Indian men were atheistic or Spinozistic thinkers – although providing several different meanings to this assumption – whilst for Heumann saying that they were such would have been to recognise their philosophical consistency and, before his eyes, that was completely unacceptable. In Heumann we cannot detect the fear of the 'Oriental atheistic plague', since according to him the Asiatic thought completely lacked the effective strength to affect European minds, which were by far more refined and capable.

3.4 Friedrich Gentzken: Asians lack morality and theoretics

In 1724, Friedrich Gentzken (1679–1757) published his *Historia Philosophiae* and the same book was inserted the year after in his renowned *Systema philosophiae*,[62] a complex manual dealing with all issues concerned with philosophy: 1. what philosophy is; 2. the history of philosophy; 3. the metaphysics; 4. the logic. He was a professor at the University of Kiel where he studied, but despite not being a direct disciple of Thomasius, he was deeply influenced by the school of Halle in matters of philosophy and historiography. The accuracy, readability and reliability of Gentzken's *Historia philosophiae* made this book become the standard manual of German university students for several decades,[63] because being more devoted to plain explanations than to theoretical analysis, it was perceived as an easy and impartial source. It responded to the historiographical need of a manual for University students, while the complex and refined investigations provided by Thomasius, Buddeus and Heumann were more fragmentary and highly critical, hence not suitable for them.

Gentzken divided the history into three general periods with their specific partitions and this model deserves to be quoted:

1. Aevi veteris
   1.1. Gentium *barbararum*: Jews, Egyptians, Chaldeans, Persians, Indians, Chinese and in a single chapter Phoenician, Thracians, Gauls and Germans
   1.2. Gentium *moratiorum*: 1.2.1. Ancient Greeks; 1.2.2. Romans
2. Aevi medi (very short)
3. Aevi recentis: 3.1. 'De veterum sectarum instauratoribus'; 3.2. 'De novatoribus in Philosophia'; 3.3. 'De sectarum conciliatoribus' (namely, eclecticism)

Apparently Gentzken did not exclude Barbarians, since they were, as usual, inserted in the ancient times, on the opposite side of the Greeks. However, the author instead of using the classical division, namely '*Extra-Graecanica*' and '*Graecanica*', proposed to call them 'Gentium *barbarorum*' and 'Gentium *moratiorum*'. Actually, the innovation introduced was relevant. The people who were not Greeks were Barbarians, thus defined through a hetero-ethnic, nothing strange since we remark who they are opposed to, i.e. 'Gentium *moratiorum*'. Greeks and Romans were 'morati', which means moral, ethical, regulated and educated; 'moratus' seems to us to be used by Gentzken instead of 'civilized'. He did not openly claim that Barbarians were immoral or uncivilized, but it was quite a natural deduction for readers.

This deduction is confirmed when the chapters on Asians are investigated. Indians were described through the usual ancient sources, but with a new focus on two moral aspects: the nakedness of those wise men and the blame of Greeks for their extreme austerity. The nakedness has always been a point of interest for European thinkers, as for Bayle himself, who discussed the topic at length. But to suggest an open blame of Greeks for Indians was not usual among historians. Generally, Greeks were reported as surprised, astonished, maybe shocked but also positively impressed by their bravery and complete detachment from life. On the contrary, Gentzken claimed that Greeks openly disdained their morality:

> And [those Greeks] dissociated themselves from their [of Indians] moral doctrines, because these were not related to social life and friendship habits, but rather to an austere damnation of the body and to the aim of reaching a solitary life devoted to meditation. It is certain that most Greeks felt offended by these doctrines.[64]
>
> ibid., 29–30

Thus we can infer that not only modern Indians – as was usual at least since Heurn – were deplorable but also ancient Indians. In modern as in ancient times, they professed an idolatrous theology along with many unreasonable and despicable opinions (ibid., 30).

In the chapter devoted to the Chinese, Chinese morality is presented, which has as ethical model the life and thought of Confucius. From the first two pages it would seem that the author had a better opinion of the Chinese, but instead Gentzken stressed that their morality was only apparent, since he presented modern Mandarins as people who follow Confucius's teaching only to have 'immunitatis privilegium' (privilege of immunity) and not for the value of his teaching (ibid., 32). Furthermore, modern followers of Confucius had many Spinozistic opinions as has already been suggested by many erudites (ibid., 33). Therefore, although the author accepted to find some good points in Confucius's norms – but never in his followers' ethics – he refused to raise this morality to a superior level:

> The philosophy of Confucius by several people, first of all the Jesuits, has been raised to touch the sky. However, we are undoubtedly obliged to recognise that in theoretical disciplines Europeans exceed by far Chinese. As regards their moral doctrine – which was at first praised – when compared with our [proves to be] markedly inferior, apart from the judge Leibniz, [who said that] regarding the conduct of life, [Chinese] even exceed the Christians themselves.[65]
>
> ibid., 34

Therefore, Leibniz took up the cudgels on the Chinese behalf, but his claims were not grounded on effective reasons, because Chinese morality was minimal and ineffective. Curiously, Gentzken did not mention Wolff and his approval of Chinese morality, probably because a direct attack against his contemporary would suggest an affinity with Pietism, something that since Thomasius the eclectics tried to avoid.

Before presenting Brucker, who provided the most complete confluence of all German Eclectic instances with a few French ones, a minor history of philosophy deserves our attention, even if somewhat briefly. It is the 'Historia philosophica' by Heineccius, that is an introductory chapter to his *Elementa philosophiae rationalis et moralis*.[66] He was a renowned professor of law, but also an esteemed philosopher; he studied at the University of Leipzig and after at the University of Halle, where he attended Thomasius's classes. He was a professor in Franeker (Netherlands), Frankfurt and finally he turned back to Halle, recalled by the King of Prussia himself.[67] The whole of his writings had two complete editions after his death, one in Geneva and one in Naples, which indisputably prove his high reputation around Europe.

According to the philosophical school of Thomasius, Heineccius considered the history of philosophy as an important prerequisite in order to achieve the goal of an effective eclectic philosophical work. Ancient philosophy is classed in two branches, Barbaric and Greek, but the first is also called 'Traditionaria':

> In our eyes it is correct to call the whole barbaric philosophy TRADITIONAL, since the traces of wisdom are willingly accepted by all barbarians, religiously protected and anew they are consigned to the following generations.[68]
>
> ibid., chap. II, §12, 5

This term, and the theory behind it, sounds very similar to the 'perennial philosophy model' about ancient wisdom, however, it is a similarity inferred at first glance. In effect, what Heneiccius argued was that barbarian philosophy was inferior to Greek philosophy, since it was a simple repetition of ancient traces of wisdom – not of the divine wisdom – which were taught within privileged families or classes. The perennialists claimed the ancient wise men to be closer to the divine truth, purer worshipers of the divine wisdom. On the contrary, Heineccius, saying that Barbarians were traditionalists, was suggesting that they were unable to produce new effective thinking and that their thinkers were the worst expression of dogmatism, on the opposite side of eclecticism and freethinking. And we also know that a philosopher very far from German Eclecticism, namely Deslandes, shared the same opinion in his *Histoire critique de la philosophie*, but from a 'proto-sociological' ground (§2.7.).

Regarding the Indians, Heineccius quoted the classic paragraphs by Strabo, but also Bayle (*Dictionnaire*) and Bernier, in order to suggest their pantheism and their theory of 'vacuum' (ibid., chap. II, §31, 13). Regarding the Chinese, he mentioned their claimed morality as described by Leibniz (*Novissima Sinica*) and Couplet, but also the Spinozism of their tenets. It is clear that for the author the chapter on barbaric philosophy was simply a residual and useless part, because true philosophy only started with the Greeks. Effectively, at first the Greeks took few traces of wisdom from the Barbarians, however they were the only people who 'made an accurate use of philosophical reason, [who] followed the leading role of reason, or at least they had the intention to follow it' (ibid., chap. III, §1, 15). Heineccius was perfectly in accordance with Thomasius, Walch, Heumann and, as we shall see, Brucker on the dismissal of Barbarian philosophy. However, this must be clear, this dismissal did not include Jewish thought, which although not being really philosophical, was the starting point of monotheistic religions. In brief, already for German Eclecticism the actual interest in ancient civilizations was mostly related to Jewish wise men and Greek philosophers, the antiquarian interest already faded.

3.5 Jakob Brucker: the unphilosophical nature of ancient Asians' thought

Although Diderot did not mention Brucker among the detractors of Chinese philosophy (§3.2), most probably because the German philosopher was his main source, we shall see that his *Historia critica* was the definitive act of German Eclecticism, thus, the accomplishment of Heumann's exclusion of barbarians from Philosophy.

Jakob Brucker (1696-1770) was Buddeus's student at the University of Jena and thanks to his professor came his extraordinary interest in historiography and philosophy, although Buddeus was a professor of Theology and not of Philosophy. Brucker was a clergyman and a Lutheran minister, at first for twenty years in the little town of Kaufbeuren (1724-44) and after in the bigger town of Augsburg, thus always far from University environments. Being far from University libraries, his literary work, full of quotes from the most complete bibliography available at that time, is even more extraordinary. Although in a peripheral position, he was a member of many renowned Academies around Europe and he even refused to become a professor of theology at the prestigious University of Halle when invited by the king of Prussia, Frederick II himself. He was said to prefer the tranquillity of his studies and of his parish church. In short, he was the effective emblem of the most moderate side of German Eclecticism, both in philosophy and in theology, never acting as a Lutheran controversialist.[69]

Brucker's contribution to the philosophical debate of the first half of the eighteenth century is remarkable, he wrote books and articles on the history of philosophy, history of politics, literature, education, theology and pastoral arguments. He wrote both in Latin and in German, as almost all German Eclectics did, reaching a large German and international audience. The most important books he wrote about the history of philosophy are certainly the *Kurtze Fragen*[70] (1731) and the widespread *Historia critica philosophiae*[71] (1742-4). In a few years the *Historia* became the reference history for the erudites of all Europe, as was the case of Diderot, who had this book as the main source for his philosophical entries of the *Encyclopédie*, together with Bayle and Deslandes.[72] In both books the Chinese and Indians are discussed at length, but we shall focus only on the *Historia critica philosphiae*, because it was the most complete achievement of Brucker's reflection and because of its larger impact on the historical discipline being written in Latin, still the European lingua franca.

After Heumann, the question of 'what is philosophy or philosophical' became unavoidable, and Brucker wrote many pages to provide his detailed answer, which was close to that of the former author but in a more coherent and elaborated form. In the 'Dissertatio praeliminaris' the author explained that philosophy and wisdom share the same object (i.e. truth) and aim (i.e. bliss), but that their forms are completely different. The (religious) wise man knows the divine truths that are cognizable for men thanks to revelation and grace, whilst the philosopher, thanks to his rational principles and logical rules, investigates the same truths as not already given. Philosophy provides clear general principles by means of rational investigations, since it explains prepositions and finally comes to terms with objections. Longo suggests that those formal aspects of Brucker's philosophy reveal a double philosophical heritage, on one side, Cartesian rationalism, as for instance fully realized in Wolff, and on the other side, the investigation of the role of philosophy, following Thomasius's school.[73] Therefore, it is correct to say that Brucker was the champion of Eclecticism and, more widely, the most representative German historian of philosophy of his age.

According to the author, philosophy was different to wisdom, thus all cultural expressions produced not by means of principles, presentations and debates were not philosophical and did not deserve to be inserted properly in a history of philosophy. However, as we shall see, Brucker provided long chapters on what he reputed not to be philosophical, because he felt the necessity of a detailed investigation even of what is excluded from philosophy to better qualify the philosophical field itself. That is the reason for the long chapters devoted to Barbarians and Asians, who, according to the author, did not produce philosophy but at the most a kind of arguable wisdom. Brucker was less explicit and violent than Heumann, but besides a more moderate language, he shared the 'exclusivist' opinions already expressed in the *Acta*.

We need to be aware of the real critical focus of Brucker, which was not on Asians or Barbarians, but rather on the historiographical theories of Neoplatonism and syncretism. He was more interested in voiding the perennial philosophy model than in attacking non-European civilizations or the Jesuits themselves (ibid., I, 16–17). On religious ground he was quite tolerant, but on the historiographical one he was determined to free the discipline from forced conciliations or accommodations. Syncretism falsified interpretations and even forged texts in accordance with a preposterous unifying vision. The Neoplatonic histories of philosophy were evidently untrustworthy and required to be consulted or quoted with constant attention.

> Brucker's polemic attacked not only the seventeenth-century scholars Otto Hernius and Georg Horn, but also the contemporary *Historire critique de la philosophie* by André-François Boureau-Deslandes, who had included under the term philosophy 'the theology of the ancients, jurisprudence and the source of all the sciences including even the very origins of peoples'.
>
> ibid., I, p. 6[74]

With Brucker the long-lasting historiographic model that we saw from Ficino or Steuco to Leibniz was definitively swept away. But, at the same time, the definition of 'what was philosophical and what was not' was also in contrast with the French

'Histoires de l'esprit', which were not rigorous and specific enough to be evaluated as reliable historiographies.[75] Brucker himself suggested that only historical Pyrrhonism might be accepted as a correct attitude when sources or interpretations are arguable or even dubious, but obviously he never mentioned Bayle as one of the first sceptical historians, since the Frenchman was associated with Spinozism and atheism.

The history of philosophy 'est Historia intellectus humani' and an 'Errorum Index' (ibid., I, 21), thus the history of the human intellect and of its mistakes and misunderstandings. It is the historical 'life' of the human intellect, the description of how it dealt with darkness and mistakes – mostly due to corrupt religious ideas – in order to gain happiness and bliss, which are to be found in the divine wisdom.[76] According to Brucker, history is a continuous process, with highs and lows, that has still not reached its aim, but instead it is always in progress. That is why a reliable history of philosophy was useful for ecclesiastic history, jurisprudence and medicine, since all sciences needed to detect mistakes; as for instance ecclesiastic history needs to understand the reasons behind heresies and atheism (ibid., I, 28–30). The same eclectic philosophy, which is the highest speculation for Brucker, has limits, because of human nature itself, which is very poor compared to the divine wisdom, hence to the divine perfection. Longo notices that:

> The reader of the *Historia critica* can readily observe the religious foundation that animated the personality of Brucker and his concept of the history of philosophy: indeed it shows the origin of natural religion, confirms the historicity of the Bible with reliable sources, explains the history of atheism and the spread of heresy, and clarifies the boundaries between revelation and reason ... Eclecticism and the defence of religion, and the exaltation of human reason with the battle against every form of atheism, are clearly to be the two fundamental points of view through which Brucker examined and judged the history of philosophy ...[77]

Therefore, it would be completely wrong to understand Brucker's history out of this context that is also the inner and never hidden aim of all his history of philosophy. Even the exclusion of Barbarian and Asian philosophies is to be understood both in the process of shaping a 'scientific'/'systematic' concept of philosophy and in the religious (i.e. Lutheran)[78] vision of the history of humankind, grounded on these unavoidable four tenets: Original sin, Revelation, Predestination and Holy Grace. As we said, Renaissance syncretism, Jesuit accommodationism and Bayle's Spinozism – although from completely different standpoints – were leading to the irrelevance of all these four tenets of Protestant theology.

The first book of the *Historia critica philosophiae* begins with the barbaric philosophy and ends with the Roman philosophers, certainly with the longest chapters devoted to the Greeks. In the first few paragraphs, Brucker provided a detailed analysis of what is the meaning of the Greek word for 'barbarian' and who is a 'barbarian'. According to the author, the term 'barbarian' originates from other ancient languages, but it was very complicated to understand from which language (i.e. Chaldean, Arabian or Egyptian). Besides its philological origin, what is worth noting is the negative and derogatory meaning of this word in the Greek use, which Brucker strongly emphasized:

> The name Barbarian, hence the negative meaning of this term, was extended from the language to the moral. Who is named barbarian is averse to the cult of erudition; thus, when correctly observed from the [side] of learned men, the barbarians are opposed to these learned men, and barbarian is a synonym of ignorance.[79]
>
> ibid., I, 47

It is clear here that Brucker shared the opinion expressed by Gentzken, who opposed 'barbarus' to 'moratus' (§3.4.). For Neoplatonists and 'inclusivists' in general, 'barbarian' was used as a geographical definition, meaning the ancient peoples of the Middle East, thus all the historical civilizations that were not Greek. On the contrary, in German Eclecticism as for Heumann, Gentzken and Brucker himself, 'barbarian' was used as a strongly derogatory definition. A barbarian was not Greek, and among the German Eclectics, the ancient Greek man was the emblem of reason, morality and science, thus the Barbarian was irrational, immoral and not gifted in science.

For Brucker the issue of what Greeks took from barbarians was a false problem, created by the authors who emphasized the presumed barbaric heritage of Greek culture. Those authors were, on one side, the Neoplatonists which were not reliable historians as we said, on the other side, a few fathers of the Church, i.e. Clement of Alexandria, who wished to trace all ancient wisdom back to the 'ancient Jewish civilization . . .',[80] thus to a presumed divine lineage that was the origin of philosophy. However, whereas this last theory could be acceptable regarding wisdom, what Brucker and Heumann before him provided was a new definition of philosophy that involved a new history separate from the history of wisdom. On that account, Brucker claimed that:

> When we could state the proper meaning of philosophy by means of norms; when a distinction would be made between, [on one side,] the different knowledge and understanding of things of common people, and, [on the other side,] philosophy; when the beginning of philosophy would be distinct from its growing and formal state; and when a distinction would be made in the way philosophy was handed down between, [on one side,] the use of parental and teaching authority and, [on the other side,] the accurate philosophising method and the investigative reflection that makes use of the cause and effect chain: only then all this controversy will disappear, because it will be disclosed as a linguistic quarrel [λογομαχὶαν] ... Whoever studied the nature of the barbaric philosophy effectively, he would admit that they had reflected only through simple notions instead of scientific analysis. Furthermore, they propagated to posterity an investigation of truth that was obtained through meditation and tradition instead of evidence. On the same questions, Greeks, who were the first who stood out of the [original] coarse habits, struggled themselves to investigate the principles of truth and good, and researched

therein the causes, and they provided others with certain truths deducted from sources by means of a precise method [grounded on] rational laws.[81]

ibid., I, 49

Philosophy was born in Greece, where a real investigation grounded on rational principles and deductions was for the first time undertaken. Before that time, there was only meditation and tradition, thus authority and repetition. Knowledge was simply handed down within familiar lineages, excluding any implement and any diffusion of the discipline itself. This was barbarian philosophy according to Brucker and Heumann – who reputed the barbarian sects 'School of Ignorance' – supported the same viewpoint. It is clear that within this *Historia* the Barbarians were inserted not as philosophers, properly speaking, but at the most as learned men, among which only Jews had a distinct good reputation. The issue of the 'barbarian philosophy' was simply a 'linguistic quarrel', due to an improper use of the term 'philosophy', which was correctly related only to the Greeks.

In his historical exposition, Brucker proposed a classification of Barbarians based on the classic four directions of Ephorus:

1. Orientis: Jews, Chaldeans, Persians, Indians, ancient Arabians and Phoenicians
2. Meridiei: Egyptians and Ethiopians
3. Occidentis: Celts/Gauls, ancient Britain tribes, Germans and ancient Romans
4. Septentrionis: 'Hyperboreorum', Scythians, Thracians, Getae.

At the top of all ancient barbarians are evidently listed the Jews, who were not properly philosophers but bearers of an indisputable wisdom (i.e. monotheism). On the contrary Brucker's criticism was incredibly harsh about Chaldeans, who had been the pivotal civilization in Neoplatonic histories, since Chaldeans had been the divine link between God or Adam and ancient peoples and Abraham was often described as Chaldean. For Brucker, all these theories lacked any historical grounds, since there were only confused and unreliable sources regarding them. Their wisdom was a blend of superstition, idolatry and unreasonable ideas; hence they did not deserve the rank of philosophers (ibid., I, 106–13). This criticism of Chaldeans has a clear reason: Brucker, like several contemporaries, aimed at outlining only one pure divine lineage and not a spread of this wisdom among ancient civilizations. On the contrary, for perennial and accommodationist historians Chaldea had been the starting place of the diffusion of philosophy, as we saw quoting De Villemandy and Thomassin (see §1.5.). We might suggest that this new historical approach was consistent with the Lutheran concept of predestination and the research of a single seed from which Christianity arose, providing one progressive and linear spread.

Regarding Persians Brucker wrote few long paragraphs, in order to investigate the several ancient men named Zoroaster, a very relevant question already investigated among our authors by Kircher. But what concerns us is only that Persians had an obscure philosophy and Brucker presented their views about God and the world in detail, which were clearly opposed to that of Jews. Therefore, the idea suggested by the

German historian was that with Persians the reader of the *Historia* was already far from Jews, who did not share their wisdom out of their blessed community. Consequently, the Indians, who lived in an even farther land, were completely out of the 'wisdom area' (Jewish), and Brucker described them as coarse and ignorant people:

> Indians are really ignorant and not gifted with the fortune of intelligence, indeed since remote times they have sustained those wise men, whom the Greeks had acknowledged as philosophers, after a comparison with the characteristics of their own habits and institutions.
>
> ibid., I, 192[82]

It is evident what Brucker was suggesting: Greeks were mistakenly calling them philosophers. These wise men were the so-called 'Brachmanes', a term which he wrongly defined as the Indian name for 'Gymnosophistae', when we know that the latter are more likely the Jaina. Brucker reported all the previous interpretations of the term 'Brachmanes', rejecting Postel's theory about the son of Abraham and Keturah (§1.2.), which afterwards was repeated by Heurn (§1.1.), or the odd assonances suggested by Horn (§1.3.). He also reported the many groups listed among them as in Strabo and Porphyry. Also the description of their strict life, the sexual regulation, the extreme practices, the self-immolation and their nakedness followed the already classical version. However, he added, that the 'Brachmanes' at his time were named 'Bahramae et Braminae' (ibid., I, 193) and were since the most remote time selected only 'per generis successionem', thus because they were born in a pure lineage and not because of merits or natural attitudes. Furthermore, those presumed wise men were extremely influential, being worshipped by the common people, and they acted as advisors and auspices ('arte consultos') of the ruling class. They were also the unique mediators with the Gods, thus they worshipped them on behalf of other classes[83] (ibid., I, 199).

Brucker openly contested the theories about the origin of part of Pythagoras's philosophy out of India. Among his most harshly criticized authors there were Georg Horn and the ancient Neoplatonicians such as Apuleius. But, above all, he accused Philostratus (*The Life of Apollonius of Tyana*), one of the main sources of Neoplatonic concordism about India, to be a faker and a swindler ('nugator'), because he had completely invented the beautiful history of the Gymnosophists without any proof of what he said and also, according to Brucker, he fostered a false positive image of the Indian philosophers devoted to rational judgements and followers of a natural morality that was untenable (ibid., I, 201–2).

After this background of rejected sources, Brucker wrote about the few Indian thinkers mentioned by name in the ancient sources and thus already quite well known among European historians. The first is 'Buddas' who was the prince of Gymnosophists, as claimed by Saint Jerome (Eusebius Sophronius Hieronymus) in his *Contra Jovianus* (I, 42 and II, 14), a common reference regarding Gymnosophists' rigid vegetarianism and refusal to kill animals, who also reported the mythical birth of Buddha: 'Buddam e latere suo virgo generarit' ('[the mother] virgin brought Buddha to life from her left flank').[84] Brucker opposed to the version of Hieronymus the widespread description of

Buddha as the founder of Manichaeism. The most relevant source of this last theory was not indicated by the author, but it was probably the entry 'Μάνης' (Manes) of the tenth century Byzantine Encyclopedia *Suda* or *Souda*, which says:

> This man, thrice-cursed, appeared under Emperor Aurelian, fantasizing that he was Christ and the Holy Ghost. With 12 disciples, as if Christ, he borrowed from every heresy any evil thing he could, and introduced into the Roman territory from Persia a private contract against God. This man, called both Manes and the Scythian, was Brahman by race. He had as his teacher a 'Buddha' (Βουδδᾶς), the one previously called Terebinthos, who had been educated in the things of the Greeks and loved the school of Empedokles, who had declared that there are two first principles opposed to each other. This Terebinthos, when he arrived, said that he had been born in Persia of a virgin and had been reared on the mountains. He also wrote four books, one The Book of Mysteries, another The Gospel, another The Treasure, another The Book of the Recapitulation. And this 'Buddha', the one also called Terebinthos, being crushed by an unclean spirit, died. A woman with whom he lodged, inheriting his money and impure books, bought a little boy of seven years, Cubricus by name, whom she taught writing and set free, making him her sole heir. Taking the books and money of 'Buddha' he travelled through Persia, calling himself Manes. Becoming expert in the wanderings of 'Buddha', he said that the books were his own labours.[85]

The birth from a virgin mother proves that the author was referring not to a Buddhist in general (i.e. a monk), but rather to the Buddha himself. This description of the life of Manes was quite diffused among the Christian anti-Manichaens authors, such as Socrates Scholasticus of Constantinople (*c.* 380–*c.* 440), usually acknowledged as a relevant source on Manichaeism together with Saint Augustine. We wish to make it clear that this theory of Buddha as master of Manichaens was not unusual or claimed only by their Christian opponents, since Manes himself proposed this link, according to his universalistic and messianic view. We quote as proof a fragment of the *Shabuhragan* (one of the foundational books of Manichaeism) as reported in the *Chronology of Ancient Nations* (*Al-Āthār al-bāqiyah*) written by the famous Islamic historian Al-Bīrūnī (973–1048):

> Wisdom and deeds have always from time to time been brought to mankind by the messengers of God. So in one age they have been brought by the messenger, called Buddha, to India, in another by Zarâdusht [Zarathustra] to Persia, in another by Jesus to the West. Thereupon this revelation has come down, this prophecy in this last age through me, Mânî [Manes], the messenger of the God of truth to Babylonia.[86]

We see that the claim of Rodrigues and Kircher (§2.1.) about the single atheistic epidemic stream of all religions of the eastern heathen might find a proof here. However, Brucker did not directly quote these well-known modern authors (i.e. Kircher) and simply rejected the claim of Buddha as master of Terebinthos, accepting the version of

Buddha as prince of Gymnosophists. Furthermore, Brucker added that this prince 'Budda' was the same as the Siamese Sommona-Codom, the Chinese Xaca and he was also worshipped in Japan. Brucker used the missionaries' tone to provide a definition of the historical role of Buddha: he was 'a renowned impostor in all of India ...'.[87] We can infer that for the writer the Gymnosophists themselves were impostors, 'Budda' being their master. However, although in this chapter Brucker denied the linking of Buddha with Manichaeism, in the chapter about modern Asians he claimed that Buddhism was a plague from Egypt as argued by Kircher.

The second Indian thinker mentioned is Dandamis, the numinous and wise philosopher who met and blamed the violence of Alexander the Great without fear of the reaction of the latter. Palladius and Saint Ambrose (Saint Ambrogio)[88] described Dandamis as a refined logician, but this philosophical expertise was obviously contested by the German historian and acknowledged as a clear misunderstanding. Connected with the adventure of the Macedonian king in India is the third man mentioned, namely Calanus or Kalanos, who followed the army before sacrificing himself in a funeral pyre. The last thinker is the mythical prince of the Gymnosophists mentioned by Dandamis himself, who lived seated on an aerial throne. Brucker stressed that the last three wise men were all described by Philostratus, thus, suggesting their forged identities. In short, we might say that of the four Indian men, one of them was an impostor and three were falsified historical characters. We might infer that Brucker was openly rejecting any positive description of the Indians as wise men and contrasting the reliability of all historical accounts about them.

The Indian religious thought was not better depicted than the thinkers. Brucker stressed as the most relevant fact that the Indian views were not originally of this land but brought there by one of the ancient men named Zoroaster (ibid., I, 205). Their main tenets were: 1. God is light or creative fire; 2. God is immanent, He pervades and rules everything; 3. God is immortal; 4. The origin of human souls is God and when the body dies ('corpusque animae indumentum', ibid., I, 207) the soul turns back to Him; 5. They worship God by means of hymns and chants; 6. They believe in a repeating cycle of births. Brucker also reported that Clement of Alexandria misunderstood this cycle as a resurrection theory, hence comparing it with the Christian regeneration after the Last Judgement, whilst the Indian theory of rebirth was simply a natural and necessary process without any moral meaning. Although Brucker was right in correcting Clement, he was wrong in suggesting that the theory of rebirth was not guided by moral actions (i.e. karman), and this claim reveals the aim of the German historians, which was the illustration of Indian immorality.

About Indian scientific and technical skills the German Eclectic was even harsher: 'The knowledge of natural philosophy among Indians is really minimal...'.[89] (ibid., I, 208). The same Megasthenes blamed their mythological explanations and their imaginary theories, because there was nothing other than allegories in their sciences. Anyway, Brucker was obliged by the Greek sources themselves to admit a certain good knowledge of astronomy and cosmogony among Indians. But immediately he added that:

> Several Pythagoric principles differ little from that of the Indian system, [however] it is easy to understand that the nature of the barbarian philosophy is very far

away from the technical reasoning and the chain of causality known by the Greek school.[90]

ibid., I, 209

The Indian knowledge was not scientific, because it was not reached through observation and reasoning, but simply through tradition and repetition. And he also claimed that this astronomical tradition did not have Indian origins, but rather it came to India from Chaldea and, as the same religious tenets, from Persia.

As we have already suggested in the chapters about perennialist historians, ancient Indians were often respected for their moral teaching and educational system. On this topic, Brucker made a summary of the book by Stolle already quoted by Heumann (§3.4.), which was considered the most complete and balanced survey of heathen morality. Globally Indians did not fear death and did not discern between good and evil. They condemned everything related to body and passions and that is why they trained their bodies to keep the most complete continence during the harder exercises (like yoga). Their educational system was completely disregarded by Brucker and also their sexual continence, two main arguments of the former leading description of their morality.

> According to this survey of moral precepts, it is evident that this [Indian] man limited his philosophy to an imitation of GOD, through the control of passions, the exercise of patience and disregarding [the fear of] death.[91]

ibid., I, 212

This expression 'imitandum DEUM' is very intriguing, since it has obviously nothing to do with the renowned *The imitation of Christ* (c. 1418–27), but more probably with the idea of the possible reaching of the divine state of being by wise men in Indian philosophy. This was the same argument moved by Bernier against all the Quietists of the world, both in the East and in the West (§2.2.). The idea of an imitable God, whose state and nature was reachable or imitable by wise men, created, as Bernier called them, several little Gods, since the wise men became divine themselves. Brucker was not so direct, but the use of the word 'imitate' is very suggestive. As proof of our understanding, we mention that, according to him, this lack of a true morality could only lead to magic and superstition, which were the consequences of the theory of the 'little Gods' as claimed by Bernier.

The last paragraph on India mentioned the Chinese and that, after Horn, is no more a surprise for us. The aim of this quote here was to note that the Chinese were named Seres in ancient times while Sinenses in modern times and both names came from the long-lasting history of the silk route. Because ancient Greeks and Romans said almost nothing about them, besides short quotes in Celsus and Origines, the account and discussion of this civilization was postponed to the section on modern Asians. As he said: 'suo loco tractanda servantes' (ibid., I, 212). This insertion in a later stage of the global plan of the history was the same provided by Horn, who introduced Chinese between the Middle Age and the Renaissance philosophers, and by Burnet when he referred to his Appendix. Furthermore, Brucker in this chapter on ancients decided to reveal in advance his suspicions concerning the modern sources available on China:

> Whatever we know of the philosophy of that people reached us through the men that were sent there to seed the Christian religion, [this knowledge] was deduced from the Chinese [written] monuments, forcedly ['arcte'] made coherent with the recent history and because of this is really hard to retrace an unmodified [/correct] order [of events].[92]
>
> ibid., I, 212

The ancient sources on Chinese were minimal and the modern were unreliable, because of the common historical attitude that made all the facts coherent. That was the missionaries' attitude, but we know that Brucker moved the same accusation also to the Neoplatonists and to every 'inclusivist perspective' connected more or less tightly with perennial philosophy. The author aimed at making that criticism completely clear before the related chapter, which is necessarily the final book. Therefore, Anne-Lise Dyck is somewhat wrong in saying that Chinese are not mentioned in the book about ancient philosophy and in claiming that they were introduced in extremis into an added booklet,[93] because the last book was an integral part of the whole work and because, before Brucker, at least Horn and Burnet did the same. And the reason for this position in a further book, although 'Eurocentric', was due to the historical division of sources: ancient sources about ancient people and modern sources, that of missionaries in the case of the Chinese, about modern people. Dyck correctly stresses the exclusion of Asians out of the philosophical field, but this exclusion was not because of the insertion in a final section, but because of the arguments raised against them.

3.6 Jakob Brucker: the contemporary 'Exotic' Asians out of philosophy

The last book of the *Historia critica* is entitled 'De Philosophia Exotica' (The exotic philosophy) and it is the second part of the fifth volume. For the first time in a history, we find the use of the word 'exotic' (exotica) about a philosophy; a word completely unfamiliar to the seventeenth-century historians and that marked the new idea of what was not European. The exotic peoples were the Persians, the Indians, the Chinese, the Japanese, the South-East Asians and the pre-Columbian Americans, hence the peoples formerly included into the old definition of 'the Indies'. Evidently, according to Brucker only ancient civilizations were barbaric, whilst modern non-European civilizations were exotic. There was already that division in Burnet, but the English historian did not provide a general definition of all non-European civilizations. And Brucker also preserved the long-lasting exception of the Arabs and the Jews, which were not barbaric, because they were part of the main stream of the true philosophy. They were both monotheistic as Christians: the Jews were the same source of monotheism, while

Arabs learned Greek philosophy and taught it to the Europeans after the Middle Ages, being an integral part of the history of philosophy in its proper meaning. Therefore, all the other civilizations of the world were 'exotic', although, as we shall see, not every civilization deserved attention from the philosophical point of view.

With a tone very similar to the one adopted by Heumann, Brucker pointed out that the use of the term philosophy about these civilizations must not be misinterpreted:

> Who upon hearing the term 'exotic philosophy' applies to it the notion of philosophy current among the European people commits a mistake. In that sense, whether we focus on whatever Chinese, Japanese or Indian sect, [there] philosophy would be unattainable both in western and in eastern India. Furthermore, since the most ancient times, among Barbarians philosophy and religion had been closely connected...[94]
>
> ibid., V, 804

He added that Barbaric and Asian philosophies were more suitable to be investigated in a history of religion than in a history of philosophy. This implied an evident secular idea of the Greek and European philosophy. As we know, for Brucker Philosophy was an instrument in the hand of religion, but from this claim against barbaric philosophy, it descended that Philosophy was a secular instrument and should not be religious in itself. When we compare with the perennial paradigm, evidently this was a drastic change. The wall erected by perennialists since Heurn between ancient Asian philosophers ('prisci theologi') and modern Asian coarse men was replaced by Brucker between the Europeans – with their double origins, i.e. Jewish and Greek – and all other civilizations. Therefore, Asian philosophies were a 'pars altera' of the manual, not being introduced among the Europeans as in Horn, but in a specific and separate section, since they were not properly philosophical.

This book is an outline of all the most important 'exotic' civilizations and it has a clear geographical trend, opposed to the spread of philosophy we investigated in the first chapter (§1.5.). The spread of philosophy for perennialists was from the East (Chaldea) to the West (Europe), despite the problems of coherence posed by India and China, whilst here the direction was from the West (Persia) to the East (Japan). This direction brings to mind Kircher and the 'atheistic plague', thus the aim of the writer was explicit. He reproposed the theory of the double spread, on one side Jewish wisdom strengthened by Greek philosophy, on the other, Egyptian atheism. The first civilization quoted was the Persian, although Brucker suggested that the ancient Persians were extinct, being defeated by the Muslims. He provided the renowned quote by Bernier on the Persian and Indian Cabala (§2.2.) that was made famous by Bayle (§2.3.), but in order to contest the interpretation of the author of the *Dictionnaire*:

> P. Bayle claims that this [system] was the system of Spinoza, however, according to us this equivalence is wrong, indeed [the Persian system] assumes an extremely wide emanation, which should not be confused with the Spinozistic modes. The first proposed [an ontological system where the modes] are similar to flasks full of water floating into the ocean, and the water although it was taken from the ocean,

because it was contained in the flasks was really distinct from the ocean itself. Whilst, according to Spinoza, the 'res omnes' that are in the universe are like little bubbles floating in the agitated ocean.[95]

ibid., V, 809

Brucker claimed that Bernier correctly described the Persian and Indian systems as a Cabala. But Bayle's philosophical association was wrong, because Spinozism was monistic, while the origin of Persian thought was the dualistic system of Zoroaster. The German Eclectic, willing to contest Bayle, interpreted the description of Bernier as dualistic: on one side the water in the flasks, on the other the water of the ocean. But this interpretation was really far from the description of Bernier, also because the French traveller was not speaking about the Zoroastrian system, but instead about the modern Sufis and Indians. Not only Bayle was correct in his interpretation of Bernier, but, as we saw in the second chapter (§2.2), he was also not the first to compare Spinoza and the Asian ontology. Nevertheless, Brucker was really certain that the writing of Bernier was related to the Zoroastrian system, which according to the former studies spread from Egypt to India.

We might suggest that this error of the German historian was due to at least two reasons. On one side, the long-lasting theories of the 'atheistic plague' that has in Kircher its most relevant advocate, to whom we added Jacob Thomasius – father of Christian Thomasius – who proved in his renowned *Schediasma historicum*[96] an original Zoroastrian dualism behind all heathen religions. On the other side, Brucker held a clear anti-comparativist approach, which led him to refuse the comparison of Spinoza with any non-European philosophy, since every comparison would mean to acknowledge the philosophical level of the non-European thinkers. And the German historian also knew that comparativism was, since Bayle, a dangerous polemic and anti-orthodox tool in the hands of libertines and early Enlightened thinkers, as it was the case with Jean-Baptiste de Boyer d'Argens in his *Lettres Juives* and *Lettres chinoises* published between the years 1738 and 1742.[97]

After the Persians, Brucker described Buddhism in accordance with the theory of the 'atheistic plague' and that confirms our hypothesis on his error regarding Bernier. Buddhism was diffused among Tatars (lat. Tartari), an undefined mix of peoples that, according to the classical conception, included Mongols and Tibetans. The author was clearly speaking about these two civilizations, because he mentioned several 'Lama' and even the 'Dalai Lama', which was the 'pontifex maximus' (ibid., V, 810). They worshipped 'Foë', that is the Chinese name for Buddha. But Buddha himself was not an Indian man as several claimed, but rather, according to La Croze, he was a 'sacerdotem atque philosophum Aegyptiacum' ('an Egyptian clergyman and philosopher').

Mathurin Veyssière de La Croze (1661–1739) was a French erudite and orientalist; he was formerly a Benedictine but when he moved to Germany converted to Protestantism and became the librarian of the Prussian Royal Library in Berlin. He wrote a very detailed outline of Indian sects,[98] where he primarily used the manuscript of the German Lutheran Bartholomäus Ziegenbalg (1682–1719), who worked for a Danish mission in Tamil Nadu (India).[99] Both writers followed the theory of the Egyptian origin of the Buddhist 'plague' that had been argued and supported especially by Kircher several decades before (§2.1). That is why we are already familiar with the word used by Brucker to describe this faith: 'pestis', namely plague (ibid., V, 813).[100] From another source, that is Couplet, Brucker took the classical description of the two doctrines, the exoteric that was idolatric and the esoteric that was atheistic (ibid., V, 817–20). Several details on both doctrines are provided, but the most interesting topic is the Spinozism of the esoteric one:

> This famous doctrine of the sect of Foë, or discipline of Xekia, is according to most [of the scholars] a form of atheism, and moreover it deserves the infamy of the Spinozism. Although somebody erroneously confuses it with Spinozism – as Magi's emanative system, which is also followed by the exoteric doctrine of Xekia – we think it is plausible that it shares some Spinozistic instances.[101]
>
> ibid., V, 820

Therefore, although Buddhism was not properly a Spinozistic thought, because we should not forget that for Brucker Oriental philosophies were not comparable with western philosophies, Buddhism shared many points of the Spinozistic system. According to the author, Magi and Indians, as we said before, were not Spinozistic being dualistic thinkers, whilst esoteric Buddhism, supporting 'that void and inane is the principle and the end of all things'[102] (ibid.), was somehow a monistic system.

The German historian also provided several proofs (at least ten) of the Egyptian origin of Buddha, taken from La Croze. We report only the most relevant: the worship of preposterous gods, which mixed animals and human features; the worship of cows (Api); the transmigration of souls; the Buddhist statues that had curly hairs that reminded to the Ethiopians' hairs; allegedly Buddha was the Indian name for Mercurius; the double doctrine, the exoteric one in order to deceive and subjugate the common people and the esoteric only for a specific caste. His aim at proving the ancient atheistic and idolatric 'Oriental plague' was clear and, within the spread of this atheistic plague, Buddhism was the worst faith, the most similar to some tenets of Spinozism, because it was strictly monistic and this single substance was an empty chaos. The Quietism (see §2.2; §2.3.) is not openly mentioned in this chapter, but the motionless worship and meditation is reported several times. We might argue that the nineteenth-century debate about the 'nihilism' of Buddhism had already begun, but hidden under the all-inclusive definition of atheism.

The second chapter of this book on the 'exotic civilizations' deals with Malabarians. This was an improper term used to refer to real Indians, instead of the Indians of 'the Indies', which also included China, Japan, South-East Asia, pre-Columbian America and so on. It was an improper definition because Malabar is the modern coast of Karnataka and Kerala, thus the south-west coast of India, which was mostly under Dutch control until the English complete occupation of India in the last years of the eighteenth century. Malabar was only a part of India and Brucker knew that (ibid., V, 828), but we might notice that missionaries stayed mostly in the south coast of India, either on the west or on the east side, thus in ancient Malabar or in Tamil Nadu and Ceylon. Therefore, the definition of Indians as Malabarians – although improper – was not inexplicable, because at that time the missionaries knew mostly that part of India, as we said, the south coasts of both sides.

The most eminent Indian class was the 'Bramanarum familia' and clearly here the author did not use the old Greek term that translated in Latin gave 'Brachmanes', but instead the modern Latinization. On the term 'Bramana' he made no further mention of the old theory suggested by Postel on the etymological origin from Abraham, but instead he correctly reported that this name came from the first God of India that was 'Brama' (skr. Brahmā) and this change indicates that the old perennialist theory of the origin of Indians from Noah or Abraham was definitively devoid of any validity. The 'Bramanae' were the wise men and they were wise not because of their studies, education or merit, but because they were born in this social class. They wore a 'funiculum', i.e. the *yajñopavīta*, the sacred thread which means that they were consecrated members of the class. And they followed a complex theory of impurity and purity, which regarded food, social exchange, marriage life, etc. All these practices, together with several others, proved their similarity with the Egyptian tradition and again this claim was taken from La Croze. 'Bramanae' had a sacred book named 'Vedam', from which they took the 'Sudraes' (*sūtra*) or aphorisms they have to learn by heart (ibid., V, 830).

La Croze in his chapter provided a wide presentation of several religious classes that did not belong to the Brahmans, because they believed either in Viṣṇu or Śiva (instead of Brahmā) and also of classes of intellectual men, which were shortly reported in the *Historia critica*. There were the 'Igigueuli' and the 'Gnanigueuli', who likely were the *Yogin* and the *Jñanin*, both classes of spiritual thinkers.

> There are two classes that may be correctly collocated among the philosophers, they are the *Yogin*, i.e. the theoreticians, and the *Jñānin*, i.e. the wise men, two classes very different from one another ...[but] all of them follow an isolated theoretical life,[103] cultivate the meditation and they enter specific penitential orders. Having left their wives, they are free; they afflict their bodies with several tortures and torments. Taking their minds under control, they reach ecstasy [when] they are in a high motionless meditation.[104]
>
> ibid., V, 831

While Deslandes (§2.7.) provided a description of eighteen schools of philosophy (*darśana*), Brucker wrote the first classification of the Indian religious and intellectual classes. Obviously, the first description was by La Croze (from Ziegenbalg), but Brucker was the first historian of philosophy who felt the necessity to report the fact that Brahmans were not the only religious and intellectual caste. The classical confused classification of Indians into Brachamanes, Gymnosophists and Sarmanes/Germanes was solved and updated with new effective insights. There were three main castes of religious thinkers and each of them followed one of the three Indian principal gods: Brahmā, Viṣṇu and Śiva. The first god was worshipped only by 'Brahmanae' and to respect them was to respect the god. The next two gods were worshipped by two classes almost opposed to one another. Furthermore, there were not only religious classes, but also the so-called intellectual classes: they did not worship a god, they rejected all the classical religious tradition and lived a contemplative and speculative life. The most relevant were the *Yogin* and the *Jñanin*, and although they were different, they shared the same style of life: meditation, detachment from the body, control of the mind and ecstasy. And this description reminds of the ancient Gymnosophists and Hyloboli that were previously wrongly confused with the Brachmanes themselves.

After the illustration of these classes, the author recalled the well-known question of Quietism, which was connected with the aforementioned 'Oriental Spinozism'. About Spinozism, he reiterated that it could be in some aspects similar to Buddhism but not to the Indian sects. It was the same for Quietism: Buddhism ('sectam Foënam') was the only Quietist sect, while the other aforementioned classes – i.e. Brahmans, *Yogin, Jñanin*, etc. – were merely to some extent influenced by their Quietism. That was because when this Quietism spread around Africa and Asia, it also infected India and the local beliefs. Therefore, for Brucker Spinozism and Quietism were related to the Buddhist sect that infected the other Indian sects, which although infected could not properly be acknowledged as Spinozistic and Quietistic. The author, who generally refused the use of European philosophical terms to describe non-European sects (i.e. comparativism), made an exception with Buddhism, the renowned 'atheismi pestis' (ibid., V, 832).

In the section about Indians of the fifth book of the *Historia critica*, Malabarian erudition was described in detail and the main source was again La Croze:

> Each part of the Malabarian erudition may be properly sized in theoretic doctrine and practical doctrine: the knowledge of nature is modest, simple and without order, it is taken from their natural theology, which is the main part of the Malabarian encyclopaedia [/culture].[105]
>
> ibid., V, 833

They did not have a proper medical science, but instead a huge number of medical practices without real theoretical basis.[106] Also their astronomy was minimal and in its few interesting points recalled Egyptian, Greek and Latin knowledge. How was that possible? The answer to this question was simple: 'When we connect the [astronomical similarities] with what we already said about the coming of Buddha [Xekia] in India, that added great similitude to the theory about the transplantation to India of the seeds of the Egyptian disciplines [sciences] and philosophy'[107] (V, 834). The same goes for their physics, which was irrelevant and in many aspects bring to mind the more developed science of Egyptians and Greeks (ibid., V, 842).

On the subject of Malabarian natural theology, Brucker argued that it was completely devoted to the single 'substantia suprema' (supreme substance), which was 'the essence of the essence of all things'[108] (ibid., V, 835). This substance was motionless, just and good, but also it understood nothing because it was detached from worldly life (ibid.). Furthermore, this was a clear emanative system and that was enough to prove again that the tenets of Indian theology had an Egyptian origin (ibid.). This supreme substance could not be represented through idols; however, from it emanated several deities that could be worshipped by men. The only symbolic statue that represented the essence of this substance being not an emanation was the 'Lingum genitalia' (skr. *liṅgaṃ*), i.e. the Phallus, which according to the author was the local representation of the Egyptian sexual rites and of the famous Bacchanal (ibid., V, 837). Brucker, always through La Croze, reported the Indian 'trinitas divina', which is the *trimūrti* (the three forms) in Sanskrit. They were 'Birum, sive Birama, Isuren and Vistnou', who are the aforementioned Brahmā, Iṣvara and Viṣṇu. Brahmā is the lord creator, not to be confused with Brahman that is the 'supreme substance', but the distinction between the two was still unknown at the time and they were often confused. Viṣṇu is the preserver God, he maintains and rules the world. He is opposed to the destroyer God that is Śiva, here named Iṣvara as according to some schools of Śaivaism (Maheṣvara).[109] For La Croze, followed here, only the Brahmans worshipped Brahmā and, as Brucker already stressed, they derived their name from the god himself. The two aforementioned religious beliefs worshipped the other two gods and each sect could be divided into several sub-sects.

The last topic raised about Indians was their morality and, quite surprisingly, Stolle's *Historie der Heÿdnischen Morale*,[110] a reference book for German Eclectics (i.e. Heumann), is not mentioned as it was in the previous chapter about ancient barbarians. In addition to La Croze, the main source of this section was the Dutch Calvinist missionary in India Abraham Rogerius (1609–49), who wrote the 'Cent Proverbes, du Payen Barthrovherri, renommé parmy les Bramines, qui demerent sur les Costes de Chormandel'.[111] According to Rogerius, the Indian wise man had to take all his passions and reactions under control, achieving an inner pacification. According to Brucker, this morality of abstinence was due to the transmigration theory, which guided all human actions and imposed a prearranged destiny. The god 'Birama' (Brahmā) influenced and ruled over the transmigration itself, thus he was depicted as a sort of inscrutable judge. Their morality of abstinence left no room for freedom, thus in the Indian system there was no room for a real moral decision. Evidently the *saṃsāra* – the cycle of birth, life, death and rebirth – and the *karman* – the theory of the consequences of the acts in the actual and in the next life – were unknown and yet to be understood, we remark that only a correct knowledge of the working of *karman* would have suggested a place, although narrow, for morality. In short, we might infer that the Indian morality is depicted in the *Historia critica* as a morality good merely for hermits. Therefore, the classical image of the spiritual India detached from reality was enriched but not changed in this history of philosophy.

It is worth noting that Brucker made wide use of La Croze's chapter, however he did not completely follow the French author. The disagreements among them were mostly on two issues: the aforementioned positive comments made by La Croze on Indian religion and sciences, but, above all, the historiographical paradigm followed by the latter, namely the 'prisca theologia', into which the Indian belief in a Supreme God was inserted. La Croze claimed that 'We find there relevant traces of the Law of Moses and histories that have an evident relation with what is reported in our Sacred books'.[112] Although La Croze, as the German historian himself, did not discuss the biblical genealogical origin of Indians, he found – as Thomas Burnet – several traces of a common background, which were completely dismissed by Brucker. However, they both agreed to blame Buddhism, which was the 'inoculator' of the Egyptian atheistic plague of immanentism (Spinozism) and Quietism. Indian philosophies were not blamed as Buddhism was, but their belongingness to a 'prisca theologia' typical of the perennialist (Neoplatonic) historiography was obviously unacceptable and inconsistent with the new historical paradigm of the German Eclecticism.

Heading east, the next civilization investigated by Brucker is China, and this chapter is the longest and the most structured of the whole book on 'exotic civilisations'. At first, Brucker devoted several pages (ibid., V, 846–52) to a comprehensive presentation of the available bibliography: on the philosophical side there were Isaac Vossius, Leibniz, Wolff, Arnauld, Thomasius, Gundling, Buddeus and Heumann, while the primary sources were mostly Couplet, Longobardi, Navarrete and Renaudot. This bibliography was likely the most complete one ever provided since that time in a history of philosophy; the only lacking author was Pierre Bayle, who was usually quoted about Chinese, but evidently that omission was not by chance.

The first topic explored was the mythological Chinese chronology, which reported the stories of the ancient emperors and founders of the Chinese civilization (ibid., V, 852–8). What concerns us of this scrupulous investigation of each emperor is only that Brucker never compared any of them with the biblical figures as formerly several thinkers did, among whom Horn was the most relevant (§1.4.). A less mythological and more historical period started with Confucius, whose Chinese name was 'KIEU CHUM NHI' that, even with some difficulties, must be Kongfuzi 孔夫子 (master Kong), which being corrupted by the Portuguese language became 'CONFUçU' and in Latin 'Confucius' (ibid., V, 859). He was the advisor of a local ruler and his life was moral and devoted to the teaching of the best ethical practices. His teaching still lasted after two millennia and, as Horn already reported almost a century before, this doctrine by Confucius was the main subject of the exams that ratified the 'Mandarinorum dignitates' (ibid., V, 861). Many rites were devoted to Confucius, but usually these rites were described as civil and not religious by Jesuits, although several interpreters disagreed on the topic, particularly the Franciscans and the Dominicans (ibid., V, 863). Brucker did not openly take part in the 'rites controversy', we might suppose because for him the question was not philosophical, and thus he devoted more attention to the criticism of the Confucian morality. He quoted the Lutheran theologian and historian Johann Lorenz von Mosheim (1693-1755), who rejected the Chinese rites and discussed negatively Confucius's ethics. According to the latter, this moral system focused on prudence and tranquillity, it did not ask men to improve themselves and to become virtuous. These ethics simply pushed men to maintain the given state of things and to adapt to the world without undertaking useless autonomous actions. The Confucian ethics was an ethics of subtraction: the aim was to reach the balance between two poles: vices and virtues. The Chinese man couldn't improve himself and his personal attitudes and skills were annihilated (ibid., V, 867–9).

After Confucius, the author introduced an unprecedented division in periods of Chinese intellectual history: the first was Confucius himself, the second was the diffusion of the three sects, the third was the sect of alchemists and modern Chinese philosophers, and the fourth was related to the introduction of European culture. Taoism was founded by 'Li lao kium' (Laozi 老子), the study of the sect was mostly about the natural course and alchemy. About Confucianism, he reported 'Memcio'

(Mengzi 孟子), who wrote a book about the most refined knowledge but, according to Brucker, this book was not a great progress and that proved the static nature of Chinese schools. Moreover, three centuries after Confucius there was the 'books burning' (*fenshu* 焚书 or *qinhuo* 秦火) decided by the emperor 'Xi-hoam-ti' (i.e. the Qin 秦 Shihuangdi 始皇帝 in 213 BCE), which destroyed almost all the ancient Chinese literature, thus an event that made the study of ancient China very difficult (ibid., V, 870). The last sect was the 'secta Foëna' (Buddhism) that reached China from India and, as we know, it brought there the Egyptian plague of immanentism, atheism and Quietism. And to better depict Buddhism the historian also quoted Ricci, i.e. the first missionary who diffused the negative image of this faith in Europe (§1.2.). We are already familiar with the words used in the *Historia critica*: 'the impiety and the fanaticism of Buddha, like a deluge, flooded the whole Chinese Empire'[113] (ibid., V, 872). And the unique Buddhist sect described was obviously the well-known '*Vu guei kiao* [*wuweijiao* 無為教], id est, *nihil agentium dicta*', emblem of the Buddhist atheism – we might say nihilism – since at least Couplet (§2.1.).

'Media Sinensium philosophia' (ibid., V, 873) – a definition that reminds of the European Middle Ages – corresponds to the third period, when the Buddhist atheism also infected the Confucian sect and alchemy pervaded almost all studies. This period should be what we call the Neo-Confucianism (*xin rujia* 新儒家) of the Song dynasty and probably also of the Ming dynasties, when, after the Buddhist assimilation, Confucianism took new eclectic and syncretic forms. The last period was that of the meeting between the atheistic or pantheistic Chinese and the modern European missionaries. The Jesuits taught mathematics and philosophy to the Chinese, who showed a great appreciation for this scientific knowledge. The German historians stressed that this great interest and fascination for our mathematics and its applications in astronomy was the proof of their sure weakness in sciences: 'the whole Chinese philosophy is lime without sand, therefore the European systems [of thought], because of their connection to the philosophical reflections, could not but excite the Chinese admiration'[114] (ibid., V, 875).

From this history of Chinese philosophy, Brucker drew his historical conclusions about the problematic issue of Chinese sources. He began providing a few historical reasons for the difficult – and unreliable – interpretations of Chinese texts. First of all, Chinese was an ambiguous and imprecise language. Secondly, there was a great corruption of texts due to the introduction of Buddhist belief in China, a thesis argued by Ricci himself and afterwards supported by all Jesuits and thinkers (which led to the 'pestis'). The last reason was the aforementioned 'book burning', which erased former literary tradition, thus the original roots of monotheism were far from being easily retraced. These were the historical effective reasons, but Brucker also accused the Jesuits of having manipulated these texts on purpose, as Renaudot and Heumann did (§3.3.). The Jesuits' interpretation of Chinese sources brings to mind the rewriting and the adaptation of ancient Greek sources that was made by the scholastics during the Middle Ages and the peripatetics in the Renaissance (ibid., V, 878). Therefore, although the Jesuits were acknowledged as learned scholars by the German Eclectic historian (ibid., V, 877), their understanding was similar to that of the Renaissance thinkers, who forced and adapted texts to their own current needs.

Brucker reported that already the quality of Chinese thought had been discussed at length: Leibniz and Wolff praised them, while many philosophers disregarded them and even a few missionaries did the same. Brucker minimized the importance of the 'Sinophile' thinkers and shortly said that: 'Chinese philosophy is lime without sand, a broken broom; it is ineffective, unable to connect properly its own principles, completely unable to reach effectively firm and definitive conclusions'[115] (ibid., V, 879). Leibniz himself, who highly praised them, was worth a thousand of Confucius (ibid., V, 881). Thus, the most eminent philosopher of China, acknowledged by everyone as the pillar of this civilization, was markedly inferior to any European thinker. That is because, as it was already claimed by many among the German Eclectics, the Chinese completely ignored logic and the art of reasoning. Logic was a Greek invention and all other civilizations either received it from the former or simply ignored it. Muslims and Europeans received Logic from the Greeks, whilst Chinese (and clearly all the 'Oriental' or 'Exotic' civilizations) were excluded from this knowledge. Brucker even conceded that they could be clever and capable thinkers, however, they actually lack any correct and systematic rational art. The same is true for their physics, which was poor and was certainly imported from other Oriental lands, likely from Egypt and from Greece thanks to the Arabs, who brought there a few good physical principles (ibid., V, 900).

The metaphysics of the Chinese was more refined than their logic, but it was overwhelmed with atheism. In each period of their history there were different forms of atheism, but a scrupulous investigation could also detect a kind of 'Ortodoxia Sinensium' (ibid., V, 883), i.e. Chinese orthodoxy, which disclosed acceptable definitions of God. However, their most acceptable definition of God was not better than the Greek definition of Jupiter (ibid., V, 886): the God of the 'Chinese Orthodoxy' was similar to the one worshipped by ancient heathen peoples. We find here again an antiquarian attitude. Therefore, there were clearly not effective traces of a true monotheism in China, despite what Ricci with his accommodation method claimed. And Brucker added also that the issue of whether the Chinese had worshipped in ancient times a monotheistic God was irrelevant, because Jesuits had to convert modern Chinese that actually did not believe in a single God but instead were atheists as Ricci himself argued. However, for the German historian the question of atheism in modern China, which was uncontroversial among all European thinkers (except Leibniz), needed important clarifications:

> the question of the atheism of the Chinese and of Confucius himself could be easily solved. Whereas we closely examine the term atheism, in our opinion it is not correct to attribute to the Chinese this impiety, because they worship the heaven animated by the divine spirit. If instead atheism would be understood as a sort of pantheism or deism according to a not uncommon understanding, we cannot envisage how the Chinese could be freed from this accuse beyond all doubt, since they connect the world with God so closely and believe that the divine spirit is in every part of the world itself.[116]
>
> ibid., V, 889

This clarification of the term 'atheism' reveals the real historical attention of the German author, far from the acrimony of Renaudot and consequently Heumann, but fully aware of the contemporary libertine debate about atheism (particularly in France and the Dutch Republic). The Chinese were not properly speaking atheists, since they believe in Heaven, which is animated by God, thus they have somehow a theistic belief (after Ricci). However, if the word atheism – according to the current debate – was taken as synonym of immanentism, pantheism and even deism, they could but be atheists. Therefore, Brucker disagreed with both Bayle and Leibniz or Wolff. He contested Bayle, because the Chinese were not atheistic thinkers, because they believed in Heaven and thus they were theists. But, at the same time, he rejected the good morality and the ancient traces of monotheism as suggested by the accommodationism of Jesuits and the harmonic perennialism of Leibniz. Chinese were pantheists, immanentists[117] and deists but not atheists, because the only Spinozistic, Quietist and atheistic sect was that of Buddhism.

Whether the ineffectiveness of Chinese Logic and sciences was suggested since several of the first accounts, their morality was renowned and esteemed by most of the European thinkers. We know that already Renaudot and Heumann openly rejected this acknowledgement, but the presumed morality of Mandarins was still a widespread opinion in the eighteenth century (i.e. among Sinophilies). Brucker already quoted Mosheim's critical understanding of Confucius's morality, but he stressed again this point at the end of the chapter:

> As regards theoretical philosophy China is childish and it is by far exceeded by us, as it clearly follows from what we said. [However,] great men – admiring and praiseful – claimed that Chinese practical philosophy even exceeded our own. At first those men were the Jesuits, but also Leibniz confirmed that theory, and his approach was followed by some great men as G.B. Bulfingers [sic.] and C. Wolf [sic.], not to mention the 'deities' of the minor peoples.[118]
>
> ibid., V, 902

The practical or moral philosophy of the Chinese had been praised for almost a century and a half, since la Mothe le Vayer. The sarcastic expression 'deities of the minor people' is quite intriguing, we could wonder who those minor people were. They probably were the libertines themselves and the Radical thinkers, while the 'deities' could be le Vayer himself, but above all Isaac Vossius and Bayle. Brucker mentioned only Leibniz, Christian Wolff and Georg Bernhard Bilfinger (1693–1750), all of whom were German Lutheran thinkers. Wolff is usually reputed a follower of Leibniz in the vision of China and Bilfinger was a pupil of Wolff, thus somehow they were included in a sort of philosophical lineage. We might suppose that Brucker reputed these three philosophers as effective philosophical interlocutors, while the other 'Sinophile' thinkers were not even worth being mentioned.

Brucker acknowledged that Chinese moral norms, as reported by the Jesuits and the aforementioned Lutheran thinkers, were certainly respectable, however, he suggested that those norms were the result of a European adjustment. The beautiful norms of Confucius were indeed beautiful but they were not Chinese. He suggested that from a deeper investigation of Chinese society would arise the real nature of their morality, which was political and not related to the heart and soul of men. The unique aim of this morality was to maintain the political control of this immense empire and Chinese history testified to its success. But, this stability of the empire required the suppression of all human instincts, passions and desires, since they could prejudice the complex and precise hierarchy of power, which was the unique frame of this society. Brucker described accurately the three most general levels of this social hierarchy: 'of the family regime, the offices of the functionaries, [and] the administration of the Empire ...'.[119] This threefold system oppressed Chinese men as three 'Russian dolls', because each level reproduced in larger scale the family unit, with the functionary and even the emperor as inscrutable fathers of their subjects. This morality did not lead men to happiness but to their most complete submission, in order to make the imperial violence less and less necessary (ibid., V, 903). Therefore, this ethics was not an effective guide for men, a means of inner and outer improvement, but instead, we can say metaphorically, the soft velvet glove hiding the imperial iron fist.

Furthermore, these oppressive norms did not need rational investigations or explanations, since their reasons were more external premises than argumentative outcomes of the mind. The imperial hierarchy and its needs were only expressed in the forms of moral norms, however, they did not need the practical philosophy to be deduced and produced. The real reason behind each norm preceded ethics, thus there was no room for a concrete moral reflection or discourse. Brucker closed the chapter addressing his critic to his most eminent German interlocutor:

> We add a few words to what we said and exhort to a last reflection: Chinese ethics ignores the definite [moral] principle. This ethics could neither determine which is the innate reason, which is the rectitude of the heart and which is its praised perfection, nor reveal the [moral] obligation. [Therefore] it is undeniable that the illustrious Wolff raised Chinese ethics at an excessive high degree.[120]
>
> ibid., V, 906

According to Brucker, Wolff, probably the writer of the most refined demonstrative-deductive critic of morality before Kant, completely misunderstood Chinese morality. Brucker stressed that his misunderstanding was obvious since Chinese morality lacked reasoning, principle and obligation, which on the contrary were the pivotal tenets of Wolffian ethics. The rule of philosophy, according to Wolff himself, was to make human life and actions perfect, thus to improve the man himself. On the contrary, Chinese morality was oppressive and its real aim was only the political suppression of dissent, thus this system had nothing in common with Wolffian practical philosophy. Therefore, grounded on his arguments against the Chinese, the eclectic historian was at ease in claiming that Wolff, who was an excellent moralist, was wrong about the Chinese, since he wrongly confused his own positive ethics with that of the Chinese and he even prejudiced the reputation of his own demonstrative system. But, as we reported before, Wolff did not compose only one text where he praised Chinese morality, but instead he did so in several of his essays and monographs during all his academic life (§3.2.).

After the Chinese, Brucker dealt shortly with the Japanese, but about them we mention only that their land was the farthest one reached by the aforementioned spreading of the 'Buddhist plague' from Egypt. The last very short chapter is about the Indo-Canadians, since they were praised by Leibniz and obviously Brucker demolished these given reasons. But more intriguing is the global opinion of the author on Africa and America:

> We have finished the Asiatic section, and moving westerly, we look at the coasts of Africa and America. However, since these immense regions are shrouded in fog, we see nothing consistent with a great history of philosophy ... Moreover, the superstition of heathens in Africa and America is so deep that we cannot figure out anything that could be consistent with our dissertation.[121]
>
> ibid., V, 919

Brucker did not provide racial claims as Deslandes, who depicted Australians and Africans as monsters (§2.7.), but his ultimate philosophical judgement was identical. Africa and America were lands of superstition and where was cultivated a thought not only inferior to the European philosophy but even to the Asiatic wisdom, thus being not even worth mentioning. Therefore, according to Brucker, the history of philosophy was the history of Greek and European philosophy, to which at the most could be added a chapter about the Asians in order to prove their philosophical ineptitude, whilst all other civilizations were so coarse that their thought could not even be discussed, since it was completely irrational and superstitious.

The last paragraph of 'De philosophia exotica', which is also the last of the entire treatise, is a 'Peroratio totius operis'. This 'Peroratio' concerns us for at least three reasons. Firstly, the author stressed that all the philosophical investigation was 'secundum leges criticam examinata'[122] ('examined by means of critical laws'). Therefore, the exclusion of Asians from the philosophical field was because their thought was not consistent with (European) rational and critical principles. Secondly, Brucker asked for God's intercession to defeat all the errors and heresies he dealt with in this long dissertation and, as we already stressed several times, the apologetic aim of his history should not be neglected when reading this disapproval of the 'exotic' wisdom. The last issue we want to mention is about the insertion of this 'Peroratio' into the book on 'exotic' civilization, without a specific title. We stress this point, because it is clear that, despite what Anne-Lise Dyck says, this book is an integral part of the work and not a supplement as it was the book on Chaldeans for Stanley. Brucker planned the book on Asians since the beginning, as Burnet did with his Appendix. Therefore, for Brucker, China and India were an integral part of the world history of thought, but these lands lost their place in the effective history of philosophy because the new 'scientific' – although apologetic – definition of philosophy excluded them.

The image of the 'exotic' or 'Oriental' civilizations provided by Brucker and hence widespread around Europe was the confluence of the different images we presented in our investigation. According to him, Indian and Chinese thinkers were immoral, irrational, illogical and incompetent in science. These countries have never had real philosophers, since the Indian wise men were clergymen or renouncers and the Chinese moralists were politicians concerned with the restriction of freedom and possible revolts. Their morality aimed at suppressing passions, free thinking and even individual life, whilst Brucker argued that a true moral system should lead men to their self-improvement and to their happiness. Asians were irrational or illogical because the literary forms of dialogue and poetry prevented any line of reasoning, deduction and argument. Furthermore, the Asiatic incompetence in the sciences was proved by their great appreciation of European sciences taught by Jesuits, mostly in China, and by their ineffective chronologies fostered by the missionaries themselves.

For Brucker this negative appraisal was related not only to the contemporary Asians, as it was to a certain extent for Heurn, Horn and Burnet – the historians we presented as 'followers' of the 'prisca theologia' model – but also to the ancient Asians and this was already the leading opinion among Eclectics. Asian ways of thinking, as every thought that did not belong to ancient Greece or modern Europe, were naturally non-philosophical, since they did not share the true concerns of philosophy. As we reported in full, Brucker did provide very detailed descriptions of the Indians and the Chinese, but in doing so he aimed at proving their distance from philosophy and their idolatric or atheistic concerns. Heumann never mentioned openly the Egyptian atheistic plague diffused in Asia through Buddhism, since 'atheism' was not according to his rigorous history a philosophical issue, but instead a religious one. On the contrary, Brucker, who aimed with his history also at detecting idolatries and heresies, accepted the theory of the Buddhist infection and provided a description of this sect as almost Spinozistic, Quietistic and, using a later term, nihilistic, thus following the long dispute of the 'Chinese rites' as his own master Buddeus did. As Günther Lottes says: 'If the only road to truth was through the Christian religion, then all other civilizations were necessary and essentially inferior to that of Europe.'[123] Therefore, in the Eclectic histories of philosophy the exclusion of the Asiatic philosophies was already complete and the reasons for this exclusion were already provided, almost a century before Hegel.

3.7 Jakob Brucker's 'system of philosophy' and Chinese thinking

In this last section of the chapter, we would like to raise a few final methodological remarks about the relevance of Brucker for the history of philosophy and the effects of his – and of German Eclecticism in general – definition of what is philosophy on Chinese histories of philosophy. Leo Catana[124] has devoted a very insightful monograph to Brucker's history of philosophy as based on the concept of a 'system of philosophy' that, when applied to Greek and early Renaissance thinkers, turns out to be a philosophical imposition and violence. Catana discusses Brucker's descriptions of philosophers such as Thales, Plato and Aristotle, but his real focus is on Giordano Bruno, a brilliant but rather unsystematic philosopher of the Renaissance. In the second part of his monograph, Catana also tries to show the long effects of the 'system of philosophy' on the 'history of philosophy' discipline. As we already saw, the label of unsystematicity is usually applied to both Chinese and Indian philosophies; their irrationality and lack of logical argument is the base of Brucker's critique. Therefore, Catana's remarks are actually more effective about Asia than about Giordano Bruno.

First of all, we need to make clear that the influence of Brucker's history of philosophy is not reducible to the influence of his books,[125] but rather to the influence of his paradigm.[126] The paradigm of the 'system of philosophy' spread into the whole nineteenth- and twentieth-century philosophical arena, on all the branches of Kantism and Hegelianism and so on.[127] We think it is useful to quote Catana's definition of this relevance in full:

> Although Hegel's history of philosophy, and his concept 'system of development', has received far more critical attention in the nineteenth and twentieth centuries than Brucker's concept 'system of philosophy', this concept of Brucker has had, I shall argue, a far deeper impact on the historiography of philosophy than Hegel's concept 'system of development'. Surprisingly, the nature and influence of this concept of Brucker has not yet been traced, even though it has played a key role in the method of the history of philosophy from the time of Brucker and up till our time.
>
> Brucker was one of the chief founders of the history of philosophy as a philosophical discipline, and this notion of his entered the discipline on such a profound level that subsequent historians of philosophy, including Hegel, have typically perceived it as a natural and inherent methodological tool of the discipline.
>
> ibid., 4

What does 'system of philosophy' mean? The scholar correctly highlights that the methodological meaning of the term 'system' did not exist in the European philosophical arena before the seventeenth century and became an unavoidable historiographical concept only since the eighteenth century, precisely among the German Eclectic thinkers. Heumann and Brucker inherited this concept from the Protestant reformer Philipp Melanchthon, who was among the first to use the term 'system' to speak about philosophical and rational methodology.[128]

For our investigation, Catana's denunciation of the use of this concept on previous philosophers as an evident risk of methodological violence, since it imposes anachronistic standards, is deeply interesting. What's worse is that Brucker used the term mostly in a critical way against the philosophers of the past and present outside the Eclectic school, in order to blame their dramatic incoherency. Catana articulates four characteristics of the 'system of philosophy' concept according to Brucker.[129] They are as follows: 1. 'autonomy of individual systems of philosophy'; 2. 'autonomy of philosophical movements inspired by a Classical Philosopher'; 3. 'deduction from Principles of individual systems of philosophy'; and 4. 'comprehensiveness in a system of philosophy'. The first characteristic suggests that any effective philosophical reflection should never be related to any non-philosophical discipline. In that way philosophy became a self-centred discipline with its own principles, completely impenetrable from outside this restricted field, thus contrary to any interdisciplinary understanding. The second characteristic is about the autonomy of each school inspired by a philosopher of the past from any other school or philosopher outside this circle. This makes any school necessarily unitary, impenetrable, inward-looking and historically coherent. The same Eclectic school, despite its name, is presented in this way. Eclectic thinkers are systematic and revolutionary.[130] The third point is about the relevance of the deduction of any argument from principles or axioms inherently philosophical and abstract, i.e. expression of the perfect reasonability and coherency of the philosophical thinking. What is useful in the historical investigation of a certain philosopher is not to expose his/her writing process in the most complete and reliable way, but rather to reduce his philosophy to a few general all-embracing principles. The last aspect is comprehensiveness; according to this characteristic any effective and coherent philosophy has to investigate all branches of philosophy and make them coherent under the aforementioned general principles.

As we can understand, a presumed strict coherency is the real and only golden rule. Catana advocates that 'the concept "system of philosophy" has served as a principle of exclusion in the history of philosophy. One notorious victim is the philosophy of the Italian Renaissance'.[131] However, we saw very clearly that extra-European or 'exotic' philosophies, as Brucker named them, are identically excluded and dismissed as any Italian Renaissance – i.e. syncretic – thinker. As we already mentioned, Asian ways of thinking – particularly Buddhism – and syncretic philosophers – mostly Neoplatonic – are both to be acknowledged as intellectual 'plagues'. Chinese philosophy is a true 'philosophical enemy', since, according to Brucker, it is the emblem of unsystematicity, thus it is not philosophy. We borrow Catana's expression saying that, according to the definition of the 'system of philosophy', extra-European philosophy – particularly Chinese because of Brucker's opposition to Jesuits and *sinophile* philosophers – is 'excluded *a priori*'.

If we contrast Chinese ways of thinking with these four strict characteristics of Brucker's system of philosophy, we face a wide distance on all of them. For the autonomy of philosophy from other subjects, we need only to say that Chinese 'philosophical' texts have never been distinguished as a specific genre. Treatises exist in Chinese literature, however, philosophical thinking was more often expressed through commentaries to the Classics, master teachings, dialogues, short thoughts, philological reflections, life anecdotes and poems. For instance, the four depositories (*siku* 四庫) in which the whole Chinese literary production was divided were the Classics (*fenjing* 分經), history (*shi* 史), 'philosophy' (*zi* 子) and collections (*ji* 集). However, what we translated as 'philosophy' actually means 'masters', in order to recall the broad idea of a learned teaching that is not defined as a specific field in contrast to others.

About the autonomy of any school derived from a philosopher, we could mention countless Chinese counterfacts, but we chose only two among the most relevant. Despite the name Confucianism that we use for describing 'followers' or 'disciples' of Confucius, in Chinese philosophy this school is named *ru* 儒; this term means cultivated or learned men in several arts and traditions, scholar and even official of the empire. Although Confucius has undoubtedly been the most influential and respected thinker in the whole of Chinese thought, there is not a school which derived its name from him. Among Chinese schools of thought, only ancient Mohists took their name from their master and founder Mo 墨. Therefore, Chinese schools of thought, despite revering a master, are usually not defined by his name. Moreover, hybridization was the norm. The School of Mystery (*xuanxue* 玄學), the Song Neo-Confucianism (*songdai xin rujia* 宋代新儒家) and several others benefited from the creative confluence of opposed theories and debates among different schools. The Chinese Empire itself promoted convergence of doctrines more than opposition, and this is rather clear in the slogan '*sanjiao heyi* 三教合一', namely 'the three doctrines are but one' (i.e. Confucianism, Daoism and Buddhism).

On the third characteristic about the deduction of incontrovertible and purely rational truths from principles, we quote Harbsmeier's lucid reflection on Chinese rhetoric and philosophical argumentation:

> Ideally, classical Chinese texts sow the seeds of meaning in the reader rather than transmitting explicitly the fruits of thought. Thus ancient Chinese texts cultivate an implicit mutual understanding. They tend to be pregnant with a socially constructed meaning, rather than directly expressive of a meaning exclusively imposed on the reader by the writer ... These texts suggest rather than impose meaning, and they may suggest certain kinds of conclusions to be drawn from this. They leave the reader a peculiar inner fertile space of freedom in which the energy of the pregnant thought expressed in the text is designed to take root and gain a life of its own, inspired by and in the spirit of the harmoniously patterned text ...[132]

For the Chinese, an explicitly demonstrative text is somehow crude or rude (*cu* 粗), and lacks the rich energy of a discourse of cultivation, which instead has to be elegant and subtle (*wei* 微). An explicit and intellectual reasoning is only good to achieve understanding and knowledge (*zhi* 知) but cannot penetrate the heart and mind (*xin* 心) of man, becoming a natural attitude, an embodiment of wisdom. The contemporary philosopher Yang Gourong usually names Chinese philosophy 'the study of human nature and Dao' (*xingdao zhixue* 性道之学),[133] since its aim is not to reach a supreme or universal truth, but rather to perfect the applied study and learning of the nature of both humanity and the cosmos.

Chinese logic and epistemology is based not on univocal and universal principles from which reason can deduce facts and truth through rational cause-effect chains, but rather on a correlative system of interpenetrating opposites. Again Harbsmeier provides an effective and to the point explanation:

> The Chinese, one might feel, were not so much interested in proving general theses as they were in correlating phenomena with supernatural agents, *shen* 神, and classifying them, e.g. under such broad categories as *yin* 陰 and *yang* 陽, 'hot' and 'cold' in medicine and natural philosophy, or *wu hsing* 五行 'five phases'.[134]

For pre-imperial and imperial Chinese learned men, 'scientific proofs' were more likely to be correlations of facts and intelligent classifications of apparently unrelated elements in order to make the cosmos intelligible.

About the last characteristic, namely the necessity to be comprehensive, it is enough to know that Chinese thought or philosophy has never been divided into fields as in Greek philosophy, particularly since Aristotle. Broadly speaking, Chinese philosophy has almost been devoted, on one side, to the understanding and perfectioning of human nature (i.e. morality and politics) and, on the other, to the understanding of the undetectable principle behind reality (i.e. the cause of change and order), named *li* 理. Fang Yizhi 方以智 (1611–71), a late Ming and early Qing thinker, classified Chinese study into three fields: *zhice* 質測, the investigation of reality, i.e. 'natural sciences', *zaili* 宰理, the study of social and moral norms, and, at the last hierarchical stage, *tongji* 通幾, the complete investigation of the ultimate and undetectable reasons of change, the unexpressed origin.[135] According to this classification, the western thought, that he knew thanks to the Jesuits, was of good quality in 'natural sciences' but extremely weak in the study of the last level, devoted to the ultimate and the principle (*li* 理).[136] This classification is clearly far from what Brucker meant with the concept of 'system of philosophy' and his sharp distinction of fields.

More recently, the twentieth-century Chinese historian of philosophy Zhang Dainian 张岱年, in his most influential work translated in English – *Key Concepts in Chinese Philosophy*[137] – attempted the titanic task of classifying Chinese philosophical fields and technical concepts that he named 'system of categories', a definition that actually reminds us of Brucker. Despite the incredible utility of this classification of terms, the main impression it perhaps leaves upon the reader of this investigation is the unsystematic use of terms in Chinese schools from all time periods. There are concepts specific to one thinker, specific to one period, crossing several fields and so on. The book looks more like a dictionary than a systematic classification, and the same Zhang is in fact the editor of an outstanding *Chinese philosophy dictionary* (*Zhongguo zhexue dacidian* 中国哲学大辞典).[138] In *Key Concepts* he classifies sixty-four terms – that he correctly presents as a selection – under three general fields: metaphysics (ontology and cosmology), anthropology (morality and psychology) and lastly, epistemology (theory of knowledge, philosophy of language and theory of truth). The same author reflects that, in Chinese terms, these three fields were actually named the 'Way of heaven', the 'Way of man' and the 'method of study'.[139] We should ask ourselves whether these translations in European terms are neutral or not. Looking at the selected terms, we can find that particularly Confucianism (as a whole) touched – in different periods and in different ways – all the three general fields, but does this mean that a Chinese thinker needs to be engaged in all of them in order to be acknowledged as a philosopher? This idea of a necessary completeness of the system would likely exclude all Daoist thinkers, all Buddhist thinkers and most of the Confucian thinkers as taken singularly. This is just to say that the idea of a system where all the parts are driven by a principle – or a very few principles – is closer to an image of thought as a geometry or a physical mechanism, two concepts both very far from a way of thinking based on the idea of the undetectableness of the principle (*li* 理), of the continuous change, of the search for an internal and external harmony (*he* 和) that can never be completely achieved. Chinese thought is closer to the idea of a historical accumulation of methods for perfectioning human nature more than to the reduction of this task to a simple rational system. Chinese thinking is historical and cumulative in itself. Therefore, if we want to find a true system as in Brucker, we need to consider the whole of Chinese thought, since, as we mentioned, the general attitude was very holistic. A comprehensive thinker as Zhu Xi of the Song dynasty has a very systematic attitude, however, his system is truly holistic; in that case, the idea of 'system' meant that his thinking was able to find convergences among divergent opinions. But Brucker's 'system of philosophy' is absolutely anti-holistic. It is strongly exclusivist. It is the means to discover and delete rational mistakes (of other thinkers of the past and present) in order to produce a new, perfect philosophical theory.

Despite this natural incompatibility, the effect of Brucker's 'system of philosophy' can be easily detected in 'histories of Chinese philosophy' written in early twentieth-century China. We quote only the first two instances, the one written by Hu Shi 胡适 in 1917 and the one by Feng Youlan, published two years later. Hu Shi's history was preceded by a short preface by the influential philosopher and educator Cai Yuanpei 蔡元培, at the time rector of the University of Beijing. Cai reported that the writing of a history of Chinese philosophy had to face two main difficulties: 1. the falsification of original documents brought on in the Qing age, softened only thanks to the *hanxue* 汉学 movement (i.e. the classical studies opposed to the imperial transmission); 2. 'a formal problem: the Chinese learning has never had a systematic (*xitong* 系统) restitution .... We need to create a system anew and we cannot rely on any of our ancient authors, on the contrary, we cannot but rely on western history of philosophy. Therefore, anyone who has never investigated western history of philosophy could not provide an appropriate analysis'.[140] The second issue very deeply reflects the influence of the systematicity of western history of philosophy as compared to the presumed unsystematicity and unreliability of the sources of Chinese philosophy. Cai was not absolutely suggesting, as Brucker did, that China does not have a philosophical tradition, however, he was completely certain that China needed western 'system of philosophy', as this was the only correct and universal way of understanding this discipline. Antonio S. Cua efficaciously outlines the merits of Hu's history according to Cai: '(1) the use of the methods of evidence; (2) the skill in distinguishing the "pure" elements of philosophical thought from those of mythological and political history of the Chinese people; (3) the ability to render impartial evaluation of the merits and demerits of different philosophies; and finally (4) the systematic character of the work'.[141] All of the qualities listed by Cai are perfectly compatible with the four characters of Brucker's 'system of philosophy'. The idea of an evaluation is intrinsic in the Eclectics' religious (Lutheran) goal of rationally detecting mistakes. What has changed between Heumann and Brucker's religious aim and Hu's laic one is the shift in attention of (western) philosophy from religious faith to faith in a universal Spirit that follows a cultural realization process (i.e. Hegel's *Geist*), in which Europe is the only apex, the expression of the universality that other civilizations have to imitate as much as possible.

Hu Shi in his *History* reveals at least two undergoing stands. On one side, he showed a great interest in any school of ancient times which did not became the imperial standard, thus he favoured the late Mohist school of logic and philosophy of language, which was more easily comparable with western schools and investigations, at the expense of Confucianism. On the other side, he revendicated a world role for Chinese philosophy together with Indian and western (i.e. ancient Greece and ancient Judaic thinking) traditions, even suggesting that, in fifty or one hundred years, the future emergence of a world philosophy would be possible.¹⁴² Furthermore, he proposed a historical subdivision of the history of thought based on the western periods, namely ancient, medieval and modern, although he completed a history of only the first of the three.

Feng Youlan's *History of Chinese philosophy* became worldly renowned thanks to the first translation in English and subsequent translations in several languages (although of a shortened and simplified version of the text). In this *History*, Feng wrote a remarkable methodological first chapter where he discussed the meaning of Chinese philosophy and its weakness. He started reporting that the word 'Philosophy' (*zhexue* 哲學) came from the West in Chinese language and, since in China philosophy was not univocal, he adhered to the foreigner meaning. He thus presents the subdivision in fields, such as ontology and cosmology, in order to define the area of the discipline.

However, the most interesting section is about the weakness of the Chinese way of thinking, particularly about the presumed Chinese logical underdevelopment, that was the result of a greater attention to human affairs instead of epistemology and language. He reports that Chinese philosophy was usually acknowledged as unsystematic (*wu xitong* 無系統), showing the long-lasting introjection of Brucker's criticism. However, Feng was fully aware of the fact that qualifying Chinese philosophy as completely unsystematic would mean to reject the possibility of it being included in the philosophical field, and he refused to even consider this possibility. Therefore, he tries his best to suggest two different meanings of the concept 'systematicity': one would be formal (*xingshi* 形式) and one real or concrete (*shizhi* 實質). According to his view, while western philosophy certainly had a stronger 'formal systematicity', Chinese philosophy had a 'concrete or essential systematicity' that was comparable to the first, although formally more fragile.¹⁴³ Antonio S. Cua interestingly suggests translating in English these two terms as 'explicit/articulate' for 'formal' and 'implicit/inchoate' for 'concrete'.¹⁴⁴ Therefore, while western philosophy would show an explicit system, Chinese philosophy would be grounded on an implicit system that does not reveal itself in its effective formality. Although he suggested this terminological reflection, Feng was certain that Chinese philosophy needed renovation, and this is the reason for tracing Chinese history of philosophy in only two periods: 1. ancient masters (*zixue* 子學) and 2. Classical learning (*jingxue* 經學). He did not use the western division into periods – i.e. Ancient, Middle Ages and Modern – however the lack of modernity is self-evident, in a certain way because of the empire's backwardness – as compared to western modern nations – Chinese thought did not overcome the 'Middle Ages'. Feng's history confirms again that, in republican China, philosophical 'systematicity' was the pivotal question, completely unavoidable when the western historiography of philosophy was taken as a universal instrument and not as a way of understanding philosophy grounded on a specific context, as was the Eclectic historiography with its long impact.

There are two open questions that our research has discussed thus far: (1) historiography and (2) philosophy. These concepts both arose in a specific western context, which we investigated and which is absolutely not neutral or universal in itself. More recently, Chinese historians of philosophy are gradually becoming aware of the "local" character of these two terms. For instance, the aforementioned Zhang Dainian

张岱年 refused to write a 'history of Chinese philosophy'. He kept only 'philosophy' (*zhexue* 哲学), writing scholarly explanations of specific terms related to Chinese ways of thinking, not considering a history the best way to explain this culture. He revendicates a linguistic specificity for Chinese philosophical thought that is not expressible into a time sequence of gradual perfectioning. On the contrary, Ge Zhaoguang 葛兆光 titled his masterpiece *History of Chinese Thought* (*Zhongguo sixiang shi* 中国思想史),[145] since he openly refuses the term philosophy in the Prefaces to both volumes. He advocates that the term 'philosophy' (*zhexue* 哲学) was used for the following reasons: 1. recognition of equal dignity (with the West), 2. because it was already a well-organized discipline suitable for Chinese university and departments adhering to the western scientific fashion. He does not look for 'philosophy' in Chinese ways of thinking, but rather for any 'refined learning in Chinese history' (中国历史上各种学问), thus creating a broader and richer 'intellectual history' or 'history of thought' (*sixiang lishi* 思想历史).[146] According to his opinion, to persist with the term 'philosophy' is 'to cut own foot to fit shoes' (*xuezu shilü* 削足适履), meaning shoes of others, too small for us.[147] The 'system of philosophy' concept is clearly the most uncomfortable shoe for an Asian thinker to wear.

Conclusion: The Tight Shoes of Philosophy

'et la seule histoire véritable, qui ne peut se faire que par entr'aide, est l'histoire universelle.'

Marc Bloch, *Apologie pour l'histoire ou métier d'historien*, 15

In the current investigation, we presented the different understandings of China and India from 1600 to 1744 within the three main historiographical paradigms of philosophy used at that time. The first one was that of 'perennialism' and 'prisca theologia', which was held – among our historians – by Otto van Heurn, Georg Horn, Thomas Burnet and Leibniz. The second paradigm is the 'natural atheism', which had Pierre Bayle as its firm advocate and which was contested by both 'perennialists' (i.e. Leibniz) and 'anti-perennialists'. The last historical paradigm is the 'scientific model' argued by the German Eclectic historians, who were Christian Thomasius, Georg Walch, Friedrich Gentzken, Christoph August Heumann and Jakob Brucker. This last model established the exclusion of all non-Greek and extra-European thought from the history of philosophy, since these civilizations did not meet the (European) standards of the discipline.

Mungello explains the philosophical attitude of the Enlightened thinkers who exalted China and India as part of the universal frame of rationality, but we contend that the same could be said also of the thinkers who excluded these civilizations. The reasons for both exclusion and inclusion were barely concerned with the effective understanding of Asian cultures, but instead were led by universalistic concerns as regards reason and religion. Mungello writes about the 'inclusivists':

> Most seventeenth-century European thinkers who showed a strong interest in non-European philosophy believed in the universal basis of knowledge. The truths that they discovered did not, in their view, end at the borders of Europe. Consequently, when these Europeans encountered other philosophies, they tried to understand the differences in terms of an absolute conception of truth and falsehood rather than regard these other philosophies as merely different or alternative paths to truth.[1]

The same 'absolute conception of truth' justified the exclusion of these civilizations, since they were judged 'unphilosophical' according to the universal definition of reason and, consequently, true (namely systematic) philosophy.

Brucker's descriptions of Indians and Chinese were the critical summary of all previous descriptions. First of all, Brucker respected Horn's twofold system of descriptions: a chapter on ancient Indians, where he invited the readers to consult a final section on contemporary Chinese and Indians. Therefore, all these historians saw these two civilizations as a problem, because they were contemporary and they both had a long tradition, certainly chronologically longer than Christianity. Brucker's chapter on ancient Indians was written as usual reporting the common ancient western sources (Megasthenes, Strabo, Diodorus Siculus, etc), while the chapter on moderns was a criticism of missionary sources. Whereas for 'perennialists' India and China had received the spreading of wisdom, Brucker, as Heumann, refused this spreading and investigated these civilizations as historically separate from the Jews and the Christians.

Brucker and Deslandes were the first European thinkers who reported in their histories the complexity of Indian culture, as opposed to the monolithic description of Greek sources, according to which Brachmanes, Gymnosophists and 'Buddhists' were a single unclear sect. Deslandes provided the first description of the Indian schools of philosophy, which were eighteen in number, two of them being the philosophies of Grammar and Vedānta. In the related chapter, we suggested that the source behind the French historian was the *Prasthānabheda* by Madhusūdana Sarasvatī, a doxography of the school of the Advaita Vedānta, a hypothesis which if confirmed would prove the influence of Vedānta in the understanding of India already in the early eighteenth century. Instead, Brucker reported La Croze's description of Indian religious and spiritual classes, the former worshipped different gods (three were the most important: Brahmā, Viṣṇu and Śiva), while the spiritual or ascetic classes were only devoted to meditation and were detached from cults and worldly life. The scientific knowledge of Indians was minimal, since they did not reach it through rational investigation and reflection, but only because it was stated in their tradition. The same was true for their ethics, which was suitable only for ascetics and it was not grounded on rational principles.

About the Chinese, Brucker presented their cultural history as divided into four stages, which were: the age of Confucius, Confucianism and the spreading of Buddhism, Neo-Confucianism and, finally, the introduction of European sciences thanks to the missionaries. Obviously, according to Brucker, the last stage represented the first and only period in Chinese history when true rational knowledge reached this country. That is true since Chinese thought completely lacked logic and rational principles. As Brucker said: 'Chinese philosophy is lime without sand, a broken broom; it is ineffective, unable to connect properly its own principles, completely unable to reach effectively firm and definitive conclusions.'[2] Moreover, the Chinese were immanentist, and immanentism was also intended as a kind of atheism. Brucker did not openly quote Bayle's 'Oriental Spinozism', but it was clear that the Chinese shared an irrational principle, which could but lead them to atheism or at least irreligion. The same was true for their morality, which was not grounded on principles and reflections but instead on political control, since the Chinese Empire in order to guarantee its stability imposed a moral of suppression and repression of human nature. Therefore, the Chinese natural morality praised by la Mothe le Vayer, Isaac Vossius, Pierre Bayle, Gottfried Leibniz, Christian Wolff, Georg Bernhard Bilfinger and several *philosophes* (i.e. French Enlightened thinkers), was completely ineffective according to Brucker and it was instead the undeniable expression of Chinese despotic system. In this civilization, morality was merely an instrument in the hand of the imperial power.

To the Chinese and Indians, we should add a sect (or group of sects), which crossed both civilizations: Buddhism (the so-called 'sect of Fo'). This sect was described since the followers of Xavier, particularly Ricci, as the atheistic thought responsible of the disappearance of the monotheistic original faith in China. The description, from time to time more negative and wide, of the spreading of Buddhism, supported the theory of the 'atheistic plague' argued by Kircher. This gradual elaboration was grounded on one prevailing element: Buddhists believed in an immanentist doctrine, which had as material and active cause emptiness or nothingness. Brucker, while he rejected any comparison of Chinese and Indian thought with western philosophy, accepted the description of the Spinozism, Quietism and atheism of Buddhism. This sect was clearly an exception and the reason was probably its diffusion out of its original cultural boundaries. Seventeenth- and eighteenth-century philosophers such as Bayle and Brucker were already aware of the spreading of the sect from India into China, Ceylon, South-East Asia, Japan, Korea, Mongolia, Tibet, etc. We might suppose that, as it was the case of the missionaries, the 'Christian' historians feared the possible 'universalism' of Buddhism. Therefore, this 'soteriological path', which proclaimed the presumed 'God-nothing' (as Cristoforo Borri suggested), could but be the worst error in human history, the most diffused and dangerous faith. Chinese and Indians sects were wrong, irrational, idolatrous and ineffective, but they were not devilish as Buddhism was. Brucker shared Kircher's hypothesis of the diffusion of the atheist Egyptian doctrine in Asia only regarding Buddhism, while Confucianism and Indian sects were described as original to the countries, already grounded in this civilization before the epidemic spread of atheism. It is evident that the definition of a nihilistic Buddhism was already embedded in the all-inclusive word 'atheism' and it is wrong to claim that this topic arose in the 1830s as Roger-Pol Droit does. In 1954, the Indologist Helmuth von Glasenapp wrote an essay, the translation of which into English was entitled *Buddhism a Non-Theistic religion*.[3] This is a provocative and intriguing title that we can understand even if we ignore the debate after Brucker, since the features of the understanding of Buddhism as atheism had already been discussed and fixed since the late seventeenth century.[4] Furthermore, the debate about the atheism and nihilism of at least some Buddhist schools is still alive today, particularly about the Madhyamaka School led by Nāgārjuna.[5]

To sum up, what we want to argue is that the description of Asian civilizations was already settled in the first half of the eighteenth century. Basically, historians contended that all extra-European civilizations faithfully followed their given traditions, which they could not challenge or change in any aspect. Moreover, these peoples were not able to provide effective reasons for their theories and practices, but only tales and metaphors, thus their morality was not rational and did not lead men to perfection, instead it was grounded on superstition, asceticism (repression of passions and feelings) or political oppression. These Asian civilizations were childish in sciences and in theoretical knowledge, since they could observe events, but they lacked a science of logic that could guide them through deductions to stable systematic theories. Therefore, these images of the Chinese and Indian people were already built up decades before the triumphant colonialism. What Bankimchandra Chattopadhyay (1838–94) complained about some of his arrogant European contemporaries also seems to be true for several of our seventeenth- and eighteenth-century historians:

> It is the logical outcome of that monstrous claim of omniscience, which certain Europeans – an extremely limited number happily – put forward for themselves. No knowledge is true knowledge unless it has passed through the sieve of European criticism. All coin is false coin unless it bears the stamp of a Western mint. Existence is possible to nothing which is hid from their searching vision. Truth is not truth, but noisome error and rank falsehood, if it presumes to exist outside the pale of European cognisance.[6]

The alleged universalism of European philosophy as rational principle was a consequence of both the Enlightenment concept of rationality and the Lutheran (anti-*philosophe*) revised concept of philosophy as a secular tool useful in order to detect religious errors. Usually, the presumed universalism of philosophy is acknowledged as a product of Enlightenment and, afterwards, of Kantian and Hegelian philosophy, since in these philosophies lay the distinction between philosophy on one side and religion or tradition on the other side. But that distinction had already occurred in the 1720s, when Heumann rejected the possibility of a philosophy of clergymen, although he did not exclude Lutheran eclectics, who had religious concerns (like himself), from the list of effective philosophers. Brucker, who was also a parish priest, did not share the anti-clerical claim of Heumann, but he asserted the same separation between philosophy and religion. Therefore, although the religious or apologetical concerns among German Eclectics were relevant, they already conceived a secular philosophy, based on rational principles, and they, unlike Wolff, provided refined histories of philosophy, which aimed at retracing the historical universality of rational philosophy. Moreover, these histories were presented as a history of humankind, as a global selection of effective thinkers, where only ancient Greeks, a few Islamic philosophers – who took ancient philosophy back to Europe – together with modern European philosophers were legitimately discussed. The thinkers of other civilizations, then those of ancient Greece and Europe, were not properly 'philosophers', since they did not meet the alleged universal standard of the 'system of philosophy'.

This exclusion of Indian and Chinese thought from philosophy is often wrongly called the 'Hegelian exclusion', whereas Hegel provided a very changeable and intense understanding of India and China, from his young writings to the *Lectures on the History of Philosophy*. Actually, the true exclusion took root in the philosophical school of Christian Thomasius, of which Heumann and Brucker represented its more refined accomplishment. After them, particularly with the Kantian[7] historians such as Tennemann, histories of philosophy did not provide chapters on extra-European civilizations and they rejected any theories suggesting the spreading of philosophy from the original divine wisdom. This change in the historiographical perspective did not regard only Asians, but also Jewish thought,[8] which was excluded from philosophy, as for instance in Tiedemann, Tennemann and Hegel, only to name the most relevant historians. Tennemann added in the second edition of his *Grundriß der Geschichte der Philosophie* a brief chapter on Oriental philosophies that was not even a condensed digest, but only a list of short bibliographical notes on the most relevant Oriental civilizations.[9] In Kantian histories there was not any place for Oriental thought. On the contrary, Hegel introduced Indian and Chinese thoughts[10] in the first chapter of his history (*Lectures*), a phase not properly philosophical, but he reputed these two civilizations as the only non-Greek and European civilizations that deserved to be discussed. Obviously, as it was claimed since the early eighteenth century by several historians following Laërtius, Hegel suggested that the real philosophy was born in Greece, where the 'dialectic mediation' was effective.

The effect of the exclusion of Asian thought from the philosophical discipline was not limited to Europe,[11] since even in Asia Hegel's critical analysis of Oriental philosophies had a wide reception. As Wilhelm Halbfass pointed out: 'Hegel's influence is not confined to Europe. There is also a significant tradition of "Hegelianism", "Neo-Hegelianism" and "Anti-Hegelianism" in India, i.e. reception of, critical response to, and comparison with, Hegel's philosophy in general. There has, however, been much less response to his specific arguments concerning Indian philosophy and religion'.[12] 'Hegel's exclusion' has been a widespread argument in India and China, although several critiques levelled against him should have been more properly levelled against more 'exclusivist' thinkers as the aforementioned German Eclectic historians or several Kantian philosophers and historians. However, nowadays Chinese and Indian contemporary philosophers are mostly concerned not with Hegel himself but rather with the presumed universalism of European philosophical, rational, scientific and religious principles. Orientalism, since the early missionaries, was born as a description of the others with western eyes and by means of western words and standards. Idolatry, atheism, religion, irrationality, devilishness, etc., were all words strictly connected with the history of European thought. As we have seen in our historiographical investigation, during the seventeenth and eighteenth centuries, the evaluation and subsequent exclusion of non-Greek and extra-European civilizations had matured according to the self-understanding of European civilization. The European identity has emerged in opposition to what was not European. European thought, this was the pivotal point, presumed to be in itself universal, as it was the emblem of reason, of a secular and systematic reason.

In 1893, during the Congress of the World Parliament of Religions in Chicago (11 to 27 September), Vivekananda (Narendranātha Datta) – within the six speeches he delivered – claimed that Indian religion as a whole was a universal religion and that every instance expressed in every civilization was contained in the unequalled philosophy of Vedānta.[13] After a few decades, Sarvapalli Rādhākrishnan, professor in a couple of Indian Universities and at Oxford University, continued this universalistic project and wrote his *Indian philosophy*[14] in order to prove the progressive and dialectic morality of Indian sects, which reached its perfection in the Advaita Vedānta. In our opinion, *Indian philosophy* has been one of the most refined late-Hegelian histories, since the model followed was that of the German Idealism, where the *Geist* is the moral principle realized in the Vedānta school of philosophy.[15] It was not by chance that Rādhākrishnan exalted Indian morality, since, as we already well know, Indian morality had been despised from the early missionaries up to Brucker and the same was true for the following European philosophers. We understand that this 'claim of universality' was a reaction to the British Rāj colonial regime, but also to the orientalist studies that were often suggesting the low philosophical quality of Indian thought during the nineteenth and early twentieth centuries. However, this response to the European negative evaluation exploits the 'weapons' of the European philosophy itself, and this reaction forced Indian thought to find its self-identity grounded on outer or extraneous principles and terms.

Jarava Lal Mehta, an Indian philosopher expert in Heidegger's philosophy – they met a couple of times – and the author of a relevant book on the German philosopher,[16] says about the exposure of Indian thinkers to the western universalism:

> Western thought as Western metaphysical thought or philosophy thus necessarily enters, very much like a Trojan horse, into the thinking of the non-Western world, not like a bullet hitting a body or a piece of stone shattering a glass pane on impact, but like a virus, to use Arend Theodoor van Leewen's word, invisibly altering our perception of reality.[17]

The 'Trojan horse' is European metaphysics, but moreover the specific terms of European philosophy, through which the tenets of extra-European philosophies are formulated and evaluated. The 'Trojan horse' is the alleged universalism of western philosophy, which pervaded Indian culture as a polemical reaction to the European colonization of the country and of the minds. This universalism charges 'the other' of 'a weak otherness' opposed to the rational and moral principles of the western self-identity. Mehta suggests that European or western identity needs to be opposed to 'other cultural identities' in order to create itself, because without a contrasting identity its self-acknowledgement is at risk. The Indian philosopher also stresses that:

> Long ago 'Asia' and the 'Orient' became almost existential categories in the European mind, sometimes projected to a vaguely defined geographical area, sometimes introjected as 'the Orient between us', sometimes ardently sought after as the land of desire and dream, then to be either excluded altogether from the realm of rationality or to be brought within control, conquered physically, economically, religiously or culturally. The history of the world, as Hegel said, has an East kat'exochen. Nothing in the Indian consciousness has ever corresponded to this geographical mythology; the West has never had that kind of symbolic value for India, far from playing the self-defined role that the Occident-Orient polarity has done in Western consciousness.[18]

Mehta, in this excerpt, stresses all the pivotal questions that have arisen from our investigation through the European histories of philosophy. In the period from the second half of the sixteenth century to the eighteenth century, European men realized a complex and difficult process of understanding of other civilizations, and the hermeneutical tools they made use of were based on the features of their own identity. At first the Jesuit missionaries described India and China in their accounts and their descriptions were necessarily influenced by their evangelic aims. The early Xavier and Postel inserted China and India within the history of Christianity, since Abraham was the founder of their civilization and Buddhism was a local version of Christianity itself. However, in the next decades, missionaries met several obstacles and opposition to their evangelization, therefore, the tone of their descriptions changed. Buddhists were the primary opponents of the Christianization of China and Japan, hence Buddhism was gradually described in negative words: as atheism, devilish sect, idolatry, the belief in nothingness, etc. The 'Confucian' sect, which had not this name before Ricci's definition – it was named *rujia* 儒家 – was the new religious, political and scientific interlocutor. Therefore, it was described not only as 'less other' than Buddhism, but even as a 'European self-identity' better realized than in the same Europe, since Confucianism was the fulfilment of Plato's *Republic*, the emblem of a meritocratic and tolerant society. Some features were truly Chinese; instead, several were part of a process of idealization necessary in order to ease conversion. On the contrary, according to the anti-Riccian missionaries and thinkers, all Asians were as the Buddhists, hence atheists and hideous men, as for Althanasius Kircher.

The historiographical insertion of China and India was realized following two directions: complete otherness and moderate selfhood. Since Heurn, modern Indians were barbarians and superstitious men, thus they were opposed to modern Europeans who were Christians and were improving their scientific knowledge. Horn introduced the Chinese among modern European thinkers, but the reason was not the validity of their thought, but instead it was due to a 'Eurocentric' attitude which could be simplified as: as far as we (Europeans) do not know something, it did not exist, at least it has no place in histories, since the historical standpoint is essentially European in itself. Ancient Oriental thinkers were acknowledged as *'prisci theologi'*, therefore inserted in the biblical framework, which was the European base of the historical identity of 'Christianity before Christianity'. The identification of the patriarch who spread the divine residual wisdom of Adam was relevant, because Abraham was clearly closer to the foundation of Jewish religion and then to Christian religion itself, whereas Noah was the earlier possible man to spread wisdom, since the Deluge (according to the universalist reading) had killed the whole humankind with the only exception of Noah and his family. What we want to contend is that historians were distancing other civilizations as much as they could. Moreover, the modern Asian heirs of this 'wisdom' had lost it and they preserved only impure traces. The civilizations that received this wisdom had already disappeared, with the exception of India. We need to understand that, from the standpoint of an effective biblical history, Indians were at risk to be the true legitimate heirs of God's wisdom, more than the recent 'European Christians'. The same occurred to China, when Figurist Jesuits, Leibniz and John Webb even claimed that China was the only preserved biblical civilization, since the Chinese language was the most ancient, hence the original divine language.[19] Clearly, these theories were supported by a very limited number of European thinkers, who were, in the case of China, the only effective Sinophiles, more than the *philosophes*. In effect, the most diffused description of Asians was based on concepts as barbarity, heathendom, atheism and already irrationality together with immorality. Therefore, they were the complete 'other'.

Mehta also suggests the idea of 'the Orient between us' and we claim that, to some extent, this was what Bayle and the *philosophes* more concerned with Asia contended. Bayle's 'moral Chinese' was the universal prototype of the rational, tolerant, anti-dogmatic and natural thinker. To say that Asian thinkers were 'Spinozist' was a way to argue the naturalness of this contested philosophy, without saying directly that 'Spinozism' was more natural than Christian factitious doctrines. Several *philosophes* made use of Oriental thought – particularly Confucianism – in order to support their call for a social and political change; since 'Confucianism' was taken as the exemplification of European pleas, hence they completely disregarded the effective principles of Chinese society and thought. Leibniz followed the Figurists and, although he exalted Chinese culture, his understanding was forcibly inserted within his own universalist and concordist philosophy, which promoted equivalences based on western principles, instead of an effective understanding.

'Barbarian' and 'Pagan' or 'Heathen' were the negative categories used by Europeans in order to define the 'otherness' of the Orient. Greeks, the alleged philosophical progenitors of Europeans, described all non-Greek civilizations as 'Barbarian' and their modern heirs did the same. Jews, the religious progenitors (or elder brothers) of Europeans, detached themselves from their former state of paganism and this process forged their identity as distinct to the rest of humankind, which was instead an undefined heathendom. The last category of otherness used by the historians we investigated is 'exoticism'. Brucker, although he seldom used this term, entitled the chapter on Asians (and Canadians): 'The exotic philosophy'. 'Exotic' in Brucker's *Historia critica* acquired a specific meaning: the other as regards to the European philosophy, which was the only universal thought. 'Exotic' does not mean simply 'other', but also 'extra', 'outer', 'external'. These civilizations were actually outside the effective history of philosophy. They were 'outside' geographically and intellectually, since the inside was the presumed universal thought of Europe. Brucker, although he also used 'barbarian' and 'heathen', chose in the title of the book not a religious term, but instead a geographical term, since he was writing the history and the geography of the philosophy of humankind, which regarded mostly ancient Greeks and European thinkers. Brucker was deeply concerned with an apology of Christian thought and a defence of its correctness against heresies and atheism. However, he fulfilled Heumann's dismissal of non-Greek and extra-European thought because of the ineffectiveness and weakness of their thought and not because of the religiosity of their philosophy.

'Exotic' is not a religious term, however, it states the identity of the other as entirely other; we could say 'ontologically other'. After Brucker, 'exotic' also entailed a positive meaning, as Mehta himself suggests, since the 'exotic lands' became the place of dream, desire and prosperity, but also the countries to exploit and subdue. Both the positive and negative meaning of this later 'exoticism', suggested a complete 'otherness' due to the intellectual weakness of these peoples. These were lands of dreams since there, life was simpler, the rules less strict and the duty less absolute; these peoples were morally and intellectually weak. The same was true for western conquerors or exploiters, since they firmly believed that these peoples belonged to a lower humanity than the rational, scientific and brave western men. 'Exoticism', in both the positive and negative meanings, was the form of 'otherness' as a fixed identity opposed to the 'selfhood' of westerners. The 'Orient' was the 'extra-West', in the historical, geographical and intellective sense. According to Brucker the 'exotic' philosophies should not even be compared to Europe's most dreaded philosophies as Spinozism; in effect, the historian argued that Buddhism was to some extent a Spinozism but not in a proper sense.

Among the historians of philosophy we investigated, Bayle was the only one who provided few effective reflections about Buddhism, revealing an understanding of the Buddhist concept of nothingness which is completely extraordinary, and this was the only moment of effective understanding. He did not adhere to the most widespread interpretation of the Buddhist first principle, which was usually translated with 'nothing' or 'nothingness'. Bayle proposed to understand this principle as nothingness in so far as it was distinct from worldly matters. The 'nothingness' was the denial of every expressions or terms in order to define this first principle: it was an emptiness of the mind as the Buddhist philosopher and monk Nāgārjuna already demonstrated in the third century CE. And Bayle even compared this emptiness with the scientific concept of 'space', which was empty but existing. However, this surprising understanding of the historian, consistent with his sceptical philosophy, did not influence other thinkers and not even Bayle himself, since he resumed in later writings the negative description of Buddhism as an incoherent and weak pantheism.

What the western philosophical arena largely ignores is that, since the last decades of the twentieth century, in both Indian and Chinese Universities, several philosophers are questioning the concepts of 'philosophy', 'religion', 'rationality', 'spirituality', etc. as applied to their own Indian or Chinese history of thought. In short, they are questioning the validity of definitions as 'history of Chinese or Indian philosophy', 'history of Chinese or Indian religions', since these terms imply a westernization of their cultures. They also complain about the lack of Chinese and Indian disciplines within the western departments of philosophy as the enduring effect of the exclusion of their thought from the history of philosophy. Jitendra Nath Mohanty, one of the most refined contemporary Indian philosophers – well known for his studies on Phenomenology and Frege – says clearly:

> Śaṁkara[20], was concerned with truth. The indologist does not share that quest with Śaṁkara but wants to find the truth *about* Śaṁkara. So even if he sincerely believes that whatever Śaṁkara says is false, he may spend a lifetime finding the truth *about* him, and not the truth *in* him ... [On the contrary] philosophy, after all, calls for a concern about truth (*or falsity*) and nothing else can replace that interest.[21]

Usually the scholars of 'Oriental philosophies' are not philosophers but philologists and their concerns are about the correctness from the philological and historical standpoints, therefore, they marginally care to uncover the possible original philosophical aims of the authors. And philosophers, who should be more suitable for a correct understanding of those extra-European texts, do not read them, not even in translation, since they still claim the preconceived unphilosophical nature of Asian thought. Mohanty stresses again this claim in one of his last books:

> Indology, like Sinology, is a strange discipline, whose subject matter is an entire country – it's history, language, religion, culture and civilization. It also includes a study of India's philosophy. But is it not remarkable that there is no such discipline whose subject matter is one of the European countries – no Deutschologie, no Frankologie? Only the non-European, or rather the Oriental countries, are made themes of such global disciplines. Is this a historical accident? Or has it something to do with what Halbfass calls 'objectification'?[22]

The Oriental disciplines, as Indology and Sinology, are 'bottlenecks' of different specializations and concerns, among which philosophy is usually quite neglected. Mohanty asks himself if western philosophers would never consider more appropriate a philologist than a philosopher to understand Kant or Hegel's writings, because that is what happens to the study of all extra-European philosophies. Moreover, the effects of this long history of misunderstanding are not limited to the western Oriental studies, but instead, as we already suggested quoting Mehta, they infected the same self-understanding of eastern people. Daya Krishna takes it to extremes when he says:

> Somehow, the context of contemporary intellectual life in India, even in the field of philosophy, has no relationship with India's intellectual traditions of the past, but rather with the way these disciplines have developed in the West and the way they are developing there at present.[23]

The modern Indian who tries to live and to understand his own tradition actually fails to do that, because his tradition has already been diverted, since it is an 'intellectual hostage' of western definitions, terms and evaluations. Mohanty reports that during a conference at the University of Hawaii – i.e. the most renowned University in the field of comparative philosophy – Daya Krishna started his speech in front of a puzzled audience arguing that: 'there is nothing called Indian philosophy'.[24] Obviously, the Indian thinker was not suggesting that India was unphilosophical, but instead that Indian thought needed a renewal in its understanding and definition not grounded on external basis and concepts. According to Daya Krishna and many further Indian philosophers, Indian philosophy exists but not as we used to describe it. The definitions of Indian philosophy as religious, soteriological, illogical, mysterious, unhistorical, monist (i.e. Vedānta) or polytheistic (i.e. many Indian goods) are no more acceptable, because they are the outcomes of the presumed universality of western philosophy, which describes all other thought as opposed to itself. Indian texts unquestionably reveal a thought well-articulated and complex, where soteriology is not the primary concern, which instead are the 'correct means of understanding' (*pramāṇa*). Western studies when applied to Indian thought usually confuse what is related to religion, sociology and literature with what concerns philosophy (which is instead mostly devoted to epistemology).[25] Vedānta, for instance, is always taken as the only effective Indian philosophical thought, and only its soteriological concerns are stressed, while

Indian philosophy is rich of many schools and of many different approaches, which also deserve to be presented to an audience of philosophers.

A similar and even wider reflection is evolving within the departments of philosophy and history in Mainland China as well as abroad. Anne Cheng, professor at the Collège de France, published a remarkable book in 2007 about the contemporary identity of Chinese thought.[26] In this book, two articles are devoted to this terminological problem, one about the question of 'religion' in China (chap. 7), and another about the question of 'philosophy' (chap. 6). Both terms emerged as debatable and pivotal questions for Chinese contemporary thinkers.[27] Joël Thoraval explains that the term religion is problematic in China, because it entails a meaning closely connected with the monotheistic roots, among which the ideas of a unique faith and a unique God, both concepts undoubtedly far from Chinese culture.[28] As we already discussed, the same is true for the term 'philosophy', which was inescapable – although problematic – for twentieth-century Chinese philosophers, while in the last two decades it is even refused by a few academic philosophers. In effect, the term *zhexue* (哲學) is the Chinese reading for the Japanese *tetsugaku*, which was an attempt of translation of the western term 'philosophy' as the 'study of wisdom'. The Chinese philosophers of the twentieth century, also being on very different sides (i.e. Pragmatism, Marxism, Confucianism, etc.), wrote several 'histories of Chinese philosophy' (中国哲學史 *zhongguo zhexue shi*) always struggling and claiming the philosophic nature of Chinese thought. As we discussed in §3.7. while evaluating the influence of Brucker's 'system of philosophy', western philosophy was the model of every comparison and it stated the level each thought should reach to be reputed 'philosophical'. Zhang Fa lucidly suggests that Chinese philosophy is 'hybrid' (*hunza* 混杂) in its own nature, a cultural combination of classic learning and western culture.[29] This is the case of Feng Youlan (1885–1990), who, although safeguarding a meaningful place for Chinese philosophy, argued that his tradition was somehow retarded and still in its Middle Ages.[30] This happens to Chinese and sometimes also to Indian thinkers, and this sociological and philosophical attitude is usually named 'self-Orientalism'.[31] Self-Orientalism is the perception of eastern thinkers of their culture by means of western Orientalism or western concepts.

On the contrary, in the last two decades – i.e. after decades of monolithic Marxist control – several Chinese philosophers have started to debate the correctness of European philosophy as a global standard with a value in itself. They do not belong to the 'reverse Orientalism'[32] side – which argues the impossible understanding of eastern values by western people – but they claim a specific path for Chinese philosophy and for its history. They refuse to consider European philosophy as the single model and they challenge the idea of a universal path towards wisdom, which is allegedly the only truly rational method available.

Li Weiwu, in his *Renewal of the Chinese philosophical tradition* of the year 2012, summarizes the actual trends in the Chinese philosophical field as follows: 1. Marxism (*Makesi zhuyi* 马克思主义) or dialectic materialism (*weiwu bianzhengfa zhexue* 唯物辩证法哲学); 2. Liberalism (*ziyou zhuyi* 自由主义); 3. Contemporary New Confucianism (*xiandai xinzruxue* 现代新儒学).[33] Obviously, the Marxists understand Chinese philosophy within the materialistic paradigm, which, although 'sinicized', is of western origins. The same is for Liberalism, which has been relevant in China since the first years of the twentieth century (John Stuart Mill was one of the first philosophers translated into Chinese), characterized by a strong pro-western attitude. The last one is the Contemporary New Confucianism, which has never disappeared but has undergone several periods of contraction under the Communist repression, and mostly flourished in Hong Kong and Taiwan. This last school is in outstanding progress since the 1980s, when began the actual ideological release of Communist repression. Li lucidly reports that the main actual Chinese attitudes towards the philosophical tradition are three: 1. to consider the past as glorious and as the real Chinese legacy and identity; 2. after the two Opium wars (1839–60) and therefore when the concrete meeting with western culture was displayed, there occurred a concrete and deep rift between Chinese traditional thought and modern thought; 3. Chinese philosophical thought has assimilated many relevant western concepts within its own tradition, without losing its specific identity. Li underlines the complexity and the refinement of this assimilation of western ideas using a precise sequence of verbs: to assimilate (*xiqu* 吸取), to digest (*xiaohua* 消化), to integrate (*zonghe* 综合) and to blend together (*rong* 融).[34]

Western academic scholars should bear in mind that this process of understanding and appropriation of western philosophy is still in progress in China today and it is far from being settled. For instance, in a recent article, Tong Shijun[35] explains in detail the problem of the correct and effective study of western philosophical texts. He underlines the linguistic issues – i.e. the use of translations; the many western languages and the multifaceted use of one term in the same linguistic tradition[36] – but also the inherent conceptual differences (*gainian qufen* 概念区分) between the two traditions, as for instance the extreme abstraction of western thought against the use of specification and examples in the Chinese method. Furthermore, Xie Xialing suggests a radical difference between western and eastern ways of thinking, since the first is devoted to the research of a static (*jingzhi* 静止) first principle, while the second search is devoted to the harmony of the moving change (*dongjing jiaoti* 动静交替), learning not from abstraction but from direct experience (*tiyan* 体验).[37] Zhang Fa compares East–West philosophies opposing the objectificating (*shiwu* 事物) attitude of the second to the vitalistic (*shengming* 生命) attitude of the first, particularly speaking about *qi* 氣 (i.e. vital energy).[38] Although these theories are arguable on both sides, this study of the differences between Chinese and western philosophy entails a remarkable point: the path of philosophy is no more unique – i.e. universal – but instead plural.

From the historiographical viewpoint, Xie Xialing proposes an interesting theory: he accuses the emperor Kangxi 康熙 (1654–1722) of the Qing for having caused the Chinese philosophical defeat of the last two centuries. According to the author, Kangxi, being a Qing and hence of foreign origin, had promoted the less relevant and more blameable sector of Confucianism – in order to control opponents easily – and, at the same time, he was so fascinated by the western thought taught by missionaries that he facilitated its spreading.[39] This theory, although being historically debatable and controversial, helps us to understand the crucial role of the historiography of philosophy in the definition of contemporary Chinese identity. Missionaries have influenced not only European historians, but also Chinese thinkers and the emperor himself. Therefore, the vulnerability of the Chinese thought since the eighteenth century was a reason of the supremacy of western thought, but according to Xie the roots of Chinese tradition are still alive and need to be at the same time restored and actualized.

For instance, the twentieth century New Confucian philosopher Mou Zongsan 牟宗三 – who was also an expert of Kant's three *Critiques* – [40] tried to solve the opposition between western and Chinese thought, without depriving both civilizations of their 'intellectual universality'. He suggested that in this debate, we face two different concepts of truth: the first is the logical abstraction of reason, and the second the empirical understanding of life as something to be endlessly perfected. Although this intriguing difference is never a complete and irreducible opposition, he named the western universal 'abstract universal' (*chouxiangde* 抽象的), because the logic or scientific universality is conceptual, it looks for confirmation of conceptualization of a truth that always belongs to a kind of 'transcendental elsewhere'. On the contrary, the Chinese concept of truth – i.e. Confucian, Buddhist and Daoist – is 'concrete' (*jutide* 具體的), since it is based on the empirical observation and contemplation of the immanent source of life and nature, that men have to bring to perfection and harmony.[41] According to Mou's description, the European thought is scientific, in the sense it has to show the whole chain of reasoning, trying to trap the opponent discourses through logical arguments, and find incontrovertible evidence. Contrarily, the Chinese thought is always devoted to something inexpressible, because words and arguments are necessary for the deconstruction of perceived reality and not for the construction of a way to truth. The way to truth is based on life practices, awareness of incessant change and reciprocity. Mou's 'philosophical device' evidently betrays a preference for Chinese thought.

According to both the Chinese and Indian philosophers, western philosophy and historiography, after having imposed the terms of the exclusion on the others, has evaded any real dialogue with them. Dipesh Chakrabarty gives a name to the nineteenth-century colonial arrogant attitude of western historians: 'waiting room'. This is the core of his intriguing thesis:

> Historicism—and even the modern, European idea of history—one might say, came to non-European peoples in the nineteenth century as somebody's way of saying "not yet" to somebody else. [...] In doing so, it converted history itself into a version of this waiting room. We were all headed to the same destination, Mill averred, but some people were to arrive earlier than others. That was what historicist consciousness was: a recommendation to the colonized to wait.[42]

We need to say that even this dramatic analysis presented by Chakrabarty is inadequate to explain what happened in the philosophical field. In fact, while in the historiographical context of Positivism the colonized people were invited to wait for their future evolution, within the philosophical context, they were acknowledged as ontologically inferior, as 'a priori excluded', without any future perspective unless they became a provincial western philosophy in foreigner lands. On the contrary, contemporary eastern philosophies are involved in a feverish process of redefinition, which western philosophy almost disregards or at least misunderstands as parochialism. Actually, those thinkers express the need to forge new identities for their civilizations, but also for western philosophy, since the presumption of universality, after the postmodern deconstruction, is no more legitimate. Whether western philosophy still evades this dialogue about the reciprocal identities, this Asian process would advance autonomously, and it would reach a definition of both Asian and western identities, which risks to be prevailing in the next decades. In order to ease this possible and still feeble dialogue, a correct understanding of when, how and on which terms the exclusion of Chinese and Indian civilizations from the history of philosophy occurred is necessary. This was the aim of this research and reaching the conclusions we might argue that, despite what the main scholars of Orientalism suggest, the roots of this exclusion of eastern people from philosophy lie not within the 'scientific Orientalism', within the Hegelian exclusion or within the colonial expansion, but instead within early missionaries' descriptions, within the biblical histories as histories of humankind, and within the claim of universalism of the European identity already in the histories of philosophy of the early eighteenth century. As Richard King suggests:

> The political, economic and ideological supremacy of the Western world since the seventeenth century tells us more about the dominance of Western discourses and paradigms in contemporary philosophical debates than any claims by Western philosophers to have discovered universal truths applicable beyond the confines of European culture and history.[43]

This investigation into the modern European historiographies aims at providing the historically correct characters of this East–West intellectual dialogue as the basis for a renovated mutual hermeneutical understanding of the past and of the future.[44]

Notes

General Introduction

1. We will discuss this point later in this Introduction.
2. We make use of both the Italian edition and the English translation (limited at vols 1 and 2). We use the following abbreviations: SSGF for the Italian edition and MHP for the English translation.
3. See Leo Catana, *The Historiographical Concept 'System of Philosophy'. Its Origin, nature, influence and legitimacy*, (Leiden: Brill, 2008) and Leo Catana, 'The history of the History of Philosophy, and the Lost Biographical Tradition', *British Journal for the History of Philosophy*, 20.3, 2012, 619–25.
4. Dimitri Levitin, *Ancient Wisdom in the Age of the New Science. Histories of Philosophy in England, c. 1640–1700* (Cambridge: Cambridge University Press, 2015).
5. Leo Catana, 'The history of the History of Philosophy, and the Lost Biographical Tradition', 621.
6. Dimitri Levitin, *Ancient Wisdom in the Age of the New Science*, 5.
7. Virgile Pinot, *La Chine et la Formation de l'esprit philosophique en France (1640-1740)* (Genève: Slatkine Reprints, 1971).
8. David E. Mungello, *Curious Land: Jesuit accommodation and the origins of Sinology* (Honolulu: University of Hawaii Press, 1989). Mungello is both a sinologue and a historian of ideas.
9. His most relevant study on Leibniz, among many publications, is Mungello, *Leibniz and Confucianism. The Search for Accord* (Honolulu: University of Hawaii Press, 1977).
10. Some of them are published in Thomas H. C. Lee (ed.), *China and Europe. Images and Influences in Sixteenth to Eighteenth Centuries* (Hong Kong: The Chinese University Press, 1991).
11. The first author who devoted a complete study to the reception of Buddhism in Europe is Henri de Lubac, *La rencontre du Bouddhisme et de l'Occident* (Paris: Aubier, 1952). De Lubac devoted intense chapters to the Jesuits and the first European understanding, however, these sections of his work are outdated nowadays when compared to Urs App, *The cult of Emptiness. The Western Discovery of Buddhist Thought and the Invention of Oriental Philosophy* (Rorschach/Kyoto: UniversityMedia, 2012).
12. Frédéric Lenoir, *La Rencontre du Bouddhisme et de l'Occident* (Paris: Albin Michel, 1999).
13. Roger-Pol Droit, *Le culte du néant. Les philosophes et le Bouddha*, 2nd enlarged edn (Paris: Éditions du Seuil, 2004).
14. Rolando Minuti, *Orientalismo e idee di tolleranza nella cultura francese del primo '700* (Firenze: Olschki editore, 2006).
15. Wilhelm Halbfass, *India and Europe. An Essay in Understanding* (Albany: SUNY, 1988).

16 Eun-Jeung Lee, *Anti-Europa. Die Geschichte der Rezeption des Konfuzianismus und der konfuzianischen Gesellschaft seit der Frühen Aufklärung* (Münster: Lit-Verlag, 2003).
17 See §3.7.

Chapter 1

1 For a complete overview on the origin of the historiographical field see MHP1, sect. 1 (SSGF1, sez. 1) by Luciano Malusa.
2 Charles B. Schmitt, '*Prisca Theologia* e *Philosophia perennis*: due temi del Rinascimento italiano e la loro fortuna' in, *Il pensiero italiano del Rinascimento e il nostro tempo*, ed. Giovannangiola Tarugi (Firenze: Olschki, 1970), 212–13.
3 Wilhelm Schmidt-Biggemann, *Philosophia perennis, Historical Outlines of Western Spirituality in Ancient, Medieval and Early Modern Thought* (Dordrecht: Springer, 2004), p. XIII.
4 Plethon was the main philosophical 'bridge' between these Hellenistic theories and Ficino. He was one of the most important Greek philosophers living in Italy in the fifteenth century; he was responsible for re-introducing Plato to European, particularly Italian, learned people. Plethon was a clear example of the ancient 'prisca theologia' model of philosophy.
5 Plethon, *Traité des Lois*, ed. Alexandre C. and trans. De Pellissier (Paris: Librairie de Firmin, 1858), I, chap. II, 31.
6 Schmidt-Biggemann, *Philosophia perennis*, 417.
7 Ibid., 418. See Roger Bacon, *The 'Opus majus'*, ed. John Henry Bridges (Oxford: William and Norgate, 1900), vol.1, pars. II, chap. 9, 46.
8 For an interesting, unfortunately unpublished, research on the influence of Greek Byzantine philosophers on Ficino with regard to the historical theories, see Eleonora Lo Presti, 'La filosofia nel suo sviluppo storico: la prospettiva storiografica di Marsilio Ficino e l'influenza dei dotti bizantini Giorgio Gemisto Pletone e Giovanni Basilio Bessarione' (PhD diss., University of Bologna, 2007).
9 See Marsilio Ficino, *Teologia platonica*, it. trans. M. Schiavone (Bologna: Zanichelli, 1965), vol. II, 404–19. We refer to chap. 1 of the book XVIII entitled 'Quod Plato non prohibet fidem adhibere Theologiae Hebraeorum, Christianorum, Arabumque communi' [Plato does not prevent to give credence to the theology of Jews, Christians and Arabians]. See also Marsilio Ficino, *Platonic theology*, lat. ed. J. Warden and J. Hankins, eng. trans. M. J. B. Allen and J. B. Allen (Harvard University Press, London 2006), vol. 6.
10 The first modern translation of this text in Latin was due to Ambrogio Traversari (1386–1439), printed in 1472, and this translation had an incredible number of editions in the fifteenth and sixteenth centuries, as it was soon translated into vernacular languages. Ambrogio Traversari, *Vitae et Sententiae Philosophorum* (Roma: Giorgio Lauer, 1472). Among the first editions: Venezia, 1475, 1490, 1493 e 1497; Brescia, 1485; Bologna, 1495; Paris, 1504 and 1505. On Ambrogio Traversari see Salvatore Frigerio (ed.), *Ambrogio Traversari: un monaco e un monastero nell'umanesimo fiorentino* (Camaldoli: Edizioni Camaldoli, 1988). Traversari submitted his manuscript translation in 1433, however it was printed only in 1472, on this see Albinia Catherine De La Mare, 'Cosimo and his Books', in *Cosimo 'il Vecchio' de' Medici, 1389-1464*, ed. F. Ames-Lewis (Oxford, New York 1992).

11 Wilhelm Schmidt-Biggemann, *Philosophia perennis,* 33ff.
12 Agostino Steuco, *De perenni philosophia libri X*, Basel: Per Nicolaum Bryling et Sebastianum Francken, 1542 (1st edn, Lyon 1540).
13 See Maria Muccillo, *Platonismo ermetismo e 'Prisca theologia'* (Firenze: Olschki, 1996), chap. I.; Luciano Malusa, MHP1, Introduction, sect. 1 (SSGF1, Introd., sez. 1) and the aforementioned Schmitt Charles B., '*Prisca Theologia* e *Philosophia perennis*: due temi del Rinascimento italiano e la loro fortuna', 221–4.
14 'Primi igitur omnium sunt Chaldaei, proxime quos et Paradisus fuit: et primi homines, qui ad partem orintalem paradisi dicuntur habitasse, hanc potissium regionem tenuerunt ... Primi igitur omnium sunt Chaldaei, ab his Hebraei, Aegyptij, Phoenices, novissimi Graeci, post Romani sunt nati ...' (Agostino Steuco, *De perenni philosophia libri X*, I, chap. III, 8).
15 Benito Pereyra, *De communibus omnium rerum naturalium Principiis et Affectionibus libri quindecim. Qui plurimum conferunt ad eos octo libros Aristotelis qui de physico audit inscribuntur, intelligendos* (Paris: apud Micaëlem Sonnio 1579).
16 'Illos etiam quos tanquam sapientes venerata est antiquitas, non Graecos, sed magnam partem Barbaros fuisse constat. Etenim Orpheus, Thrax fuit, Thales, Phoenix, Mercurius, Ægyptius; Zoroaster, Persa, Athlas, Lybicus, seu Phryx: Anacha[r]sis, Scyta; Pherecydes, Syrus: Deinde apud Hispanos, olim magistratus gerebant viri sapientia clari, differentes de natura, Deo et moribus. Apud Gallos sapientes habebantur Druidae; Apud Ægyptios, Sacerdotes; Apud Babylonios, Caldaei, apud Persas, Magi, Apud Indos, Gymnosophistae; Apud Hebraeos, Prophetae.'
17 'sive aliarum quoque gentium qui sapientes vel philosophi habiti sunt, Atlantici Libyes, Aegyptii, Indi, Persae, Chaldaei, Scythae, Galli, Hispani, ...' (Augustine, *De Civitate Dei*, VIII, IX, §9).
18 Joan-Pau Rubiés, 'From Antiquarianism to Philosophical History: India, China, and the World History of Religion in European Thought (1600-1770)', in Peter N. Miller, François Louis (eds), *Antiquarianism and Intellectual Life in Europe and China. 1500-1800* (Ann Arbor: University of Michigan Press 2012), 314.
19 Peter N. Miller, 'Taking Paganism Seriously: Anthropology and Antiquarianism in Early Seventeenth-Century Histories of Religion', *Archiv für Religionsgeschichte*, 3. Band, 2001, 186.
20 See the two aforementioned essays by Rubiés and Miller, together with Giuliano Mori, 'Natural Theology and Ancient Theology in the Jesuit China Mission', unpublished article retrieved from https://www.academia.edu/37948679/Natural_Theology_and_Ancient_Theology_in_the_Jesuit_China_Mission
21 Otto van Heurn, *Barbaricae philosophiae antiquitatum/ libri duo: I Chaldaicus,/ II Indicus. / Opus historicum et philosophicum* (Leyden: ex Officina Plantiniana, Academiae Lugduno-Bat. Typographum, 1600).
22 On Heurn's life see Ilario Tolomio in MHP1, 107 (SSGF1, 104).
23 Eric Jorink, 'Heurnius, Otto', in *The dictionary of Seventeenth and Eighteenth-century Dutch philosophers* (Bristol: Thoemmes Press, 2003), vol. 1, 431.
24 We will further discuss the question of the 'system of philosophy' at the end of the third chapter dealing with Brucker.
25 According to Paulinus a Sancto Bartolomaeo, also known as Filip Vesdin (*Systema Brahmanicum Liturgicum mythologicum civile Ex monumentis indicis Musei Borgiani Velitris Dissertationibus Historico-criticis*, Rome: apud Antonium Fulgonium, 1791), this theory has an early advocate in Saint Epiphanius ('Brahmanes ab Abraham ex Ketura progenitos fuisse existimavit S. Epiphanius', ibid., 44).

26 In §1.2. we report his theory.
27 'Tanto autem, tamque multipici exercitio corpori robur afflabant, ut mentes confirmarent, immobilesque in iudiciis ac consultationibusque redderent. Omnisque eorum Philosophia finem ac terminum illum unicum habebat, ut bonam vitam pia mors terminaret'
28 On Osório see Donald F. Lach, *Asia in the making of Europe* (Chicago-London: University of Chicago Press, 1965–77), vol. I, book 1, 196.
29 We used Hieronymi Osorii, *De rebus Emmanuelis Lusitaniae Regis invictissimi* (Colonia: In Officina Birckmannica, sumptibus Arnoldi Mylii, 1597), but the 1st edition is dated 1586. This text was quite widespread during the first half of the seventeenth century; it was translated into Portuguese, French and English (a paraphrase, therefore we could not quote this text). The letter by Metelli, dated 1580, being the 'Preface', was clearly only attached at the beginning of the text.
30 'Adorant Bramanes vaccas, easque non mactandas docent. Deum existimant nigrum esse, hunc colorem, sibi quod sit familiaris, pulcherrimum arbitrantes. Hinc ipsorum idola nigrore horrendo sunt conspicua, impuroque oleo delibuta: adeo tetra ac foeda visu, ut eorum aspectus intuenti horrorem incutiat.' This text is a paraphrase of Metelli, *Preface*, 31v.
31 Daniel Barbu, 'Idolatry and the History of Religions', *Studi e Materiali di Storia delle Religioni*, 82/2, 2016.
32 'Deum caeli et terra creatorem adorantes, hanc sententiam subinde repetentes, Adoro te, o Deus, cum tua gratia et auxilio in aeternum.' Osorii, *De rebus Emmanuelis Lusitaniae,* 148 (also Metelli, *Preface*, 31v). Heurn did not quote a further 'Christianized' detail provided by Metelli: the God creator of heaven and earth stays in heaven ('creatorem coeli et terrae, qui in ceolis est').
33 A missionary as Roberto de Nobili tried to overcome this condition, pretending to be a *brahman* according to his noble native origin in Italy and to his surname.
34 Metello quoted the Chinese a few lines after Indians, but Heurn kept the usual list, without mentioning this people. As we will see in the next paragraph, the first widespread book on China was Ricci's account of the Jesuit mission in China, published by Trigault in 1615, several years after Heurn's investigation.
35 It was not really China but more accurately Chinese Tartary or Cathay. For a comprehensive and short account see Michael Robson, *The Franciscans in the Middle Ages* (Woodbridge (UK): Boydell Press, 2006), chap. 9, titled 'The mission to China'. Several Franciscans sources – i.e. by Montecorvino – on China are edited in Henry Yule, *Cathay and the way Thither* (London: Hakluyt Society, 1866), but see also Guillaume de Rubrouck, *The mission of Friar William of Rubruck (1253-55),* trans. P. Jackson (London: The Hakluyt Society, 1990) and Giovanni Di Plano Carpini (Giovanni da Pian del Carpine), *The story of the Mongols whom we call the Tartares,* trans. E. Hildinger (Boston: Branden Publishing Company, 1996).
36 For a survey of Xavier's life and letters see Henry J. Coleridge, *The life and letters of Saint Francis Xavier* (London: Burns Oates, 1881) or Francis Xavier, *The letters and instructions of Francis Xavier*, ed. and trans. M. Joseph Costellope, (Anand: Gujarat Sahitya Prakash, 1993).
37 See Marion Kuntz, *Guillaume Postel, Prophet of the Restitution of All Things, His Life and Thought* (The Hague: Martinus Nijhoff Publishers, 1981), 13ff.
38 On Postel and the quest for the 'lingua humana' as the original universal language see Lach, *Asia in the making of Europe*, vol. II, book 3, 509–25.

39 'Nam Græci ob rerum nuditatem, et voluntariam paupertatem Gymnosopfistas vocarunt: alii, ut hodie sacerdotes Guzrati Narsingæ et præcipuis Indiæ regnis, vocant Abrahmanes, seu Brahmanas, aut Brahminos, ab ipso Abrahamo, authore illius disciplinæ …' *De originibus* (Basel: per Ioannem Oporinum, 1553), 69–70.

40 Postel, Guillaume. *Des merveilles du monde, et principalemét [sic] des admirables choses des Indes, et du nouveau monde : histoire extraicte des escriptz tresdignes de foy, tant de ceulx qui encores sont a present audict pays, come de ceulx qui encores vivantz peu paravat en sont retournez* (No editor and date, possibly 1553). Bibliothèque nationale de France, dép. Réserve des livres rares, Rés. D2 5267). The title is the incipit of the book, which seems to be a draft, since it has several hand emendations. Another copy is in The Houghton Library at Harvard University (see Kuntz, *Guillaume Postel*, 191). We will quote the original French of the text in notes, without emendations.

41 At the end and on page 83v.

42 The pages from 9r to 40r of this book of Postel are edited in Henri Bernard-Maitre, 'L'orientaliste Guillaume Postel et la découverte spirituelle du Japon en 1552', in *Monumenta Nipponica*, vol. 9 no. 1/2 (Avril), 1953, 82–108.

43 Postel translated a couple of paragraphs from Xavier's Letter 59 of the Schurhammer edition (§15–18), which is dated 20 January 1548, while Postel says 1549. The reference edition is Georg Schurhammer, *Francis Xavier. His life, his time*, eng. trans. J. Costelloe, 4 vols (Rome The Jesuit Historical Institute, 1973–82), this is a trans. of the German original: Georg Schurhammer, *Franz Xavier. Sein Leben und sein Zeit* (Freiburg i.B.: Herder, 1955–73).

44 A first analysis of this text in the context of the European understanding of Buddhism is in Henri de Lubac, *La rencontre du Bouddhisme et de l'Occident* (Paris: Aubier, 1952), 53–7.

45 Although we know of previous cultivated travellers such as Filippo Sassetti, a Florentine man of letters.

46 Juan Ruiz-de-Medina, *Documentos del Japon 1547-1557* (Rome: Monumenta Historica Japoniae II, 1990), doc. 8, 'Nicolao Lancillotto, Informacion sobre Japon [1]', 44–69.

47 According to Medina (*Documentos*), the interview by Torres was edited and modified by Lancillotto.

48 Guillaume Postel, *Des merveilles du monde*, 12r–38r. Postel's copious glosses are clearly identifiable, being in italic.

49 'Le comun argument de leur sermon est qu'il est un seul Dieu createur de toutes choses, et qu'il y ha un paradis ou lieu lá ou vont les bienhereulx, et au contraire un lieu deputé pour les meschantz, don't le diable est le capitain et chef: et un pour ceulx qui sont moyens, qui sont ceulx, qu'il faut purger' (ibid., 17v–18r)

50 'Cecy me conferme en la sentence que ie tiens que ce soit doctrine des Abrahmanes enfantz des concubines d'Abraham, lesquelz il env[o]ya eu orient soubz l'heureuse influence, et m'y rendz confermé par unes letres qu'escrivit par le passé ledict M. Françoys Sch[i]abier a M. Ignace de Loyola chef de ladicte compagnie de Iesus, qui dedens Paris en feist le fondement il y ha 15. ou 16. ans, lá ou ledict Schiabier dist, qu'il y eut un desdictz Abrahamanes lesquelz Marc Paulo appelle Abrahmin, et eulx se disent Brahmin mangeant la lettre a, voyant que si librement il luy monstroit les commen cementz de nostre religion, entre beaucoup de propos luy dist, nous avons bien la mesme Doctrine que vos ensegnes, entre nos prestres mais iamais ne l'enseignerions au peuple, et n'y ha que les Brahmains, qui entre eulx, qui entre eulx

et pour eulx la doibuent scavoir, ansi dist ledict Brahmin, ce que ie croy. Car combien qu'Abraham veist que les enfantz des son concubines ne vouloient pas obeir a Isaac et renoncoient en ce a la Catholique Eglise, neantmoins il ne les envoya pas en l'orient sans leur bailler Doctrine Divine avec leur Magike ou Astrologie, don't iusques auiourd'huy ilz retiennent l'odeur avec tresgrande et a tout le monde superieure cognoissance d'Astrologie, ce qui außi est en Giapan.'

51 Postel named him 'Schiaca' and also suggested that Xaca was the Spanish version of the name, being in this language the sound 'Schi' written as X (ibid., 22r). Postel was very close to the honorific name of Buddha, which is Śākyamuni (i.e. the wise man of the Śākya, being this his patronymic).

52 Ruiz-de-Medina attributes this strong and forced concordism between Christian and Buddhist beliefs to Lancillotto.

53 'Cecy est la vraye confirmation que XACA soit là adoré pour IESUS CHRIST CRUCIFIE.' (ibid., 31v, capital letters in the text).

54 Obviously, Buddha did not go to China or Japan, but Buddhist monks did, a few centuries after his death, more or less in the first and second century A D.

55 Actually, it is the *bodhisattva* of compassion Avalokiteśvara, called Kannon in Japanese. A *bodhisattva* is a future Buddha, who is waiting to disappear in his enlightenment – i.e. becoming a Buddha – in order to help people to reach liberation or enlightenment. In Chinese iconography often this *bodhisattva* looks like a sweet woman or even a mother. Avalokiteśvara is one of the most worshiped 'deities' of Buddhist pantheon in East Asia.

56 Actually, Postel created many problems for Ignatius and to the whole Jesuit order, because of his controversial statements critical of the power of papacy within the Church (see Kuntz, *Guillaume Postel*, 60ff).

57 'Cathai' was often larger than Chinese Empire, because it included also countries subject to Chinese influences.

58 'N'ayant donc iamais abandonné la cognoissance du Roy des Iuifz ladicte province de Catay doibt estre tenue la plus hereuse du monde.'

59 'Ainsi nous voyons la vertu de la souveraine puissance de nostre Dieu et pere Iesus Christ, qui aux deux extremitez de son monde ha voulu sans communication de puissance, de lettres, et de ceremonies, planter et maintenir sa tressaincte doctrine et loy, ce qui est le plus merveilleux et necessaire argument du monde.'

60 Juan Gonzáles de Mendoza, *Historia de las cosas mas notables, ritos y costumbres, del gran Reyno dela China* (Rome Bartholome Grassi, 1585).

61 Juan González de Mendoza, *Dell'Historia della China*, trans. Francesco Avanzi (Rome: Bartholome Grassi, 1586).

62 Juan Gonzáles de Mendoza, *Histoire du Grand Royaume de la Chine*, trans. Luc de La Porte (Paris: chez Ieremie Perier, 1588). The French editions were really copious and important, one of which was read by Montaigne.

63 Juan Gonzáles de Mendoza, *The Historie of the Great and mightie Kingdome of China, and the situation thereof*, trans. Robert Parke (London: Edward White, 1588). We quote from the reprint edition: ibid., *The history of the great and mighty Kingdom of China and of the situation thereof*, ed. G. T. Staunton (London: The Hakluyt Society, 1853).

64 A very insightful and detailed investigation on Mendoza's book and its reception in Europe is in Donald F. Lach, *Asia in the making of Europe*, vol. 1, book 2, 742–94.

65 Gaspar da Cruz, *Tractado em que se contam muito por estenso as cousas da China* (Evora: em casa de Andre de Burgos, 1569). An English translation is in: Charles Raph Boxer (trans.), *South China in the Sixteenth Century : being the narratives of Galeote Pereira, Fr. Gaspar da Cruz O.P., Fr. Martin De Rada O.E.S.A. (1550-1575)* (London: The Hakluyt Society, no.106, 1953, reissue Bangkok: Orchid Press, 2004).
66 Ruiz-de-Medina, *Documentos*, 48, where the author quoted a letter by Valignano suggesting that '[the author of *Informacion*] wished to adjust Japanese things to ours [Christian], with strong exaggeration' ('queriendo acomodar las cosas de Japón a las nuetras, muchas van exageradas').
67 Alessandro Valignano, *Catechismus Christianae Fidei, in quo Veritas nostrae religionis ostenditur, et sectae Iaponenses confutantur* (Lisbon: Antonius Riberius, 1586).
68 Antonio Possevino, *Bibliotheca selecta* (Rome Typ. Apostolica Vaticana, 1593).
69 For further details on Valignano's interpretation of Buddhism, see Alessandro Valignano, *Historia del Principio y Progresso de la Compania de Jesus en las Indias Orientales (1542-64)*, which stayed unpublished since 1899 in *Monumenta Xaveriana* (Madrid: Typis Augustini Avrial, 1899-1900), 111-19. Thierry Meynard wrote a masterful article on Valignano's *Catechismus Japonensis* as a model for Ricci's *Tianzhu shiyi* 天主實義, he suggests that Valignano was unsatisfied with his catechism and when reading Ruggeri's and Ricci's reports and letters, he came to understand the role of Confucianism and shared the accommodation approach. See Thierry Meynard, 'The Overlooked Connection between Ricci's *Tianzhu shiyi* and Valignano's *Catechismus Japonensis*', *Japanese Journal of Religious Studies* 40/2, 303-22.
70 See Song Liming, 'Father Matteo Ricci's change in status in light of four Chinese Poems', in *Matteo Ricci. Encounter Between Civilizations in Ming Dynasty China*, ed. Filippo Mignini (Milan: Regione Marche/24 ORE Motta Cultura, 2010), 92-9.
71 See Lionel M. Jensen, *Manufacturing Confucianism* (Durham: Duke University Press, 1997). Against this controversial theory see Nicolas Standaert, 'The Jesuits Did NOT Manufacture "Confucianism"', *East Asian Science, Technology and Medicine*, 16, 1999, 115-32.
72 It is assumed that this text was written around the last two years of Ricci's life (1608-10).
73 See Matteo Ricci, *Storia dell'Introduzione del Cristianesimo in Cina*, in *Fonti Ricciane*, ed. Pasquale M. D'Elia (Rome: La Libreria dello Stato, 1942), by now *Storia*. We quote from the new edition Matteo Ricci, *Della entrata della compagnia di Giesù e Christianità nella Cina*, ed. Maddalena del Gatto (Macerata: Quodlibet, 2000), by now *Della entrata*.
74 Matteo Ricci, *De Christiana expeditione apud Sinas suscepta ab Societate Iesu*, ed. Nicolas Trigault (Augsburg: apud Christoph Mangium, 1615). We use the edition London: Sumptibus Horatii Cardon, 1616, by now *De Christiana*.
75 Matteo Ricci, *Histoire de l'expédition chrestienne au royaume de la Chine*, ed. Nicolas Trigault (Lyon: pour Horace Cardon, 1616), by now *Histoire*.
76 See *Della entrata*, 90; *Storia*, 109.
77 'legge naturale', *Della entrata*, 90; *Storia*, 109.
78 Michael Lackner contends a similar interpretation of Ricci as an advocate of a Chinese 'prisca theologia' in ibid., 'Jesuit Figurism', in *China and Europe. Images and Influences in Sixteenth to Eighteenth Centuries*, ed. Thomas H. C. Lee (Hong Kong: The Chinese University Press, 1991), 130-1.
79 See *Della entrata*, 91-3; *Storia*, 110-14.
80 Ricci seldom used 'setta', only about Buddhists ('setta degli idoli', *Storia*, 116).

81 'tutto questo mondo sta composto di una sola sustantia e che il creatore di esso con il Cielo e la terra, gli huomini e gli animali, alberi et herbe con i quattro elementi tutti fanno un corpo continuo, e tutti sono membri di questo corpo; e da questa unità di sustantia cavano la charità che habbiamo d'aver gli uni con gli altri; con il che tutti gli huomini possono venire a esser simili a Dio per esser della stessa sustantia con esso lui. Il che noi procuriamo di Confutare non solo con ragioni, ma anco con autorità de' loro Antichi, che assai chiaramente insegnorno assai differente dottrina.' (*Storia*, 116; *Della entrata*, 95).

82 See §2.3.

83 'E conciosia che loro nè comandino, nè prohibiscano niente di quello che si ha da credere delle cose dell'altra vita, e molti di loro seguono, insime con questa sua le altre due sette, venessimo a conchiudere che non è questa una legge formata, ma solo è propriamente un'Academia, instituita per il buon governo della Republica, e così possono esser di questa Academia e farsi Christiani, posciaché nel suo essentiale non contiene niente contra l'essentia della fede Catholica, nè la fede Catholica impedisce niente, anzi agiuta molto alla quite e pace della repubblica, che i suoi libri pretendono.' (*Storia*, 120, *Della entrata*, 98)

84 'hebbero notitia de' nostri Philosophi.' (*Storia*, 123; *Della entrata*, 99).

85 'dicono tante falsità che oscurano tutta la luce che, dalla verità delle cose pigliate da noi, si potrebbe scorgere . . .' (*Storia*, 124; *Della entrata*, 100). The heaviest falsity they profess is temporariness of Heaven and Hell.

86 Ricci was aware of the falsity of this accusation, furthermore he read almost nothing about Buddhist texts, because he focused his attention solely on ancient Confucian texts. He accused Buddhism evidently without knowing its sources and foundations. This correct analysis of Ricci apologetics was formulated by the Buddhist scholar Yu Deyuan, who had a direct epistolary exchange with Ricci (1608–9) in *Posthumous Dispute* (*Bianxueyidu* 辯學遺牘). The *Posthumous Disputes* can be divided into two sections. The first section is composed of two letters, one written by Yu Deyuan 虞德园 (1553–1621) – also named Yu Chunxi 虞淳熙 – to Ricci and the second is Ricci's reply. These two letters discuss topics related to Jesuits' critiques of Buddhism; Yu invites Ricci to study Buddhist texts instead of rejecting blindly their contents. The second part is really a dispute and it is the first available dispute between a Christian and a Buddhist monk. The Buddhist Chan monk is Lianchi 莲池 (1535–1615) – better known as Shen Zhuhong 沈袾宏 – , who, in his *Three Notes of the Bamboo Window* (*Zhuchuang sanbi* 竹窗三笔), inserted four chapters entitled 'Discourses on Heaven' (*Tianshuo* 天說), where he rejected Christian faith. A Christian author, or a Jesuit or an early converted, wrote a point-by-point aggressive reply to each chapter, using rhetoric, scientific proofs and logic in order to reject Buddhist tenets. The authorship was traditionally attributed to Ricci, but recent studies mostly suggest Xu Guangqi 徐光启 (1562–1633) as the author, although the question of the authorship according to our opinion is still open. The most ancient edition available today was printed in 1626, in Li Zhizao 李之藻, *Tian Xue Chu Han* 天学初函, [First Collection of Christian Studies], (first edition of 1626, reprinted as photographic copy), Taipei 1953, vol.2, 637–88 (photographic copy). The most recent modern edition of the text is in Zhu Weizheng 朱維錚, *Li Madou zhongwenzhu yiji* 利瑪竇中文著譯集 [A reasoned collection of Matteo Ricci's Chinese writings] (Shanghai: Fudan Daxue Chubanshe, 2001), 653–87 – under the title *Fu Yu Chunxi* 復虞淳熙 [Reply to Yu Chunxi]. For a discussion on the authorship see Sun Shangyang 孫尚揚, *Bianxueyidu zuozhe kao* 《辩学遗牍》作者考 [Research on the authorship of *Posthumous Disputes*], in *Jidujiao yu ming mo ruxue* 基督教与明末儒学 [Christian teaching and

the late Ming Confucianism], (Beijing: Dongfang chubanshe, 1994) and Erik Zürcher, 'Xu Guangqi and Buddhism', in *Statecraft and Intellectual Renewal in late Ming China. The Cross-Cultural Synthesis of Xu Guangqi (1562-1633)*, ed. Catherine Jami, Peter Engelfriet and Gregory Blue (Leiden–Boston–Köln: Brill, 2001), 155–69. On the dispute see also Selusi Ambrogio, 'Secular Reason as a Tool of the Early Jesuit Mission to China', in *Asiatische Studien / Études Asiatiques*, 72.4 (Nov. 2018), 1195–1213.

87 For an English translation see Matteo Ricci, *The True Meaning of the Lord of Heaven (T'ien-chu Shih-i)*, ed. D. Lancashire and P. Hu Kuo-chen (Taipei–Paris–Hong Kong: Ricci Institute, 1985).

88 Only an Italian translation with Chinese text is available: Matteo Ricci, *Dieci capitoli di un uomo strano*, ed. Filippo Mignini, Italian trans. Wang Suna (Macerata: Quodlibet, 2010).

89 Ines G. Županov and Po-Chia Hsia, 'Reception of Hinduism and Buddhism', *The Cambridge History of Christianity*, vol. 6. *Reform and Expansion 1500-1660*, ed. Po-Chia Xsia (Cambridge: Cambridge University Press, 2008), 595.

90 *Storia*, 127; *Della entrata*, 102.

91 *Storia*, 132; *Della entrata*, 106.

92 'volendo seguire tutte le leggi, vengono a restare senza nessuna, per non seguire nessuna di cuore. E così altri chiaramente confessando la loro incredulità, altri ingannati dalla falsa persuasione di credere, vengono la magior parte di questa gente a stare nel profondo dell'atheismo.' (*Storia*, 132; *Della entrata*, 106)

93 Georg Horn, *Historiae philosophicae libri septem, quibus De origine, successione, sectis et vita Philosophorum ab orbe condito ad nostram aetatem agitur* (Leiden: apud Johannem Elsevirium, 1655).

94 It is not surprising that both Heurn and Horn were living and teaching in the tolerant Netherlands, since this country received Jesuit accounts very early and with great interest; on the impact of China Jesuits in the Dutch Republic see Thijs Weststeijn, 'The Middle Kingdom in the Low Countries. Sinology in the Seventeenth century Netherlands', in *The Making of the Humanities II: From Early Modern to Modern Disciplines* (Amsterdam: Amsterdam University Press, 2012), 209–42.

95 There was a long series of books on this topic inaugurated by the influential Jesuit José de Acosta (*Historia natural y moral de las Indias*, Seville 1590).

96 'He contrasted genuine philosophical study, restored by the Reformation and by humanist methodology ('that philosophy which is both natural and very ancient), with Sofistry, the search for the novel where there was emptiness and error . . . He believed that the proper interpretation of new ideas must stem from the fundamental categories used in reading ancient texts and analysing historical accounts, and that this resulted in the rediscovery of what was timeless and original, real and well-founded, always new and always vital', Luciano Malusa, MHP1, 241 (SSGF1, 258). Henry Krop also stresses the tolerant political and religious beliefs of the author, typical expression of a moderate Dutch philosophy able to connect Republicanism and admiration for the House of Orange (see 'Hornius, Georgius', *The dictionary of Seventeenth and Eighteenth-century Dutch philosophers*, Bristol: Thoemmes Press, 2003, vol. 1, 452).

97 See Daniel Barbu, 'Idolatry and the History of Religions', *Studi e Materiali di Storia delle Religioni*, 82/2, 2016, 553.

98 In a way, this approach recalls that of Renaissance thinkers, such as Ficino and Pico della Mirandola. It is worth noting that Horn defended the authority of the Bible in all circumstances, particularly on chronology, as we will see in the next paragraph. Instead of rejecting contrasting sources, Horn chose to try a conciliation.

99 See §3.5.
100 Horn indicated 'lib. III, cap. 7', but it is lib. III, chap. 50: 'genus plenum iustitiae'.
101 'Postea multis seculis abditi quasi et ignoti, Europaeorum notitiam fugerunt, donec sub Cathaeorum nomine Persis, inde Saracenis innotescerent' (ibid., 308).
102 In Mongolian *Khagan* means '*Khan* of the *Khans*', prince of all princes, often translated as 'Magnum Canem', 'Gran *Khan*'.
103 Horn remembered Gerardus Mercator and Abraham Ortels, who were both out of Flanders.
104 Actually, Marco Polo used the Persian name and not the Latin one which came from Greek.
105 'Academias in China nullas adhuc compertas: studia ipsorum esse linguam Mandarinorum, Historias, Leges Civiles, Proverbia, Physica quaedam eos habere et Mathematica, sed αμεθοδικά. Comoediis et Historiis deditissimos esse. Omnem eorum eruditionem revera in legendo et scribendo consistere. Theologiam nullam habere' (as quoted by Horn, ibid., 309).
106 Today we know that these books had not been written by Confucius, who probably did not write anything.
107 'In sola igitur Sina regnant Philosophi, ibique voti sui compos Plato factus est'.
108 There are many well-done researches on this topic, among which the most interesting and specifically related to China is the old but still useful Virgile Pinot, *La Chine et la Formation de l'esprit philosophique en France 1640-1740* (Genève: Slatkine Reprints, 1971), 189ff (1st edn, Paris 1932).
109 The quoted Gonzáles de Mendoza, *Histoire du grand Royaume de la Chine*.
110 Martino Martini, *Historiae sinicae decas primas* (Munich: typis Lucae Straubi, 1658).
111 For further details, see Pinot, *La Chine et la formation*, 194 and Mungello, *The Great Encounter of China and the West*, 1500-1800, 91–2. The Vulgate version is a fourth-century Latin translation of the Bible, made from several texts of different traditions. We might say that it is a compound Bible, therefore, it is not properly speaking the Hebrew Bible translated in Latin. However, among modern historians, it was usually called the Hebrew Bible, because the sections about chronology (i.e. Genesis) were taken from the Jewish version of the text.
112 The Septuagint version is also called the 'Greek old Testament', because it was written in Greek. The legend tells that Ptolomey II of Egypt sponsored this translation on behalf of Egyptian Jews, who did not have a command of Hebrew.
113 This incisive expression is provided in Günther Lottes, 'China in European Political Thought (1750-1850)', in *China and Europe. Images and Influences in Sixteenth to Eighteenth Centuries*, 68.
114 We use Isaac La Peyrère, *I Preadamiti / Praeadamitae*, ed. and it. trans. G. Lucchesini (Macerata: Quodlibét, 2004). Lucchesini edited and translated the anonymous edition of *Praeadamitae sive Exercitatio [. . .] quibus inducuntur Primi Homines ante Adamum conditi*, [Amsterdam] 1655 (without place or editor).
115 The most detailed and insightful book on this author is Richard H. Popkin, *Isaac La Peyrère (1596-1676), His Life, Work and Influence* (Leiden: E. J. Brill, 1987). Popkin investigates, together with La Peyrère's arguments, the former theories about Pre Adamism since the most ancient times.
116 'Conciliari Genesim et Evangelium, cum Astronomia veterum, Historia et Philosophia gentium vel antiquissimarum. Itaque si venerint Chaldaei ipsi, vetustissimi illi Astronomi, penes quos erant rationes cursus syderum, a multis retro centenis annorum millibus (ut aiunt) compositae et confectae: si venerint

antiquissimi Aegyptiorum Chronologi, cum antiquissimis Regum suorum dynastiis: si venerit Aristoteles ipse: si venerint cum Aristotele Sinenses, philosophi et chronologi for sean eximii: vel si qui olim reperientur sagaces apud Australes et Septentrionales incognitos: quibus, sicut et Sinensibus, Aegyptiis, et Chaldaeis, suae sibi sint epochae, a pluribus annorum myriadibus traditae et cognitae: Accipiant ultro illi omnes expositione hac historiam Geneseos, et fiant lubentius Christiani.', chap. XXVI, in Isaac La Peyrère, *I Preadamiti / Praeadamitae*, 138-40 [edn 1655, 69-70].

117 See Sergio Zoli, *Europa libertina tra Controriforma e Illuminismo* (Bologna: Cappelli Editore, 1989), 157.

118 On his personality of erudite libertine, see Rudolf de Smet, 'Vossius, Isaac', *The dictionary of Seventeenth and Eighteenth-century Dutch philosophers* (Bristol: Thoemmes Press, 2003), vol. 2, 1049-2. Voss was truly a secularist, a Radical thinker ante-litteram, he strenuously refused the last sacraments. 'Vossius was above all an erudite libertine with a broad horizon, devoted to the truth, an encyclopaedic scholar who, on the one hand, was aware of his universal knowledge (he knew that he knew all there was to be known), but who was also eager to unearth facts from the past which could refute or supplement the universal knowledge of his time.' (ibid., 1051). See also Eric Jorink and Dirk van Miert (ed.), *Isaac Vossius (1618-1689) between science and scholarship* (Leiden: Brill, 2012) and William Poole, 'Heterodoxy and Sinology: Isaac Vossius, Robert Hooke, and the Early Royal Society's use of Sinology'. *The Intellectual Consequences of Religious Heterodoxy 1600-1750*, ed. Sarah Mortimer and John Robertson (Leiden–Boston: Brill, 2012), 145-8.

119 Isaac Vossius, *De dissertatio de vera aetate mundi* (Hague: ex Typ. Adriani Vlacq, 1659).

120 'Scriptores habent ipso etiam Moyse antiquiores' (ibid., XLIV–XLV).

121 '[the Jewish] deluge was not universal, on the contrary, there had been diverse deluges in different times and places' ('diluvium non fuisse universale, sed diversis temporibus et locis diversa quoque fuisse diluvia.', ibid., p. LII).

122 'pour justifier l'admiration frénétique qu'il avait pour la Chine.' (Virgile Pinot, *La Chine et la formation*, 202).

123 As it is correctly pointed out by Israel in 'Spinoza, Confucius, and Classical Chinese Philosophy' (Jonathan I. Israel, *Enlightenment contested*, New York: Oxford University Press, 2006, chap. 25).

124 Eusèbe Renaudot, *Anciennes relations des Indes et de la Chine. De deux voyageurs Mahometans qui y allerent dans le neuvième siècle, avec Des Remarques sur les principaux endroits de ces Relations traduites d'arabe* (Paris: chez Jean-Baptiste Coignard, 1718). This text was partially translated in German by Heumann in his *Acta* (see §3.3. where Renaudot and Heumann are presented in detail).

125 Isaac Vossius, *Variarum observationum liber* (London: apud Robertum Scott Bibliopolam, 1685), 56-85.

126 'Soli in hoc nostro mundo sunt Seres, qui jam à quinque sere annorum millibus perennem et nunquam interruptam conservavere literaturam ..', ibid., 69-70.

127 'Soli illi inter omnes fuere mortales, qui pluribus quam quatuor annorum millibus regnum et rempublicam suam sine armis in summa pace et tranquillitate conservaverunt ..', ibid., 84.

128 Jonathan I. Israel, 'Admiration of China and Classical Chinese Thought in the Radical Enlightenment', *Taiwan Journal of East Asian Studies*, vol. 4, no. 1 (Iss.7), June 2007, 3. On Vossius as precursor of Bayle's interpretation of Chinese culture see also Thijs

Weststeijn, '*Spinoza sinicus*: An Asian Paragraph in the History of Radical Enlightenment', *Journal of the History of Ideas*, vol. 68, no. 4 (October 2007).
129 Peter Lambec, *Prodromus Historiae literariae*, (Leipzig – Frankfurt: Ex Officina Christiani Liebezeit, 1710), 1st edn, Hamburg 1659).
130 Georg Horn, *Dissertatio de vera aetate mundi qua sententia illorum refellitur qui statuunt Natale Mundi tempus annis minimum 1440 vulgarem aeram anticipare* (London: apud Elsevirium-Leffen, 1659).
131 Georg Horn, *Arca Noae sive Historia Imperiorum et Regnorum a condito orbe ad nostra Tempora* (London: ex Officina Hackiana, 1666).
132 Chinese, Egyptians, Chaldeans and Assyrians as Horn made explicit after a few lines.
133 'unde veritatem sacrarum Scripturarum haud obscure illustrare ac illis gentibus fontes ipsos, unde sua hauserint, recludere possimus.'
134 For further details on this topic, see Pinot, *La Chine et la Formation*, 209–11.
135 The already quoted E. Renaudot, *Anciennes relations des Indes et de la Chine*.
136 Pierre de Villemandy, *Manuductio ad Philosophiae Aristoteleae, Epicureae, et Cartesianae, Parallelismum*, (Amsterdam: apud Henricos Wetstenium et Desbordes, 1685). The historical part is on pp. 41–76.
137 'Unicum esse Deum, qui omnia ex nihilo condiderit; Animos esse immortales; Omnia sapientissime Divina Providentia Regi; Futuram aliquando corporum resurrectionem, etc.'
138 We changed the passive in an active sentence to make it more readable.
139 'Verum, quemadmodum Orientales plage solis nascentis lumine primum illustrantur, tum Meridionales, postremo Occiduae; sic nascentis Philosophiae radiis Orientales plagae primum illustrate fuerunt; a quibus deinde ad Meridionales transmissi sunt, ut inde ad Occiduas deferrentur' (in chap. *Philosophiae Nascentis sectae*, 58).
140 De Villemandy said clearly that Indian philosophy is derived from Abraham, thus he followed Postel (ibid., 57).
141 Louis Thomassin, *La Methode d'étudier et d'enseigner Chrêtiennement et solidement la Philosophie par rapport à la Religion Chrestienne et aux Ecritures* (Paris: chez François Muguet, 1685).
142 In French Thomassin used 'des Indes', hence India, China, Siam, etc. The contact between China and India, as we have seen with Matteo Ricci, was well known; although it was not clear that Buddhism was the key of their contact. Historians often spoke of Brachmanes or Gymnosophists who influenced Chinese culture, but we know that correctly they were Buddhists.
143 'De là comme d'une source commune le genre humain s'étendit d'un costé vers l'Orient, où la Sagesse se répandant en mesme temps, forma les Brachmanes, ou les Gymnosophistes des Indes; et de l'autre vers l'Occident, où les Pheniciens, les Egyptiens et plusieurs autres nations eurent des Sages de diverses sortes, quoy que tous émanez d'une mesme origine.'
144 'du cours naturel des choses humaines, qui semblent suivre le cours des astres, et passer toûjours de l'Orient à l'Occident, comme fait le genre humain mesme, par la providence de celuy qui a créé et qui gouverne le Ciel et la terre. Ou bien c'est un effet du progrez naturel des hommes, et de tout ce qui vient d'eux, le cours des années et la suite des siecles leur ajoûte ordinairement quelque nouvelle perfection.'
145 We follow Luciano Malusa (MHP1, I, chap. 1 and 3), who investigates the most relevant English historians of philosophy of the seventeenth and eighteenth centuries, who were Stanley and two Cambridge Platonists, namely Thephilius Gale (1628–78) and Thomas Burnet.

146 Thomas Stanley, *History of Philosophy: Containing the Lives, Opinions, Actions and Discourses of the Philosophers of every Sect* (London: for H. Moseley and Th. Dring, 1656–62).
147 Published as Thomas Stanley, *Historia philosophiae orientalis recensuit, ex anglica lingua in latinam, notis in Oracula chaldaica et indice philologico auxit Johannes Clericus* (Amsterdam: apud Swart, 1690).
148 On Stanley and on the Latin editions of his *History of Philosophy* see Luciano Malusa, MHP1, 177–8 (SSGF1, 182–3). See also the same chapter for an interesting overview of the Baconian historical method, named more properly 'literary history and arts'.
149 On the second page (without number) of the *Preface*.
150 Thomas Burnet, *Archaeologiae Philosophicae: sive Doctrina antiqua de Rerum Originibus, libri duo* (London: Typis R. N. Impensis Kettilby, 1692). We use this edition for the first book.
151 This book was the fulfilment of his renowned *Telluris theoria sacra*, typis R. N. (i.e. R. Norton) (London: impensis Gual. Kettilby, 1691), this is the first of many editions and translations.
152 Thomas Burnet, *Archaeologia Philosophicae: or, the Ancient Doctrine Concerning the Origininals of Things, written in Latin by Thomas Burnet, Faithfully translated into English, with Remarks thereon, by Mr. Foxton* (London: Printed for E. Curll in the Strand, 1729). For quoting the Appendix we use this edition, which has autonomous numbers (from 1 to 9), whilst the Latin edition has number in sequence with the former books (from 352 to 358).
153 Thomas Burnet, *Archaeologia Philosophicae: or, the Ancient Doctrine Concerning the Origininals of Things, written in Latin by Thomas Burnet, to which is added, Dr Burnet's Theory of the Visible World, by way of Commentary on his own Theory of the Earth; being the second Part of his Archiologiae Philosophicae. Faithfully translated into English, with Remarks thereon, Printed and fold by J. Fisher* (London: Tom's Coffe-House in Cornhill, 1736).
154 It was also translated alone in Charles Blount, *Oracles of Reason*, London 1693, 77–86. A book written in defence of the same Burnet, when he was accused by the archbishop of Canterbury because of the theological theories argued in *Archaeologiae Philosophicae*. The deist Blount also provided the first English translation of the account of Apollonius Tyaneus, the most debated and influential book on Indian philosophy since Renaissance times (Charles Blount, *The Two First Books of Philostratus concerning the Life of Apollonius Tyaneus*, London: Nathaniel Thompson, 1680).
155 Mirella Pasini, *Thomas Burnet. Una storia del mondo tra ragione, mito e rivelazione* (Firenze: La Nuova Italia editrice, 1981), 71.
156 In 1687, as master of the Charterhouse School, he opposed the Catholic King James II who proposed the Catholic Andrew Popham as a new pensioner of the School.
157 MHP1, 331 (SSGF1, 358).
158 M. Pasini, *Thomas Burnet*, 2 and Sergio Zoli, *Europa libertina tra Controriforma e Illuminismo* (Bologna: Cappelli Editore, 1989), 164–5, 198 (n. 16).
159 Burnet quoted Strabo (*Geo.* I, II, §28), who takes this classification from Ephorus (in his *Universal history*).
160 'Quum vero Indorum nomine plures Gentes confuse intellexerint antiqui, cum eo perventum fuerit, utendum erit novo apparatu ...' (*ibid.*, 5).
161 Origen, *Against Celus*, trans. Frederick Crombie, in *Ante-Nicene Fathers*, ed. Schaff Philip, facsimile of American ed. 1885 (Grand Rapids: Erdmans Publishing

Company, 2001), vo. 4, 1498. The reference of Origene's original text is book VII, chap. 62.

162 Burnet reported here the 'books burning' (*fenshu* 焚书 or *qinhuo* 秦火) of Qin Shi Huangdi 秦始皇帝 – the first emperor and unifier of China – which happened in 213 BCE. The emperor ordered the destruction of all books (with the exception of technical books), because he aimed at erasing all cultural diversities in his fragmented empire.

163 'Habent nonnullas Archaeologias Philosophicas, de *Diluvio*, de ortu rerum *ex Ovo*, et observationes coelestes mirandae vetustatis' (italics in the original text).

164 'Sinenses cum hodiernis Europaeis comparentur, non dubito nostratibus illos multum inferiores esse; sive disciplinas Mathematicas spectemus, puras vel mixtas; sive Physiologiam.'

165 'Haec de antiquis Brachmanis intelligo; de quorum vita et moribus multa occurrunt apud veteres, de doctrina paucissima'

166 'Certissimum est superesse adhuc ordines et tribus Philosophorum apud Indos, atque eos uti, in conservanda sua philosophia, lingua sacra, (hoc est, non vulgari vernacula) et antiquissima; ut non incredibile sit mansisse per tot saecula eandem Philosophiam, vel ejusdem philosophiae corpus, licet varie dictorum et novis fabulis quasi incrustatum. Hujus notitias aliquas nobis attulerunt viri docti, qui apud Indos diu versati sunt, et ex eorum scriptis quaedam specimina, cum opportunum fuerit, in sequenti forsan libro afferemus.'

167 'Sua dogmata tradunt plerumque nude et simpliciter, nulla praesunte dissertatione, nullis munita rationibus: ab ipso nutu et authoritate docentis recipienda.'

168 'Recte notat Clemens Alexandrinus, Philosophiam antiquo-barbaram fuisse facilem brevemque, per quaesita et responsa: non argumentativam et contentiosam, ut eat postea Graeca.'

169 'Hinc satis constare videtur: Priscorum Philosophiam fuisse traducem sive traditivam ...'

170 On this important topic, we cannot examine in depth here, see ibid., 63–4 (chap. 7, on Jews and their Cabala).

171 'Idem docent hodierni Brachmanes apud Indos.'

172 'Haec et hujusmodi capita complexa est priscorum philosophia; Quae, licet multis maculis conspersa, aut sordibus involuta, ad nos feros homines, ultimam fere Noachidarum progeniem, post aliquot millennia, pervenerit: veritate tamen aliunde reperta et explorata; has labes eluere non penitus arduum est; et in his Antiquorum gemmis, vetustate licet decoloratis, vividas adhuc relucere scintillas, non sine admiratione saepius adverti.'

173 In the Latin version he used 'Oriente' (*ibid.*, 352).

174 As Frédéric Lenoir pointed out, Tibetans were known in Europe since at least Marco Polo (see Frédéric Lenoir, *La rencontre du Bouddhisme et de l'Occident*, Paris: Albin Michel, 1999, pars I, chap. 3). However, they were absent in the histories of philosophy, we suggest that this could be because of their fame as magicians and not as thinkers.

175 Roth wrote maybe the first grammar of Sanskrit language, see for references Stephen Neill, *The history of Christianity in India, The beginnings to AD 1707* (Cambridge: Cambridge University Press, 1984), 417–19.

176 Athanasius Kircher, *China Monumentis qua sacris qua profanis, nec non variis naturae et artis spectaculis, aliarumque rerum memorabilium argumentis illustrate* (Amsterdam: Apud Iacobum à Meurs, 1677), usually shortened as *China illustrata*. That book

proposed two influential theories: 1. the direct relation between Egyptians hieroglyphics and Chinese characters; 2. the diffusion of the Egyptian idolatry through Persia, India and China, which was became Buddhism in Asia. On Kircher see §2.1.
177 Burnet suggested in brackets to see chap. 7 of the first book, in the Latin version. Obviously, the Appendix in Latin (p. 354) was more precise suggesting pages 63ff, where the doctrine of emanation is presented.
178 Constable, London 1630. See the new edition: Henry Lord, *A discovery of the Banian religion and the religion of the Persees : a critical edition of two early English works on Indian religions*, ed. Will Sweetman (Lewiston: Edwin Mellen Press, 1999).
179 François Bernier, *Suite des Mémoires du sieur Bernier sur l'empire du grand Mogol* (Paris: chez Claude Barbin, 1671). Burnet was probably referring to the 'Letter to M. Chapelain, describing the Gentiles of Hindustan' (in French 'Lettre à Monsieur Chapelain, envoyer de Chiraz en Perse le 4 octobre 1667'). Recently, this letter has been edited in F. Tinguely (ed.), *Un libertin dans l'Inde Moghole. Le voyages de François Bernier 1656-1669* (Paris: Editions Chandeigne, 2008), 301–44.
180 Simon de la Loubère, *Du Royame du Siam*, 2 vols (Amsterdam: chez Abraham Wolfang, 1691). For a good overview of the image of Siam in the late seventeenth and early eighteenth centuries see Rolando Minuti, *Orientalismo e idee di tolleranza nella cultura francese del primo '700* (Firenze: Olschki editore, 2006), 47–78.
181 Guy Tachard, *Voyage de Siam des pères Jesuites, envoyés par le roy, aux Indes et à la Chine* (Paris: A. Seneuze & D. Hortemels, 1686).
182 Broadly speaking, it was the Tamil coast of India, thus the south-eastern coast. This included sometimes also Sri Lanka (the north coast was culturally Tamil).
183 Malabar was the south-west coast of India, specifically the Kerala coast.
184 This is the renowned myth of the cosmic egg of Pangu 盤古.
185 Jonathan I. Israel, *Radical Enlightenment* (New York: Oxford University Press, 2001), 15 (italics in the original).
186 De la Mothe le Vayer François, *De la vertu des payens* (Paris: chez François Targa, 1642), republished in the several editions of his *Oeuvres*, we consulted the edition Paris 1662-3, I, 584–705.
187 'Iamais personne raisonnable n'a douté que la Vertu ne meritast d'estre honorée.'
188 'C'est pourquoy comme les Fideles ne laissent pas d'estre assez souvent vicieux, il n'est pas impossible non plusqu'un Infidele ne puisse exercer quelques vertus, quoy qu'elles ne soient pas accompagnées du merite que donne la grace qui vient de la Foy.'
189 On Le Vayer's libertine use of Confucius as Socrates (both without Original sin and saved without grace) see Sergio Zoli, *Europa libertina tra Controriforma e Illuminismo* (Bologna: Cappelli Editore, 1989), chap. 2, 125–39.
190 'ne doute point que beaucoup de vertueus Chinois n'ayent peu se sauver en observant la simple Loy de nature, et avec le secours special du seul Dieu qu'ils reconnoissoient pour Autheur du Ciel et de la terre'. Obviously Ricci is quoted from Trigault's translation.
191 'Or les Payens qui ont vescu vertueusement suivant les lumieres du droit de Nature, et soumettans leur liberal arbitre à la raison, ont fait tout ce qui estoit de leur pouvoir puis qu'ils ne connoissoient point d'autre loy que la naturelle ... ceste loy gravée dans nos coeurs qui comprend toute celle de Moyse ...'
192 'Les Chinois ... n'ont reconnu de temps immemorial qu'un seul Dieu, qu'ils nommoient le Roy du Ciel; et l'on peut voir par leurs annales de plus de quatre mille ans, qu'il n'y a point eu de Payens qui l'ayent moins offencé qu'eus de ce costé-là, et dont le reste des actions se soient plus conformées à ce que prescrit la droite raison.'

193 'le plus homme de bien, et le plus grand Philosophe qu'ait veu l'Orient, a esté un nommé Confutius Chinois . . .' (ibid., 280). It is quite hard to translate properly 'homme de bien', it is slightly different from 'good man'.

194 Scholars suggest 479 BCE as Confucius' year of death, whilst Socrates should have been born in 469 BCE.

195 'De sorte qu'on peut dire que Confucius fit descendre aussi bien que Socrate la philosophie du Ciel en terre, par l'authorité qu'ils donnerent tous deus à la Morale . . .'.

196 Laurent Bordelon, *Théatre philosophique, sur lequel On represente par des Dialogues dans le Champs Elisées les Philosophes anciens et modernes* (Paris: Chez Claude Barbin et Jean Musier, 1692), Dialogue XXV, 349–60.

197 'tous les Arts liberaus et toutes les Sciences ont eu cours à la Chine aussi bien que parmy nous'

198 'Certes ce n'est pas une petite gloire à Confutius, d'avoir mis le Sceptre entre les mains de la philosophie, et d'avoir fait que la force obeysse paisiblement à la Raison.'

199 Cristoforo Borri, *Relatione della Nuova Missione delli PP. della Compagnia di Giesù, al Regno della Cocincina* (Rome: per Francesco Corbelletti, 1631).

200 Cristoforo Borri, *Relation de la Nouvelle Mission des Pères de la Compagnie de Iesu, au Royaume de la Cochinchine*, trans. Antoine de la Croix (Lille la Bible d'Or, 1631). We present Borri in §2.1.

201 'Condemnons donc ceste Indolence, ou ceste exemption de toute douleur, dont Xaca faisot nostre parfaitte beatitude; et reconnoissons encore que ses termes touchant la Divinité ne peuvent estre reçeus.'

202 The Buddhist apathy has already been discussed in Valignano's *Catechismus* (see §1.2.).

203 For instance, Bernier wrote a letter to him that was published at the beginning of the second tome of *Voyages de François Bernier*, where the voyager described in detail Indian cities and royal palaces. Bernier also quoted Le Vayer in his letters to M.me de la Sabliere regarding his appraisal of Confucius (see 'Introduction à la lecture de Confucius' published 7 June 1688 in *Journal de Sçavans* pour l'année 1688, II, Paris: chez Jean Cusson, 1688, 22).

Chapter 2

1 Urs App, *The cult of Emptiness. The Western Discovery of Buddhist Thought and the Invention of Oriental Philosophy*, Rorschach/Kyoto: UniversityMedia, 2012. This monograph is an excellent and updated investigation on the shaping of Buddhist understanding among the Jesuits in China and Japan. App quotes many unpublished sources or sources published in more recent times, whilst we use only accounts published in the seventeenth century, because our aim is to understand the image of the Asiatic thought in Europe and not in Asia. Nevertheless, this paragraph is in several points indebted to App's excellent analysis.

2 On this dispute see App, *Discovery*, 143.

3 On the topic, see both App, *Discovery*, part. II, and the aforementioned Virgille Pinot, *La Chine et la formation*.

4 Cristoforo Borri, *Relatione della Nuova Missione delli PP. della Compagnia di Giesù, al Regno della Cocincina*, (Rome: per Francesco Corbelletti, 1631). We already mentioned this book presenting Thomas Burnet in §1.6.

5 Cristoforo Borri, *Relation de la Nouvelle Mission des Pères de la Compagnie de Iesu, au Royaume de la Cochinchine*, trans. Antoine de la Croix, (Lille: la Bible d'Or, 1631).

6. 'pare habbia voluto il Demonio fare tra gentili un ritratto della bellezza…' and 'se alcuno entrasse novamente in quella Terra [Cocincina], potrebbe facilmente persuadersi, essere ivi stati nei tempi antichi Cattolici, e Christiani, tanto ha voluto il Demonio imitare le cose nostre' (ibid., 198, 200).
7. 'I Gentili Orientali, le cui sette hebbero già origine da un gran metafisico chiamato Xaca, nativo del Regno di Siam, antico molto più d'Aristotile, et à lui nella capacità, et conoscimento delle cose naturali niente inferiore. Mosso costui dall'acutezza del suo ingegno alla consideratione della natura, et fabrica del mondo, contemplando li principij, et fini delle cose particolarmente della natura humana… determinò, che tutte le cose tanto fisiche, e naturali, quanto morali eran nulla da nulla, e per nulla…'
8. 'Dalche tutto conchiudeva, che essendo queste cose nulla, havevano origine come da una causa non già efficiente, ma materiale, da un principio, ch'era nulla sì, ma nulla eterno, infinito, immenso, immutabile, omnipotente e finalmente Dio nulla, et origine del niente.'
9. In Buddhist words this is the 'useful or skillful means', in skr. *upāya-kauśalya*, the theory of the different possible means leading to freedom or liberation, not based on one orthodoxy, but rather in accord with the specific skills of each person. This doctrine is the heart of the Mahāyāna, one of the three major branches of Buddhism.
10. Alvarez Semedo, *Histoire universelle du Grand Royaume de la China* (Paris: chez Cramoisy, 1645).
11. Semedo also quoted the prohibited White Lotus Sect (白莲教 he transcripted as 'Peliankico') as a real danger for imperial stability.
12. Alexandre de Rhodes, *Histoire du Royaume de Tunquin,* trans. H. Albi (Lyon: chez Iean Baptiste Devenet, 1651).
13. 'Mais les Diables qui gouvernoient l'esprit de ce malheureux Prince, n'ignorans pas que l'Atheisme est pire, et plus pernicieux que l'Idolatrie, comme celuy qui fait planche à toutes sortes de vices, persuaderent à cét esprit impie de se dédire sur la fin de ses jours. Ce qu'il fit, non pas devant le peuple, mais seulement devant les plus ingenieux, et les plus malins de ses disciples, ausquels il declara que la doctrine des Idoles qu'il avoit enseignée durant quarante ans, n'estoit que pour amuser le simple peuple […] deux grands maux dont il avoit esté l'Autheur; l'un de l'Idolatries dans lequelle le peuple trompé et enchanté des contes de ses fables, s'est ietté, et a depuis perseveré; et l'autre de l'Atheisme, duquel font encore profession les esprit les plus deliez, s'abandonnans sans crainte à toutes sortes de vices…'
14. 's'arresta en l'Inde; et là s'estant addressé aux Brachmanes, et ayant eu communication du Livre, et de la doctrine de leur *Budda*, (c'est à dire) *le Sage*, qui est le nom qu'ils ont donné au Thicca dont nous avons parlé, il l'apporta au Roy de la Chine…'
15. Clement of Alexandria in *Stromata* (I, 15) and more likely Saint Jerome (Eusebius Sophronius Hieronymus) in his *Contra Jovianus* (I, 42 and II, 14), who use the transcription 'Budda', whilst Clement wrote βούττα.
16. Since Megasthenes (*Indika*) who was quoted by, to mention only the most relevant authors, Diodorus Siculus (*Bibliotheca historica*, II, 35–42) and Strabo in *Geographica* (XV, I, 39–73).
17. Accounts from India were really scarce and Buddhism had already disappeared from Indian lands, while it survived only in Ceylon.
18. Giovanni Filippo de Marini, *Delle missioni de' padri della Compagnia di Giesù, nella Provincia del Giappone, e particolarmente di quella di Tumkino* (Rome: per Nicolò Angelo Tinassi, 1658).

19 'ivi gionti non curarono passar più avanti, ad altri Regni più Occidentali, ove era fama corresse legge migliore, qual si osservava nel Regno di Canbaya [Khambat, India], e Sinde, vicino al fiume Indo [zona di Hyderabad, Pakistan], dove que' popoli adoravano il celebre Idolo chiamato *O My To*, ma perché videro, che quivi nell'India era maggiore il seguito di un'altra Setta, perché più libera, e più infame del Rama, Idolo più moderno dell'*O My To* . . . [lo scelsero.] L'autore di questa mala setta nell'India si chiama Rama nella Cina *Xé Kian*, nel Giappone *Faca*, nel Tunkino *Thic Ca*. Sparse quest'Idra il suo veleno in tanti Regni, in quanti la maggior parte di quest'Asia si divide, ma dove fe' sentire più esitiale la sua peste, fu ne' Regni dell'India, del Bengala, Perú [Pegu, ie. Birmania], Siám, Cambogia, Lao. Nacque questo mostro nell'India di mezzo . . .'

20 Many books have been published on the topic, we suggest Kamaleswar Bhattacharya, *L'ātman-Brahman dans le Bouddhisme ancien* (Paris: Adrien-Maisonneuve, 1973).

21 'vi è tutta l'arte dell'hipocrisia de' Farisei; il temerario delle bestemmie degli Atei, e tutto il sordido dell'heresie de' Novatori, massimamente di Lutero e Calvino.' For a Protestant and anti-Jesuit answer to these sentences see Mathurin Veyssière de La Croze, *Histoire du christianisme des Inde* (La Haye: chez les frères Vaillant, & N. Prévost, 1724), vol. 6, 509–10 (La Croze is presented in §3.6., since he was Brucker's main source on India).

22 Athanasius Kircher, *China monumentis qua Sacris qua Profanis, nec non variis naturae et artis spectaculis, aliarumque rerum memorabilium argumentis illustrate* (Amsterdam: apud Jacobum à Meurs, 1667). We quote from the English translation: ibid., *China Illustrata*, trans. Charles D. Van Tuyl (Bloomington Indiana University, 1987).

23 David E. Mungello, *Curious land: Jesuit accommodation and the origins of Sinology* (Honolulu: University of Hawaii Press, 1989), 179, 336–337.

24 See Sergio Zoli, *Europa libertina tra Controriforma e Illuminismo*, 148–50.

25 Unpublished until 2001: João Rodrigues, *João Rodrigues's Account of Sixteenth-Century Japan*, ed. and trans. M. Cooper (London: Hakluyt Society, 2001), 355–6.

26 Michael Cooper, 'Rodrigues in China. The Letters of João Rodrigues, 1611-1633', *Kokugoshi e ni michi*, vol. 2, Tokyo: Sanshodo, 1981. Quoted in App, *Discovery*, 104.

27 App, *Discovery*, 103–4, he speaks of 'revolutionary view'.

28 See Schmidt-Biggemann, *Philosophia perennis*, 418 and 427. It was already in *Berossus* that Ham was described as the father of black magic.

29 Michael Cooper, 'Rodrigues in China', 311–12. Quoted in App, *Discovery*, 105.

30 Domingo Fernandez Navarrete, *Tratados historicos, politicos, ethicos, y religiosos de la monarchia de China* (Madrid: Imprenta Real, 1676). Only in 1704 was it translated in English.

31 'La dicha secta literaria professa un puro Atheismo, como largamente se probarà en su proprio lugar, de los Missionarios mas doctos y graves de la Compañia [di Gesù] . . .'

32 'Y assi el Padre Iuan Ruiz, en el Tratado que hízo de estas controversias, prueba con mucha probabilidad, que Fo Hi, fue a quel gran Zoroastres Rey de Bactriana, y Principe de los Magos Chaldeos, el quel dio princípio a todas las Sectas del Occidente, y despues vino a este Oriente, y fundò el Reyno de la China con la Secta que llaman de los Letrados. De donde nace, que como esta Secta de China, con las de aquellas Gentilidades, salieron de la mesma fuente, y por obra del mesmo demonio, assi tienen entre si grandissima semejança, y por la mesma traça, y arte llevan a los hombres engañados al infierno.'

33 'el primer príncipio, y ultimo fin, era la materia primera, ò el Chaos, lo qual significan por estas dos lettras Kung, y Hiu, que es lo mesmo que vacuo, y que fuera desto no avia otra cosa que buscar, ní esperar.'
34 Antoine Arnauld, *La Morale pratique des Jesuites: divisé en sept parties: où l'on represente leur conduite dans la Chine, dans le Japon, et dans l'Ethyopie: le tout tiré de livres très-autorisez, ou de pieces très-authentiques* (Cologne: chez Gervinus Quentel, 1682).
35 On Arnauld's opposition to both Le Vayer and the Jesuits see Sergio Zoli, *Europa libertina tra Controriforma e Illuminismo*, 132–5.
36 Philippe Couplet, *Confucius sinarum philosophus, sive scientia sinensis latine exposita, studio et opera, Prosperi Intorcetta, Christiani Herdtrich, Francisci Rougemont, Philippi Couplet Patrum societatis Jesu* (Paris: Apud Danielem Horthmels, 1687).
37 For a short survey of the Chinese texts translated before and after the *Confucius sinarum philosophus* within Jesuit works, see Knud Lundbaek, 'The first European Translations of Chinese Historical and Philosophical Works', in Thomas H. C. Lee (ed.), *China and Europe*, 29–43.
38 See App, *Discovery*, 138–40.
39 '*vacuum* igitur et *inane* (*Cum hiu* Sinae vocant) primum scilicet rerum omnium principium, nihil esse quod quaeratur, nihil in quo collecentur spes nostrae.' Le Clerc translated with 'vuide et un néant reel', in Jean Le Clerc, *Bibliotheque universelle et historique de l'année 1687*, tome VII (December, XIV), Amsterdam: chez Wolfang, Waesberge, Boom, et van Someren, 1688, 406.
40 On the name of this school see App, *Discovery*, 179.
41 Gita Dharampal-Frick, *Indien im Spiegel deutscher Quellen der Frühen Neuzeit 1500–1750* (Tübingen: Max Niemeyer Verlag, 1994), 342–8.
42 Bernier quoted Roth, whom he called 'Roa', as the source of his knowledge of the principles of the Sanskrit language and as source of Kircher, who published a list of Sanskrit letters in *China illustrata*.
43 François Bernier, *Suite de memoires du Sieur Bernier sur l'Empire du Grand Mogol* (Paris: chez Claude Barbin, 1671). Each letter is paginated separately, thus the number refers to the single Letter not to the whole book. This letter to Chapelain is translated in English in F. Bernier, *Travels in the Mogul Empire (1656-1658)*, trans. Archibald Constable, London 1891; we quote from the 2nd revised by Vincent A. Smith printed at London: Oxford University Press, 1916 (there are several reprints in Delhi).
44 Robert Flud or Fludd (1574-1637) was an English Paracelsian physician and Cabalist who belonged to the Rosicrucians. Gassendi wrote the *Examen Philosophiae Fluddanae* (1630) against his Neoplatonic and cabalist theories.
45 We suggest it might be the Sanskrit *acala*, which means motionless.
46 'Biapek' or 'Byapek' is certainly *vyāpaka* in Sanskrit, which means pervading, all-inclusive, from the root *vi-ĀP*: to spread, to get in all directions.
47 'Il n'est pas que vous ne sçachiez la doctrine de beaucoup d'anciens Philosophes, touchant cette grande ame du Monde, don't ils veulent que nos ames, et celles des animaux, soient des portions: Si nous penetrions bien dans Platon et dans Aristote, peut-estre que nous trouverions qu'ils ont donné dans cette pensée; C'est la Doctrine comme universelle des Pendets Gentils des Indes, et c'est cette mesme Doctrine qui fait encore à present la Cabale des Soufys, et de la pluspart des gens de lettres de Perse, . . . Comme ç'a esté celle-là mesme de Flud que nostre grand Gassendy a refutée si doctement, et celle où se perdent la pluspart de nos Chimiques. Or ces Cabalistes ou Pendets Indous que je veux dire; poussent l'impertinence plus avant que tous ces

Philosophes, et pretendent que Dieu ou cet Estre souverain qu'ils appellent Achar, immobile, immuable, ait non seulement produit ou tiré les ames de sa propre substance, mais generalement encore tout ce qu'ill y a de materiel et de corporel dans l'Univers, et que cette production ne s'est pas faite simplement à la façon des causes efficientes, mais à la façon d'une Araignée qui produit une toile qu'elle tire de son nombril, et qu'elle reprend quand elle veut; La creation donc, disent ces Docteurs imaginaires, n'est autre chose qu'une extraction et extension que Dieu fait de sa propre substance... Il n'est donc rien, disent-ils, de réel et d'effectif de tout ce que nous croyons voir, oüir ou falairer, goûter ou toucher, tout ce Monde n'est qu'une espece de songe et une pure illusion... Mais demandez-leur un peu quelque raison de cette imagination, ou qu'ils vous expliquent comme se fait cette sortie et cette reprise de substance, cette extension, cette diversité apparente, ou comme il se peut faire que Dieu n'estant pas corporel, mais Biapek, com e ils avoüent et incorruptible, il soit neantmoins divisé en tant de portions de corps et d'ame, il ne vous payeront jamais que de belles comparaisons; Que Dieu est comme un Ocean immense dans lequel se mouveroient plusieurs fioles quelque part qu'elles pussent aller, se trouveroient toûjours dans le mesme Ocean, dans le mesme eau, et que se venant à rompre, leurs eaux se trouveroient en mesme temps unies à leur tout, à cet Ocean don't elle estoient des portions: Ou bien ils vous diront qu'il en est de Dieu comme de la Lumiere, qui est la mesme par tout l'Univers, et qui ne laisse pas de paroître de cent façons differentes selon la diversité des objets où elle tombe, ou selon les diverses couleurs et figures des verres par où elle passe. Il ne vous payeront, dis-je, jamais que de ces sortes de comparaisons qui n'ont aucune proportion avec Dieu et qui ne sont bonnes que pour jetter de la poudre aux yeux d'un peuple ignorant; et il ne faut pas esperer qu'ils vous répondent solidement...' (Bernier, *Suite de memoires du Sieur Bernier*, 127–34).

48 On Bernier's negative interpretation of India as despotic and superstitious see Joan-Pau Rubiés. 'Race, Climate and Civilization in the Works of François Bernier'. *Collection Puruṣārtha,* 2013, 53–76.
49 *Muṇḍaka Upaniṣad* (1.6-7)
50 *Cūlikā* or *Mantrika Upaniṣad*. The allegory or metaphor of water was already reported in Kircher, *China Illustrata*, vol. 3, chap. 5, 145. As we said, the source for both Bernier and Kircher was Roth (see App, *Discovery*, chap. 12).
51 'Qi'il n'y a Opinions si ridicules et si extravagantes don't l'esprit de l'homme ne s'avise' (ibid., 135)
52 François Bernier, *Abregé de la Philosophie de Gassendi*, 2nd enlarged edn, 2 vols (Lyon: chez Anisson, Posuel et Rigaud, 1684).
53 'Aussi ne seaurois-je trop m'etonner comment cette Opinion a pû si generalement s'emparer de l'Esprit des hommes, et que pour ne rien dire de nos Cabalistes, et de plusieurs de nos Chymistes qui ont de la peine à en revenir, elle ait infecté une bonne partie de l'Asie: Car je me suis aperceu en voyageant dans ces Pays là, que la pluspart des Derviches des Turcs, et de Souphis, ou des Scavans de Perse en sont entestez; et j'ay appris de personnes dignes de foy qu'elle a penetré jusques à la Chine, et au Japon; desorte que presque tous ceux qui passent pour Doctes en Asie font gloire, quoy qu'en particulier, de dire qu'ils sont de parcelles de la Substance Divine, et en quelque facon de petis Dieux: Mais voyez je vous prie, jusques ou le Bragmanes ont poussé la fiction, et la reverie.'
54 Noël Aubert de Versé, *L'Impie convaincu, ou dissertation contre Spinosa* (Amsterdam: chez Jean Crelle, 1685).
55 'C'estoit là les sentiment des anciens Gnostiques, celui des Priscillianiste, et c'est celui de la plupart des Cabbaliste, des nouveaux Adamites ou illuminez, et d'une infinité de

Philosophes de l'Asie et des Indes.' The 'Avertissement' has no page numbers, thus, the quote is from the seventh page of it. The translation is from App, *Discovery*, 172.
56 Jean Le Clerc, *Bibliotheque universelle et historique de l'année 1687*, tome VII (December, XIV), 387–455.
57 'Que nous, tous les èlemens et toutes les créatures, faisons partie de ce vuide; Qu'ainsi il n'y a qu'une seule et même substance, qui est differente dans les êtres particuliers, par les seules figures et par les qualitez ou la configuration intérieure; à peu près comme l'eau, qui est toûjours essentiellement de l'eau, soit qu'elle ait la forme de la neige, de grêle, de pluye ou de glace. Ceux qui voudront s'instruire plus amplement de la Philosophie des Indiens et de Chinois, qui n'est pas fort différent du systeme des Spinosistes, s'ils en ont un, peuvent lire le voyage de l'Indostan de Mr Bernier.'
58 François Bernier, 'Introduction à la lecture de Confucius' (8 June 1688), in *Journal des Sçavans*, pour l'année 1688, ed.-S. Regis (Paris: chez Jean Cusson, 1688), 14–22.
59 François Bernier, 'Memoire de Mr. Bernier sur le Quietisme des Indes', in *Histoire des ouvrages des Sçavans*, Sept. 1688, ed. H. B. de Beauval (Rotterdam: chez Renier Leers, 1688), 47–2.
60 Miguel Molinos, *Recueuil de diverses pieces concernant le quietisme ou Molinos, ses sentiments et ses disciples*, ed. J. C. Lacroze (Amsterdam: chez Wolfang et Savouret, 1688).
61 See App, *Discovery*, 180–1, where a complete translation of the argument against Couplet's description of Buddhism as Quietism is provided.
62 'Le Pere Couplet ne fait pas lui-même la comparaison; mais on sent bien par la lecture des paroles qu'on vient de citer, par le tour de sa narration, et par toute la suite de ses raisonnemens, qu'il a voulu laisser au Lecteur le plaisir de la faire. Quoi qu'il en soit, c'est la grande accusation qu'on fait aux Quiétistes de réduire toute la Religion à la contemplation du vuide ou d'une idée vague et confuse …'
63 'Comme depuis cinq ou six mois je n'entents parler que du *Quietisme*, cela m'a fait souvenir de nos Quietistes des Indes, et m'a donné la curiosité de revoir mes vieux memoires de ce pays-là.'
64 'et, ce qui est à remarquer, dans un parfait repos, dans une absolüe inaction, en un mot dans un Quietisme très-parfait.'
65 'C'est faire Dieu corporel, et par consequent divisible, corruptible, etc. ce qui repugne à la souveraine et absolüe perfection de Dieu.'
66 It is the local term for Buddhist monks.
67 'Au rest je ne pretens point icy qu'il en soit de ce Quietisme ou Molinisisme qui fait tant de bruit, comme du Quietisme des Joguis des Indes, ou des Bonzes de la Chine, ou des Talapois de Siam. Je veux bonnement croire qu'il y aura plus de devotion et de d'extravagance, que de méchanceté. Cependant ce grand rapport de ce deux Quietismes, cet abyme de contemplation, cette grande inaction, cette grande union de nostre ame a Dieu, et cent autres choses qu'on en dit, me sont fort suspectes, et me font soupçonner que toute cette grande et extraordinaire devotion ne tende, ou ne puisse mener à quelque espece d'irreligion, ou de libertinage. C'est ce que nous pourrons un jour examiner, si les veritables originaux de Molinos nous peuvent tomber entre les mains, et si ses amis jugent qu'ils meritent qu'on se donne la peine de les lire.'
68 On Bayle as atheist or Calvinist, among many outstanding works, see Richard Popkins, *The history of Scepticism. From Savonarola to Bayle* (New York: Oxford University Press, 2003), chap. 18 and Israel, *Enlightenment contested*, (New York: Oxford University Press, 2006), chap. 3 or ibid., *Radical Enlightenment* (New York: Oxford University Press, 2001), chap. 18. Popkin argues that Bayle's personal Calvinist

faith should be distinguished from the sceptical and somewhat atheistic attitude of the historian; instead, Israel supports the atheism of the thinker. As far as we are concerned, we share Israel's opinion, since from the investigation of the 'natural and virtuous atheist', Bayle's sceptical atheism seem to descend almost necessarily.

69 Pierre Bayle, *Dictionnaire historique et critique* (Amsterdam–Leyde–La Haye–Utrecht 1740), retrieved from https://artfl-project.uchicago.edu/content/dictionnaire-de-bayle. Each entry is quoted as follows: title of the entry, number of volume of this edition, number of page.

70 These are all the entries we found, by means of 'Table de matières', where China and India are discussed or simply mentioned: 1. Brachmanes; 2. Cesalpin André; 3. Gymnosophistes; 4. Golius; 5. Hali-Beigh; 6. Japon; 7. Maldonat; 8. Mendozza; 9. Milton; 10. Spinoza; 11. Sommona-Codom.

71 Gymnosophistes, II, 551–2.

72 Gymnosophistes, II, 552 e Brachmanes, I, 651. In Brachmanes rem. A, Bayle acknowledged the most extreme practices as fairy tales.

73 Brachmanes, I, rem. B.

74 Gymnosophistes, II, rem. A.; Bayle suggested that they were not completely naked but rather with covered pubis.

75 Brachmanes, I, 652; Gymnosophistes, II, 552. Unfortunately, in both entries, Bayle did not examine in depth this interesting topic.

76 Since Buddhism is listed as the third sect, we suspect that Bayle did not use Ricci, *De Christiana expeditione*.

77 'sentimens fort bizarres sur le néant.'

78 'que le Monde n'est qu'une illusion, un songe, un prestige; et que les choses, pour exister véritablement, doivent cesser d'estre en eux-mesme, et se confondre avec le néant, qui par sa simplicité fait la perfection de tous les Estres.'

79 'les Chinois et les Siamois fort différens d'Epicure; ils nient l'existence de Dieu, et admettent une providence.'

80 'les loix et les sympathies naturelles qui ont lié selon eux la vertu avec le bonheur, et le vice avec le malheur, sont un motif et un frein aussi puissant, que le sauroit être la fois d'une providence éclairée.'

81 'Ce n'est pas un lieu, mais une maniere d'être: car à parler juste, disent-ils, Sommona-Codom n'est nulle part, et il ne jouit d'aucune félicité: il est sans nul pouvoir, et hors d'état de faire ny bien ny mal aux hommes: expressions que les Portugais ont renduës par le mot d'anéantissement' (ibid., rem. A, 238). The source is Simon de la Loubère, *Du Royaume de Siam*, I, chap. 24, 533–4. This text was published several times from 1700 under the title *Description du Royaume de Siam*.

82 '[...] leurs idées sont si confuses qu'elles leur permettent d'affirmer le blanc et le noir ... Les notions de leur esprit sont différentes du sentiment de leur cœur, c'est pourquoi leur théorie ne s'accorde pas avec leur pratique ...'

83 Antoine Arnauld, *Cinquiéme denonciation du Philosophisme c'est à dire de la nouvelle heresie du Peché philosophique* (Cologne: chez Nicolas Schouten, 1690). The long quote is from pp. 35 to 36.

84 Arnauld largely used Longobardi, *Traité sur quelques points de la religion des Chinois* (Paris: chez Louis Guerin, 1701). There is a critical edition in: Gottfried Wilhelm Leibniz, *Discours sur la Theologie Naturelle des Chinois*, ed. Wenchao Li & Hans Potter (Frankfurt am Main: Vittorio Klostermann, 2002), 113–58. This text was the allegedly lost refutation of Ricci's theory that was used by Navarrete, but published for the first time only in this edition of 1701.

85 For instance, Spinoza is the main philosophical origin of the Radical thinkers' philosophy according to Jonathan I. Israel, author of the renowned triad about Enlightenment.
86 Sergio Zoli, *Europa libertina tra Controriforma e Illuminismo*, 172 and 164.
87 'Il [Spinoza ndr] a été un Athée de Système, et d'une méthode toute nuovelle, quoi que le fonds de sa Doctrine lui fût commun avec plusieurs autres Philosophes anciens et modernes, Européens et Orientaux (A). A l'égard de ces derniers on n'a qu'à lire ce que je rapporte dans la Remarque D de l'Article du Japon, et ce que je dis ci-dessous concernant la Théologie d'une Secte de Chinois (B)'. The English translation is from App, *Discovery*, 228, where this entry is richly presented and discussed.
88 Obviously, this entry is connected with the likewise remarkable entry on Manicheans, where Bayle claimed the reasonability of the 'nothing comes out of nothing' theory, an immanentist standpoint against the Christian 'creatio ex nihilo'.
89 On the 'rites controversy' see David E. Mungello, *The Chines rites controversy: its history and meaning* (Nettetal: Steyler Verlag, 1994).
90 Pierre Jurieu, *Jugement du public et particulièrement de l'abbé Renaudot sur le dictionnaire historique et critique*, (Rotterdam: chez Abraham Acher, 1697), pub. first half of September. The real author was Eusèbe Renaudot himself, it was well known, as Bayle addressed to him a defence against this attack at the end of the second edition of the *Reflexion*, where Bayle strenuously defended himself from the accusation of being atheist.
91 See Pinot, *La Chine et la formation*, 110–1.
92 'S'il est monstrueux de soutenir que les plantes, les bêtes, les hommes, sont réellement la même chose, et le fonder sur la prétention que tous les êtres particuliers sont indistincts de leur principe, il est encore plus monstrueux de débiter que ce principe n'a nulle pensée, nulle puissance, nulle vertu ... Spinoza n'a point été si absurde ...'
93 Jean de La Bruyère, *Dialogues posthumes du sieur de la Bruyere sur le Quietisme* (Paris: chez Charles Osmont, 1699).
94 'Je ne faurois me persuader qu'elle [la setta dei Buddhisti, ndr] prenne le mot de néant dans la signification exacte, et je m'imagine qu'elle l'entend comme le peuple quand il dit qu'il n'y a rien dans un coffre vuide'.
95 'Sur ce pied-là le Disciple de Confucius seroit coupable du Sophisme que l'on nomme *ignoratio elenchi*; car il auroit entendu par *nihil* ce qui n'a aucune existence, et ses Adversaires auroient entendu par ce même mot ce qui n'a point les propriétez de la matiere sensible. Je croi qu'ils entendoient à-peu-près par ce mot-là ce que les Modernes entendent par le mot d'espace; les Modernes, dis-je, qui ne voulant être ni Cartésiens, ni Aristotéliciens, soutiennent que l'espace est distinct des corps, et que son étendue indivisible, impalpable, pénétrable, immobile, et infinie, est quelque chose de réel. Le Disciple de Confucius avroit prouvé aisément qu'une telle chose ne peut pas être le prémier principe, si elle est d'ailleurs destituée d'activité, comme le prétendent les contemplatifs de la Chine'.
96 Isaac Newton, 'Scholium on Time, Space, Place and Motion', in *Philosophiae Naturalis Principia Mathematica*, trans. Andrew Motte (1729), revision Florian Cajori (Berkeley: University of California Press, 1934), vol. 1, 6–12. (we used https://plato.stanford.edu/entries/newton-stm/scholium.html). The quote is from the Tenth Definition related to the concept of motion.
97 See Nishida Kitarō, *Place and Dialectic: Two Essays by Nishida Kitarō*, trans. by John W. M. Krummel and Shigenori Nagatomo (New York: Oxford University Press, 2012).

98 See Narasingha Charan Panda, 'Concept of Bhūmi in the Buddhist Literature with special reference to the Daśabhūmika Sūtra', in ibid., *Perspectives of Indian Thought* (Delhi: Bharatiya Kala Prakashan, 2007), 106–19.
99 Pierre Bayle, *Pensées diverses à l'occasion de la Comète*, in *Oeuvres diverses*, III, 1, La Haye 1727, reprint, edited by Elisabeth Laborusse (Hildesheim: Georg Olms Verlagsbuchhandlung), 1966 (by now *OD3*). The 1st edition 1681, 2nd revised edition 1682. In 1694 there was the *Addition aux Pensées diverses*.
100 Pierre Bayle, *Continuation des Pensés diverses*, in *OD3*. The 1st edition was published chez Reinier Leers, Rotterdam 1704 (August).
101 Pierre Bayle, *Réponse aux questions d'un provincial*, in *OD3*. The *Réponse* was published in four parts (1703–4; 1705–6; 1706–7; 1707), the last was published posthumously; the 1st edition of the whole four parts was published chez Reiner Leers in Rotterdam.
102 Alan Charles Kors, *Atheism in France, 1650-1729* (Princeton: Princeton University Press, 1990), vol. 1, 137.
103 See also Sergio Zoli, *Europa libertina tra Controriforma e Illuminismo*, chap. 1, 5 and 6.
104 Kors, *Atheism in France*, 140.
105 For a deep analysis of Bayle's psychology of atheism, see Gianluca Mori, *Bayle philosophe* (Paris: Honoré Champion Éditeur, 1999), chap. 5 ('Athéism et Fidéism').
106 'Que l'Atheisme n'est pas un plus grand mal que l'Idolatrie' (*Pensées*, chap. CXIV, 75).
107 'Athéïsme se seroit tout au plus glissé parmi quelques peuples barbares, et feroces.'
108 'l'on ne s'étonne plus que tant de Païens se rangent sous les enseignes d'un Dieu crucifié, et qu'ils donnent leur consentement à des doctrines si peu conformes au idées naturelles; mais les esprits forts ne croïent ni les miracles, ni l'opération intérieure de la grace, font obligez de chercher d'autres principes, pour donner raison de ces changemens de foi, et ils n'en trouvent point de plus spécieuses, que de dire que l'on gagne les Chinois en les étonnant d'abord par le terreur des enfers …'
109 'nation savante et ingénieuse autant qu'acune autre.' (*Continuation*, chap. XIX, 212).
110 Bayle suggested: as it is evident, Le Comte was only the 'scapegoat' of accommodationism for the prosecution. The argument of Sorbonne's censure is in chaps XXVII–XIX, 226–31.
111 Particularly *Continuation*, chap. XXIX, 231.
112 'Ironically, the Chinese "weapon" which the freethinkers of the early Enlightenment used so effectively in their criticism of religion had been forged by the Church itself. The Church had reacted to the growing awareness of a wider world beyond the narrow confines of Christian Europe by reasserting the universality of the Christian religion and by launching a missionary campaign; the absolute nature of the truth or revelation left it no choice.' (Günther Lottes, 'China in European Political Thought, 1750-1850', 67).
113 See *Continuation*, chap. CIV, 329ff.
114 'pour vous donner un example non seulement plus moderne, mais aussi plus éclatant, je n'ai qu'à vous prier de jetter les yeux sur la morale de Spinoza.' (*Continuation*, chap. CXLIV, 397)
115 'Je ne vous dirai pas que Confucius qui a laissé d'excellens préceptes de morale étoit Athée. Ceux qui l'afirment trouvent des contredisans, je passe donc à des faits non contestez. Le Dieu Fo est la principale idole de la Chine'
116 As we have seen in §1.2., also Ricci asserted the atheism of all Chinese, but not of the ancients.

117 We see here an early instance of the theory of the 'good savage'.
118 In *Réponse*, II, chap. XCVff .
119 Jacques Bernard (ed.), *Nouvelles de la République des Lettres* (Amsterdam: chez Desbordes-Pain, 1705), reprinted Genère: Slatkine Reprints, 1966, vol. 7. This Journal was formerly directed by Bayle himself and afterwards by Le Clerc.
120 Discussed in *Réponse*, II, chap. XCVIII.
121 'rien n'est plus propre à chagriner que le témoignages qui concernent l'Athéisme des Philosophes de la Chine. C'est n'est pas un simple Athéisme négatif, comme celui des Sauvages de l'Amerique; c'est un Athéisme positif: car ces Philosophes ont comparé ensemble le système de l'existence de Dieu, et le système oposé. Ils se conforment même quant à l'extérieur à l'idolatrie du païs: les loix de l'Etat, et leur propre Politique les y engagent.'
122 'ces Missionaires ne parlent pas en Controversistes, mais en purs Historiens …' (*Réponse*, III, chap. XI, 927).
123 All this scheme is presented in *Réponse*, III, chap. XIII, 932. For further details, see Gianluca Mori, *Bayle philosophe*, 212–17.
124 Kors, *Atheism in France*, 248.
125 'Vous voïez par là que pour être non Théiste, ou Athéiste, il n'est pas nécessaire d'afirmer que le Théisme est faux; il faut de le regarder comme un problême …' (*Réponse*, III, chap. XIII, 932).
126 *Réponse*, III, chap. XX, 955.
127 'il a cessé d'afirmer mentalement qu'il y a un Dieu, il faut croire qu'il s'abstient de le nier mentalement; car les objections contre l'Athéisme lui ont dû paroître insolubles. Il doit donc se tenir comme une piece de fer entre deux aimans de même force.'
128 'Que s'il s'agit des Athées de la Chine, il y a de l'aparence que la plupart nient l'existence de la Divinité. Ils aprenent dès l'enfance un système de philosophie qui est un Atheïsme tout pur. Or la plupart des disciple d'un Philosophe afirment toute leur vie ce qu'ils l'ont vu afirmer, et principalement lors qu'ils n'ont que du mépris pour les autres Philosophes. Telle est la situation de la secte des Lettrez; ils méprisent souverainement les Bonzes, ou les Prêtres de l'Idolatrie, qui en effet sont très-méprisable, soit par leurs dogmes, soit par leurs mœurs.'
129 *Réponse*, III, chap. XXIX, 987–8.
130 'Il [Dieu] a donc connu nécessairement les choses telles qu'elles sont. Donc leur essence ne dépend ni de son intelligence ni de sa volonté, ni de sa liberté … La Vertu étoit donc bonne morellement avant que Dieu la connût telle, et ce n'est point parce que Dieu l'a connue telle qu'elle a été telle, mais Dieu la connuë telle parce que qu'elle étoit telle.'
131 See Giovanni Bonacina, *Filosofia ellenistica e cultura moderna: epicureismo, storicismo e scetticismo da Bayle a Hegel* (Milan: Le Lettere, 1996).
132 See Kors, *Atheism in France*, 258–9, no. 136, 137.
133 Pierre-Daniel Huet, *Traité philosophique de la foiblesse de l'esprit humain* (Amsterdam: chez Hensi du Sauzet, 1723), 1st ed. Parigi 1722.
134 '59. Si nous passons aux Nations étrangères, nous en trouverons plusieurs dans ce même sentiment, qi'il faut suspendre son jugement et sa créance. Diogene de Laërte raporte qu'Anaxarque et Pyrrhon apprierent des Mages, et de Gymnosophistes des Indes, cette excellente methode de philosopher, qui défend de croire que rien puisse être compris, et de donner sur rien son consentement et sa créance.
60. Les Brachmanes, selon le témoignage de Strabon et de Megasthene, soûtenoient qu'il n'y a rien de bon ni de mauvais, par ce que ce qui semble bon à l'un, semble

mauvais à l'autre. Ce que je viens de dire fait voir, que la Philosophie Sceptique a pénétré jusqu'aux extrêmitez de l'Orient.'

135 We remember that we use the categories 'inclusivist' and 'exclusivist' historians in order to denote the historians who included or excluded in their histories the non-Greek and extra-European civilizations.
136 See Sergio Zoli, *Europa libertina tra Controriforma e Illuminismo*, chap. 3.
137 Jean Lévesque de Burigny, *Histoire de la Philosophie Payenne ou sentimens des philosophes et des peuples payens les plus celèbres sur Dieu, sur l'Ame et sur les devoirs de l'Homme* (La Haye: chez Gosse-Dehondt, 1724). The book was re-edited and slightly modified after thirty years with the new title: *Théologie payenne; ou sentimens des philosophes et des peuples payens les plus celèbres sur Dieu, sur l'Ame et sur les devoirs de l'Homme* (Paris: chez De Bure l'aîné, 1754). We use the first edition.
138 Jean Pierre de Crousaz, *Examen du Pyrrhonisme ancien et modern* (La Haye: chez Pierre de Hondt, 1733).
139 On de Crousaz see Simone Zurbuchen, 'Crousaz, Jean-Pierre de', in *The dictionary of Seventeenth and Eighteenth-century Dutch philosophers* (Bristol: Thoemmes Press, 2003), vol. 1, 234–7.
140 'Je demande qu'on me conçoive dans quelque coin des Indes, en conference avec un Philosophe judicieux, et curieux de savoir sur quel pié les Sciences sont en Europe. Pour le satisfaire, je reprendrois ce sujet d'un peu loin, je lui dirois que les Sciences avoient premiérement fleuri dans la Gréce, ou du moins que nous ne pouvons pas remonter plus haut, parce que nous n'avons pas les Livres des autres Nations, dont il se peut que les Grecs ayent emprunté leurs conoissances.'
141 In Johann Franz Buddeus, *Analecta historiae philosophicae* (Halle: Sumptibus Orphanotrophii, 1706), 263–99.
142 Ibid., 309–59.
143 Johann Franz Buddeus, *Theses theologicae de atheismo et superstitione variis observationibus illustratae et in usum recitationum academicarum editae* (Jena: apud Bielckium, 1717). References from Latin original.
144 Johann Franz Buddeus, *Traité de l'athéisme et de la superstition*, trans. Louis Philon & J.C. Fischer (Amsterdam: chez Pierre Mortier, 1740).
145 Buddeus, *Theses theologicae de atheismo*, 156–63.
146 On the differences between Bayle and Buddeus on atheism as expressed in the *Theses* see Kors, *Atheism in France*, 239–44.
147 Johann Franz Buddeus, *Compendium Historiae philosophicae, observationibus illustratum,* pref. J.G. Walch (Halle: Typis & impensis Orfanotrophii, 1731).
148 According to Buddeus the origin of ancient philosophy was Jewish. We add that he studied Oriental literature (mostly Jewish) at the University of Wittenberg.
149 On Pythagoras and barbarians, see also the first dispute published in Buddeus, *Analecta*.
150 'Sed hi cum adhuc hodie sapientiae studia colant, dicemus de iis, * cum ad recentiores philosophorum sectas fuerit ventum'
151 It is worth noticing that those notes had a very long redaction; Mario Longo, MHP2, 353 (SSGF2, 384) suggests the years from 1703 to 1729.
152 Georg Horn, *Historiae philosophicae libri septem, quibus De origine, successione, sectis et vita Philosophorum ab orbe condito ad nostram aetatem agitur* (Leiden: apud Johannem Elsevirium, 1655).
153 Maturin Veyssière La Croze, *Histoire du Christianisme des Indes* (La Haye: chez Vaillant-Prevost, 1724). The chap. 6 was a detailed description of Indian sects.

154 'Nisi quod apud Indos reliquiae quaedam priscae philosophiae, si non nullis credimus, reperiuntur, et Sinenses sapientiae sibi gloriam prae reliquis omnibus orbis gentibus vindicent...'
155 Here Buddeus recalled the dissertation published in *Analecta* on Chinese rites.
156 Here the Dissertation on 'Spinozismo ante Spinozam' is mentioned for a deeper analysis.
157 Among several writings, we quote: Oliver Roy, *Leibniz et la Chine* (Paris: Librairie philosophique J. Vrin, 1972).
158 Lai Yuenting, 'Leibniz and Chinese thought', in *Leibniz, mysticism and religion*, ed. A. P. Coudert, R. H. Popkin and G. M. Weiner (Dordrecht: Kluwer Academic Publishers, 1998), 136-68. In this article, the author provided a complete overview of Leibniz's interests in China, from the linguistic to the religious aspects. We follow the classification of Leibniz's oriental writings provided in this article. Already in 1945 Donald F. Lach published in *Journal of the history of ideas* an article where he outlines Leibniz's use of China within his universal theory, the article is 'Leibniz and China', republished in Julia Ching, Willard G. Oxtoby (ed.), *Discovering China. European interpretations in the Enlightenment*, (Rochester: University of Rochester Press, 1992), 97-116
159 John Webb, *The Antiquity of China Or an Historical Essay: Endeavouring a Probability that the Language of the Empire of China is the Primitive Language, Spoken Through the Whole Word, Before the Confusion of Babel* (London: Nath. Brook, 1669). John Webb argued that Noah before the Deluge had lived in China, the only place in the world where the people already possessed the technical skills necessary to build an Ark; thus only after the Deluge Noah moved to the West. Evidently, Webb was supporting the antediluvian origin of Chinese civilization. On Webb's radical view of China see also William Poole, 'Heterodoxy and Sinology: Isaac Vossius, Robert Hooke, and the Early Royal Society's use of Sinology', in *The Intellectual Consequences of Religious Heterodoxy 1600-1750*, ed. Sarah Mortimer and John Robertson (Leiden - Boston: Brill, 2012), 136-40.
160 On Jesuit Figurists and Leibniz see Arnold H. Rowbotham, 'The Jesuit figurists and eighteenth-century religious thought', in Ching-Oxtoby (ed.), *Discovering China. European interpretations in the Enlightenment*, (Rochester: University of Rochester Press, 1992), 39-53.
161 Michael Lackner, 'Jesuit Figurism', in Thomas H. C. Lee (ed.), *China and Europe*, 136. We might quote also: 'To understand such a perennial intellectual attitude – "perennial" was indeed the basic device of Figurism – it may be useful to study the first encounters of Figurism with Chinese thought', ibid., 143.
162 The Preface is published in G. W. Leibniz, *Discours sur la théologie naturelle des Chinois, plus quelques écrits sur la question religieuse de Chine*, ed. Christiane Frémont (Paris: L'Herne, 1987).
163 Gottfried Wilhelm Leibniz, *Discours sur la Theologie Naturelle des Chinois*, ed. Wenchao Li & Hans Potter (Frankfurt am Main: Vittorio Klostermann, 2002). The Wenchao and Potter edition is more updated than the one by Ch. Frémont, however, that edition has a good introduction and a few further short texts by Leibniz on China.
164 For a detailed rejection of Malebranche by Leibniz, see the critical notes collected in André Robinet, *Malebranche et Leibniz, relations personnelles, Bibliothèque des textes philosophique* (Paris: Librairie Philosophique J. Vrin, 1955), 483-9. The same notes – even more readable – are reported in the edition of the *Entrétien* in Gottfried Wilhelm Leibniz, *Discours sur la Théologie Naturelle des Chinois*.

165 Published in Gottfried Wilhelm Leibniz, *Discours sur la Théologie Naturelle des Chinois*, 225–53.
166 For a detailed and balanced analysis of the *Entrétien* see David E. Mungello, 'Malebranche and Chinese philosophy', *Journal of the History of Ideas*, vol. XLI, no. 4, October–December 1980, 551–79.
167 Ibid., 245.
168 Leibniz stressed several times in the *Discours* his complete agreement with Ricci, against Longobardi and Sainte-Marie.
169 Gottfried Wilhelm Leibniz, *Discours sur la Theologie Naturelle des Chinois*, 71.
170 Ibid., 103.
171 Daniel J. Cook, Henry Rosemont, 'The Pre-established harmony between Leibniz and Chinese Thought', *Journal of the History of Ideas*, vol. XLII, no. 2, April–June 1981, 260.
172 Charles B. Schmitt, 'Perennial Philosophy: from Agostino Steuco to Leibniz', *Journal of the history of ideas*, vol. XXVII, no. 4, October–December 1966, 530–1.
173 Oliver Roy, *Leibniz et la Chine*, 166. 'Leibniz et la Chine, l'histoire d'un échec? Leibniz s'est retrouvé dans le champ des perdants, dans la querelle des rites comme dans la langue universelle. En fait, c'est l'irénisme qui échoue.'
174 See Gregorio Piaia, MHP2, 178ff (SSGF2, 199ff).
175 André-François Boureau-Deslandes, *Histoire critique de la Philosophie*, Nouvelle edition (Amsterdam: chez François Changuion, 1756). The first edition was anonymously published in Amsterdam in 1737 and it was never acknowledged by Deslandes, who waited almost twenty years before publishing the *Histoire* under his name.
176 The Roman number is for the volume, the Arabic number for pages.
177 'Ce grand crédit, cette réputation qu'avoit la Philosophie chez le Barbares, furent cause qu'on l'enveloppa d'une infinité de symboles, d'allégories, d'énigmes et de métaphores. Les Prêtres et ceux de la Famille Royale en avoient seuls la clé; ... Tous les autres sont condamnés à une ignorance humiliante et générale'.
178 'La différance des Climats, de l'air, de la nourriture, cause des différances infinies dans les ames, tout immatérielles qu'elles sont'.
179 'le berceau du Genre-Humain et la source commune des Arts et des Sciences'.
180 'Nous avons jusqu'ici parcouru beaucoup de terres ingrates et stériles, où la Philosophie n'avoit fait que couler légerement ... L'ancienne érudition Orientale est plus estimable qu'on ne se l'imagine d'ordinaire ...'
181 This reference is not collected in Henry Yule, *Cathay and the way Thither*, but, for instance, it was quoted and discussed by Thomas Burnet, see §1.6.
182 'Mais ce qui distingue la Chine des autres Pays de l'Europe, c'est que la même langue s'y parle depuis le commencement de la Monarchie, et qu'on n'y a jamais été curieux d'en apprendre d'étrangeres. Cette espece d'immobilité de la langue à mis les Chinois en état de repasser leurs origines, d'entendre leurs plus anciens Auteurs, de perpétuer, pour ansi dire, leurs pensées et leurs sentimens, de n'en point avoir qui ne fussent à eux: au lieu que les autres Nations en moins de trois siécles ont vu changer tout leur langage, sans pouvoir y apporter de remede.'
183 'Combien de talens ont été anéantis par l'injustice de la fortune, ou par le peu de discernement des personnes en place? Combien de fois le mérite humble et timide a t-il été abandonné dans l'obscurité, d'où il ne cherchoit point à sortir!'
184 'C'est des Indiens, ou plutôt des Orientaux en général, que sont venus les prosternemens, les génufléxions, les divers panchemens de tête et du corps; enfin

toutes les marques exterieures de respect et de déférence. Ces marques ont passé peu à peu dans l'Occident, moins déplié, moins démonstratif au-dehors'

185 'A l'égard des sentimens de ces Gymnosophistes, ils n'ont point changé depuis l'âge le plus reculé. Plusieurs d'entr'eux faisoient profession ouverte d'Athéïsme, et malgré cela ils vivoient avec beaucoup de sagesse et de retenue; ils remplissoient exactement tous les devoirs de la Société. Cette Secte d'Athées subsiste encore, et on ne voit chez elle aucun culte extérieur de Religion ... Mais tous les autres reconoissoient un Dieu qui anime, qui remplit, qui pénetre l'Univers de toutes parts ...'

186 As far as we know, the only manuscript preserved of Roz is the 'De Erroribus Nestorianorum Qui in Hac India Orientali Versantur'. This manuscript was found by Father Castets and edited by Father Irénée Hausherr: Francisco Roz, 'De Erroribus Nestorianorum Qui in Hac India Orientali Versantur', in *Orientalia Christiana* vol. XI/I (= no. 40), Rome: Pont. Inst. Orientalium Studiorum, 1928, 1–35.

187 'Les Sciences que cultivent ces Brachmanes, et où ils réussissent à proportion de ce qu'ils se sentent de force et de génie, se peuvent réduire à dixhuit. La premiere est une espece de Grammaire, qui contient les principes et le fondemens du *Grandham*: c'est la langue privilégiée dont ils se servent pour écrire, et pour converser ensemble. Les autres Sciences s'entresuivent avec assez de justesse, et on monte comme par degrés, du simple et du facile, à ce qu'il y a d'épineux et de compliqué. La derniere enfin s'appelle *Veddata* ou *Vendata*, ce qui veut dire la fin, le term de toutes choses. C'est aussi une espece de Méthaphysique et de Théologie, que les Brachmanes reçoivent non par voye d'examen, mais avec une pleine et rapide soumission. Il se trouve peu de Novateurs entr'eux, parce qu'ils sont dans la pensée décourageante qu'on ne peut point ajouter à ce que leurs Ancêtres ont pensé: mais aussi ils n'avancent ils ne perfectionnent rien. L'esprit s'use à rester immobile, à ne point faire d'effort ni de tentatives, même aux risques de s'égarer.'

188 South Indian languages do not belong to the Indo-European root as Sanskrit or Hindi, instead to the Dravidian languages, which are completely different; therefore, the use of a specific local alphabet to represent Sanskrit was usual. Roz was archbishop of Cranganore, a town in what is now Kerala, where 'Grantha' was used as in Tamil Nadu.

189 On the Indian doxographies and particularly Madhusūdana, we refer to Andrew J. Nicholson, *Unifying Hinduism. Philosophy and identity in Indian intellectual history* (New York: Columbia University Press, 2010), chap. 8 and also Wilhelm Halbfass, *India and Europe. An essay in Understanding* (Albany: SUNY, 1988), chap. 19.

190 Among many essays we quote only one of the latest: Andrew J. Nicholson, *Unifying Hinduism*, chap. 7.

191 'L'Afrique n'étale que des monstres, des créatures hideuses et réduites à un instinct plus grossier que celui des animaux. L'Amérique est presque toute semblable, ce vaste et malheureux pays, le cimetiere de tant d'hommes égorgés par des trahisons et des cruautés inouïes, où pour avoir assouvir notre avarice, il se fait encore un trafic si honteux. Les terres Australes renferment des habitans, en qui la figure humaine est presque méconnoissable, et ce qui en reste se doit haïr. L'Asie paroît en quelques lieux plus cultivée. Mais encore, quelle culture! quelle différence de ce qu'elle est à ce qu'elle a été! Comment tant de barbarie a-t-elle succédé à tant de politesse? Comment tant de ronces et d'épines ont-elles couvert des jardins autrefois si fleuris? Je ne dis rien de l'Europe. Quel amas de mœurs, de systêmes, de goûts, de passions, de loix et de coutumes, s'y trouve épars? On pense tout différemment dans un Pays que dans un autre, et au lieu de se tolérer mutuellement parmi cette variété infinie d'opinions, et de se souffrir avec doucer, on se tourmente, on se tue de sang froid.'

192 See Gregorio Piaia, MHP2, 177 (SSGF2, 199), where is quoted Macary, *Masque et Lumières au XVIIIe. André-François Deslandes 'citoyen et philosophe', 1689-1757* (The Hague: M. Nijhoff, 1975), p. IX.

Chapter 3

1 'Dadurch geriet der Monopolanspruch der Philosophia perennis zwar zunächst noch nicht ins Wanken, aber es begannen sich zwei Typen von Philosophiegeschichte herauszubilden, einer, der an der Philosophia perennis orientiert war, ein anderer, der der griechischen Vorgabe des Diogenes Laertius folgte', Wilhelm Schmidt-Biggemann, 'Jacob Bruckers philosophiegeschichtliches Konzept', in W. Schmidt-Biggemann, T. Stammen (ed.), *Jacob Brucker (1696-1770), Philosoph und Historiker der europäischen Aufklärung* (Berlin: Akademie Verlag, 1998).
2 See René Étiemble, *L'Europe chinoise* (Paris: Éditions Gallimard, 1989). This book is not a reliable source but it is full of interesting details and it created the interesting dichotomy 'Sinophilie-Sinophobie'.
3 Danielle Elisseeff-Poisle, *Nicolas Fréret (1688-1749). Réflexions d'un humaniste du XVIIIe siècle sur la Chine* (Paris: Mémoires de l'Institut des Hautes Études Chinoises, 1978), vol. XI,. The scholar says about Fréret's work on China: 'Frèret, aussi éloigné de la querelle de rites que des idéologies physiocratiques, refusa de faire de la Chine une arme de guerre ... Fréret se contentait de réunir des documents sur l'organisation des divers groupes sociaux antiques, refusant une unité du monde qui lui paraissait artificielle, et se gardant des idées préconçues.' (ibid., 89).
4 A more complete list of Sinophile philosophers may be found in Walter W. Davis, 'China, the Confucian Ideal, and the European Age of Enlightenment', in Julia Ching, Willard G. Oxtoby, *Discovering China. European interpretations in the Enlightenment* (Rochester: University of Rochester Press, 1992), 16.
5 On the quarrel see Marc Fumaroli, *La Querelle des Anciens et des Modernes* (Paris: Gallimard-Folio, 2001).
6 René Rapin, *Les comparaisons des Grands Hommes de l'Antiquité, qui ont le plus excellé dans les belles Lettres* in *Oeuvres diverses du R. P. R. Rapin concernant les belles Lettres*, vol. I (Amsterdam: chez Abraham Wolfgang, 1686). From *Les comparaisons* we quote *La comparaison de Platon et Aristote*.
7 René Rapin, *Les Réflexions sur la philosophie ancienne et modern* (Paris: chez Muguet et Barbin, 1676).
8 Descartes is presented quite faithfully and not openly criticized, while all his followers are blamed.
9 'tous neanmoins demeurent d'accord que les Grecs ont esté les premiers Philosophes du monde. Ce n'est pas que les autres Nations qui les ont precedez, n'ayent eu le connoissance de quelque partie de la Philosophie, et que selon la nature ou la situation de leur païs, la necessité, qui est la premiere maistresse de toutes les sciences, ne leur ai enseigné celles qui étoint propres à leurs besoin'.
10 'Tous ces peuples ne sçavoient ces choses que par une simple experience, et ils n'avoient point encore reduit en preceptes les connoissances qu'ils avoint aquises'.
11 Pierre Coste, 'Discours sur la Philosophie, où l'on voit en abregé l'histoire de cette Science', in *Cours entier de Philosophie, ou Systeme General selon les principes de M. Descartes*, ed. Regis Pierre Silvain (Amsterdam: Huguetan, 1691). The text by Coste lacks numbers, so we consider from pp. 1 to 44.

12 'Tout le monde tombe d'accord que la Philosophie est venûë des Orientaux; mais les Orientaux ne s'accordoient pas eux-même sur les premiers inventeurs de cette Science.'
13 'Quoy qu'il en soit, cette premiére Philosophie étoit si informe, qu'à peine merite-t-elle ce nom. On pourroit l'appeller à plus juste titre une *Théologie superstitieuse* ...'
14 On the figure of Christian Thomasius see Francesco Tomasoni, *Christian Thomasius. Spirito e identità culturale alle soglie dell'illuminismo europeo* (Brescia: Morcelliana, 2005) and Roberto Bordoli, 'Una biografia illuministica: Christian Thomasius', *Giornale critico della filosofia italiana*, vol. LXXXVI, II (May–June), 'Discussioni e postille', Firenze 2007, 373–82.
15 Christian Thomasius, *Introductio ad Philosophiam Aulicam, seu Linae Primae libri de Prudentia cogitandi et ratiocinandi, ubi ostenditur media inter praejudicia Cartesianorum, et ineptias Paeripateticorum, veritatem inveniendi via*. Editio altera (Halle: Prostat in Officina Libraria Rengeriana, 1703; 1st edn, Halle 1702). This is a different edition from the 1688 one published in Leipzig.
16 'At inquiunt, difficilissimum est esse Eclecticum. Respondeo (1) ita saltem dicunt homines pigri et inepti. (2) Sectarium esse multo elaboriosus, quippe Philosophia Eclectica laborem requirit ingenuo homine dignum, Sectaria asininum'
17 The lecture was published in 1726 as *Oratio de Sinarum Philosophia practica* (Frankfurt: Apud Joh. B. Andreae et Henr. Hort. 1726). Edited text as Christian Wolff, *Oratio de Sinarum philosophia practica. Rede über die praktische Philosophie der Chinesen*, ed. Michael Albrecht (Hamburg: Felix Meiner Verlag, 1985). The Preface by Albrecht is full of details of the Wolffian controversy. There is an English translation of the *Oratio* together with a few further texts by Leibniz and Wolff on Chinese philosophy in Julia Ching and Willard G. Oxtoby (ed.), *Moral Enlightenment: Leibniz and Wolff on China* (Nettetal: Steyler Verlag, 1992).
18 He was probably referring to his reviews of Francisco Noël's *Observationes Mathematicae et Physicae in India et China factae ab anno 1684 usque annum 1708* (Prague: per Joachimum Joannem Kamenicky, 1710) published in *Acta eruditorum* in the year 1711 and of the same Noël, *Sinensi imperii libri classici sex* (Prague 1711). See Christian Wolff, *Sämtliche Rezensionen in den Acta Eruditorum (1705-1731). 2, 1711-1718*, ed. Hubert A. Laeven und Lucy J. M. Laeven-Aretz (Hildesheim: G. Olms, 2001). The book of Francisco Noël would be important in the French Enlightenment when translated into French in the 1780s.
19 *Oratio* as translated in Ching–Oxtoby, *Moral Enlightenment*, 183.
20 In Jonathan I. Israel, *Enlightenment Contested* (New York: Oxford University Press, 2006), 657, where the author cross-refers Michael Albrecht, 'Einleitung to Wolff' in Ch. Wolff, *Oratio*, Hamburg 1985, p. LXXIII.
21 This edition has been lost.
22 The long history of the edition of the *Oratio* is reported in Ching–Oxtoby, *Moral Enlightenment*, and in Donald F. Lach, 'The Sinophilism of Christian Wolff (1679-1754)', in ed. Ching–Oxtoby, *Discovering China. European interpretations in the Enlightenment*, 121–3. This last article by Lach, although published in 1953 in *Journal of the history of ideas*, is still a useful essay on Wolff and China.
23 Georg Bernhard Bilfinger, *Specimen Doctrinae Veterum Sinarum Moralis et Politicae* (Frankfurt am Main: apud Andreae & Hort, 1724). But more interesting is his explanation of Wolff's philosophy where he merged his master's dialectic philosophy with that of Chinese thought, see ibid., *Dilucidationes philosophicae de Deo, anima humana, mundo et generalioribus rerum affectibus* (Tübingen: Johannis Georgii Cottae, 1768), 1st edn 1725. This book according to Scönfeld even influenced Kant's definition

of dialectic (Martin Schönfeld, 'Kant's Philosophical Development' (2007), in *The Stanford Encyclopedia of Philosophy* (Winter 2012 Edition), Edward N. Zalta (ed.), (http://plato.stanford.edu/archives/win2012/entries/kant-development/).

24 Christian Wolff, *De rege philosophante et philosopho regnante* in *Horae subsecivae Marburgenses, quibus philosophia ad publicam privatamque utilitatem captar* (Frankfurt–Leipzig: Officina Rengeriana, 1731–2), vol. 2, 563–632. This book is translated in the aforementioned Ching-Oxtoby, *Moral Enlightenment*.

25 Johann Jakob Walch, *Historia artis Logicae generatim*, in *Parerga Academica ex Historiarum atque antiquitatum monimentis collecta* (Leipzig: sumtu Io. Frieder. Gleiditschii, B. Filii, 1721), 453–848.

26 'Simplex fuit modus philosophiam tractandi apud has gentes . . .'

27 'Il est vrai que Budée, Thomasius, Gundling, Heumann, et d'autres écrivains dont les lumières sont de quelques poids, ne nous peignent pas les *Chinois* en beau . . .' in 'Philosophie des Chinois', *Encyclopédie*, III, 342. We use *Encyclopédie, ou dictionnaire raisonné des sciences, des arts et des métiers, etc.*, ed. University of Chicago: ARTFL Encyclopédie Project (Spring 2011 Edition), ed. Robert Morrissey, http://encyclopedie.uchicago.edu/

28 Christoph August Heumann, *Acta philosophorum, das ist: Gründliche Nachrichten aus der Historia philosophica*, (Halle: zu finden in der Rengerischen Buchhandl, 1715–27). Despite a few short articles written by others, all the numbers are authored by Heumann.

29 Mario Longo, MHP2, 403–4 (SSGF2, 442).

30 The eighteen parts of the *Acta* has been published in three volumes, thus the Roman number refers to the volume, the Arab number to the Stück or part and the page number follows.

31 'eine Untersuchung und Erforschung nützlicher Wahrheiten aus festen Gründen und principiis'.

32 'welche die Pfaffen im Heydenthum geschrieben habth /und die man Philosophiam barbaricam nennet'.

33 The clear parallel made between Catholic priests and Barbaric ones is undeniable.

34 'Allein ich aus denen bisher gesetzten Gründen gewiß / daß alle diese Collegia sacerdotum Aegyptiorum, Orphaicorum, Eumolpiadarum, Samothracum, Magorum, Brachmanum, Gymnosophistarum und Druidum . . ., daß / sage ich / dieses alles keine Schulen der Weißheit / sondern der Thorheit gewesen / in welchem man di superstition in formam artis zu bringen / und von dem betragen Volcke zu profitieren gesuchet . . .'

35 'so war das Monarchische Regiment in denen Barbarischen Ländern der Philosophie gar sehr præjudicirlich', I, 2, 212.

36 I, 3, 462–72.

37 '*in stricto sensu* hier keine *Philosophos* finden . . .'

38 'das sie wenigstens *empirice philosophi*ret haben . . .'. On Egyptians see the related chapter on II, 11, chap. 1, 659–97.

39 This organic division is from the 5th *Einleitung* on Philosophy, see I, 2, 293–4.

40 '[soll] eine Art von der *Philosophie* zu finden seyn: welches wir zu seiner Zeit / *si per fata licet*, schon untersuchen wollen.'

41 *Acta phil.*, II, XI Stuck (year 1720), chap. 4, 717–86.

42 It is something between a translation and a review (in classical seventeenth-eighteenth century style).

43 Eusèbe Renaudot, *Anciennes relations des Indes et de la Chine. De deux voyageurs Mahometans qui y allerent dans le neuvième siècle, avec Des Remarques sur les principaux endroits de ces Relations* (Paris: à la Bible d'or, 1718).

44 We don't agree with Lottes when he says that Renaudot was 'a mediocre anti-Jesuit controversialist' (Günther Lottes, 'China in European Political Thought', 71). We claim instead his historical pivotal role in the exclusion of China from philosophy.
45 Heumann quoted Buddeus, 'De superstitio mortuorum apud Chinenses cultum' as best summary of the 'rites controversy' (see §2.5.).
46 Isaac Vossius, *Variarum Observationum liber*, in *De antiquæ Romæ magnitudine*, London, 1685, republished in Grævius, *Thesaurus Antiquitatum Romanorum*. vol. IV (see §2.3.)
47 *Anciennes rel.*, p. XVIII–XIX, 340–1; *Acta phil.*, II, 717–8. Obviously not being a real translation, we indicate the pages that likely correspond.
48 'So findet man auch nicht, daß die Sineser etwas sonderliches entdecket hätten in der *Botanic*, noch weniger in der *Chymie*: und, wenn man hiervon in ihren Schrifften etwas findet, so muß man sich wohl vorsehen, ob diselben Bücher auch alt sind, und ob nicht von denen *Missionariis* sind vermehret und verbessert worden; gleichwie dieselben dieses an den Astronomischen Schrifften der Sineser gethan haben.'
49 'blosse *Invention* der Europäer, und insonderheit des *P. Martini*.'
50 *Anciennes rel.*, 390; *Acta phil.*, II, 779–81 (Heumann is more insistent on this point).
51 Here Heumann quoted Horn, *Historiae philosophicae*, VI, chap. 7, 310 (see §1.3.).
52 'Man hat vor langer Zeit gesaget, daß dasjenige Volck glücklich sey, bey welchem entweder die Könige *Philosophi* wären, oder *Philosophi* das Regiment führeten. Nun kan man mit Wahrheit sagen, daß, wenn iemahls ein Land gewesen, in welchem *Philosophi* regieret haben, so ist das Königreich *Sina*. Denn di *Mandarini*, welche alle miteinander gelehrte Leute und Schüler des *Confucii*, und folglich *Philosophi* sind, haben viele hundert Jahre her alle vornehme so wohl Krieges-als Staats-Aemter verwaltet.'
53 *Acta phil.*, II, 11, 767.
54 *Anciennes rel.*, 377; *Acta phil.*, II, 11, 768.
55 Joan-Pau Rubiés, 'Oriental despotism and European orientalism: Botero to Montesquieu', *Journal of Early Modern History*, Leiden: Koninklijke Brill, 2005, 9, 1–2, 109–80. See also Joan-Pau Rubiés, 'Race, Climate and Civilization in the Works of François Bernier', *Collection Puruṣārtha*, 2013, 61–4 and ibid., 'The Discovery of New Worlds and Sixteenth-century Philosophy', *Routledge Companion to Sixteenth-century Philosophy*, ed. Henrik Lagerlund and Benjamin Hill (New York – London: Routledge, 2017), 74–5.
56 See Walter Demel, 'China in the Political Thought of Western and Central Europe, 1570-1750', in Thomas H. C. Lee (ed.), *China and Europe*, 55–7.
57 *Anciennes rel.*, 381–2 (where he criticizes again Vossius); *Acta phil.*, II, 773–9.
58 'Endlich sehe ich auch nicht, wie man aus einer solchen *Morale* and *Politic* ein grosses Wesen machen kan, welche gar keine Principia hat, sondern nur in gemeinen Sprüchen bestehet, ohne das menschliche Thun und menschlichen Affecten gründlich zu betrachten'. Translation of *Ancienne rel.*, 378.
59 Gottlieb Stolle, *Historie der Heÿdnischen Morale* (Jena: Christian Pohl, 1714).
60 'daß diese Völcker keine Philosophia Moralem gehabt / ob sie gleich dann und wann einen und andern Spruch / der recht un nützlich ist / vorgebracht haben.'
61 Heumann did not agree with Bayle on many issues, however he reputed the historical method of the French thinker as an effective scientific model. He even met Bayle in Rotterdam, see MHP2, 399–400 (SSGF2, 437). Thomasius was his master of philosophy, whilst Bayle the master of the historical method, not of philosophy.
62 We use the first edition: Friedrich Gentzken, *Historia philosophiae in qua philosophorum celebrium vitae eorumque hypotheses notabiliores, ac sectarum fata a*

longa rerum memoria ad nostra usque tempora succinte et ordine sistuntur. In usum lectionum academicarum (Hamburg: Apud Theodor. Christoph. Felginer, 1724).

63 Mario Longo, MHP2, 449 (SSGF2, 495).
64 'Et cum illorum doctrina moralis in eo aberraret, quod non ad vitam sociabilem et amicam consuetudinem cum aliis hominibus fuerit comparata, sed in austera corporis damnatione, et remota vitae usu contemplationis voluptate acquieverit, factum est, ut multi Graecorum Philosophorum in hoc ipso offenderint.'
65 'Hanc Confucii philosophiam haut pauci et imprimis Jesuitae ad coelum esque extollunt. Enim vero in disciplinis theoreticis Europaeos multum Sinensibus praestare demum fateri coguntur; et moralis eorum doctrina, quam inprimis admirantur, cum nostra collata multis parasangis inferior, nisi quod iudice Leibnizio ipsos Christianos vitae regimine vincant.'
66 We use Joh. Gottlieb Heineccius, 'Historia philosophica' in *Elementa philosophiae rationalis et moralis* (Frankfurt: Impens. Io. Christian Kleybii, 1745), that is the 9th enlarged edition. The first edition was published in 1728. The *Elementa* were also published in the edition comprising the entire writing of the author in Geneva (1771) and Naples (1753–77).
67 Mario Longo, MHP2, 457 (SSGF2, 504).
68 'Nobis aurem tota philosophia barbarica TRADITIONARIA dici posse videtur, quum barbari omnes, reliquias sapientiae, a maioribus acceptas, sancte custodierint, easque rursus commendarint posteris.'
69 Mario Longo, MHP2, 479–81 (SSGF2, 529–31).
70 Jakob Brucker, *Kurtze Fragen aus der Philosophischen Historie, von Anfang der Welt bis auf die Geburt Christi, mit ausführlichen Anmerkungen erläutert* (Ulm: apud Erster Theil, 1731–7).
71 Jakob Brucker, *Historia critica philosophiae a mundi incunabulis ad nostram usque aetatem deducta* (Leipzig: Literis et impensis Bern. Christoph Breitkopf, 1742–4).
72 On the conspicuous influence of Brucker's *Historia critica* on Diderot's philosophical entries of the *Encyclopédie*, see Paolo Casini, *Diderot 'philosophe'* (Bari: Editori Laterza, 1962), 254–61. Casini identifies forty-three entries of which the *Historia critica* is the main source.
73 Mario Longo, MHP2, 486–7 (SSGF2, 537).
74 Mario Longo, MHP2, 485 (SSGF2, 535).
75 For instance, the historian of philosophy he most harshly criticized was Deslandes, accused of unfaithfulness and arrogance (ibid., I, 37–8). For a brief but useful overview of the polemic between Brucker and Deslandes see Mario Longo, MHP2, 206–7 (SSGF2, 232–3).
76 See also Leo Catana, *The Historiographical Concept 'System of Philosophy'. Its Origin, nature, influence and legitimacy* (Leiden: Brill, 2008), 14.
77 Mario Longo, MHP2, 494 (SSGF2, 544–5).
78 Catana highlights the influence of the Protestant reformer Philipp Melanchton, see Leo Catana, *The Historiographical Concept 'System of Philosophy'*, 8–10.
79 'Nomen itaque vitii hac vox, barbarus, fuit, a lingua tamen ad mores traducta fuit, barbarusque dictus est, qui ab eruditionis cultu alienus erat: unde docte observatum est viris eruditis, barbaras gentes opponi doctis, barbarumque cum imperito idem dicere.'
80 'priscam Hebraeorum gentem...' (ibid., I, 49).
81 'Quod si enim philosophiae propria significatio pro norma fuisset adhibita, si distinctum fuisset, inter eruditionem et cognitionem rerum a vulgo diversam, et inter

philosophiam, si philosophandi initia ab incrementis et formali habitu fuissent separata, si modus tradendi sapientiam per auctoritatem parentis et magistri a philosophandi methodo accurata et meditatione cuncta per causas et principia sua inquirente fuisset segregatus, facile tota controversia in λογομαχίαν abitura evanuisset ... Quisquis vero barbaricae philosophiae indolem perdidicit, fatebitur, eos simplici potius cognitione, quam scientifica, quod ajunt, meditatione veritatem indagasse, et traditione potius, quam demostratione ad posteros propagavisse, Graecis, ubi a ruditate morum primum emerserunt, in id contendentibus, ut veri atque boni principia investigarent, in ejus causas inquirerent, et ex fontibus deductas veritates certa et ratiocinandi legibus adstricta methodo aliis proponerent.'

82 'Est vero Indorum quidem gens natura rudis, et non adeo magna ingenii felicitate praedita, aluit tamen a vetustissimis temporibus viros sapientes, quos Graeci ad suos mores et instituta componentes, philosophos dixere.'

83 This theory about Indian worship is enlarged and rectified in the added book on modern Asians.

84 *Adversus Iovinanum*, I, 42. For an introduction to the quote see C. Dognini, *Primi contatti fra cristianesimo e buddhismo*, in *Gli Apostoli in India*, in ed. Dognini-Ramelli ed (Milano: Ed. Medusa), 2001, 100–2. The tale of the mythical birth is very common among Buddhists and it is enriched in the *Jātaka*, the tale of all the lives of Buddha.

85 Translation from 'Suda On Line: Byzantine Lexicography' (http://www.stoa.org/sol/).

86 Edward Sachau, *The Chronology of Ancient Nations* (London: by W.H. Allen & Co, 1879), 190. Similar quotes may also be found in the different fragments of *Kephalaia* translated by professor Prods Oktor Skjærvø in a free PDF from the website http://www.fas.harvard.edu/~iranian/Manicheism/

87 'celeberrimo Indiae totius impostore ...' (ibid., I, 202).

88 *De gentibus Indiae et bragmanicus* by Pseudo-Palladius and *De moribus brachmanorum* by (pseudo-) Saint Ambrogio (Ambrose) are two almost identical texts, which adapt in a Christian shape the tale of the meeting of Alexander and the Gymnosophist Dandanis. It is useful to remember that the *Alexander Romance*, as it is usually called, was really omnipresent in late antiquity and the Middle Ages. The number of versions of this tale was huge in the Middle East languages and in the European vernaculars. The alleged author was Callisthenes (360–328 BCE), who was a companion of Alexander in India, but philological studies has proved that the author was a Pseudo-Callisthenes of the third century CE. The Greek text has been translated into Latin by Julius Valerius in the fourth century and that version was translated into ancient vernacular French and English (from around the twelfth century). See among many articles and essays on the topic, the most recent that is Richard Stoneman, *Alexander the Great: A Life in Legend* (New Haven: Yale University Press, 2008).

89 'Naturalis philosophiae cognitio apud Indos exigua fuit ...'

90 'Ceterum Pythagoreum systema Indico quoad principia non admodum dissimile esse, facile nobis persuaderi patimur, tota tamen artificialis ejus ratio et conclusionum consecutio scholam Graecam sapit, et ab indole philosophiae barbaricae est alienissima.'

91 'Ex quo praeceptorum moralium specimine patet, homines hos ad domandos affectus, imitandum DEUM, exercendam patientiam et contemnendam mortem suam philosophiam reduxisse.'

92 'Omnia enim, quae de hujus gentis philosophia nobis constant, recentissimis temporibus per eos, qui religionis Christianae inter illam gentem plantandae causa eo missi sunt, pervenere ad nos, et ex domesticis Sinensium monumentis desumta sunt, et arcte cum recentiori historia cohaerent, ut difficile divelli illaeso ordine queant.'

93 Anne-Lise Dyck, 'La Chine hors de la philosophie: essai de généalogie à partir des traditions sinologique et philosophique françaises au XIXe siècle', in *Y a-t-il une philosophie chinoise? Un état de la question*, ed. Anne Cheng (Saint-Denis: Presses Universitaire de Vincennes, 2005), 18–19.

94 'Falluntur autem, qui philosophiae exotica nomen audientes, eam sibi philosophiae notionem fingunt, quae apud Europeas gentes obtinet. Hoc enim sensu, si Sinensium, Iaponensium et Indorum sectas quasdam excipias, philosophiam neque in India orientali neque in occidentali reperias. Sed ut antiquissimis temporibus inter gentes barbaras religionem et philosophiam arctissimo vinculo colligatas fuisse . . .'

95 'Hoc ipsissimum Spinozae systema esse P. BAYLE contendit, perperam quidem si quid iudicamus, nam apertissime emanationem supponunt, quae cum modificatione Spinozistica confundi non debet, et ipsum, quod de vasculis aqua plenis et in oceano natantibus petere solent simile, satis prodit, diversam hanc esse hypothesin a Spinozistica, eo quod vasculorum comprehensione aqua ex oceano hausta realiter distinguitur ab ipso oceano, cum secundum Spinozae hypothesin res omnes, quae in universo sunt, simile modo sint bullulis minimis in oceano agitato natantibus'.

96 Jakob Thomasius, *Schediasma historicum* (Leipzig: P. Fuhrmanni, 1665).

97 This thinker and the French comparativism are investigated in a detailed and long chapter in Rolando Minuti, *Orientalismo e idee di tolleranza*, chap. 3.

98 Mathurin Veyssière de La Croze, *Histoire du christianisme des Inde* (La Haye: chez les frères Vaillant, & N. Prévost, 1724), book VI ('De l'Idolatrie des Indes').

99 For a detailed investigation on Ziegenbalg and La Croze, see Urs App, *The Birth of Orientalism* (Philadelphia: University of Pennsylvania Press, 2010), chap. 2 and also Gita Dharampal-Frick, *Indien im Spiegel deutscher Quellen der Frühen Neuzeit 1500-1750* (Tübingen: Max Niemeyer Verlag, 1994), 348–73.

100 It is meaningful to note that the same term 'plague' is used by Brucker also to denominate philosophic syncretism, particularly that of the Renaissance thinkers, i.e. Pico della Mirandola. See Leo Catana, *The Historiographical Concept 'System of Philosophy'. Its Origin, nature, influence and legitimacy* (Leiden: Brill, 2008), 29, where an English translation of Brucker's cutting remark on Pico is provided.

101 'Haec famosa illa Foënae sectae, sive Xekianae disciplinae doctrina est quae apud plerosque atheismi, et imprimis Spinozismi infamia meruit. Quam tamen perperam cum Spinozismo confundi, et systema magis emanativum, quo etiam exoterica Xekiae doctrina nititur, quam Spinozisticum continere, nobis valde est verisimile'.

102 'Vacuum sive inane esse principium finemque rerum omnium'.

103 This is evidently the Aristotelian 'theoretical life' (*biòs theoricòs*), which is the superior life of the philosophers or seekers of the truth. The 'theoretical life' is described in the *Nicomachean Ethics*, I, 5, 1096a4 and above all X, 8 1178a9-1178a32, where it is reputed to be the best possible human way of life.

104 'Dantur tamen inter eas duae quoque classes aliae, quae non inepte inter philosophos referri possunt, nempe Iogigueuli, sive theoretici, et Gnanigueuli, sive sapientes, quae classes valde inter se differunt . . . toti vitae theoreticae invigilantes solitudinem et meditationem colunt, et in poenitentium ordine recte collocantur. Relictis enim uxoribus liberisque, multis molestiis et cruciatibus corpus affligunt, et imprimis spiritum continendo ecstasin affectant, altissima meditatione sopiti'.

105 'Omnem vero eruditionis Malabaricae circulum, in theoreticam et practicam doctrinam commodo dispescere licet: quae enim de rebus naturalibus tradere solent, pauca sunt, facileque et sine ordinis neglectu ad naturalem theologiam, quae magnam partem in encyclopaediae Malabaricae constituit, trahi possunt'.

106 Although La Croze reported positively on Indian medicine and even reported that many Europeans in India made use of it, Brucker chose to avoid those positive aspects.
107 'Quae si cum iis comparentur, quae supra de Xekiae adventu in India coniecimus, magnam addent isti opinioni verisimilitudinem, quae ex Aegypto disciplinarum et philosophiae semina ad Indos translata esse statuit.'
108 'essentia essentiarum rerumque omnium'.
109 Iṣvara is the conceivable form of the aforementioned supreme entity Brahman, but it is also a Sanskrit term that means 'lord', hence it is used in several religious names that are compounds.
110 Gottlieb Stolle, *Historie der Heÿdnischen Morale* (Jena: Christian Pohl, 1714).
111 Published in Abraham Rogerius, *La Porte Ouverte, par parvenir à la connaissance du Paganisme caché* (Amsterdam: chez Jean Schipper, 1670). Barthrovherri is an early transcription of the name of the renowned Indian poet and grammarian Bhartṛhari, who lived in the fifth century.
112 'On y trouve des traces sensibles de la Loi de Moyse, et des Histoires qui ont un raport visible à celles qui sont raportées dans nos Livres Sacrez.' La Croze, *Histoire*, 496.
113 'Foënam impietatem et fanaticismum totum imperium Sinicum velut diluvium quoddam inundasse'.
114 'tota enim Sinensium philosophia calx sine arena est, unde systemata Europeorum non potuere non ob connexionem meditationum philosophicarum, illis admirationem excitare'.
115 'philosophia Sinensem esse calcem sine arena, scopasque dissolutas, nihil cohaerere, nihil apte suis principiis connecti, nihil quod certas et definitas conclusiones efficere valeat afferri.'
116 'vero questio de atheismo Sinensium ipsiusque Confucii, dirìmi facile potest. Si enim vocem atheismi premamus, impietas ista Sinis nostro iudicio tribui nequit, qui coelum quidem coluerunt, at spiritu divino animatum. Ast si more haud inusitato atheismus etiam pantheismum, vel deismum quendam, innuat, non videmus, qui ab ea suspicione possint Sinae toti liberari, qui mundum cum Deo arctissime copulando, omnibus partibus inesse spiritus divinos crediderunt.'
117 Brucker, willing to prove without any doubts the immanentist nature of Chinese thought, scrutinized in depth Chinese cosmological system. On p. 901, he reports for the first time in a history of philosophy a diagram with *yin* 陰 and *yang* 陽, translated improperly as 'imperfectum' and 'perfectum', and the eight trigrams (with transcriptions) at the base of the sixty-four exagrams of the *Yijing* 易經 (*Classic of Change*).
118 'Infantes esse in philosophia theoretica Sinas, et valde a nobis superari, ex dictis est manifestissimum. Ast superari nos quoque a Sinensi philosophia practica, magni viri non sine admiratione et insignibus laudibus fatentur. Faciunt id imprimis Iesuitae, quibus pollicem hoc quoque loco premit LEIBNIZIUS, quem more suo sequuntur celeberrimi viri G. B. BULFINGERUS et C. WOLFIUS, ut deos minorum gentium taceamus.'
119 'de regimine familiae, de officiis magistratuum, de administratione Imperii . . .' (ibid., V, 906).
120 'Nos pauca supra dictis addimus, et considerare iubemus: ignorare ethicam Sinensem certum principium, nec definire posse, quae sit ea ratio congenita, quae cordis rectitudo, quae laudata illa perfectio, nec posse nexum ostendere. Fassus id est, qui immensum in modum Sinicam ethicam extulit, illustris Wolfius.'

121 'Absolvimus iter Asiaticum, inque occidentem versi, littora iam Africae, Americaeque intuemur. Ast, inter denissimas nebulas, quibus amplissimae regiones cinguntur, nihil videmus, quod ad historiam philosophicam magnopere pertineat ... Gentilis autem superstitio per Africam et Americam tanta est, ut quid ad nostram tractationem pertinens erui possit, non inveniamus.'
122 Ibid., V, 923.
123 Günther Lottes, 'China in European Political Thought, 1750-1850', 67.
124 Leo Catana, *The Historiographical Concept 'System of Philosophy'. Its Origin, nature, influence and legitimacy*, (Leiden: Brill, 2008).
125 On the influence of this history of philosophy among others see Peter K. J. Park, *Africa, Asia, and the History of Philosophy. Racism in the Formation of the Philosophical Canon, 1780–1830* (Albany: State University of New York Press, 2013), 14–15.
126 'Brucker's method of the history of philosophy became an integral part of the discipline as it evolved over the following centuries', Leo Catana, *The Historiographical Concept 'System of Philosophy'. Its Origin, nature, influence and legitimacy* (Leiden: Brill, 2008), 3.
127 Catana recognizes the influence of this paradigm particularly within the Hegelian *Geistesgeshichte*, but also within the thinking of more recent philosophers such as Richard Rorty and Hans-Georg Gadamer (ibid., 297–304).
128 Ibid., 20.
129 See ibid., 3, 32–3, 285–92.
130 See ibid., 25.
131 Ibid., 297.
132 Christoph Harbsmeier, 'The rhetoric of premodern prose style', in *The Cambridge History of Chinese Literature*, ed. Kang-I Sun Chang and Stephen Owen (Cambridge: Cambridge University Press, 2010), vol. 1, chap. 43, 882–4.
133 See Yang Guorong 杨国荣, *Zhongguo zhexue sanshi jiang* 中国哲学三十讲 [Thirteen lessons on Chinese Philosophy] (Beijing: Zhonghua shuju, 2015), chap. 1.
134 Christoph Harbsmeier, *Language and Logic. Part I*, in *Science and civilization in China*, ed. Joseph Needham, vol. 7. (Cambridge: Cambridge University Press, 1998), 262.
135 Lim Jongtae, 'Restoring the Unity of the World: Fang Yizhi and Jie Xuan's Responses to Aristotelian Natural Philosophy', in *The Jesuits, the Padroado and East Asian Science (1552–1773)*, ed. Luís Saraiva and Catherine Jami, (Singapore: World Scientific Publishing, 2008), 145.
136 Kang Ouyang (2003): 'Fang Yizhi', in *The Encyclopedia of Confucianism*, ed. Yao Xinzhong (Oxon: Routledge, 2003), 209–211.
137 Zhang Dainian, *Key Concepts in Chinese Philosophy* (Beijing: Foreign Languages Press, 2002).
138 Zhang Dainian 张岱年, *Zhongguo zhexue dacidian* 中国哲学大辞典 [The Dictionary of Chinese Philosophy], (Shanghai: Shanghai cishu chubanshe, 2014).
139 Zhang Dainian, *Key Concepts in Chinese Philosophy*, p. XX.
140 '第二是形式问题：中国古代学术从没有编成系统的记载…我们要编成系统，古人的著作没有可依傍的，不能不依傍西洋人的哲学史。所以非研究过西洋哲学史，不能构成适当的形式。', Cai Yuanpei 蔡元培. Xu 序 [Preface], in Hu Shi 胡适, *Zhongguo zhexueshi dagang* 中国哲学史大刚 [Outlines of Chinese history of philosophy] (Chongqing: Congqing Chubanshe, 2013), p. I.
141 Antonio S. Cua, 'The emergence of the History of Chinese Philosophy', in *History of Chinese Philosophy*, ed. Bou Mou, (Oxon (London – New York): Routledge 2009), 49.

142 Ibid., 6.
143 Feng Youlan 冯友兰, *Zhongguo zhexueshi* 中国哲学史, *Zhongguo zhexueshi* 中国哲学史 [History of Chinese Philosophy] (Beijing: Shangwu yinshuguan chuban, 2006), 7.
144 Antonio S. Cua, 'The emergence of the History of Chinese Philosophy', 52.
145 Ge Zhaoguang 葛兆光, *Zhongguo sixiang shi* 中国思想史 [History of Chinese Thought] (Shanghai: Fudan daxue chubanshe, 2001).
146 Ibid., 5–6.
147 Several similar 'forced feet' expressions by contemporary Chinese scholars are reported in Carine Defoort, 'Is "Chinese Philosophy" a Proper name? A Response to Rein Raud', *Philosophy East & West*, 56. 4 (Oct. 2006), 645 (no. 28).

Conclusion

1 David E. Mungello, 'European philosophical responses to non-European culture: China', in *The Cambridge History of Seventeenth-Century Philosophy*, ed. D. Garber, M. Ayers (New York: Cambridge University Press, 1998), 87.
2 'philosophia Sinensem esse calcem sine arena, scopasque dissolutas, nihil cohaerere, nihil apte suis principiis connecti, nihil quod certas et definitas conclusiones efficere valeat afferri.' (Brucker, *Historia critica*, V, 879).
3 Helmuth von Glasenapp, *Buddhism a not-theistic religion* (London: George Allen and Unwin Ltd, 1970).
4 See Urs App, *Discovery* as the most comprehensive investigation of the understanding of Buddhism between the sixteenth and seventeenth centuries; it is properly a study of 'Orientalism' before the 'Scientific Orientalism'.
5 Among several monographs on the Buddhist philosopher rejecting nihilism, we recommend the philosophical investigation in Guy Bugault, *L'Inde pense-t-elle?* (Paris: Presses Universitaire de France, 1994), chap. 8–10.
6 Bankimchandra Chattopadhyay, 'The intellectual superiority of Europe' (1882), published in ibid., *Baṅkim racanābalī*, ed. Yogeś'cāndra Bāgal (Kolkata: Sāhitya Saṃsad, 1990), vol. 3, 210. The excerpt is quoted in Saverio Marchignoli, *Indagine sul dharma. Bankimchandra Chattopadyay e il discorso sulla religione nell'India colonizzata. Con la prima traduzione della* Dharmajijñāsā (Bologna: Libreria Bonomo editrice, 2005), 29.
7 Martin Schönfeld argues that Kant himself was influenced by eastern thought, although he was not fully aware of the extent of this influence, mostly through the works of Georg Bernhard Bilfinger. Schönfeld says: 'in terms of culture, Kant's early views may be placed in a Eurasian rather than a purely western context. Recent research suggests that key ideas of Kant's natural philosophy also have sources in Taoist and Confucian thought, which were disseminated in continental Europe by Jesuits based in China, popularized by Leibniz and Wolff, and further developed by Wolff's Sinophile student Bilfinger. One example is the idea of dialectics that Bilfinger found in the Chinese classics, and which Kant encountered in the proceedings of the Russian academy. Kant was unaware of the Far Eastern roots of the notions that influenced him, and the historical irony is that he dismissed non-western cultures while being deeply influenced by their insights.' (Martin Schönfeld, 'Kant's Philosophical Development' (2007), in *The Stanford Encyclopedia of Philosophy* (Winter 2012 Edition), ed. Edward N. Zalta, retrieved from http://plato.stanford.edu/archives/win2012/entries/kant-development/). The author also quotes a monographic

issue he edited specifically on Kant and eastern philosophy, where several interesting essays may be read on Chinese influences on Kant: Martin Schönfeld (ed.), 'Kant and Confucianism', Special Issue, *Journal of Chinese Philosophy*, vol. 33, Issue 1, March 2006, 1–157.

8   On the anti-Judaism and the definition of religion and philosophy out of the biblical framework, see Guy G. Stroumsa, *A New Science. The discovery of religion in the age of reason* (Cambridge (Mass.) – London: Harvard University Press, 2010), particularly chap. 7 (related to China) and 'Epilogue' (related to India and the nineteenth-century Indophiles).

9   Among them, Tennemann listed the Jews, but they completely lost the primary role still acknowledged by German Eclectics. Therefore, we can understand how the religious concerns were lessening, since the triumph of the universal thought was accomplished. The second and third edition contains this list, but the order of civilizations is changed between the second, where Egyptians are the first, and the third, where Indians gain the first position. See Wilhelm Gottlieb Tennemann, *Grundriß der Geschichte der Philosophie für den akademishen Unterricht* (Leipzig: bey Johann Ambrosius Barth, 1816), while the third edition was revised by Amadeus Wendt and published by the same editor in 1820. For a critical overview of Judaism between Kant and the Hegelians see Francesco Tomasoni, *La modernità e il fine della storia. Il dibattito sull'ebraismo da Kant ai giovani hegeliani* (Brescia: Morcelliana, 1999).

10 He was quite aware of the new knowledge about Asia thanks to the works of Henry Thomas Colebrooke – on India – and to his meeting with Abel Rémusar – first holder of a chair of Sinology in Europe (at the College de France) – on China.

11 The contemporary effects of this prejudiced exclusion are so alive and persistent today that Van Norden felt the need to write an intriguing and effective essay – written as a provocative Manifesto – in order to denounce this long-lasting attitude that is killing philosophy itself. See Bryan W. Van Norden, *Taking back Philosophy. A Multicultural Manifesto* (New York: Columbia University Press, 2017), particularly chap. 1.

12 Halbfass, *India and Europe*, 99.

13 This is the reason we insisted that behind Deslandes's description of Indian schools there was a Vedāntin doxography. For the six speeches see: https://belurmath.org/swami-vivekananda-speeches-at-the-parliament-of-religions-chicago-1893/

14 Sarvapalli Radhakrishnan, *Indian Philosophy* (London: Muirhead Library of Philosophy by Unwin Brothers Limited, 1929).

15 Rādhākrishnan is presented as 'absoluter Idealist' by Ronald Sequeira, *Die Philosophien Indiens* (Aachen: ein-FACH-verlag, 1996), 194–205.

16 Jarava Lal Mehta, *Martin Heidegger: The way and the Vision* (Honolulu: The University Press of Hawaii, 1976). This book had two editions, one in 1967 and this edition in 1976 (almost identical except for the titles). Martin Heidegger himself read the edition of 1967 and Mehta reported that the German philosopher appraised the book but not the static and systematic title: *The Philosophy of Martin Heidegger*. He reports: 'In making this change in the title I am thankful accepting Professor Heidegger's hint in a letter …' (Mehta, *The way*, p. XIV). A second positive opinion is reported by Jitendra Nath Mohanty prefacing a book of Mehta: 'Hanna Arendt, during a conversation at the New School, said to me: "Do you know that the best book on Heidegger, in any language, is written by an Indian?" This remark, coming from no less a person than her, filled me with joy and pride (being J. L. Mehta's fellow countryman)' (J. N. Mohanty,

Preface, in J. Mehta, *Philosophy and Religion, Essays in Interpretation* (Delhi: Indian Council of Philosophical Research, 1990), p. V).
17 Mehta, *Philosophy and Religion*, 38. Mehta was probably referring to Arend Theodoor van Leewen, *Christianity in world history. The meeting of the faiths of East and West* (London: Edinburgh House Press, 1964).
18 Mehta, *Philosophy and Religion*, 187.
19 See David. E. Mungello, *Curious Land. Jesuit accommodation and the origins of Sinology* (Honolulu: University of Hawaii Press, 1989), chaps 6 and 7.
20 Śaṅkara (*c.* 700–*c.* 750) is the foremost Indian philosopher of Advaita-Vedānta.
21 Jitendra Nath Mohanty, *Essays on Indian Philosophy Traditional and Modern*, edited by Purushottama Bilimoria (New Delhi: Oxford University Press, 1993), 209 (italics in the text).
22 Jitendra Nath Mohanty, *Explorations in Philosophy*, vol. I, *Indian Philosophy*, edited by Bina Gupta (New Delhi: Oxford University Press, 2001), 57.
23 Daya Krishna, *Indian Philosophy. A Counter Perspective* (Delhi: Oxford University Press, 1991), p. VII.
24 Mohanty, *Essays*, 212.
25 See also Jitendra Nath Mohanty, *An Autobiography, Between two Worlds, East and West* (New Delhi: Oxford University Press, 2002) and Bimal Krishna Matilal, *The Collected Essays of Bimal Krishna Matilal. Ethics and Epics. Philosophy, Culture and Religion,* ed. Jonardon Ganeri (New Delhi: Oxford University Press, 2002).
26 Anne Cheng (ed.), *La pensée en Chine aujourd'hui* (Paris: Gallimard, 2007).
27 On the appropriateness of the use of the term 'philosophy' see also the well-known debate on *Philosophy East and West* between Defoort and Raud. Carine Defoort, 'Is there Such a Thing as Chinese Philosophy? Arguments of an Implicit Debate', *Philosophy East and West*, vol. 51, no. 3, July 2001, 393–413; Ibid. 'Is 'Chinese Philosophy' a Proper name? A Response to Rein Raud', *Philosophy East & West*, 56. 4, Oct. 2006, 625–60 and Rein Raud, 'Philosophies versus Philosophy. In Defense of a Flexible Definition'. *Philosophy East and West*, vol. 56, no. 4, October 2006, 618–25; Ibid., 'Traditions and Tendencies: A Reply to Carine Defoort', *Philosophy East and West*, vol. 56, no. 4, October 2006, 661–4.
28 Anne Cheng (ed.), *La pensée en Chine aujourd'hui,* chap. 7.
29 Zhang Fa 张法, *Hewei zhongguo zhexue yu zhongguo zhexue hewei* 何为中国哲学与中国哲学何为 [Chinese Philosophy: why and for what?], *Tianjing shehui kexue* 天津社会科学 [Tianjing Social Science], no. 3, issue *Zhongguo zhexue xuekede jianshe yu fazhang* 中国哲学学科的建设与发展 [The shaping and development of the discipline Chinese Philosophy], 2004, 39.
30 The use of European historical periods (ancient, medieval and modern) is still common for both Indian and Chinese traditions. Already Brucker used the term 'Chinese Middle Ages' (see §3.6.)
31 Sean Golden, 'Orientalism in East Asia. A theoretic model', in *Inter Asia Papers*, no. 12 (Barcelona: Instituto de Estudios Internacionales e Interculturales Bellaterra, 2009), 8.
32 Ibid., 9.
33 Li Weiwu (李维武), 中国哲学的转统更新 [*Renewal of the Chinese Philosophical tradition*] (Beijing: Renmin chubanshe, 2012), 13.
34 Ibid., 17–8.
35 Tong Shijun (童世骏), 西方哲学的中国研究：思想风险及其应对方法 (*Studying Western Philosophy in China: Intellectual Risks and the Ways of Dealing with Them*), in

中西哲学论衡 (*Comparative Philosophy: East and West*), 上海书店出版社, Shanghai: 2012, 158–71.

36 Very interesting is his overview of the problematic translation of 'Sein' or 'Being' (already the English translation is debatable!) in Chinese, a language that explains the concept of 'being' in several different ways. Ibid., 167ff.
37 Xie Xialing (谢遐龄), 中心文化差异及其哲学解释 [*A Philosophical Explanation of the Cultural Differences between China and the West*], in 中西哲学论衡 [*Comparative Philosophy: East and West*], (Shanghai: Shanghai shudian chubanshe 2012), 138.
38 Zhang Fa 张法. '*Hewei zhongguo zhexue yu zhongguo zhexue hewei* 何为中国哲学与中国哲学何为 [Chinese Philosophy: why and for what?]', *Tianjing shehui kexue* 天津社会科学 [Tianjing Social Science], no. 3, issue *Zhongguo zhexue xuekede jianshe yu fazhang* 中国哲学学科的建设与发展 [The shaping and development of the discipline Chinese Philosophy], 2004, 40–1.
39 Ibid., 144.
40 Mou's most relevant philosophical contribution is a critique of Kantian intellectual intuition. According to Kant only God can have intellectual intuition (of principles/ noumena), instead, for Mou, Chinese philosophy shows the human capacity to have insight or intuition (*jue* 覺) into them. The most relevant study on Mou's intellectual intuition is Sébastien Billioud, *Thinking Through Confucian Modernity. A Study of Mou Zongsan's Moral Metaphysics* (Leiden – Boston: Brill, 2012), chaps 3 and 4.
41 Mou Zongsan 牟宗三, *Zhongguo zhexue shijiu jiang* 中國哲學十九講 [Nineteen Lectures on Chinese Philosophy], in *Mou Zongsan xianshengquanji* 牟宗三先生全集 29 [The Complete Work of Mou Zongsan, no. 29] (Taipei: Lianjing chubanshe, 2003), 36.
42 Dipesh Chakrabarty, *Provincializing Europe. Postcolonial Thought and Historical Difference* (Princeton – London: Princeton University Press, 2000), 8.
43 Richard King, *Indian philosophy. An Introduction to Hindu and Buddhist Thought* (Edinburgh: Edinburgh University Press, 1999), 14.
44 We suggest also reading an essay written by the historian Tortarolo for a Chinese public; the author raises similar conclusions from different standpoints: Edoardo Tortarolo, 'World history on the Twenty-first Century and Its critics', *Taiwan Journal of East Asian Studies*, vol. 1, no. 2, December 2004, 331–42. In the historical studies of pre-Colombian America similar views have been proposed by two French historians, i.e. Serge Gruzinski and François Hartog (see Bibliography).

Bibliography

Primary sources

Acosta, José de. *Historia natural y moral de las Indias*. Seville: en Casa de Juan de León, 1590.
Acosta, Josef de. *Historia Natural y Moral de las Indias*. Ed. Fermín del Pino Diáz. Madrid: Consejo Superior de Investigaciones Científicas, 2008. Retrieved from http://www.fondazioneintorcetta.info/pdf/biblioteca-virtuale/documento1182/HistoriaNatural.pdf
Ambrogio (Saint). *Il modo di vivere dei Brahmani / De moribus Brachmanorum*. Trans. Ilaria Santomanco. Milano: La vita felice, 2004.
Apuleius, Lucius. *The Apologia and Florida of Apuleius of Madure*. Trans. H. E. Butler. Oxford: Clarendon Press, 1909.
Arnauld, Antoine. *La Morale pratique des Jesuites: divisé en sept parties: où l'on represente leur conduite dans la Chine, dans le Japon, et dans l'Ethyopie: le tout tiré de livres très-autorisez, ou de pieces très-authentiques*. Cologne: chez Gervinus Quentel, 1682.
Arnauld, Antoine. *Cinquiéme denonciation du Philosophisme c'est à dire de la nouvelle heresie du Peché philosophique*. Cologne: chez Nicolas Schouten, 1690.
Arriano (di Nocomedia). *L'India / Indiké*. Trans. Alessandra Oliva. Milano: BUR, 2000.
Bacon, Roger. *The 'Opus majus'*. Ed. John Henry Bridges. Oxford: William and Norgate, 1900.
Bailly, Jean Sylvain. *Histoire de l'astronomie ancienne*. Paris: Debure, 1775.
Bailly, Jean Sylvain. *Lettres sur l'origine des sciences et sur celle de peuples de l'Asie*. Londres – Paris: chez Elmesly – De Bure l'aîne, 1777.
Bayle, Pierre. *Pensées diverses à l'occasion de la Comète*, in *Oeuvres diverses*, III, 1, La Haye 1727. Reprint, edited by Elisabeth Laborusse, Hildesheim: Georg Olms Verlagsbuchhandlung, 1966 (1st edn, 1681; 2nd rev. edn, 1682; 1694 with *Addition aux Pensées diverses*).
Bayle, Pierre. *Continuation des Pensés diverses*. In *Oeuvres diverses*, vol. III, 1, La Haye 1727. Reprint, edited by Elisabeth Laborusse, Hildesheim: Georg Olms Verlagsbuchhandlung, 1966 (1st edn, Rotterdam: chez Reinier Leers, 1704).
Bayle, Pierre. *Réponse aux questions d'un provincial*. In *Oeuvres diverses*, III, 1, La Haye 1727. Reprint, edited by Elisabeth Laborusse, Hildesheim: Georg Olms Verlagsbuchhandlung, 1966. (originally published posthumously in four parts Rotterdam: chez Reiner Leers: 1703-4, 1705-6, 1706-7, 1707).
Bayle, Pierre. *Dictionnaire historique et critique*. 5th edn. Amsterdam, Leyde, La Haye, Utrecht, 1740 (1st edn, 1695-7; 2nd enlarged edn, 1702) retrieved from https://artfl-project.uchicago.edu/content/dictionnaire-de-bayle
Bayle, Pierre. *Réponse aux questions d'un provincial*. Amsterdam: chez Reinier Leers, 1704-7.
Bernard, Jacques (ed.). *Nouvelles de la République des Lettres*. Amsterdam: chez Desbordes-Pain, 1705. Reprint, Genère: Slatkine Reprints, 1966.
Bernier, François. *Suite des Mèmoires sur l'Empire du grand Mogol*. La Haye: chez Arnout Leers, 1671.

Bernier, François. *Abregé de la Philosophie de Gassendi*. 2nd enlarged edn. Lyon: chez Anisson, Posuel et Rigaud, 1684
Bernier, François. 'Introduction à la lecture de Confucius'. In *Journal de Sçavans*, ed. P.-S. Regis, II (8 June), 14–22. Paris: chez Jean Cusson, 1688.
Bernier, François. 'Memoire de Mr. Bernier sur le Quietisme des Indes'. In *Histoire des ouvrages des Sçavans*, ed. H. B. de Beauval (Sept.), 47–52. Rotterdam: chez Renier Leers, 1688.
Bernier, François. *Travels in the Mogul Empire (1656-1658)*. Trans. Archibald Constable, revised by Vincent A. Smith. London: Oxford University Press, 1916.
Bilfinger, Georg Bernhard. *Specimen Doctrinae Veterum Sinarum Moralis et Politicae*. Frankfurt-am-Main: apud Andreae & Hort, 1724.
Bilfinger, Georg Bernhard. *Dilucidationes philosophicae de Deo, anima humana, mundo et generalioribus rerum affectibus*. New edn. Tübingen: Johannis Georgii Cottae, 1768 (1st edn, 1725).
Blount, Charles. *The Two First Books of Philostratus concerning the Life of Apollonius Tyaneus*. London: Nathaniel Thompson, 1680.
Blount, Charles (pub. anonymously). *Oracles of Reason*, London 1693
Bordelon, Laurent. *Théatre philosophique, sur lequel On represente par des Dialogues dans le Champs Elisées les Philosophes anciens et modernes*. Paris: Chez Claude Barbin et Jean Musier, 1692.
Borri, Cristoforo. *Relatione della Nuova Missione delli PP. della Compagnia di Giesù, al Regno della Cocincina*. Roma: per Francesco Corbelletti, 1631.
Borri, Cristoforo. *Relation de la Nouvelle Mission des Pères de la Compagnie de Iesu, au Royaume de la Cochinchine*. Trans. Antoine de la Croix. Lille: la Bible d'Or, 1631.
Boureau-Deslandes, André-François. *Histoire critique de la Philosophie*. New edn. Amsterdam: chez François Changuion, 1756 (1st edn, pub. anonymously, Amsterdam in 1737).
Brucker, Jakob. *Kurtze Fragen aus der Philosophischen Historie, von Anfang der Welt bis auf die Geburt Christi, mit ausführlichen Anmerkungen erläutert*. Ulm: apud Erster Theil, 1731-7.
Brucker, Jakob. *Historia critica philosophiae a mundi incunabulis ad nostram usque aetatem deducta*. Leipzig: Literis et impensis Bern. Christoph Breitkopf, 1742-4.
Bruyère, Jean de La. *Dialogues posthumes du sieur de la Bruyere sur le Quietisme*. Paris: chez Charles Osmont, 1699.
Buddeus, Johann Franz. 'De superstitio mortuorum apud Chinenses cultu' (1701). In *Analecta historiae philosophicae*, Johann Franz Buddeus, 263–99. Halle: Sumptibus Orphanotrophii, 1706.
Buddeus, Johann Franz. 'De Spinozismo ante Spinozam' (1701). In *Analecta historiae philosophicae*, Johann Franz Buddeus, 309–59. Halle: Sumptibus Orphanotrophii, 1706.
Buddeus, Johann Franz. *Theses theologicae de atheismo et superstitione variis observationibus illustratae et in usum recitationum academicarum editae*. Jena: apud Bielckium, 1717.
Buddeus, Johann Franz. *Compendium Historiae philosophicae, observationibus illustratum cum praefatione Io. Georgii Walchii*. Halle: Typis & impensis Orfanotrophii, 1731.
Buddeus, Johann Franz. *Traité de l'athéisme et de la superstition*. Fr. trans. Louis Philon & J.C. Fischer. Amsterdam: chez Pierre Mortier, 1740.
Burigny, Jean Lévesque de. *Histoire de la Philosophie Payenne ou sentimens des philosophes et des peuples payens les plus celèbres sur Dieu, sur l'Ame et sur les devoirs de l'Homme*. La Haye: chez Gosse-Dehondt, 1724.

Burigny, Jean Lévesque de. *Théologie payenne; ou sentimens des philosophes et des peuples payens les plus celèbres sur Dieu, sur l'Ame et sur les devoirs de l'Homme*. Paris: chez De Bure l'aîné, 1754.
Burnet, Thomas. *Archaeologiae Philosophicae: sive Doctrina antiqua de Rerum Originibus, libri duo*. London: Typis R. N. Impensis Kettilby, 1692.
Burnet, Thomas. *Archaeologia Philosophicae: or, the Ancient Doctrine Concerning the Origininals of Things, written in Latin by Thomas Burnet, Faithfully translated into English, with Remarks thereon, by Mr. Foxton*. London: E. Curll in the Strand, 1729.
Burnet, Thomas. *Archaeologia Philosophicae: or, the Ancient Doctrine Concerning the Originals of Things*. London: Printed and fold by J. Fisher, over-against Tom's Coffe-House in Cornhill, 1736.
Cai Yuanpei 蔡元培. Xu 序 [Preface]. In Hu Shi 胡适, *Zhongguo zhexueshi dagang* 中国哲学史大刚 [Outlines of Chinese history of philosophy], I-III. Chongqing: Congqing Chubanshe, 2013.
Casini, Paolo. *Diderot 'philosophe'*. Bari: Editori Laterza, 1962.
Clement of Alexandria (Titus Flavius Clemens), *Stromata*. Trans. William Wilson, in *Ante-Nicene Fathers*, ed. A. Roberts, J. Donaldson and A. C. Coxe., vol. II. Grand Rapids: Erdmans Publishing Company, 2001 (facsimile of American edn, 1885).
Clerc, Jean Le. *Bibliotheque universelle et historique de l'année 1687*. Vol. VII (December, no. XIV). Amsterdam: chez Wolfang, Waesberge, Boom, et van Someren, 1688.
Coleridge, Henry J. *The life and letters of Saint Francis Xavier*. London: Burns Oates, 1881.
Coste, Pierre. 'Discours sur la Philosophie, où l'on voit en abregé l'histoire de cette Science'. In *Cours entier de Philosophie, ou Systeme General selon les principes de M. Descartes*, ed. Regis Pierre Silvain, published anonymously before the text and not paginated. Amsterdam: Huguetan, 1691.
Couplet, Philippe (ed.). *Confucius sinarum philosophus, sive scientia sinensis latine exposita, studio et opera, Prosperi Intorcetta, Christiani Herdtrich, Francisci Rougemont, Philippi Couplet (Patrum societatis Jesu)*. Paris: Apud Danielem Horthmels, 1687.
Crousaz, Jean-Pierre de. *Examen du Pyrrhonisme ancien et moderne*. La Haye: chez Pierre de Hondt, 1733.
Croze, Mathurin Veyssière de La. *Histoire du christianisme des Inde*. La Haye: chez les frères Vaillant, & N. Prévost, 1724.
Cruz, Gaspar da. *Tractado em que se contam muito por estenso as cousas da China*, em casa de Andre de Burgos, Evora 1569. (modern English trans. in *South China in the Sixteenth Century : being the narratives of Galeote Pereira, Fr. Gaspar da Cruz O.P., Fr. Martin De Rada O.E.S.A. (1550-1575)*, trans. Charles Raph Boxer, London: The Hakluyt Society, 1953; reissue Orchid Press, Bangkok 2004).
Diderot, Denis. 'Philosophie des Chinois'. In *Encyclopédie*, III, 342. (used *Encyclopédie, ou dictionnaire raisonné des sciences, des arts et des métiers, etc.*, University of Chicago: ARTFL Encyclopédie Project (Spring 2011 Edition), ed. Robert Morrissey, http://encyclopedie.uchicago.edu/).
Feng, Youlan 冯友兰. *Zhongguo zhexueshi* 中国哲学史 [History of Chinese Philosophy]. Beijing: Shangwu yinshuguan chuban, 2006.
Ficino, Marsilio. *Teologia platonica*. Trans. M. Schiavone, Bologna: Zanichelli, 1965.
Ficino, Marsilio. *Platonic theology*. Textual lat. ed. J. Warden and J. Hankins, trans. M. J. B. Allen and J. B. Allen. London: Harvard University Press, 2006.

Gentzken, Friedrich. *Historia philosophiae in qua philosophorum celebrium vitae eorumque hypotheses notabiliores, ac sectarum fata a longa rerum memoria ad nostra usque tempora succinte et ordine sistuntur. In usum lectionum academicarum.* Hamburg: Apud Theodor. Christoph. Felginer, 1724.

Hegel, Georg Wilhelm Friedrich. *Vorlesungen über die Geschichte der Philosophie.* In *Werke*, no. 18, ed. Eva Moldenhauer & Karl Markus Michel. Frankfurt am Main: Suhrkamp Verlag, 1986.

Heineccius, Joh. Gottlieb. 'Historia philosophica'. In ibid., *Elementa philosophiae rationalis et moralis*, 9th enlarged ed., Frankfurt am Main: Impens. Io. Christian Kleybii, 1745 (1st edn, 1728)

Heumann, Christoph August. *Acta philosophorum, das ist: Gründliche Nachrichten aus der Historia hilosophica.* Halle: zu finden in der Rengerischen Buchhandl, 1715–27.

Heurn, Otto van. *Barbaricae philosophiae antiquitatum/ libri duo: I Chaldaicus, II Indicus. Opus historicum et philosophicum.* Leiden: ex Officina Plantiniana, Academiae Lugduno-Bat. Typographum, 1600.

Horn, Georg. *Historiae philosophicae libri septem, quibus De origine, successione, sectis et vita Philosophorum ab orbe condito ad nostram aetatem agitur, apud Johannem Elsevirium.* Leiden: apud Johannem Elsevirium, 1655.

Horn, Georg. *Dissertatio de vera aetate mundi qua sententia illorum refellitur qui statuunt Natale Mundi tempus annis minimum 1440 vulgarem aeram anticipare.* London: apud Elsevirium-Leffen, 1659.

Horn, Georg. *Arca Noae sive Historia Imperiorum et Regnorum a condito orbe ad nostra Tempora.* London: ex Officina Hackiana, 1666.

Hu Shi 胡适. *Zhongguo zhexueshi dagang* 中国哲学史大刚 [Outlines of Chinese history of philosophy]. Chongqing: Congqing Chubanshe, 2013

Huet, Pierre-Daniel. *Traité philosophique de la foiblesse de l'esprit humain.* Amsterdam: chez Hensi du Sauzet, 1723 (1st edn, Paris 1722).

Jurieu, Pierre. *Jugement du public et particulièrement de l'abbé Renaudot sur le dictionnaire historique et critique.* Rotterdam: chez Abraham Acher, 1697.

Karttunen, Klaus. *India in early Greek literature.* Helsinki: Studia orientalia / Finnish oriental society, 1989.

Karttunen, Klaus. *India and the Hellenistic world.* Helsinki: Studia orientalia / Finnish oriental society, 1997.

Kircher, Athanasius. *China Monumentis qua sacris qua profanis, nec non variis naturae et artis spectaculis, aliarumque rerum memorabilium argumentis illustrata.* Amsterdam: Apud Iacobum à Meurs, 1677.

Kircher, Athanasius. *China Illustrata.* Trans. Charles D. Van Tuyl. Bloomington: Indiana University, 1987.

Lambec, Peter. *Prodromus Historiae literariae.* Leipzig–Frankfurt: Ex Officina Christiani Liebezeit, 1710 (1st edn, Hamburg 1659).

Leibniz, Gottfried Wilhelm. *Discours sur la Théologie naturelle des Chinois.* Paris: ed. Ch. Frémont, 1987.

Leibniz, Gottfried Wilhelm. *Discours sur la Theologie Naturelle des Chinois.* Ed. Wenchao Li & Hans Potter. Frankfurt am Main: Vittorio Klostermann, 2002.

Li, Zhizao 李之藻. *Tian Xue Chu Han* 天学初函 [First Collection of Christian Studies]. Photographic copy of the first edition of 1626, vol. 2, 637–88. Taipei, 1953,

Longobardi, Niccolò. *Traité sur quelques points de la religion des Chinois.* Paris: chez Louis Guerin, 1701 (critical edition in Gottfried Wilhelm Leibniz, *Discours sur la Theologie Naturelle des Chinois*, 113–58. Frankfurt am Main: Vittorio Klostermann, 2002).

Lord, Henry. *A discovery of the Banian religion and the religion of the Persees : a critical edition of two early English works on Indian religions*. Ed. Will Sweetman. Lewiston: Edwin Mellen Press, 1999.

Loubère, Simon de la. *Du Royame du Siam*, 2 vols. Amsterdam: chez Abraham Wolfang, 1691.

Malebranche, Nicolas. *Entrétien d'un Philosophe Chrétien et d'un Philosophe Chinois* (1708). In Gottfried Wilhelm Leibniz. *Discours sur la Theologie Naturelle des Chinois*, ed. Wenchao Li & Hans Potter (ed.), 225–53. Frankfurt am Main: Vittorio Klostermann, 2002.

Marini, Giovanni Filippo de. *Delle missioni de' padri della Compagnia di Giesù, nella Provincia del Giappone, e particolarmente di quella di Tumkino*. Rome: per Nicolò Angelo Tinassi, 1658.

Martini, Martino. *Historiae sinicae decas primas*. Munich: typis Lucae Straubi, 1658.

Matalio Metello, Giovanni, 'Praefatio'. In *De rebus Emmanuelis Lusitaniae Regis invictissimi*, ed. Osório, Jerónimo, 2r–50f. Cologne: In Officina Birckmannica, sumptibus Arnoldi Mylii, 1586.

Mendoza, Juan Gonzáles de. *Historia de las cosas mas notables, ritos y costumbres, del gran Reyno dela China*. Rome: Bartholome Grassi, 1585.

Mendoza, Juan Gonzáles de. *Dell'Historia della China*. It. trans. Francesco Avanzi. Rome: Bartholome Grassi, 1586.

Mendoza, Juan Gonzáles de. *Histoire du Grand Royaume de la Chine*. Fr. trans. Luc de La Porte. Paris: chez Ieremie Perier, 1588.

Mendoza, Juan Gonzáles de. *The Historie of the Great and mightie Kingdome of China, and the situation thereof*. Eng. trans. Robert Parke. London: Edward White, 1588 (reprint edition: *The history of the great and mighty Kingdom of China and of the situation thereof*, ed. G. T. Staunton, London: The Hakluyt Society, 1853).

Molinos, Miguel. *Recueuil de diverses pieces concernant le quietisme ou Molinos, ses sentiments et ses disciples*. Ed. J. C. Lacroze. Amsterdam: chez Wolfang et Savouret, 1688.

Navarrete, Domingo Fernandez. *Tratados historicos, politicos, ethicos, y religiosos de la monarchia de China*. Madrid: Imprenta Real, 1676.

Newton, Isaac. 'Scholium on Time, Space, Place and Motion'. In *Philosophiae Naturalis Principia Mathematica*, Trans. Andrew Motte (1729), revision Florian Cajori, vol. 1, 6–12. Berkeley: University of California Press, 1934 (we used https://plato.stanford.edu/entries/newton-stm/scholium.html).

Nishida, Kitarō. *Place and Dialectic: Two Essays by Nishida Kitarō*. Trans. John W. M. Krummel and Shigenori Nagatomo. New York: Oxford University Press, 2012.

Noël, Francisco. *Observationes Mathematicae et Physicae in India et China factae ab anno 1684 usque annum 1708*. Prague: per Joachimum Joannem Kamenicky, 1710.

Origen. *Against Celus*. Trans. Frederick Crombie, in *Ante-Nicene Fathers*, Ed. Schaff Philip. Vol. 4. Grand Rapids: Erdmans Publishing Company, 2001 (facsimile of American ed. 1885).

Palladio (Pseudo). *Le genti dell'India e i brahmani / De gentibus Indiae et bragmanibus*. It. trans. Giovanni de Santis. Rome: Città nuova editrice, 1992.

Pereyra, Benito. *De communibus omnium rerum naturalium Principiis et Affectionibus libri quindecim. Qui plurimum conferunt ad eos octo libros Aristotelis qui de physico audit inscribuntur, intelligendos*. Paris: apud Micaëlem Sonnio, 1579.

Peyrère, Isaac La. *I Preadamiti / Praeadamitae*. Ed. and it. trans. G. Lucchesini. Macerata: Quodlibet, 2004 (1st edn, *Praeadamitae sive Exercitatio [...] quibus inducuntur Primi Homines ante Adamum conditi*, [Amsterdam?] 1655).

Plano Carpini, Giovanni Di (Giovanni da Pian del Carpine). *The story of the Mongols whome we call the Tartares*. Trans. E. Hildinger. Boston: Branden Publishing Company, 1996.
Plethon, Gemistus. *Traité des Lois*. Ed. Alexandre C. and trans. De Pellissier. Paris: Librairie de Firmin, 1858.
Polo, Marco. *Il Milione*. Ed. Marcello Ciccuto. Milano: BUR, 1995.
Possevino, Antonio. *Bibliotheca selecta*. Rome: Typ. Apostolica Vaticana, 1593.
Postel, Guillaume. *Abrahami patriarchae Liber Jezirah*. Paris (No editor), 1552.
Postel, Guillaume. *De originibus, seu, de varia et potissimum orbi Latino ad hanc diem incognita, aut inconsyderata historia, quuntotius Orientis, tum maxime Tartarorum, Persarum, Turcarum, et omnium Abrahami et Noachi alumnorum origins, et mysteria Brachmanum retegente: Quod ad gentium, literarumqae quib. Utuntur, rationes attinet.* Basel: per Ioannem Oporinum, 1553.
Postel, Guillaume. *Des merveilles du monde, et principalemét ["sic"] des admirables choses des Indes, & du nouveau monde : histoire extraicte des escriptz tresdignes de foy, tant de ceulx qui encores sont a present audict pays, come de ceulx qui encores vivantz peu paravat en sont retournez*. No editor and date, possibly 1553. Bibliothèque nationale de France, dép. Réserve des livres rares, Rés. D2 5267.
Rapin, René. *Les Réflexions sur la philosophie ancienne et modern*. Paris: chez Muguet et Barbin, 1676.
Rapin, René. *Les comparaisons des Grands Hommes de l'Antiquité, qui ont le plus excellé dans les belles Lettres* in *Oeuvres diverses du R. P. R. Rapin concernant les belles Lettres*. Vol. 1. Amsterdam: chez Abraham Wolfgang, 1686.
Renaudot, Eusèbe. *Anciennes relations des Indes et de la Chine. De deux voyageurs Mahometans qui y allerent dans le neuvième siècle, avec Des Remarques sur les principaux endroits de ces Relations* (traduites d'arabe). Paris: chez Jean-Baptiste Coignard, Imprimeur ordinaire du Roy (ruë S. Jacques, à la Bible d'or), 1718.
Rhodes, Alexandre de. *Histoire du Royaume de Tunquin*. Fr. trans. H. Albi. Lyon: chez Iean Baptiste Devenet, 1651.
Ricci, Matteo. *De Christiana expeditione apud Sinas suscepta ab Societate Iesu*. Ed. and lat. trans. Nicolas Trigault. London: Sumptibus Horatii Cardon, 1616 (1st edn, Augsburg: apud Christoph Mangium, 1615).
Ricci, Matteo. *Histoire de l'expédition chrestienne au royaume de la Chine*. Ed. and fr. trans. Nicolas Trigault. Lyon: pour Horace Cardon, 1616.
Ricci, Matteo. *Storia dell'Introduzione del Cristianesimo in Cina*. In *Fonti Ricciane*, ed. Pasquale M. D'Elia. Rome: La Libreria dello Stato, 1942.
Ricci, Matteo. *The True Meaning of the Lord of Heaven (T'ien-chu Shih-i)*. Ed. and trans. D. Lancashire and P. Hu Kuo-chen. Taipei–Paris–Hong Kong: Ricci Institute, 1985.
Ricci, Matteo. *Della entrata della compagnia di Giesù e Christianità nella Cina*. Ed. Maddalena del Gatto. Macerata: Quodlibet, 2000.
Ricci, Matteo. *Dieci capitoli di un uomo strano*. Ed. Filippo Mignini, it. trans. Wang Suna. Macerata: Quodlibet, 2010.
Rodrigues, João. *João Rodrigues's Account of Sixteenth-Century Japan*. Ed. and trans. M. Cooper. London: Hakluyt Society, 2001.
Rogerius, Abraham. *La Porte Ouverte, par parvenir à la connaissance du Paganisme cache*. Amsterdam: chez Jean Schipper, 1670.
Roz, Francisco. 'De Erroribus Nestorianorum Qui in Hac India Orientali Versantur'. In *Orientalia Christiana* vol. XI/I (=no. 40), ed. Irénée Hausherr, 1–35. Rome: Pont. Inst. Orientalium Studiorum, 1928.

Ruiz-de-Medina, Juan. *Documentos del Japon 1547-1557*. Rome: Monumenta Historica Japoniae II (Instituto Histórico de la Compañía de Jesús), 1990.
Sachau, Edward. *The Chronology of Ancient Nations*. London: W.H. Allen & Co, 1879.
Semedo, Alvarez. *Histoire universelle du Grand Royaume de la China*. Paris: chez Cramoisy, 1645.
Siculo, Diodoro. *Biblioteca storica, (v. I, books 1-3)* with Greek. Ed. and it. trans. Giuseppe Cordiano & Marta Zorat. Milano: BUR, 2004.
Skjærvø, Prods Oktor (trans. and ed.). *Kephalaia*, Free Pdf retrieved from the website http://www.fas.harvard.edu/~iranian/Manicheism/
Stanley, Thomas. *History of Philosophy: Containing the Lives, Opinions, Actions and Discourses of the Philosophers of every Sect*. London: printed for H. Moseley and Th. Dring, 1656–62.
Stanley, Thomas. *Historia philosophiae orientalis recensuit, ex anglica lingua in latinam, notis in Oracula chaldaica et indice philologico auxit Johannes Clericus*. Amsterdam: apud Swart, 1690.
Steuco, Agostino. *De perenni philosophia libri X*. Basel: Per Nicolaum Bryling et Sebastianum Francken, 1542 (1st edn, Lyon 1540).
Stolle, Gottlieb. *Historie der Heÿdnischen Morale*. Jena: Christian Pohl, 1714.
Suda. In 'Suda On Line: Byzantine Lexicography', retrieved from http://www.stoa.org/sol/
Tachard, Guy. *Voyage de Siam des pères Jesuites, envoyés par le roy, aux Indes et à la Chine*. Paris: A. Seneuze & D. Hortemels, 1686.
Thomassin, Louis. *La Methode d'étudier et d'enseigner chrêtiennement et solidement la Philosophie par rapport à la Religion Chrestienne et aux Ecritures*. Paris: chez François Muguet, 1685.
Thomasius, Jakob. *Schediasma historicum*. Leipzig P. Fuhrmanni, 1665.
Thomasius, Christian. *Introductio ad Philosophiam Aulicam, seu Linae Primae libri de Prudentia cogitandi et ratiocinandi, ubi ostenditur media inter praejudicia Cartesianorum, et ineptias Paeripateticorum, veritatem inveniendi via*. Halle: Editio altera, Prostat in Officina Libraria Rengeriana, 1703 (1st edn, Halle 1702).
Traversari, Ambrogio. *Vitae et Sententiae Philosophorum*. Rome: Giorgio Lauer, 1472.
Valignano, Alessandro. *Catechismus Christianae Fidei, in quo Veritas nostrae religionis ostenditur, et sectae Iaponenses confutantur*. Lisbon: Antonius Riberius, 1586.
Valignano, Alessandro. *Historia del Principio y Progresso de la Compania de Jesus en las Indias Orientales (1542-64)*. In *Monumenta Xaveriana*. Madrid: Typis Augustini Avrial, 1899–1900.
Vayer, François De la Mothe le. *De la vertu des payens*. Paris: chez François Targa, 1642 (republished in several editions of his *Oeuvres*, ed. Paris 1662, I, 584–705).
Versé, Noël Aubert de. *L'Impie convaincu, ou dissertation contre Spinosa*. Amsterdam: chez Jean Crelle, 1685.
Vesdin, Filip (Paulinus a Sancto Bartolomaeo). *Systema Brahmanicum Liturgicum mythologicum civile Ex monumentis indicis Musei Borgiani Velitris Dissertationibus Historico-criticis*. Rome: apud Antonium Fulgonium, 1791.
Villemandy, Pierre de. *Manuductio ad Philosophiae Aristoteleae, Epicureae, et Cartesianae, Parallelismum*. Amsterdam: apud Henricos Wetstenium et Desbordes, 1685.
Voltaire, Arouet François-Marie. *Essai sur les moeurs et l'esprit des nations et sur les principaux faits de l'histoire depuis Charlemagne jusqu'à Louis XIII*. Ed. R. Pomeau. Paris: Garnier, 1963 (1st edn, 1756).
Voltaire, Arouet François-Marie. *Lettres chinoises, indiennes et tartares à Monsieur Paw*. Paris (no editor), 1776.

Vossius, Isaac. *De dissertatio de vera aetate mundi*. Hague: ex Typ. Adriani Vlacq, 1659.
Vossius, Isaac. *Variarum Observationum liber*. London: apud Robertum Scott Bibliopolam, 1685 (on China p. 56–85).
Walch, Johann Jakob. *Historia artis Logicae generatim*. In ibid., *Parerga Academica ex Historiarum atque antiquitatum monimentis collecta*, p. 453–848. Leipzig: sumtu Io. Frieder. Gleiditschii, B. Filii, 1721.
Webb, John. *The Antiquity of China Or an Historical Essay: Endeavouring a Probability that the Language of the Empire of China is the Primitive Language, Spoken Through the Whole Word, Before the Confusion of Babel*. London: Nath. Brook, 1669.
Wolff, Christian. *Oratio de Sinarum philosophia practica. Rede über die praktische Philosophie der Chinesen*. Ed. Michael Albrecht, Philosophische Bibliothek, vol. 374. Hamburg: Felix Meiner Verlag, 1985 (English trans. in Ching-Oxtoby, *Moral Enlightenment*).
Wolff, Christian. *De rege philosophante et philosopho regnante*. In ibid., *Horae subsecivae Marburgenses, quibus philosophia ad publicam privatamque utilitatem captar*, vol. II, 563–632. Frankfurt and Leibzig: Officina Rengeriana, 1731-2 (English trans. in Ching-Oxtoby, *Moral Enlightenment*).
Wolff, Christian, *Sämtliche Rezensionen in den Acta Eruditorum (1705-1731)*. Ed. Hubert A. Laeven and Lucy J. M. Laeven-Aretz, vol. 2, 1711–18. Hildesheim: G. Olms, 2001.
Xavier, Francis. *The letters and instructions of Francis Xavier*. Ed. and trans. M. Joseph Costellope. Anand: Gujarat Sahitya Prakash, 1993.
Yule, Henry. *Cathay and the way Thither*. London: Hakluyt Society, 1866.

Secondary sources

Ambrogio, Selusi. 'Secular Reason as a Tool of the Early Jesuit Mission to China'. *Asiatische Studien / Études Asiatiques*, 72.4 (Nov 2018), 1195–1213.
Ambrogio, Selusi. 'Atheism, wisdom, enlightened Empire and irrationality. The changing influence of Jesuits' China on European histories of philosophy (1600-1744)'. *New Perspective in the Studies on Matteo Ricci*, ed. Filippo Mignini, 243–62. Macerata: Quodlibet, 2019.
App, Urs. *The Birth of Orientalism*. Philadelphia: University of Pennsylvania Press, 2010.
App, Urs. *The cult of Emptiness. The Western Discovery of Buddhist Thought and the Invention of Oriental Philosophy*. Rorschach/Kyoto: UniversityMedia, 2012.
Barbu, Daniel. 'Idolatry and the History of Religions'. *Studi e Materiali di Storia delle Religioni*, 82/2, 2016 (special issue *Religion as a Colonial Concept in Modern History. America, Asia*), 537–70.
Bernard-Maitre, Henri. 'L'orientaliste Guillaume Postel et la découverte spirituelle du Japon en 1552'. In *Monumenta Nipponica*, vol. 9 no. 1/2 (Avril), 83–108. Tokyo: Sophia University, 1953.
Bhattacharya, Kamaleswar. *L'ātman-Brahman dans le Bouddhisme ancien*. Publication de l'École Française d'Extrême-Orient, vol. XC. Paris: Adrien-Maisonneuve, 1973.
Billioud, Sébastien. *Thinking Through Confucian Modernity. A Study of Mou Zongsan's Moral Metaphysics*. Leiden-Boston: Brill, 2012.
Blackwell, Constance. 'Brucker, Johann Jacob (1696–1770)'. *The Bloomsbury Dictionary of Eighteenth-Century German Philosophers*, ed. Heiner F. Klemme and Manfred Kuehn, 100–6. London: Bloomsbury, 2010.

Bloch, Marc. *Apologie pour l'histoire ou métier d'historien*. 6th edn. Paris: Armand Colin, 1967.
Bonacina, Giovanni. *Filosofia ellenistica e cultura moderna: epicureismo, storicismo e scetticismo da Bayle a Hegel*. Coll. Fondo studi Parini-Chirio, v. 4. Milan: Le Lettere, 1996.
Bordoli, Roberto. 'Una biografia illuministica: Christian Thomasius'. *Giornale critico della filosofia italiana*, vol. LXXXVI, II (May–June), 'Discussioni e postille', 373–82. Firenze 2007.
Breloer, Bernardus, and Franziscus Bomer. *Fontes historiae religionum indicarum*. Bonn: apud Ludovicum Rohrscheid, 1939.
Bugault, Guy. *L'Inde pense-t-elle?* Paris: Presses Universitaire de France, 1994.
Catana, Leo. *The Historiographical Concept 'System of Philosophy'. Its Origin, nature, influence and legitimacy*. Leiden: Brill, 2008.
Catana, Leo. 'The history of the History of Philosophy, and the Lost Biographical Tradition', *British Journal for the History of Philosophy*, vol. 20, no. 3, 2012, 619–25.
Chakrabarty, Dipesh. *Provincializing Europe. Postcolonial Thought and Historical Difference*. Princeton – London: Princeton University Press, 2000.
Chattopadhyay, Bankimchandra. 'The intellectual superiority of Europe' (1882). Republished in ibid., *Baṅkim racanābalī*, ed. Yogeścāndra Bāgal, vol. 3. Kolkata: Sāhitya Saṃsad, 1990.
Cheng, Anne. *Histoire de la pensée Chinoise*. Paris: Éditions du Seuil, 1997.
Cheng, Anne (ed.). *Y a-t-il une philosophie chinoise? Un état de la question*. Saint-Denis: Presses Universitaire de Vincennes, 2005.
Cheng, Anne (ed.). *La pensée en Chine aujourd'hui*. Paris: Gallimard, 2007.
Ching, Julia, and Willard G. Oxtoby. *Moral Enlightenment: Leibniz and Wolff on China*. Monumenta Serica monograph series, vol. XXVI. Nettetal: Steyler Verlag, 1992.
Clark, John James. *Oriental Enlightenment. The encounter between Asian and Western thought*. London: Routledge, 1997.
Cook, Daniel J., and Henry Rosemont. 'The Pre-established harmony between Leibniz and Chinese Thought'. *Journal of the History of Ideas*, vol. XLII, no. 2, April–June 1981, 253–67.
Cooper, Michael. 'Rodrigues in China. The Letters of João Rodrigues, 1611-1633'. *Kokugoshi e ni michi*, vol. 2, Tokyo: Sanshodo, 1981, 231–355.
Cua, Antonio S. 'The emergence of the History of Chinese Philosophy'. In *History of Chinese Philosophy*, ed. Bou Mou, 43–68. Oxon (London & New York): Routledge, 2009.
Davis, Walter W. 'China, the Confucian Ideal, and the European Age of Enlightenment'. In *Discovering China. European interpretations in the Enlightenment*, ed. Julia Ching and Willard G. Oxtoby, 1–26. Rochester (New York): University of Rochester Press, 1992.
Defoort, Carine. 'Is there Such a Thing as Chinese Philosophy? Arguments of an Implicit Debate'. Philosophy East and West, vol. 51, no. 3, July 2001, 393–413.
Defoort, Carine. 'Is "Chinese Philosophy" a Proper name? A Response to Rein Raud'. Philosophy East & West, 56. 4, Oct. 2006, 625–60.
Dharampal-Frick, Gita. *Indien im Spiegel deutscher Quellen der Frühen Neuzeit (1500-1750)*. Tübingen: Max Niemeyer Verlag, 1994.
Dyck, Anne-Lise. 'La Chine hors de la philosophie: essai de généalogie à partir des traditions sinologique et philosophique françaises au XIXe siècle'. In *Y a-t-il une philosophie chinoise? Un état de la question*, ed. Anne Cheng, Saint-Denis: Presses Universitaire de Vincennes, 2005.

Dognini, Cristiano. 'Primi contatti fra cristianesimo e buddhismo'. In *Gli Apostoli in India*, ed. C. Dognini, I. Ramelli. Milano: Ed. Medusa, 2001.

Droit, Roger-Pol. *Le culte du néant. Les philosophes et le Bouddha*. 2nd enlarged edn. Paris: Éditions du Seuil, 2004.

Elisseeff-Poisle, Danielle. *Nicolas Fréret (1688-1749). Réflexions d'un humaniste du XVIIIe siècle sur la Chine*, Mémoires de l'Institut des Hautes Études Chinoises, vol. XI. Paris: Collège de France, 1978.

Étiemble, René. *L'Europe chinoise*. Paris: Gallimard, 1988.

Fasana, Enciro and Giuseppe Sorge (ed.). *Civiltà indiana ed impatto europeo nei secoli XVI-XVIII. L'apporto dei viaggiatori e missionari italiani*. Milano: Edizioni Universitarie Jaca, 1988.

Fasana, Enciro and Giuseppe Sorge (ed.). *India tra Oriente e Occidente. L'apporto dei viaggiatori e missionari italiani nei secoli XVI-XVIII*. Milano: Edizioni Universitarie Jaca, 1991.

Frigerio, Salvatore (ed.). *Ambrogio Traversari: un monaco e un monastero nell'umanesimo fiorentino*. Camaldoli: Edizioni Camaldoli, 1988.

Fumaroli, Marc. *La Querelle des Anciens et des Modernes*. Paris: Gallimard-Folio, 2001.

Garin, Eugenio. *Dal Rinascimento all'Illuminismo. Studi e ricerche*. Pisa: Nistri-Lischi, 1970.

Ge, Zhaoguang 葛兆光. *Zhongguo sixiang shi* 中国思想史 [History of Chinese Thought]. Shanghai: Fudan daxue chubanshe, 2001.

Germana, Nicholas A. *The mythical Image of India and Competing Images of German National identity*. Newcastle upon Tyne: Cambridge Scholars Publishing, 2009.

Gernet, Jacques. *Chine et christianisme. La première confrontation*. Paris: Gallimard, 1991 (engl trans. *China and the Christian impact*. Cambridge: Cambridge University Press, 1985).

Glasenapp, Helmuth von. *Buddhism a not-theistic religion*. London: George Allen and Unwin Ltd, 1970.

Golden, Sean. 'Orientalism in East Asia. A theoretic model'. *Inter Asia Papers*, no. 12, Instituto de Estudios Internacionales e Interculturales Bellaterra. Barcelona: Universitat Autònoma de Barcelona, 2009.

Goodman, Hananya. *Between Jerusalem and Benares: Comparative Studies in Judaism and Hinduism*. Albany: State University of New York Press, 1994.

Gruzinski, Serge. *La machine à remonter le temps. Quand l'Europe s'est mise à écrire l'histoire du monde*. Paris: Librarie Arthème Fayard, 2017.

Halbfass, Wilhelm. *India and Europe. An essay in Understanding*. Albany: State University of New York Press, 1988.

Harbsmeier, Christoph. *Language and Logic. Part I*. In *Science and civilization in China*, edited by Joseph Needham, vol. 7. Cambridge: Cambridge University Press, 1998.

Harbsmeier, Christoph. 'The rhetoric of premodern prose style'. In *The Cambridge History of Chinese Literature*, ed. Kang-I Sun Chang and Stephen Owen, vol. 1, chap. 43, 881–908. Cambridge: Cambridge University Press, 2010.

Hartog, François. *Anciens, modernes, sauvages*. Paris: Point, 2008.

Israel, Jonathan I. *Radical Enlightenment*. New York: Oxford University Press, 2001.

Israel, Jonathan I. *Enlightenment contested*. New York: Oxford University Press, 2006.

Israel, Jonathan I. 'Admiration of China and Classical Chinese Thought in the Radical Enlightenment'. *Taiwan Journal of East Asian Studies*, vol. 4, no. 1 (Iss.7), June 2007, 1–25.

Israel, Jonathan I. *Democratic Enlightenment*. New York: Oxford University Press, 2011.

Jensen, Lionel M., *Manufacturing Confucianism*. Durham: Duke University Press, 1997.
Jorink, Eric, 'Heurnius, Otto'. *The dictionary of Seventeenth and Eighteenth-century Dutch philosophers*, vol. 1. Bristol: Thoemmes Press, 2003.
Jorink, Eric and Dirk van Miert (ed.). *Isaac Vossius (1618-1689) between science and scholarship*. Leiden: Brill, 2012.
Kang, Ouyang. 'Fang Yizhi'. In *The Encyclopedia of Confucianism*, ed. Yao Xinzhong, 209-211. Oxon: Routledge, 2003.
King, Richard. *Indian philosophy. An Introduction to Hindu and Buddhist Thought*. Edinburgh: Edinburgh University Press, 1999.
Kors, Alan Charles. *Atheism in France, 1650-1729*. Princeton: Princeton University Press, 1990.
Krishna, Daya. *Indian Philosophy. A Counter Perspective*. Delhi: Oxford University Press, 1991.
Krop, Henry. 'Hornius, Georgius'. *The dictionary of Seventeenth and Eighteenth-century Dutch philosophers*, vol. 1, 452. Bristol: Thoemmes Press, 2003.
Kuntz, Marion. *Guillaume Postel, Prophet of the Restitution of All Things, His Life and Thought*. The Hague: Martinus Nijhoff Publishers, 1981.
La Mare, Albinia Catherine de. 'Cosimo and his Books'. In *Cosimo 'il Vecchio' de' Medici, 1389-1464*, ed. F. Ames-Lewis. New York: Oxford University Press, 1992.
Lai, Yuenting. 'Leibniz and Chinese thought'. In *Leibniz, mysticism and religion*, ed. A. P. Coudert, R. H. Popkin and G. M. Weiner, 136-68. Dordrecht: Kluwer Academic Publishers, 1998.
Lach, Donald F. 'The Sinophilism of Christian Wolff (1679-1754)'. In *Discovering China. European interpretations in the Enlightenment*, ed. Julia Ching, Willard G. Oxtoby, 117-30. Rochester: University of Rochester Press, 1992.
Lach, Donald F. 'China in Western Thought and Culture'. In *Dictionary of the History of Ideas* (1968-73), ed. Wiener Philip, vol. 1, 353-73. New York: Charles Scribner's Sons, 1968-73 (retrieved from http://xtf.lib.virginia.edu/xtf/view?docId=DicHist/uvaBook/tei/DicHist1.xml;chunk.id=dv1-48;toc.depth=1;toc.id=dv1-48;brand=default).
Lach, Donald F. *Asia in the making of Europe*. Chicago-London: University of Chicago Press, 1965-77.
Lach, Donald F. 'Leibniz and China'. Republished in *Discovering China. European interpretations in the Enlightenment*, ed. Julia Ching, Willard G. Oxtoby, 97-116. Rochester: University of Rochester Press, 1992.
Lackner, Michael. 'Jesuit Figurism'. In *China and Europe. Images and Influences in Sixteenth to Eighteenth Centuries*, ed. Thomas H. C. Lee, 129-49. Hong Kong: The Chinese University Press, 1991.
Lee, Eun-Jeung. *Anti-Europa. Die Geschichte der Rezeption des Konfuzianismus und der konfuzianischen Gesellschaft seit der Frühen Aufklärung*. Münster: Lit-Verlag, 2003.
Lee, Thomas H. C. (ed.). *China and Europe. Images and Influences in Sixteenth to Eighteenth Centuries*. Hong Kong: The Chinese University Press, 1991.
Lehner, Georg. *China in European Encyclopaedias, 1700-1850*. Leiden – Boston: Brill, 2011.
Lenoir, Frédéric. *La rencontre du Bouddhisme et de l'Occident*. Paris: Albin Michel, 1999.
Levitin, Dimitri. *Ancient Wisdom in the Age of the New Science. Histories of Philosophy in England, c. 1640-1700*. Cambridge: Cambridge University Press, 2015.
Li, Weiwu 李维武. *Zhongguo zhexuede chuantong bianxin* 中国哲学的转统更新 [Renewal of the Chinese Philosophical Tradition]. Beijing: Renmin chubanshe, 2012.
Lim, Jongtae. 'Restoring the Unity of the World: Fang Yizhi and Jie Xuan's Responses to Aristotelian Natural Philosophy'. In *The Jesuits, the Padroado and East Asian Science*

(1552-1773), ed. Luís Saraiva and Catherine Jami, 139–160. Singapore: World Scientific Publishing, 2008.

Lo Presti, Eleonora. 'La filosofia nel suo sviluppo storico: la prospettiva storiografica di Marsilio Ficino e l'influenza dei dotti bizantini Giorgio Gemisto Pletone e Giovanni Basilio Bessarione'. PhD diss., University of Bologne, 2007.

Longo, Mario. *Geistige Anregungen und Quellen der Bruckerschen Historiographie.* In *Jacob Brucker (1696-1770), Philosoph und Historiker der europäischen Aufklärung*, ed. W. Schmidt-Biggemann, T. Stammen, Colloquia Augustana vol. 7, pp. 159–86. Berlin: Akademie Verlag, 1998.

Lottes, Günther. 'China in European Political Thought (1750-1850)'. In *China and Europe. Images and Influences in Sixteenth to Eighteenth Centuries*, ed. Thomas H. C. Lee, 65–98. Hong Kong: The Chinese University Press, 1991.

Lubac, Henri de. *La rencontre du Bouddhisme et de l'Occident.* Paris: Aubier, 1952.

Lundbaek, Knud. 'The first European Translations of Chinese Historical and Philosophical Works'. In *China and Europe. Images and Influences in Sixteenth to Eighteenth Centuries*, ed. Thomas H. C. Lee, 29–43. Hong Kong: The Chinese University Press, 1991.

Mackerras, Colin. *Western images of China.* Hong Kong: Oxford University Press, 1989.

Marchignoli, Saverio. *Indagine sul dharma. Bankimchandra Chattopadyay e il discorso sulla religione nell'India colonizzata. Con la prima traduzione della* Dharmajijñāsā. Bologna: Libreria Bonomo editrice, 2005.

Marchignoli, Saverio. *Materiali per lo studio della controversistica religiosa nell'India coloniale 1. Haracandra Tarkapañcānana*, Mataparīkṣottaram (*Replica all'Esame delle dottrine religiose*). Bologna: Libreria Bonomo editrice, 2008.

Marchignoli, Saverio. *Tradurre la Gītā. La ricezione europea di un testo indiano nell'età di Goethe.* Bologna: Eurocopy-Format, 2008.

Matilal, Bimal Krishna. *The Collected Essays of Bimal Krishna Matilal. Ethics and Epics. Philosophy, Culture and Religion.* Ed. Jonardon Ganeri. New Delhi: Oxford University Press, 2002.

Mehta, Jarava Lal. *Martin Heidegger: The way and the Vision.* Honolulu: The University Press of Hawaii, 1978.

Mehta, Jarava Lal. *Philosophy and Religion, Essays in Interpretation.* Delhi: Indian Council of Philosophical Research, 1990.

Meynard, Thierry. 'The Overlooked Connection between Ricci's *Tianzhu shiyi* and Valignano's *Catechismus Japonensis*'. *Japanese Journal of Religious Studies,* 40/2, 303–22.

Miller, Peter N. 'Taking Paganism Seriously: Anthropology and Antiquarianism in Early Seventeenth-Century Histories of Religion'. *Archiv für Religionsgeschichte*, vol. 3, 2001, 183–209.

Minuti, Rolando. *Oriente barbarico e storiografia settecentesca. Rappresentazioni della storia dei Tartari nella cultura francese del XVIII secolo.* Venezia: Marsilio, 1994.

Minuti, Rolando. *Orientalismo e idee di tolleranza nella cultura francese del primo '700.* Firenze: Olschki editore, 2006.

Mohanty, Jitendra Nath. *Essays on Indian Philosophy Traditional and Modern.* Ed. Purushottama Bilimoria. New Delhi: Oxford University Press, 1993.

Mohanty, Jitendra Nath. *An Autobiography, Between two Worlds, East and West.* New Delhi: Oxford University Press, 2002.

Mohanty, Jitendra Nath. *Explorations in Philosophy*, vol. 1 ("Indian Philosophy"). Ed. Bina Gupta. New Delhi: Oxford University Press, 2001.

Mori, Gianluca. *Bayle philosophe.* Paris Honoré Champion Éditeur, 1999.

Mori, Giuliano. 'Natural Theology and Ancient Theology in the Jesuit China Mission', unpublished article retrieved from https://www.academia.edu/37948679/Natural_Theology_and_Ancient_Theology_in_the_Jesuit_China_Mission

Mou, Zongsan 牟宗三. *Zhongguo zhexue shijiu jiang* 中國哲學十九講 [Nineteen Lectures on Chinese Philosophy]. In *Mou Zongsan xianshengquanji* 牟宗三先生全集29 [The Complete Work of Mou Zongsan, no. 29]. Taipei: Lianjing chubanshe, 2003.

Muccillo, Maria. *Platonismo ermetismo e «Prisca theologia»*. Firenze: Olschki editore, 1996.

Mungello, David E. *Leibniz and Confucianism. The Search for Accord*. Honolulu: University of Hawaii Press, 1977.

Mungello, David E. 'Malebranche and Chinese philosophy'. *Journal of the history of Ideas*, vol. XLI, no. 4, October–December 1980, 551–79.

Mungello, David E. *Curious land: Jesuit accommodation and the origins of Sinology*. Honolulu: University of Hawaii Press, 1989.

Mungello, David E. 'European philosophical responses to non-European culture: China'. In *The Cambridge History of Seventeenth-Century Philosophy*, ed. D. Garber and M. Ayers, 87–100. New York: Cambridge University Press, 1998.

Mungello, David E. *The Chines rites controversy: its history and meaning*. Monumenta Serica no. XXXIII. Nettetal (Germany): Steyler Verlag, 1994.

Mungello, David E. *The Great Encounter of China and the West, 1500-1800*. Lanham (Maryland): Rowman & Littlefield Publishers, 1999.

Neill, Stephen. *The history of Christianity in India, The beginnings to AD 1707*. Cambridge: Cambridge University Press, 1984.

Nelson, Eric S. *Chinese and Buddhist Philosophy in Early Twentieth-Century German Thought*. London: Bloomsbury, 2017.

Nicholson, Andrew J. *Unifying Hinduism. Philosophy and identity in Indian intellectual history*. New York: Columbia University Press, 2010.

Panda, Narasingha Charan. 'Concept of Bhūmi in the Buddhist Literature with special reference to the *Daśabhūmika Sūtra*'. In ibid., *Perspectives of Indian Thought*, 106–19. Delhi: Bharatiya Kala Prakashan, 2007.

Park, Peter K. J. *Africa, Asia, and the History of Philosophy. Racism in the Formation of the Philosophical Canon, 1780–1830*. Albany: State University of New York Press, 2013.

Pasini, Mirella. *Thomas Burnet. Una storia del mondo tra ragione, mito e rivelazione*. Firenze: La Nuova Italia editrice, 1981.

Pinot, Virgile. *La Chine et la Formation de l'esprit philosophique en France (1640-1740)*. Genève: Slatkine Reprints, 1971.

Poole, William. 'Heterodoxy and Sinology: Isaac Vossius, Robert Hooke, and the Early Royal Society's use of Sinology'. The Intellectual Consequences of Religious Heterodoxy 1600-1750, ed. Sarah Mortimer and John Robertson, 135–53. Leiden – Boston: Brill, 2012.

Popkin, Richard H. *Isaac La Peyrère (1596-1676), His Life, Work and Influence*. Leiden: E. J. Brill, 1987.

Popkin, Richard H. *The history of Scepticism. From Savonarola to Bayle*. New York: Oxford University Press, 2003.

Pretto, Davide de. *L'oriente assoluto. India, Cina e "mondo Buddhista" nell'interpretazione di Hegel*. Milano – Udine: Mimesis 2010.

Rādhākrishnan, Sarvapalli. *Indian Philosophy*. London: Muirhead Library of Philosophy by Unwin Brothers Limited, 1929.

Raud, Rein. 'Philosophies versus Philosophy. In Defense of a Flexible Definition'. *Philosophy East and West*, vol. 56, no. 4, October 2006, 618–25.

Raud, Rein. 'Traditions and Tendencies: A Reply to Carine Defoort'. *Philosophy East and West*, vol. 56, no. 4, October 2006. 661–4.

Robson, Michael. *The Franciscans in the Middles Ages*. Woodbridge (UK): Boydell Press, 2006.

Robinet, André. *Malebranche et Leibniz, relations personnelles, Bibliothèque des textes philosophique*. Paris: Librairie Philosophique J. Vrin, 1955.

Rowbotham, Arnold H. 'The Jesuit figurists and eighteenth-century religious thought'. In *Discovering China. European interpretations in the Enlightenment*, ed. Julia Ching, Willard G. Oxtoby, 39–53. Rochester: University of Rochester Press, 1992.

Roy, Olivier. *Leibniz et la Chine*. Paris: Librairie philosophique J. Vrin, 1972.

Rubiés, Joan-Pau. 'Oriental despotism and European orientalism: Botero to Montesquieu'. *Journal of Early Modern History*, 9, 1–2, 109–80. Leiden: Koninklijke Brill, 2005.

Rubiés, Joan-Pau. 'Theology, Ethnography, and the Historicization of Idolatry'. *Journal of the History of Ideas*, 67, 4, October 2006, 571–96.

Rubiés, Joan-Pau. 'From Antiquarianism to Philosophical History: India, China, and the World History of Religion in European Thought (1600-1770)'. In *Antiquarianism and Intellectual Life in Europe and China. 1500-1800*, ed. Peter N. Miller, François Louis, 313–67. Ann Arbor: University of Michigan Press 2012.

Rubiés, Joan-Pau. 'Race, Climate and Civilization in the Works of François Bernier'. *Collection Puruṣārtha* (EHESS), *L'Inde des Lumieres*, Paris 2013, 53–76.

Rubiés, Joan-Pau. 'The Discovery of New Worlds and Sixteenth-century Philosophy'. *Routledge Companion to Sixteenth-century Philosophy*, ed. Henrik Lagerlund and Benjamin Hill, 54–82. New York – London: Routledge, 2017.

Rubrouck, Guillaume de. *The mission of Friar William of Rubruck (1253-55)*. Trans. P. Jackson. The London: Hakluyt Society, 1990.

Said, Edward W. *Orientalism*. 2nd edn. New York: Pantheon Books, 1995.

Santinello, Giovanni, Mario Longo, Luciano Malusa, Gregorio Piaia, Ilario Tolomio, *et ali*. (ed.), *Storia delle storie generali della filosofia* (SSGF)

v. 1, *Dalle origini rinascimentali alla "historia philosophica"* (SSGF1). Brescia: Editrice La Scuola, 1981 (English trans. *Models of the History of Philosophy: From Its Origins in the Renaissance to the "Historia Philosophica"* (MHP1). Ed. Blackwell, C. W. T. & Philip Weller. Dodrecht-Boston-London Kluwer: Academic Publishers, 1993).

v. 2, *Dall'età cartesiana a Brucker* (SSGF2). Brescia: Editrice La Scuola, 1979 (English trans. *Models of the History of Philosophy: From the Cartesian Age to Brucker*, (MHP2), Dotrecht-Heidelberg-London-New York: Springer, 2011).

v. 3/1 and 3/2, *Il secondo illuminismo e l'età kantiana*, Padova: Editrice Antenore, 1988.

v. 4/1, *L'età hegeliana. La storiografia filosofica nell'area tedesca*, Padova: Editrice Antenore, 1995.

v. 4/2, *L'età hegeliana. La storiografia filosofica nell'area neolatina, danubiana e russa*. Roma-Padova Editrice Antenore, 2004.

v. 5, *Il secondo Ottocento*, Roma-Padova: Editrice Antenore, 2004.

Schmidt-Biggemann, Wilhelm. 'Jacob Bruckers philosophiegeschichtliches Konzept'. In *Jacob Brucker (1696-1770), Philosoph und Historiker der europäischen Aufklärung*, ed. W. Schmidt-Biggemann, T. Stammen, Colloquia Augustana, vol. 7, 113–34. Akademie Verlag, Berlin 1998.

Schmidt-Biggemann, Wilhelm, *Philosophia perennis, Historical Outlines of Western Spirituality in Ancient, Medieval and Early Modern Thought*. Dordrecht: Springer, 2004.

Schmitt, Charles B. 'Perennial Philosophy: from Agostino Steuco to Leibniz'. *Journal of the history of ideas*, vol. XXVII, no. 4, October–December 1966, 505–32.

Schmitt, Charles B. '*Prisca Theologia* e *Philosophia perennis*: due temi del Rinascimento italiano e la loro fortuna'. In *Il pensiero italiano del Rinascimento e il nostro tempo*, ed. Giovannangiola Tarugi. Firenze: Olschki, 1970.

Schönfeld, Martin (ed.). 'Kant and Confucianism' (Special Issue). *Journal of Chinese Philosophy*, vol. 33, Issue 1, March 2006, 1–157.

Schönfeld, Martin. 'Kant's Philosophical Development' (2007). *The Stanford Encyclopedia of Philosophy* (Winter 2012 Edition), ed. Edward N. Zalta, retrieved from http://plato.stanford.edu/archives/win2012/entries/kant-development/

Schurhammer, Georg. *Francis Xavier. His life, his time*. Trans. J. Costelloe (Engl. Trans.), 4 vols. Rome: The Jesuit Historical Institute, 1973–82 (original edn *Franz Xavier. Sein Leben und sein Zeit*, Freiburg i.B.: Herder, 1955–73).

Sequeira, Ronald. *Die Philosophien Indiens*. Aachen: ein-FACH-verlag, 1996.

Smet, Rudolf de. 'Vossius, Isaac'. In *The dictionary of Seventeenth and Eighteenth-century Dutch philosophers*, vol. 2, p. 1049–2. Bristol: Thoemmes Press, 2003.

Song, Liming. 'Father Matteo Ricci's change in status in light of four Chinese Poems'. In *Matteo Ricci. Encounter Between Civilizations in Ming Dynasty China*, ed. Filippo Mignini, 92–9. Milan: Regione Marche/24 ORE Motta Cultura, 2010.

Standaert, Nicolas. 'The Jesuits Did NOT Manufacture "Confucianims"'. *East Asian Science, Technology and Medicine*, 16, 1999, 115–32.

Stoneman, Richard. *Alexander the Great: A Life in Legend*. New Haven: Yale University Press, 2008.

Stroumsa, Guy G. *A New Science. The discovery of religion in the age of reason*. Cambridge (Mass.) – London: Harvard University Press, 2010.

Sun, Shangyang 孫尚揚, *Bianxueyidu zuozhe kao* 《辩学遗牍》作者考 [Research on the authorship of *Posthumous Disputes*]. In *Jidujiao yu ming mo ruxue* 基督教与明末儒学 [Christian teaching and the late Ming Confucianism], ed. Sun Shangyang, 40–8. Beijing: Dongfang chubanshe, 1994.

Tang, Yijie. 'Constructing the "Chinese Philosophy". *Procedia Social and Behavioral Sciences*, vol. 2 (Selected Papers of Beijing Forum 2005), 2010, 7312–15.

Tennemann, Wilhelm Gottlieb. *Grundriß der Geschichte der Philosophie für den akademishen Unterricht*. Leipzig: bey Johann Ambrosius Barth, 1816.

Tinguely, Frédéric (ed.). *Un libertin dans l'Inde Moghole. Le voyages de François Bernier (1656-1669)*. Paris: Editions Chandeigne, 2008.

Tomasoni, Francesco. *La modernità e il fine della storia. Il dibattito sull'ebraismo da Kant ai giovani hegeliani*. Brescia: Morcelliana, 1999.

Tomasoni, Francesco. *Christian Thomasius. Spirito e identità culturale alle soglie dell'illuminismo europeo*. Brescia: Morcelliana, 2005.

Tong, Shijun 童世骏, '*Xifang zhexuede zhongguo jangjiu: sixiang fengxian jiqi yingdui fangfa* 西方哲学的中国研究：思想风险及其应对方法' [Studying Western Philosophy in China: Intellectual risks and the Ways of Dealing with Them]. In *Zhongxi zhexue lunheng* 中西哲学论衡 (*Comparative Philosophy: East and West*), ed. Yu Zhiping 余治平, 158–71. Shanghai: Shanghai shudian chubanshe, 2012.

Tortarolo, Edoardo. 'World history on the Twenty-first Century and Its critics'. *Taiwan Journal of East Asian Studies*, vol. 1, no. 2, December 2004, 331–42.

Vaghi, Massimiliano. *L'idea dell'India nell'Europa moderna (secoli XVII-XX)*. Milano-Udine: Mimesis, 2012.

Van Norden, Bryan W. *Taking back Philosphy. A Multicultural Manifesto*. New York: Columbia University Press, 2017.

Vivekānanda, Swāmi (Narendranath Dutta). 'Swami Vivekananda's Speeches at the World's Parliament of Religions', Chicago, 1893. Retrieved from https://belurmath.org/swami-vivekananda-speeches-at-the-parliament-of-religions-chicago-1893/

Weststeijn, Thijs. 'Spinoza sinicus: An Asian Paragraph in the History of Radical Enlightenment'. *Journal of the History of Ideas*, vol. 68, no. 4, October 2007, 537–61.

Weststeijn, Thijs. 'The Middle Kingdom in the Low Countries. Sinology in the Seventeenth century Netherlands'. In *The Making of the Humanities II: From Early Modern to Modern Disciplines*, ed. Jaap Maat, Rens Bod and Thijs Weststeijn, 209–42. Amsterdam: Amsterdam University Press, 2012.

Wu, Jiang. *Enlightenment in Dispute. The Reinvention of Chan Buddhism in Seventeenth-Century China*. New York: Oxford University Press, 2008.

Xie, Xialing 谢遐龄, *Zhongguo wenhua chayi jiqi zhexue jieshi* 中心文化差异及其哲学解释 [A Philosophical Explanation of the Cultural Differences between China and the West]. In *Zhongxi zhexue lunheng* 中西哲学论衡 (*Comparative Philosophy: East and West*), ed. Yu Zhiping 余治平, 134–44. Shanghai: Shanghai shudian chubanshe, 2012.

Yang, Guorong 杨国荣. *Zhongguo zhexue sanshijiang* 中国哲学三十讲 [Thirteen lessons on Chinese Philosophy]. Beijing: Zhonghua shuju, 2015.

Zhang, Dainian. *Key Concepts in Chinese Philosophy*. Beijing: Foreign Languages Press, 2002.

Zhang, Dainian 张岱年. *Zhongguo zhexue dacidian* 中国哲学大辞典 [The Dictionary of Chinese Philosophy]. Shanghai: Shanghai cishu chubanshe, 2014.

Zhang, Fa 张法. '*Hewei zhongguo zhexue yu zhongguo zhexue hewei* 何为中国哲学与中国哲学何为 [Chinese Philosophy: why and for what?]', *Tianjing shehui kexue* 天津社会科学 [Tianjing Social Science], no. 3, issue *Zhongguo zhexue xuekede jianshe yu fazhang* 中国哲学学科的建设与发展 [The shaping and development of the discipline Chinese Philosophy], 2004, 37–41.

Zhu, Weizheng 朱維錚, *Li Madou zhongwenzhu yiji* 利瑪竇中文著譯集 [A reasoned collection of Matteo Ricci's Chinese writings], 653–87. Shanghai: Fudan Daxue Chubanshe, 2001.

Zoli, Sergio. *Europa libertina tra Controriforma e Illuminismo*. Bologna: Cappelli Editore, 1989.

Županov, Ines G. and Po-Chia Hsia. 'Reception of Hinduism and Buddhism'. *The Cambridge History of Christianity*, vol. 6. *Reform and Expansion 1500-1660*, ed. Po-Chia Xsia, 577–97. Cambridge: Cambridge University Press, 2008.

Zurbuchen, Simone. 'Crousaz, Jean-Pierre de'. In *The dictionary of Seventeenth and Eighteenth-century Dutch philosophers*, v. 1, 234–7. Bristol: Thoemmes Press, 2003.

Zürcher, Erik. 'Xu Guangqi and Buddhism'. In *Statecraft and Intellectual Renewal in late Ming China. The Cross-Cultural Synthesis of Xu Guangqi (1562-1633)*, ed. Catherine Jami, Peter Engelfriet and Gregory Blue, 155–69. Leiden – Boston – Köln: Brill, 2001.

Index

Abraham, Abrahamic 4, 12, 16, 17, 18, 19, 21–2, 32, 35, 40, 44, 51, 53, 56, 57, 59, 89, 126, 127, 135, 159, 178 n.140
accommodation 6, 26–7, 38, 44, 59, 61, 67, 79, 85–6, 90, 91, 93, 95–6, 103, 115, 123–4, 126, 140–1, 173 n.69, 190 n.110
Acosta, José de 34, 175 n.95
Adam 11, 16, 32, 36, 39, 40, 53, 92, 111, 126, 159; *see* Pre Adamism
Africa 85, 101–2, 114, 136, 143
Ambrose, Saint (Saint Ambrogio) 93, 129, 201 n.88
Annals (Chinese) 15, 35, 38–9, 39, 44, 59, 115
antiquarianism, antiquarian 8, 14–5, 17–18, 27, 32 n.7, 45, 60, 97, 98, 122, 140
apology, apologetic (Christian) 1–3, 5, 6, 8, 31, 41, 60, 103, 115, 118, 143, 156, 160, 174 n.86
App, Urs 6–7, 9, 61, 67, 69, 182 n.1, 202 n.99, 205 n.4
Apuleius, Lucius 127
Aquinas, Thomas (Saint) 18–20, 87
Arabian(s) 44, 125, 126, 168 n.9
Arnauld, Antoine 69, 78, 79, 84, 111, 138, 185 n.35
atheism 30–1, 60, 63–4, 68, 83, 85–7, 190 n.105; *see* Spinozism
atheistic plague (Buddhism) 57, 60, 65, 72, 87, 119, 129, 132–4, 137, 139, 143, 144, 155
 pestis 67, 70, 134, 136, 139
Augustine of Hippo, Saint 11–14, 128, 169 n.17
Australia (Australian) 36, 54, 102, 143

Bacon, Francis (Francesco Bacone) 83
Bacon, Roger 11–12, 16, 42, 67, 83, 168, n.7
 Baconian 42, 179, n.148

barbarity, 42, 48, 51
 barbarian(s) 5, 13–15, 19, 32, 37, 45–7, 49, 51, 57, 83, 85, 92–3, 102–3, 106, 114, 121–2, 124–6, 129, 137, 159–60, 192 n.149
Bayle, Pierre 2, 4–5, 7, 8, 15, 29, 44, 49, 53, 55–7, 60–1, 64, 72, 73, 76–89, 90–5, 96, 100, 102–4, 105, 108, 110, 111, 115, 119, 120–1, 122, 124, 132–3, 138, 141, 153–5, 160, 161, 177 n.128, 187, n.68, 188 n.69–76), 189 n.88, 189 n.90, 190 n.105, 190, n.110, 191 n.119, 192 n.146, 199 n.61
Bernier, François 4, 6, 8, 49, 56–7, 60, 70–6, 77, 80, 91, 99, 103, 111, 117, 121, 130, 132–3, 181 n.179, 182 n.203, 185 n.42, 186 n.48, 186 n.50.
bhūmi 81–2
Bible 15, 32, 35–9, 40, 43, 53, 59, 115, 124, 175 n.98, 176 n.111
Bilfinger, Georg Bernhard 110–11, 141, 154, 205 n.7
Blount, Charles 179 n154
books burning (*fenshu* 焚书) 44, 139, 180 n.162
Borri, Cristoforo 55, 62–4, 66, 155
Boureau-Deslandes, André-François 2, 19, 60, 88, 96–102, 103–4, 107, 121, 122–3, 135, 143, 154, 194 n.175, 200 n.75, 206 n.13
Brahmā 65, 135, 137, 154
brahmans (Brahmanae) 12, 16–18, 21, 43, 50, 70, 113, 128, 135–7
Brucker, Jakob 1, 2, 3, 5, 33, 38, 48, 49, 57, 76, 77, 89, 91, 93, 94, 96, 98, 100, 102, 104, 106, 112, 118, 121, 122–44, 144–50, 153–6, 158, 160, 161, 163, 184 n.21, 200 n.72, 202 n.100, 203 n.106, 203 n.117, 204 n.126, 207 n.30
Bruyère, Jean de La 80

Buddeus, Johann Franz 2, 5, 49, 60–1,
    91–4, 103, 111, 118, 119, 122, 138,
    144, 192 n.146, 192 n.149,
    193 n.155, 199 n.45
Buddha (Budda, Foe, Schiaca, Sichia, Xaca,
    XeKia, Xaka, Xakia Thicca, Thic) 23,
    24, 27, 29, 55, 62–6, 73, 77, 80, 85,
    93, 127–9, 133–4, 136, 139, 172
    nn.51–5, 201 n.84; see Buddhism,
    Sommona-codom
Buddhism (Buddhist) vii, 24–7, 28, 29–30,
    56, 61–5, 68–70, 72, 74–6, 78, 80–2,
    85, 87, 98, 99, 103, 128–9, 133–4,
    136, 137–9, 140, 143, 144, 146, 147,
    148, 154–5, 159, 161, 165, 167 n.11,
    171 n.44, 172 n.52–5, 173 n.69,
    174 n.86, 178 n.142, 181–2 n.176,
    182 n.202, 182 n.1, 183 n.9,
    183 n.17, 187 n.61, 188 n.76,
    205 n.4, 205 n.5; see Buddha,
    atheistic plague
Burigny, Jean Lévesque de 90
Burnet, Thomas 2, 4, 5, 15, 19, 42–52, 56–5,
    59, 67, 70, 93–4, 98, 102, 105, 114,
    130, 131, 137, 143–4, 153, 178 n.145,
    180 n.162, 181 n.177, 181 n.179,
    194 n.181

Cai, Yuanpei 蔡元培 149
Cain 36, 39
Catana, Leo 3, 144–6, 200 n.78, 204
    mn.126–7
Chaldea, Chaldean(s) 9, 11–14, 16, 20, 32,
    33, 36, 37, 38, 40, 41, 43, 44, 67, 68,
    108, 109, 114, 119, 126, 130, 132, 143
Chattopadhyay, Bankimchandra 156
Cheng, Anne 163
Chinese language 34, 94, 96, 98, 117, 139,
    159, 208 n.36
Chinese/Confucian ethics 27–9, 34, 45, 51,
    55, 57, 63, 74, 82, 85, 103, 109–10
    Weakness of Chinese ethics 106, 116,
    120, 138, 142
chronology, chronological 5, 12, 15, 17, 23,
    31, 33, 35, 37–40, 54–7, 59, 62–3, 67,
    101, 115–16, 138, 144, 154, 175 n.98,
    176 n.111
Clement of Alexandria 11, 12, 14, 16, 47,
    51, 56, 125, 129, 183 n.15

Clerc, Jean Le 42, 73–4, 80, 185 n.39,
    191 n.119
comparativism, comparative (philosophy)
    133, 136, 162, 202 n.97
Confucius (Confucian, Kongzi 孔子) 15,
    27–8, 29, 30, 34, 40, 45, 53–6, 63, 74,
    81, 85, 93, 115–20, 138–41, 146, 154,
    176 n.106, 181 n.189, 182 n.194,
    182 n.203; see Confucianism
    Confucius sinarum philosophus 31,
    69–70, 73–5, 80, 93, 185 n.37
Confucianism (Rujia 儒家) 15, 26–31, 50,
    54, 55, 60, 61, 62, 67–9, 75, 82, 98,
    110, 111, 138–9, 146–9, 154, 155,
    159, 160, 163, 164, 173 n.69,
    174 n.86; see Neo-confucianism,
    New Confucianism
Coste, Pierre 107–8
Couplet, Philippe 69–70, 74–7, 80, 93, 103,
    115, 121, 134, 138, 139, 187 n.61
Crousaz, Jean-Pierre de 90–1, 192 n.139
Croze, Mathurin Veyssière de La 6, 93,
    133–7, 154, 202 n.99, 203 n.106
Cruz, Gaspar da 25, 27
Cua, Antonio S. 149–50

Daoism (daojia 道家), Daoist 27, 30, 98,
    147, 148, 165; see Laozi
Defoort, Carine 205 n.147, 207 n.27
despotism, despotic 104, 107, 113, 116,
    117, 155, 186 n.48, 199 n.55
Diderot, Denis 7, 97, 111, 122, 200 n.72
diffusion, diffused 5 (revelation), 11
    (philosophy), 12 (wisdom), 24
    (Buddhism), 25 (Christian faith), 30
    (Bud), 40–2 (wis/Egyptian/Bud), 42
    (devilish faith), 50 (wis/Egyp/dev),
    64 (Bud), 67 (heresy), 87 (atheism),
    126 (ph), 133 (Bud), 138
    (Confucianism), 155 (Bud),
    180–1 n.176 (Egyp)

Egypt, Egyptian(s) 9, 12, 13, 14, 16, 32,
    36–7, 38, 42, 50, 66–7, 70, 90, 103,
    125, 129, 132–7, 139, 140, 143, 144,
    155, 176 n.112, 181–2 n.176
emanation, emanative (philosophy) 47–9,
    132, 134, 136, 181 n.177; see Noah,
    immanentism

emptiness, empty 55, 68–9, 73, 75, 80–2, 90, 134, 155, 161, 175 n.96
Encyclopédie 2, 88, 99, 100, 102, 104, 122, 200 n.72
Enlightenment, Enlightened 2, 3, 4, 7, 53, 88, 97, 99, 102–4, 109, 111, 133, 153, 155, 156, 190 n.112
Eurocentric (Eurocentrism) 4, 5, 131, 159
exclusivist (exclusivism) 5, 13, 16, 90, 105, 108, 123, 149, 157, 192 n.135
exotic, exoticism 131, 140, 160–1

Feng, Youlan 冯友兰 149–50, 163
Ficino, Marsilio 11–13, 33, 96, 123, 168 n.4, 168 n.8, 175 n.98
Fréret, Nicolas 107, 196 n.3

Ge, Zhaoguang 葛兆光 151
Gentzken, Friedrich 119–22, 125, 153
German Eclecticism 6, 39, 61, 94, 102, 104, 121–2, 123, 124, 125, 144
grace (God's) 14–15, 19, 31, 51, 53, 69, 83–4, 123, 181 n.189
Gruzinski, Serge 208 n.44
Gymnosophists 14, 21, 41, 64, 77, 89, 99–100, 113, 127, 129, 135–6, 154, 178 n.142

Halbfass, Wilhelm 7–8, 162
Ham 12, 32, 42–3, 57, 67–8, 94, 184 n.28
Harbsmeier, Christoph 147
heathen (heathens) vii, 14, 23, 36, 47, 52, 53, 54, 57, 61, 62, 66, 67, 71, 74, 82, 83, 84, 90, 103, 112, 114, 128, 130, 133, 140, 143, 160
  heathendom 159–60
Hegel, Georg Wilhelm Friedrich (Hegelianism, Hegelians) 2, 3, 144, 145, 149, 156–7, 158, 162, 166, 204 n.127, 206 n.9
Heineccius, Joh. Gottlieb 121–2
heresy (heresies) 42, 66–7, 76, 86, 103, 106, 124, 128, 143, 144, 160
Heumann, Christoph August 2, 5, 38, 39, 57, 80, 93, 106, 111–19, 122–3, 125–6, 130, 132, 137, 138, 139, 140, 141, 144, 145, 149, 153, 154, 156, 160, 124 n.177, 199 n.61

Heurn, Otto van 1–5, 14–15, 16–19, 28, 31, 42, 45, 46, 48, 51, 56–7, 59, 120, 127, 132, 144, 153, 159, 169 n.22, 170 n.32, 170 n.34, 175 n.94
Hindu, Hinduism 65–6
historical paradigm(s) 3, 5, 6, 11, 49, 51, 105, 138, 153
Horn, Georg 2, 4, 5, 8, 15, 31–5, 38–9, 42, 44, 53, 56–7, 59, 67, 68, 84, 93, 114, 123, 127, 130–2, 138, 144, 153, 159, 175 n.94, 175 n.98, 178 n.132.
Hu Shi (胡适) 149
Huet, Pierre-Daniel 60, 89–90

idolatry, idolatric 56, 63–4, 75, 83, 87, 134, 144 157
immanentism, immanentist 26, 76
immorality, immoral 18, 69, 79, 82–3, 103, 116, 120, 125, 129, 143, 160
inaction 75–6; *see* quietism
inclusivist(s) 5, 16, 82, 90, 108, 131, 192 n.135
Indian ethics 77, 154
inferior, inferiority (to the ancient Greek or western modern philosophy) 5, 27, 32, 45, 51, 108, 120–1, 140, 143–4, 165
irrationality, irrational 3, 5, 107, 125, 143–4, 154–5, 157, 160; *see* rationality, reason
Israel, Jonathan I. 37, 38, 52, 59, 118, 177 n.123, 187–8 n.68

Jews (Jewish) vii, 32, 33, 35–8, 39, 44, 53, 67, 86, 98, 108, 113, 114, 119, 122, 125–7, 132, 154, 156, 159, 160, 176 n.111, 176 n.112, 192 n.148, 206 n.9

Kant, Immanuel (Kantian, Kantism) 2, 142, 145, 156, 157, 162, 165, 197–8 n.23, 205 n.7, 206 n.9, 208 n.40
karman (karma) vii, 129, 137
Kephalaia 201 n.86
King, Richard 166
Kircher, Athanasius 8, 42, 47, 48, 50, 57, 66–7, 69, 70, 73, 87, 91, 94, 103, 126, 128, 129, 132, 133, 134, 155, 159, 185 n.42, 186 n.50

Kors, Alan Charles 82–3, 86
Krishna, Daya 162

Lach, Donald F. 110, 193 n.158
Lambec, Peter 38
language (universal, divine) 12, 94, 96, 159, 170 n.38
Laërtius, Diogenes 13, 16, 38, 89, 90, 105–6
Laozi (老子) 30, 138
Leibniz, Gottfried Wilhelm 2, 4, 5, 7, 34, 57, 59, 60, 94–6, 103, 107, 109, 110, 115, 120–1, 123, 138, 140–1, 143, 153, 154, 159, 160, 167 n.9, 193 n.158, 193 n.160, 193 n.164, 194 n.168, 205 n.7
Li, Weiwu 李维武 163
Li, Zhizao 李之藻 174 n.86
logic, logical (lack of logic) 80–1, 96, 106, 111, 114, 117–18, 123, 140, 143–4, 147, 149, 150, 154–5, 165
Longo, Mario 123–4
Longobardi, Niccolò 68, 95, 138, 188 n.84, 194 n.168
Lord, Henry (Captain) 49
Loubère, Simon de la 49, 188 n.81

Magi 12, 14, 32, 68, 113, 134
Manes (Manicheans) 128; see Zoroaster
Malebranche, Nicolas 95, 97, 193 n.164
Marini, Giovanni Filippo de 64–6, 73
Martini, Martino 8, 33–4, 39, 74, 115
Matalio Metello, Giovanni 17
Megasthenes 14, 56, 89, 93, 129, 154, 183 n.16
Melanchton, Philip 200 n.78
Mendoza, Juan Gonzáles de 24–5, 27, 29, 35
Mencius, Mengzi 孟子 (Memcio) 138–9
Mehta, Jarava Lal 158, 160, 162, 206 n.16, 207 n.17
Meynard, Thierry 173 n.69
migration (theory) 12–13, 41, 49, 56, 89, 97
Mohanty, Jitendra Nath 161–2, 206 n.16
Molinos, Miguel 74, 76
monism, monistic, monist 63, 68, 71–3, 79, 133–4, 164
moral, morality 3, 4, 5, 14, 15, 17, 18, 24, 27–8, 34, 37, 46, 50–6, 60, 62, 68–9, 74, 78, 82–6, 88, 93, 95, 99, 103, 106–7, 109–11, 116, 118, 120–1, 125, 127, 129, 130, 137–8, 141–4, 148, 154–5, 157–8, 160; *see* immorality, ethics
Moses 11, 37, 54, 92, 137
Mou, Zongsan 牟宗三 165, 208 n.40
Mungello, David E. 6, 8, 153
mythology, mythological 30, 38, 48, 129, 149, 158

Navarrete, Domingo Fernandez 62, 67–9, 138, 188 n.84
Neo-Confucianism (*Xinrujia* 新儒家) 31, 139, 147, 154
Neoplatonism, Neoplatonic, Neoplatonists 4, 11–12, 32, 105–6, 123, 125, 126–7, 138, 146, 185 n.44
New Confucianism (*xiandai xinrujia* 现代新儒家) 163–4
Newton, Isaac 43, 81
Nishida, Kitarō 81
Noah, Noahic (wisdom) 4, 11–12, 32, 33, 35, 39, 42, 47–52, 56–7, 59, 67–8, 89, 94, 135, 159, 193 n.159
Noël, Francisco 197 n.18
nothingness, nothing 40, 62–4, 68–9, 71–3, 75, 77, 80–1, 136, 155–6, 159, 161, 189 n.88

Orientalism 2, 6–8, 89, 157, 163, 166, 205 n.4
   Self-orientalism 163
Origen 44, 98

pantheism, pantheistic, pantheists 3, 5, 99, 139, 141
paradigm, paradigmatic (historical) 1, 3–7, 11–13, 14–15, 42, 49, 51–2, 59, 105, 116, 132, 137–8, 145, 153, 163, 166, 204 n.127
perennial philosophy (*philosophia perennis*), perennialist 4, 5, 11–13, 15, 16, 19, 21, 25, 28, 32, 35, 40, 42, 46, 47, 49, 51, 57, 60, 67, 76, 82, 87, 89, 90, 93, 94–6, 97, 105, 103, 106, 108, 111, 113, 116, 121, 123, 130, 131, 138
Pereyra, Benito 14
Persia, Persian(s) 8, 9, 11, 13–14, 16, 28, 33, 43, 44, 50, 61, 66, 67, 70–3, 74, 76,

109, 111, 114, 119, 126, 127, 128, 130–3, 180–1 n.176
Peyrère, Isaac La 35–7, 39, 79, 115
Pico, Giovanni, conte della Mirandola e Concordia (Pico della Mirandola) 175 n.98, 202 n.100
Pinot, Virgile 6, 37
Plano Carpini, Giovanni Di (Giovanni da Pian del Carpine) 170 n.35
Plethon, Gemistus 12, 168 n.4
polyhistory, polyhistoric 37, 38, 45–6, 76, 102
Polo, Marco 16, 22, 33, 176 n.104, 180 n.174
Possevino, Antonio 26
Postel, Guillaume 12, 15, 17, 21–5, 27, 29, 35, 44, 56, 127, 135, 159, 170 n.38, 172 n.51, 172 n.56
pratītyasamutpāda 29
Pre Adamism, Pre Adamitic, Pre Adamist 36–8, 176 n.115
prisca theologia 4, 11, 13, 19–21, 40, 41, 46, 47, 51, 67, 68, 85, 94, 96, 105, 113, 137, 138, 144, 153, 168 n.4, 173 n.78
Pythagoras 11, 34, 40, 54, 55, 70, 92, 116, 127, 192 n.149

quietism, quietist(s) 4, 56–7, 60, 70, 74–6, 77, 80, 94, 103, 130, 134, 136, 137, 139, 141, 144, 155, 187 n.61

Rādhākrishnan, Sarvapalli 157–8, 206 n.15
Rama 65–6, 73
Rapin, René 107–8
rationality, rational 5, 15, 20, 38, 46–7, 52, 54, 57, 83, 87–8, 89, 95, 103, 108–9, 110, 123, 126, 127, 140, 142–3, 145, 147–9, 153–5, 156–8, 160, 161, 163; *see* irrationality, reason
Raud, Rein 207 n.27
reason, reasonable, reasonability, reasoning 27, 43, 47, 53–5, 63, 82–3, 87–9, 103, 106, 110, 112, 118, 122, 124–5, 130, 140, 142 (innate), 144, 146, 147–8, 153, 157, 165, 189 n.88; *see* rationality, irrationality
natural reason 15, 83, 87–9

Renaudot, Eusèbe 37, 39, 79–80, 106, 115–17, 138, 139, 140, 141, 189 n.90, 199 n.44
revelation (Christian or Jewish) 4, 5, 12, 14–15, 23–4, 31, 33, 46, 54, 109, 113, 123–4, 128, 190 n.112
Rhodes, Alexandre de 63–5, 73
Ricci, Matteo (Riccian) 8, 15, 19, 21, 25, 26–31, 33, 34, 35, 38, 44, 45, 50, 53–7, 59, 61–70, 78, 82, 85, 86, 91, 93, 94, 95, 96, 103, 139–41, 159, 170 n.34, 173 n.69, 173, n.78, 174 n.86, 188 n.84, 190 n.116, 194 n.168
Rodrigues, João 61, 62, 67–9, 128
Rogerius, Abraham 137
Roth, Heinrich (Henry) 48, 70, 180 n.175, 185 n.42, 186 n.50
Ruiz-de-Medina, Juan 22, 171 n.47, 172 n.52, 173 n.66

Said, Edward W. 3
Sanskrit 18 (sk), 20, 46 (sk), 48 (sk), 50 (ind), 70 (sk), 100 (sk), 180 n.175 (sk), 185 n.42 (sk)
Sarmanes (Germanes) 64, 135
Scepticism, sceptic, sceptical 4, 60, 86, 89–90, 110
Schmidt-Biggemann 12, 105
Schmitt, Charles B. 11, 96
science, scientific, scientist 3–5, 11, 13, 16–17, 20, 27, 33, 38, 42–3, 46, 49, 55, 63, 95, 98, 100–1, 103, 106, 108, 109, 112, 114, 124–5, 129, 137, 139, 143, 147–8, 153, 157, 159, 165, 174 n.86, 199 n.61
lack of scientific thought 34, 45–6, 49, 51, 55, 115–16, 129–30, 136, 139, 141, 143–4, 154, 155
Semedo, Alvarez 63
Shem 32, 94
Śiva 65, 135, 137, 154
Sommona-codom 77–8, 129
Spinoza, Baruch 29, 59, 60, 73, 77–80, 84–6, 88, 90–3, 111, 132–3, 189 n.85
Spinozism, Spinozistic 4, 57, 59, 60, 73, 76, 78–9, 87–8, 89, 90, 91, 93, 94, 100, 103, 105, 107, 110, 111, 119, 120, 124, 132–4, 136, 137, 141, 144, 154, 155, 161

spreading (of wisdom, philosophies, religions and atheism) 4, 5, 8, 13–16, 23, 25, 28, 30, 32, 33, 36, 39, 40–3, 46, 48, 50, 53, 56–7, 59, 65–7, 70, 76, 90, 106, 111, 113–14, 124, 126, 132–3, 134, 136, 143, 154, 155, 156, 159; see diffusion
Stanley, Thomas 2, 42–3, 52, 143, 178 n.145
Steuco, Agostino 13–14, 96, 123
Stolle, Gottlieb 117–18, 130, 137
Stroumsa, Guy G. 206 n.8
Syncretism, syncretic, syncretist(s) 13, 15, 32, 60, 105, 123, 124, 139, 146, 202 n.100
system of Philosophy 8, 144–6, 148, 149, 151, 156, 163, 169 n.24
Suda 128

Tachard, Guy 49
Thomas (Saint) the Apostle 20, 25
Thomassin, Louis 40–2, 67, 126, 178 n.142
Thomasius, Christian 2, 60, 106, 108–11, 112, 114, 118, 119, 121, 122, 133, 138, 153, 156, 197 n.14, 199 n.61
Thomasius, Jakob 133
transmigration 134, 137
Traversari, Ambrogio 168 n.10
Trigault, Nicolas 15, 27–8, 31, 33, 34, 35, 56, 61

universalism, universal, universalistic, universalist (Christian faith/ perennialism) 4–5, 20, 21, 22, 23, 32, 35, 36, 47, 51, 57, 67, 82, 92, 94–6, 103, 110, 115, 119, 153, 159, 160, 190 n.112; see perennial philosophy
  of Buddhism 128, 155; see Buddhism
  of European philosophy 92, 114, 118, 149, 153, 156, 157, 158, 160, 166, 206 n.9; see apology
  of Chinese thought 147, 149, 150, 160, 163–5
  of Indian thought 157–8, 162
universal, universality (of history) 7–8, 23, 31, 36–9 (Bible), 48, 57, 60, 110, 156

universal consent (*consensus gentium*) 20, 32, 82–5, 88, 89, 95, 103

vacuum (*kongxu* 空虛) 68, 69, 121; see emptiness, empty
Valignano, Alessandro 26, 61–2, 173 n.66, 173 n.69, 182 n.202
Van Norden, Bryan W. 206 n.11
Vayer, François De la Mothe le 15, 52–6, 57, 74, 79, 82, 83, 116, 141, 154, 181 n.189, 182 n.203, 185 n.35
Veda, ṚgVeda 65, 100–1
Vedānta, 100–1, 154, 157–8, 162, 207 n.20
Versé, Noël Aubert de 73, 78
Vesdin, Filip (Paulinus a Sancto Bartolomaeo) 169 n.25
Villemandy, Pierre de 40–2, 67, 114, 126, 178 n.140
Viṣṇu 65, 135, 137, 154
Vivekānanda, Swāmi (Narendranath Dutta) 157
void 81, 134; see emptiness
Voltaire, Arouet François-Marie 2, 7, 8, 79, 97, 102, 107
Vossius, Isaac 15, 37–8, 52, 53, 56, 98, 107, 110, 115, 116, 138, 141, 154, 177 n.118, 177 n.128

Walch, Johann Jakob 92, 110–11, 117, 122, 153
Webb, John 94, 159, 193 n.159
Wolff, Christian (Wolfian) 5, 7, 94, 103, 108–11, 115, 121, 123, 138, 140–2, 154, 156, 197 n.17, 197 n.23, 205 n.7
wuwei 無為 (*wuweijiao* 無為教) 70, 80

Xavier, Francis 7, 19–24, 26, 76, 155, 159

Yang, Guorong 杨国荣 147

Zhang, Dainian 张岱年 148, 150
Zoli, Sergio 79
Zoroaster 11–14, 17, 32, 42–3, 57, 67–8, 126, 129, 133

www.ingramcontent.com/pod-product-compliance
Lightning Source LLC
Chambersburg PA
CBHW072107010526
44111CB00037B/2023